The Human Reimagined

Posthumanism in Russia

Cultural Revolutions: Russia in the Twentieth and Twenty-First Centuries

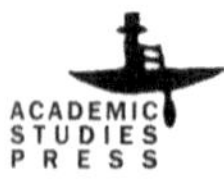

The Human Reimagined

Posthumanism in Russia

EDITED AND INTRODUCED BY
Colleen McQuillen and
Julia Vaingurt

Boston
2018

Library of Congress Cataloging-in-Publication Data

Names: McQuillen, Colleen, 1972- editor. | Vaingurt, Julia, editor.

Title: The human reimagined : posthumanism in Russia / edited and introduced by Colleen McQuillen and Julia Vaingurt.

Description: Boston: Academic Studies Press, 2018.

Series: Cultural revolutions: Russia in the twentieth and twenty-first centuries | Includes bibliographical references.

Identifiers: LCCN 2018018538 (print) | LCCN 2018031853 (ebook) | ISBN 9781618117335 (ebook) | ISBN 9781618117328 (hardcover) | ISBN 9781618117793 (pbk.)

Subjects: LCSH: Humanism in literature. | Human body and technology in literature. | Russian literature—20th century—History and criticism. | Humanism in art. | Human body and technology in art. | Art—Soviet Union.

Classification: LCC PG3020.5.H85 (ebook) | LCC PG3020.5.H85 H86 2018 (print) | DDC 891.709/384—dc23

LC record available at https://lccn.loc.gov/2018018538

ISBN 978-1-618117-32-8 (hardback)
ISBN 978-1-618117-33-5 (electronic)
ISBN 978-1-618117-79-3 (paperback)

Book design by Kryon Publishing Services (P) Ltd.
www.kryonpublishing.com

On the cover: Love, by Misha Most (from the series "The Future of the Past," 2017); reproduced by the author's permission.

Published by Academic Studies Press
28 Montfern Avenue
Brighton, MA 02135, USA
press@academicstudiespress.com
www.academicstudiespress.com

Table of Contents

Acknowledgments

This volume came out of the Workshop on Russian Modernism, "The Human Reimagined: Robots, Clones and Artificial Others," held in 2013 as part of the annual series at the University of Illinois at Chicago (UIC). We wish to thank the participants of the Workshop and the University sponsors who made this event possible: UIC's School for Literatures, Cultural Studies and Linguistics (LCSL), The Institute for the Humanities, and the Departments of Biological Sciences, History, and Slavic and Baltic Languages and Literatures. Additionally, we would like to express our gratitude to LCSL for the book subvention that defrayed the cost of including illustrations and an index.

We also wish to thank the individuals who contributed to the realization of this volume. First and foremost, we are grateful to the scholars whose work comprises this book, both for their expertise and patience. Anton Svynarenko provided much-needed support as our research assistant and translator. We thank Boris Wolfson, Editor of the series Cultural Revolutions: Russia in the Twentieth and Twenty-First Centuries, for believing in this project. We would also like to express our appreciation to Oleh Kotsyuba, Olga Livshin, Kira Nemirovsky, Faith Wilson Stein, and Ekaterina Yanduganova at Academic Studies Press for helping to move this project forward. We are profoundly indebted to the manuscript reviewers who offered invaluable feedback. Artist Misha Most graciously allowed us to use his painting *Love* (2017) for the book cover.

Finally, we would like to acknowledge the stimulating events that helped us develop our thinking about posthumanism: the ninth global conference "Visions of Humanity in Cyberculture, Cyberspace and Science Fiction," which took place at Mansfield College, Oxford University, in July 2014; and "All Things Living or Not: An Interdisciplinary Conference on Post-anthropocentric Perspectives," held at Columbia University in February 2017. Last but certainly not least, we benefited from Bruno Latour's workshop "Political Ecology as Practice: A Regional Approach to the Anthropocene" at UIC in November 2017.

List of Illustrations

Part One

Introduction

Colleen McQuillen and Julia Vaingurt

A. CRITICAL POSTHUMANISM

"And I understood the very essence of human beings. Man was a MEAT MACHINE."[1] Made by the protagonist of Vladimir Sorokin's *Bro* of *Ice Trilogy*, this damning assessment of human essence precedes his defamiliarizing description of the way "meat machines" function. The protagonist is not just the meat machine's Other but aspires to be such, to belong to a more dignified form of being. This more enlightened form of being, organized on the principles of purity and harmony, is lighter than the state in which humans find themselves, in more ways than one: it requires reduction of bodily materiality (corporeality makes human beings animalistic and machinistic at once) and its mode of operation is the heart's emission of communicative rays. In the frigid atmosphere of *Ice Trilogy*, the triumph of truth, harmony, and light is incompatible with the existence of the human race, and the reader is forced to make a choice between inhuman and inhumane perfection and filthy, fallible, yet human life. Paradoxically, nothing in this apocalyptic scenario is unprecedented or otherwise surprising. The reassessment of the concept of life, the less than favorable prognosis of the human place in it, the choice between the compromised human and the perfect inhuman—all these aspects of the trilogy are part of the discourse this volume will identify as posthumanist.

In current philosophical and culturological debates, this term has joined the group of other post-isms: poststructuralism, postmodernism, postcommunism, postcolonialism, and postfeminism. But in contrast to all of them, it refers less to a new temporal phase and more to the end of time—taken here as a product of human consciousness—all together. Posthumanism can be understood as a rejection of humanism, but what this rejection signals is the underlying crisis

1 Vladimir Sorokin, *Ice Trilogy*, trans. Jamey Gambrell (New York: New York Review of Books, 2011), 177.

not just of the doctrine of humanism but of the concept of a human being at its center. Questioning the value and validity of human life, posthumanism is radical in its negative thrust.

Russian culture is no stranger to eschatological thinking. Religious philosopher Nikolai Berdyaev remarks, "Among Russians there is always a thirst for another life, another world; there is always discontent with that which is. An eschatological bent is native to the structure of the Russian soul."[2] It would be inconsistent of us to indulge in presumptions about the Russian soul or practice any other kind of essentialism in a volume on posthumanism, but we can certainly acknowledge the overwhelming presence of eschatology in Russian written culture. With that in mind, we organized this volume, provoked by the desire to explore the extent to which Russian culture, with "its eschatological bent," contributed to the development of posthumanism that has become a prevalent paradigm of thought today.

Posthumanism, however, refers not only to a discourse, or a way of conceptualizing life, but also to a current state of accelerated technological development that radically transforms humanity's conditions and capabilities. This volume also aims, then, to explore the range of Russian artistic responses to these immense changes in the human environment. The conversations touch upon multiple spheres of life, such as politics, bioethics, technology, engineering, education, medicine, religion, social media, and, of course, the arts.[3]

Humanism

Humanism paves the way to posthumanism, and therefore by necessity our examination of the latter must begin with a glance at the former. There are multiple definitions of humanism. Posthumanist thought strives to oppose humanism that posits the human being as the rational, moral, and free agent of teleologically ordered life. This humanism is predicated on the idea that there is an essential feature that defines "human nature" and differentiates the human from the non-human. It has been held at least since the times of René Descartes that rational thought is this core human feature as it is, in the words of the philosopher, "the only thing that makes us men and distinguishes us from the beasts."[4] Neil Badmington calls Descartes "one of the principal architects of

2 Nikolai Berdyaev, *The Russian Idea,* trans. R. M. French (Hudson, NY: Lindisfarne Press, 1992), 197.

3 The sexist overtones of "man" notwithstanding, this volume uses "man" and "mankind" interchangeably with "human" and "humankind" in order to reflect the double meaning of the Russian words *chelovek* and *chelovechestvo*.

4 René Descartes, *Discourse on Method, Optics, Geometry, and Meteorology,* trans. Paul J. Olscamp (Indianapolis: Hackett Publishing Company, 2011), 4.

humanism," demarcating the Enlightenment period as the time that gave rise to the doctrine of secular humanism with the human at the center of the universal order.[5] However, Rosi Braidotti proposes that the Cartesian subject, the self-aware possessor of consciousness, along with many other self-congratulatory ideas of the Enlightenment, was constructed on the ideals of classical Antiquity and the Italian Renaissance: "At the start of it all there is He: the classical ideal of 'Man,' formulated first by Protagoras as 'the measure of all things,' later renewed in the Italian Renaissance as a universal model and represented in Leonardo da Vinci's Vitruvian Man."[6] There was just one logical step from the Renaissance belief in the infinite process of human perfectibility to the Enlightenment's conviction that reason is the instrument for the achievement of this potential.

Yet it is already at the very core of the humanist doctrine that a potential for crisis lurks. If humanity manifests itself in its drive toward self-perfection, then its nature is unstable and mutable rather than universal and fixed. Humanism carries seeds for implosion within itself; posthumanism, therefore, is not a sudden, fashionable change that we are currently experiencing but a process of questioning and doubt about the nature of humanity that begins almost simultaneously with the advent of Western humanism. There are, however, easily identifiable stages when the crisis of humanism gets clearly exacerbated.

A Brief Genealogy of Posthumanism

The onslaught on the Enlightenment concept of the human continued throughout the nineteenth century and touched upon many spheres of knowledge, ranging from biology to philosophy and to political economy.

The great precursor of the twentieth-century wave of anti-humanism is Friedrich Nietzsche. In *The Order of Things*, Michel Foucault establishes a link between Nietzsche's announcement of the death of God and the irreparable damage to the image of permanent human nature or essence that this proclamation implied: "In our day, and once again Nietzsche indicated the turning-point from a long way off, it is not so much the absence or the death of God that is affirmed as the end of man (that narrow, imperceptible displacement, that recession in the form of identity, which are the reason why man's finitude has become his end)."[7] Foucault makes a point here that if Nietzsche was not the initiator

5 Neil Badmington, ed., *Posthumanism* (New York: Palgrave, 2000), 3.

6 Rosi Braidotti, *The Posthuman* (Cambridge: Polity, 2013), 13.

7 Michel Foucault, *The Order of Things: An Archeology of Human Sciences* (London: Routledge, 2005), 420.

of this ontological uncertainty, then at least he proclaimed it loudly. Darwin was the first to question the divine origin of human nature, but it was Nietzsche who articulated the conclusions that must be drawn from this fact. Godlessness promised humans freedom to construct their existence, but under less than favorable conditions, their freedom limited by the very knowledge of their own finitude. In this limited state, the human intellect is far from what the philosophers of the Enlightenment took it to be: the instrument for figuring out and realizing the progress of humanity toward perfection. On the contrary, reason is a means by which "the most unfortunate, the most delicate, the most transient beings" preserve themselves; and it works by dissimulation rather than truth. In "Truth and Falsity in an Ultramoral Sense," Nietzsche writes: "That haughtiness connected with the cognition and sensation, spreading blinding fogs before the eyes and over the senses of men, deceives itself therefore as to the value of existence owing to the fact that it bears within itself the most flattering evaluation of cognition. Its most general effect is deception."[8] The transvaluation of all values and the recognition that human life is not a blueprint to be acted out but a task of self-conceptualization and self-creation incite Nietzsche to call for a coming of a new type of human being who will rise above all restrictive conditions of existence and design a more vigorous and creative variant of life. To think that humanity is in the process of becoming is to imply that there is much that is non-human within it. This recognition, intensified by a rather circumspect attitude toward human reason, coexists uneasily with a joyful anticipation of a new form of being that consciousness relieved from any moral constraints will bring forth. In this way Nietzshean thought encapsulates the whole spectrum of attitudes toward the concept of volatile and evolving humanity today: from critical, circumspect, and apprehensive (poststructuralist, feminist anti-humanism) to euphoric about radical transformations of humanity and devoid of any regrets and nostalgic yearnings (transhumanism).

While Marxism strived to reduce human alienation and bring forth a more just and humane society, and was proclaimed by its followers "the real humanism," this system of thought made its own dent in the shiny edifice of the Cartesian subject.[9] Much of Marxist thought conforms to the humanist

8 Friedrich Nietzsche, "Truth and Falsity in an Ultramoral Sense," in *Critical Theory Since Plato,* ed. Hazard Adams (New York: Harcourt Brace Jovanovich, 1992), 634.

9 Marx and Engels use the term "real humanism" a few times in *The Holy Family* to refer to materialism and contrast it with idealist humanism: "Real humanism has no more dangerous enemy in Germany than spiritualism..." (Karl Marx and Friedrich Engels, *Collected Works* (New York: International Publishers, 1975), 4:7. On Marxist anti-humanism and on the concept of "real humanism," see Louis Althusser, *For Marx* (New York: Verso, 2006).

doctrine; it does, after all, offer a vision of history as a progressive movement toward the most humane form of social order that would be rationally organized and allow for the full realization of human potential. However, upon reading *Capital*, human beings encountered the possibility that they were not autonomous and free agents at the center of the order of things, but products of economic conditions and social relations, their whole being fully conditioned by the mode of production in which they were merely factors. Furthermore, being a part of productive forces, humans could hardly deem themselves more exceptional or valuable than such other factors of production as land and capital.

While Marx exposed how deeply human beings are enmeshed in the external non-human world and dependent upon it, the psychoanalytic method led Freud to discover the unconscious and exhibited the extent to which the human is internally entangled with the non-human. If rational thought is the marker of humanity, its opposite, irrational drives, must, by default, diminish humanity and make it come closer to other irrational beings. The irrational aspects of human nature have always provided a challenge to the unconditional belief in human exceptionalism. However, Freud's argument that it is precisely the unconscious that is the driving force behind human behavior questions the very basis of humanism.[10]

The first half of the twentieth century witnessed a chain of cataclysmic events that brought about the destruction of innumerable masses of people on an unprecedented scale. The record levels of humanity's self-extermination in the two world wars were made possible by strides in modern technological innovation; and the mass extermination of people in Nazi and Soviet concentration camps was sanctioned as part of the daring civilizational, Enlightenment projects. The Soviet experiment of creating new socialist subjects and restructuring Russian society along rational and scientific parameters was heavily indebted to the Enlightenment's conceptualization of humanity. Lenin's famous motto "Communism equals Soviet power plus the electrification of the whole country" underscores the civilizing and progressive mission of the Soviet project that went beyond the narrower goal of social justice.[11]

10 In addition to Darwin, Marx, and Freud, Stefan Herbrechter names Saussure and Weber as "antihumanist precursors [...] who all engage in a critique of anthropocentric metaphysics." Stefan Herbrechter, *Posthumanism: A Critical Analysis* (London: Bloomsbury, 2013), 7.

11 Furthermore, Sheila Fitzpatrick argued that the French Revolution offered Russians not only a model for the October Revolution proper but also a pattern for dealing with the opposition, consolidating power, and ensuring continuity of the initiated changes through post-revolutionary terror and violence. See Sheila Fitzpatrick, *The Russian Revolution* (Oxford: Oxford University Press, 2008), 14.

While there is no scholarly consensus on whether German National Socialism was a by-product of the Enlightenment or its negation, it is hardly contestable that the Nazi ideology heavily relied on the following set of familiar concepts: the progressive movement of history and the view of man as a rational agent of political, social, and biological advancement. Dr. Gerhard Wagner, who was the head of the Nazi organization of physicians, in his speech on Nazi racial policy given at the 1936 Nuremberg Rally cloaked the future destruction of European Jewry in terms of the rational enhancement of the human makeup: "We want to rescue a dying people from the edge of the abyss and lead it back to the paths that will lead, according to human reason, to a future in the coming millennium. We must oppose the three great dangers of racial and biological decline that have repeatedly destroyed states, peoples, and cultures in the past if they did not succeed in resisting them in good time." [12]

These developments could not but shake the faith of many in such modern ideas as the progressive movement of history, the inevitable correlation between technological advancement and human perfectibility, and the rational core of human nature. Hence, in the second half of the twentieth century, continental philosophy initiated a sustained assault on the doctrine of humanism and the concept of human therein. Anthropocentrism was one of those grand metanarratives toward which postmodernity felt its defining and definite incredulity, to adopt Lyotard's catchy phrase. Poststructuralists argued for the instability of language and meaning; equipped with the Saussurian notion of the arbitrariness of the sign, they set out to deconstruct all metaphysical assumptions.

One of the strategies of the Derridean deconstructive method is to locate binary oppositions in which human thought tends to operate, privileging one side of the binary. Dismantling such binary oppositions as reason/emotion, mind/body, man/woman, civilization/barbarism, writing/speech, and inside/outside, poststructuralists started off a critique of logocentrism and phallocentrism, two pillars of humanist discourse. A paragon of enlightened humanity, the autonomous Cartesian subject was always conceived as a Western male. Endorsing difference and mutability, and questioning stable boundaries between categories,

12 Randall L. Bytwerk, ed., *Landmark Speeches of National Socialism* (College Station, TX: Texas A&M University Press, 2008), 69. On the relationship between the Enlightenment and the Holocaust, read Theodor Adorno and Max Horkheimer, *Dialectic of Enlightenment,* (Stanford, CA: Stanford University Press, 2007); Zygmunt Bauman, *Modernity and the Holocaust* (Ithaca: Cornell University Press, 2001); and Lawrence Birken, *Hitler as Philosophe: Remnants of the Enlightenment in National Socialism* (Westport, CT: Praeger, 1995).

poststructuralists paved the way for the racial, postcolonial, and feminist critiques of humanism. As Foucault argued in *Discipline and Punish* and *The History of Sexuality*, the unitary human subject is a product of the discourse of normativity created by those in power for the purposes of domination, exclusion, and control. The postcolonial and feminist critiques of humanism did not intend to eradicate the concept of human completely but rather to diminish its universalizing, restrictive, and normative aspects. The principles of multiplicity, heterogeneity, and plasticity were introduced to expand the understanding of what comprises humanity.

The final (at this stage) and present challenge to humanism arises not from the realm of philosophical thought, but rather from the recent environmental changes and technological advances. It becomes harder and harder to draw discreet boundaries between nature, technology, and humanity. In *A Thousand Plateaus*, Gilles Deleuze and Felix Guattari adopt the botanical "rhizome" as a model for a non-hierarchical, flexible, and heterogeneous cultural system.[13] Many contemporary developments manifest the rhizomatic nature of human interactions with the world: the continuous cyborgization and prosthetization of the body, the technologization of reproductive practices (that were previously considered natural), the rapidly growing sophistication of artificial intelligence machines, and the increasing presence and influence of digital environments and virtual spaces in daily life and identity formation.

Contemporary Posthumanist Debates

Today, when it is more difficult than ever to make a distinction between the human and the non-human, various voices in science, philosophy, literature, the arts, and popular culture venture to develop a response to this posthuman predicament. Responses range from complete acceptance and euphoria at the prospect of the disappearance of the human as we know him to a leveled and critical attitude that gauges the positives and negatives of the current technological developments, and to desperate lamentation over the loss of humanism and efforts to mobilize in order to fight for its salvation. Anyone who broaches the subject of humanity's new status and champions a particular vision of human life is engaged in this posthumanist discourse, whatever his or her attitude toward traditional humanism might be.

13 Gilles Deleuze and Felix Guattari, *A Thousand Plateaus: Capitalism and Schizophrenia*, trans. Brian Massumi (Minneapolis: University of Minnesota Press, 1987).

It is perhaps telling that transhumanism, which is the most unconditionally accepting of all philosophical stances on both current and imminent transformations of humanity, is also in many ways the most direct inheritor of Enlightenment humanism. It fully upholds two fundamental ideas of traditional liberal humanism: progressivism and the privileging of reason (as the defining human trait). That is why the very first paragraph of *The Transhumanist Reader* makes a point of distancing transhumanism from posthumanism.[14] Accepting such posthumanist ideals as mutability and hybridity, transhumanism nevertheless looks forward to the evolutionary changes in which the human race will be superseded by a species with more developed forms of intelligence, and to the embodiment of human intellect in a more enduring form of hardware than a human body. For transhumanists, the body in its very materiality presents a variety of obstacles to the realization of human potential. "The Transhumanist Declaration" announces the resolve of its adherents to overcome such problems as "aging, cognitive shortcomings, involuntary suffering, and our confinement to planet Earth."[15] It's the body that makes humans vulnerable to pain, suffering, and death, and imprisoned on a dying planet. It's the body that limits humanity both temporally and spatially, while the mind always gravitates toward expansion.

The issue of embodiment is a major point of contention in posthumanist discourse. Humanism prioritized the mind and spirit over the body, marking them as the loci of human uniqueness and superiority, and embroiling them in its discriminatory practices against non-humans and those deemed subhuman. The body charged with natural, animalistic impulses was on the contrary the element of human beings that incorporated them into the surrounding environment. Thereby, many posthumanists and anti-humanists came to underscore the importance of human materiality. At the core of posthumanist thought is the desire to break through the isolation of the human that came about as the result of anthropocentrism and to treat the body as the point of convergence, networking, and connection with the environment.

Feminist theorists such as Donna Haraway and N. Katherine Hayles were among the first to find political and ethical advantages in the dissolution of the boundaries between the human and the machine on one hand, and the human and the animal on the other. In Haraway's seminal essay "A Cyborg Manifesto" (1984), her cyborg is the metaphor for "social and bodily realities in which people

---

14 Max More and Natasha Vita-More, eds., *The Transhumanist Reader: Classical and Contemporary Essays on the Science, Technology and Philosophy of the Human Future* (Chichester: Wiley-Blackwell, 2013), 1.

15 Ibid., 54.

are not afraid of their joint kinship with animals and machines, not afraid of permanently partial identities and contradictory standpoints."[16] But Haraway does not speak only metaphorically: the cyborg world also signals a transition from the analog to digital technologies, which offers a possibility for remapping or recoding the body. As a result of these developments, the body ceases to be an object of knowledge and turns into "an information-processing device," a conduit of freely flowing information.[17] In *How We Became Posthuman: Virtual Bodies in Cybernetics, Literature, and Informatics* (1999), N. Katherine Hayles offers a more embodied version of feminist posthumanism. She finds the erasure of embodiment to be a point of similarity between Haraway's cybernetic posthumanism and liberal humanism. In contrast, Hayles believes that the departure from the traditional humanist subject should allow her to bring back "the flesh." Hayles wishes to celebrate the materiality of the human body, the condition of its finitude, and thereby its dependence on cooperation with the rest of the material world: "[M]y dream is the version of the posthuman that embraces the possibilities of information technologies without being seduced by fantasies of unlimited power and disembodied immortality, that recognizes and celebrates finitude as a condition of human being, and that understands human life as embedded in a material world of great complexity, one on which we depend for our continued survival."[18]

Hayles's materialist standpoint resonates with most contemporary posthumanists. Diana Coole and Samantha Frost in their introduction to *New Materialisms: Ontology, Agency, and Politics* make an explicit link between newly emerged materialist philosophies and the posthumanist worldview.[19]

---

16 Donna Haraway, "A Cyborg Manifesto: Science, Technology and Socialist-Feminism in the Late Twentieth Century." In *The Cybercultures Reader*, ed. Barbara M. Kennedy and David Bell (London: Routledge, 2007), 295.

17 Ibid., 303.

18 N. Katherine Hayles, *How We Became Posthuman: Virtual Bodies in Cybernetics, Literature, and Informatics* (Chicago: The University of Chicago Press, 1999), 5. A similar defense of human finitude is proposed by Jean-François Lyotard in "Can Thought go on without a Body?" (Lyotard, *The Inhuman* [Stanford, CA: Stanford University Press, 1988], 8–24). In this essay, the French philosopher questions the transhumanist vision of disembodied reason not on the basis of its desirability but rather on the basis of its viability. The complexity of human thought is conditioned by its encasement in the suffering, finite human body. Lyotard's objection to the prospect of disembodiment, then, is that thinking machines will be too effortless and complete and would therefore be unable to arrive at the incredible complexity of human thought.

19 Diana Coole and Samantha Frost, "Introducing the New Materialisms." In *New Materialisms: Ontology, Agency, and Politics*, ed. Diana Coole and Samantha Frost (Durham, NC: Duke University Press, 2010), 7.

These new materialist theories are endorsing a non-hierarchical, non-anthropocentric approach to the environment consisting of both human and non-human entities. For example, Jane Bennett's vital materialism is based on the premise of the vitality of all matter. In her book *Vibrant Matter: A Political Ecology of Things,* Bennett attempts to disprove the humanist principle that human bodies possess agency and autonomy, while non-human bodies are passive and inert. She draws attention to the capacity of things to affect human behavior, to prevent or incite human plans and actions. She admits the influence of Bruno Latour's actor-network theory.[20] In *We Have Never Been Modern,* Latour defines modernity as a condition in which two sets of opposing practices exist simultaneously but separately. The epistemological strategy of purification separates the human world from the natural world, while the practice of translation breaks through these boundaries and creates hybrids.[21] Latour proposes to combine the opposite strategies of translation and purification to arrive at a form of ontological model that presupposes a continuous interaction and cooperation between human and non-human actors (or actants). Such a model necessitates a reconsideration of the principles of agency and causality, which new materialists enthusiastically endorse. As Coole and Frost write,

> [T]he human species is being relocated within a natural environment whose material forces themselves manifest certain agentic capacities and in which the domain of unintended or unanticipated effects is considerably broadened. [...] It is in these choreographies of becoming that we find cosmic forces assembling and disintegrating to forge more or less enduring patterns that may provisionally exhibit internally coherent, efficacious organization: objects forming and emerging within relational fields, bodies composing their natural environment in ways that are corporeally meaningful for them, and subjectivities being constituted as open series of capacities and potencies that emerge hazardously and ambiguously within a multitude of organic and social processes.[22]

Philosophically, the return to matter can also be explained by the growing dissatisfaction with poststructuralist stress on linguistic and social constructivism

20 Jane Bennett, *Vibrant Matter: A Political Ecology of Things* (Durham, NC: Duke University Press, 2010), viii–ix.

21 Bruno Latour, *We Have Never Been Modern* (Cambridge, MA: Harvard University Press, 1991), 10–11.

22 Coole and Frost, *New Materialisms,* 10.

and a desire for a philosophy that would allow for more political engagement. The aim of new materialisms is ultimately political, to offer a Marxist, materialist counter-offensive against the harmful fallouts of global capitalist consumerism as well as the ruthless consumption of natural resources leading to global warming and the entrance into the geological age of the Anthropocene. Like vital materialists, speculative realists such as Graham Harman and Quentin Meillassoux oppose their object-oriented philosophy to both poststructuralist idealism and liberal humanism.[23] However, their view of the interaction between various objects is much less encouraging than the views espoused by Latour and the new materialists. They question the knowability of any objects and the possibility of relationality and interaction between objects proposed by the assemblage and network theorists. The inaccessibility of objects is a principle driven by the rejection of "correlationism," or the belief that the essence of an object is reducible to the subject's thought about it.

This direful assessment of human limitedness (in contrast to Hayles's celebration of finitude) also characterizes studies on the relation between life and politics, specifically, the work of Giorgio Agamben. In the seminal *Homo Sacer: Sovereign Power and Bare Life* (1998), Agamben radicalizes Foucault's concept of biopolitics and the intrusion of state power into man's biological life, and indicts contemporary democracy. The politicization of embodied subjects' private lives takes place via the demarcation of what constitutes the proper, qualified human life (*bios*) from the improper, animal existence (bare life or *zoē*) with the result that biological life, due to its bareness, is banished from bios immediately upon its inclusion therein. Considering that the non-human element, bare life, is an essential part of the life of humans, biopolitics turns by necessity into thanatopolics, the right to protect life becomes indistinguishable from the right to mete out death, and "the [concentration] camp—as the pure, absolute and impassable biopolitical space (insofar as it is founded solely on the state of exception)—will appear as the hidden paradigm of the political space of modernity."[24] For Agamben, it is precisely the vulnerability of biological life—its susceptibility to death—that drives its owners to seek protection and give themselves to power, and ultimately leads to its extermination. To produce the human, to delineate the realm of humanity is by necessity to wield

23 For a compilation of writings by speculative realists, see Levi Bryant, Nick Srnicek, and Graham Harman, eds., *Speculative Turn: Continental Materialism and Realism* (Melbourne: re.press, 2011).

24 Giorgio Agamben, *Homo Sacer: Sovereign Power and Bare Life* (Stanford, CA: Stanford University Press, 1998), 120.

destruction. In his later works, such as, notably, *The Open: Man and Animal* (2004), Agamben attempts to modify this bleak prognosis, that is, the extinction to which humanity has condemned itself in the process of self-definition, and arrives at his own posthumanist solution. Agamben proposes to find sustenance in the very indeterminacy of our species' state. Instead of trying to close the chasm between the animal and the human within, Agamben advocates for leaving it open:

> In our culture, man has always been thought of as the articulation and conjunction of a body and a soul, of a living thing and a logos, of a natural (or animal) element and a supernatural or social or divine element. We must learn instead to think of man as what results from the incongruity of these two elements. [...] What is man, if he is always the place—and, at the same time, the result—of ceaseless divisions and caesurae?[25]

Agamben admits that abstaining from further articulations of the conception of the human and refraining from fixing the void at its core is taking a risk: "To render inoperative the machine that governs our conception of man will therefore mean no longer to seek new—more effective or more authentic —articulations, but rather to show the central emptiness, the hiatus that—within man—separates man and animal, and to risk ourselves in this emptiness."[26]

The language of risk-taking is not unique to Agamben; rather, it reminds us of the declaration made by new materialists Coole and Frost that the endeavor they undertake will bring about new "capacities and potencies" that will be both "hazardous and ambiguous" (see the quote above). It is not surprising, therefore, that a number of thinkers find both theories and practices that devalue and transcend humanism fraught with danger.

Among the more vociferous defenders of humanism and advocates for the preservation of human nature is political scientist Francis Fukuyama. The thrust of Fukuyama's critique, expounded in *Our Posthuman Future: Consequences of the Biotechnology Revolution* (2002), is directed against newly emergent biotechnological advances (specifically, gene technology) that threaten to radically alter human nature.[27] Warning against unforeseen harmful consequences of

---

25 Giorgio Agamben, *The Open: Man and Animal* (Stanford, CA: Stanford University Press, 2003), 16.

26 Ibid., 92.

27 A similarly cautionary attitude about genetic engineering and its challenges to ethics is promoted in Jürgen Habermas's *The Future of Human Nature* (Cambridge: Polity, 2003).

gene manipulation, Fukuyama advances a sustained defense of the liberal humanist notion of human nature. According to Fukuyama, human beings are social creatures and they find great satisfaction in shared values and norms. The only truly universal essential component that all human beings share is their humanness, "the very grounding of the human moral sense, which has been a constant ever since there were human beings."[28] Altering human nature, we abandon the very basis of "natural standards for right and wrong."[29] Such concepts as justice and rights that democratic societies hold dear are dependent on the notion of the "inviolability of human dignity." Fukuyama credits religion, specifically the religious notion of "soul" from which the concept of human dignity is derived, with explaining more about what it means to be human than natural sciences could ever do.[30] A scholar of classical philosophy, Martha Nussbaum subscribes to the Aristotelian view that the understanding of essential human nature is the foundation of ethical reasoning.[31] Nussbaum indefatigably strives to recuperate humanistic values and the value of humanity in the age of technology-driven global economy and its concomitant instrumentalization of every sphere of life, and specifically education. Attempting to fight against the devaluation of the humanities in education, Nussbaum has written several books arguing for the need to raise critical, contemplative, and empathetic citizens.[32] A staunch defender of liberal humanism, Nussbaum provides a thoughtful justification for the ideal of universalism that would be inclusive of pluralism and multiculturalism.

Positioned between euphoric and dystopic assessments of the posthuman condition are approaches of critical posthumanists, such as Stefan Herbrechter, Cary Wolfe, Rosi Braidotti, and Neil Badmington. Critical posthumanists welcome the intellectual challenges posited by the current posthuman turn. They see how the evolution in the way we think about our species can carry ethical

---

28 Francis Fukuyama, *Our Posthuman Future: Consequences of the Biotechnology Revolution* (New York: Picador, 2002), 102.

29 Ibid.

30 Ibid., 161-62.

31 Nussbaum explicates the mechanism by which ethical judgment is based on assumptions or knowledge about essential human nature in her article "Aristotle on Human Nature and the Foundations of Ethics" in *World, Mind, and Ethics: Essays on the Ethical Philosophy of Bernard Williams,* ed. J. E. J. Altham and Ross Harrison (Cambridge: Cambridge University Press, 1995): 86-131.

32 See Martha Nussbaum, *Cultivating Humanity: A Classical Defense of Reform in Liberal Education* (Cambridge, MA: Harvard University Press, 1997), *Not for Profit: Why Democracy Needs the Humanities* (Princeton, NJ: Princeton University Press, 2010) and *Creating Capabilities: The Human Development Approach* (Cambridge, MA: Belknap Press, 2013).

and political benefits, but they do not take lightly the concerns and reservations of those who find the idea of posthumanity threatening and misguided.[33] The task of critical posthumanism is to offer balanced analysis of current technological developments as they impact and bring forth cultural changes and to "develop alternative, more egalitarian, democratic and just models for a future posthuman(ist) society."[34] These alternative ethical models of posthuman society will be built not on fear, anxiety, and shared vulnerability but rather on discovering new empowering relations and activities.[35] Ultimately, critical posthumanists are driven by the desire to arrive at a more humane (i.e., compassionate and considerate) life. As such, their ideas and aspirations are fundamentally humanist (in the sense that they wish to impart all life, including that of humans, with value). Braidotti is clear on this point: "[…] to be posthuman does not mean to be indifferent to the humans, or to be de-humanized. On the contrary, it rather implies a new way of combining ethical values with the well-being of an enlarged sense of community, which includes one's territorial and environmental inter-connections."[36]

B. POSTHUMANISM IN RUSSIA

While the discourse of posthumanism as such is distinctively postmodern and Western, the questions associated with it transcend time and geography. Looking to nineteenth-century Russia, one finds writers and philosophers thoughtfully probing the nature of man and humanity's relationship to: God; non-human forms of life; matter and the plane of material existence; society, including laws, governments, morals; the body and sexuality (reproduction); acts of creation (theurgy), art, and language; nature and natural forces, including aging, death, and the natural elements; the cosmos; the end of being (eschatology); and consciousness and subjectivity. Utopian and speculative thinking about the future of *Homo sapiens*, especially its liberation from natural

---

33 Braidotti offers the following précis: "Important liberal thinkers like Habermas (2003) and influential ones like Fukuyama (2002) […] express deep concern for the status of the human, and seem particularly struck by moral and cognitive panic at the prospect of the posthuman turn, blaming our advanced technologies for it. I share their concern, but as a posthuman thinker with distinct anti-humanist feelings, I am less prone to panic at the prospect of a displacement of the centrality of the human and can also see the advantages of such an evolution." See Braidotti, *The Posthuman*, 64.

34 Stefan Herbrechter, *Posthumanism: A Critical Analysis* (London: Bloomsbury, 2013), 23.

35 Braidotti, *The Posthuman*, 195.

36 Ibid., 190.

and manmade forms of oppression, gained currency by the end of the century. Engaging with native and Western scientific discoveries and ideologies ranging from those of Orthodox Christianity to Darwin and Marx, Russian and early Soviet thinkers elaborated programs for bodily transformation, rejuvenation, and immortality, many of which are undergirded by a monist belief in the interconnectedness of all matter.

As we have already established, the discourses of posthumanism emerged in part as a critique of the idealistic humanism of the European Enlightenment. In *The Russian Idea*, Nikolai Berdyaev explains that humanism in Russia was conflated with humanitarianism, an attitude toward one's fellow man colored by the Christian values of compassion and pity. Writing on the contrast between Russian humaneness (*chelovechnost'*) and European humanism (*gumanizm*), Berdyaev asserted, "Humanism in the European sense of the word formed no part of the experience of Russia. There was no Renaissance among us, but we did experience, and it may be with some particular sharpness, the crisis of humanism, and its inner dialectic was disclosed."[37] The crisis of humanism, as Berdyaev saw it, was the conflict between the charitable values of Eastern Orthodoxy and the Russian imperial state's tendency toward cruelty, violence, and oppression.

According to Berdyaev, it was Dostoevsky in Russia and Nietzsche in Europe who proclaimed the crisis of humanism. Dostoevsky began his critique of reason in *Notes from the Underground* (1864) by polemicizing with the utilitarianism of Jeremy Bentham and John Stuart Mill. The Underground Man questions their dictate that man should always maximize his personal advantage based on rational calculations of self-interest. He argues for the freedom to make choices that defy the pragmatic principles of rationalism, utility, and individual benefit. The Underground Man seeks freedom from humanistic, socially proscribed behavior and challenges the notion of a universal definition of advantage. While arguing that free will and desire are what make us human, Dostoevsky also shows how individualistic behaviors may be in conflict with the social.

If the Underground Man begins the crisis of humanism with his critique of reason and extreme individualism, the character Kirillov in Dostoevsky's *Demons* (1872) deepens it by illustrating the fatal consequence of humanism's godlessness and hubris. When man feels himself outside of or beyond God, he is in the condition of mangodhood (*chelovekobozhestvo*), the antithesis of Godmanhood

---

37 Nicolas Berdyaev, *The Russian Idea*, trans. R. M. French (New York: The Macmillan Company, 1948), 86, https://archive.org/details/russianidea017842mbp.

(*bogochelovechestvo*). Kirillov, the exemplar of mangodhood, prophesied the arrival of "a new man, happy and proud," who will become a god by overcoming fear and pain. He speculates that this new man will be categorically different in all regards: "Man will become a god and will change physically. And the world will change, and affairs will change, and ideas, and all feelings."[38] As Berdyaev concluded, "Compassion and humaneness in Dostoevsky are turned into inhumanity and cruelty when man [Kirillov] arrives at the stage of man-as-God, when he reaches self-deification."[39] Berdyaev further suggested that the supreme individualism expressed in the idea of rational self-interest as dictated by European humanism was antithetical to Russianness. The Russian Idea, as he called it, was "that individual salvation is impossible, that salvation is corporate [*kommunotarno*], that all are answerable for all."[40] The figure whose philosophy most vividly exemplifies this Russian Idea is Nikolai Fedorov (1829–1903).

Fedorov is regarded as the father of Russian Cosmism, a philosophical movement that attempted to reconcile evolutionary history, scientific determinism, and Christian thought. His radical proposal to resurrect our ancestors in order to transcend mortality and his bold vision of human potential inspired religious philosophers, writers, artists, scientists, engineers, and Bolshevik revolutionaries.[41] *The Philosophy of the Common Task* (published in 1906) is the name Fedorov's mentees gave to the posthumous compilation of his essays and teachings. In a nutshell, this philosophy rests on the daring assertion that the Christian doctrine of resurrection provides the sole viable goal for scientific-technological progress (and for all human activity, in general). The only conceivable ethical as well as rational use of technology is abolishing death and resurrecting human life (specifically, ancestors). Any other uses of technology, such as the temporary goals of material progress and plenitude, are rendered superfluous by the unfortunate fact of dying.

Fedorov's call to action, to control the blind force of nature by imposing rational direction, evinces a materialist vision of paradise on earth (notwithstanding his critique of Marx's "materiocracy"). Irene Masing-Delic sees a

38 Unless noted otherwise, all translations in the introduction are by the editors. F. M. Dostoevsky, *Besy* [Demons]. In *Sobranie sochinenii v 15-i tomakh* [Collected works in 15 volumes] 7: 112 (Leningrad: Nauka, 1990). http://rvb.ru/dostoevski/toc.htm.

39 Berdyaev, *The Russian Idea*, 89.

40 Ibid., 200.

41 See Irene Masing-Delic, "The Transfiguration of Cannibals: Fedorov and the Avant-Garde," in *Laboratory of Dreams: The Russian Avant-garde and Cultural Experiment*, ed. John E. Bowlt and Olga Matich (Stanford, CA: Stanford University Press, 1999), 17–36; and George Young, *The Russian Cosmists: The Esoteric Futurism of Nikolai Fedorov and His Followers* (Oxford: Oxford University Press, 2012).

link between Dmitrii Pisarev's positivist vision of man's ability to attain full knowledge of and control over nature and Fedorov's emancipatory aspirations of overcoming nature.[42] Differing from traditional Christian doctrine that focuses on the separation of body and spirit and promises a transcendent paradise, Fedorov's religious philosophy imagines a utopia achievable through bodily and terrestrial modification. His faith in science and his interest in perfecting the material existence of humankind parallels the Marxist-Leninist belief in rational progress and the quest to attain ideal circumstances for human life on earth, although his project's success required mankind's accompanying spiritual development. Fedorov also saw a "common task" as essential for restoring fraternal love and equality among men, which harmonizes with the Soviet socialist emphasis on working together in collective action for the benefit of all members of society. It is no wonder then that Fedorov's utopian materialist ideas were compatible with the agenda of socialism building in early postrevolutionary Russia, as evidenced by the Biocosmism and Makovets movement of the early 1920s (to which we will return).

Religious Cosmism

Based on Fedorov's ideas, Russian Cosmism gained adherents first in the early twentieth century and again in the post-Soviet era. Scholar Svetlana Semenova argues that early Cosmism was a unique school of thought because it demonstrated the concept of "active evolution," the term she uses to express the singular importance of human agency:

> This idea of active evolution is humanity taking the steering wheel of evolution into its own hands, it is the need for a new conscious stage of world development, which humanity directs according to reason and moral feeling, by taking the helm of evolution, as it were. Thus, it will be more accurate to define this movement not so much as cosmic as active-evolutionary. For active-evolutionary thinkers, man is a transitional being that finds himself in the process of growth, far from perfected but at the same time consciously creative, destined to transfigure not only the external world, but also his very own nature.[43]

42 Irene Masing-Delic, *Abolishing Death: A Salvation Myth of Russian Twentieth-Century Literature* (Stanford, CA: Stanford University Press, 1992), 69.

43 S. G. Semenova and A. G. Gacheva, eds., *Russkii kosmizm: Antologiia filosofskoi mysli* [Russian cosmism: anthology of philosophical thought] (Moscow: Pedagogika-Press, 1993), 4, https://fzrw.org/lib/Cosmism_anthology.pdf.

With its celebration of human intelligence and agency, Cosmism prefigures contemporary Transhumanist thought, which also conceives of humankind as capable of and even obligated ethically to take control of enhancing, and thereby advancing, our species (as discussed earlier in this Introduction). The Transhumanist Manifesto declares:

> We favor allowing individuals wide personal choice over how they enable their lives. This includes use of techniques that may be developed to assist memory, concentration, and mental energy; life extension therapies; reproductive choice technologies; cryonics procedures; and many other possible human modification and enhancement technologies.[44]

The active role man is to play in shaping his lived experience thus characterizes both Cosmist and contemporary Transhumanist thought, although biotechnological innovations are making such extreme bodily transformation possible only now, in the twenty-first century.

In *The Russian Cosmists: The Esoteric Futurism of Nikolai Fedorov and His Followers,* George Young offers a thorough genealogy of Cosmism, highlighting precursors to Cosmist thinking found in the work of such unexpected figures as Alexander Radishchev and Alexander Sukhovo-Kobylin. The proto-Cosmist paradigm of Sukhovo-Kobylin, which the nineteenth-century playwright elaborated in *The Teaching of the Allworld: Engineering-Philosophical Epiphanies* (*Uchenie Vsemir: Inzhenerno-filosofskie ozareniia*), is striking for its techno-utopian spirit. He delineated three stages of human development, the last of which would represent the perfection of humanity: first, the telluric or earthbound man, confined to planet Earth; next, the solar man, inhabiting the solar system; and finally, the sidereal man, who inhabits the entire universe (*vsemir*). Sukhovo-Kobylin envisioned man becoming a flying spirit that could

44 The Transhumanist Declaration was originally crafted in 1998 by an international group of authors: Doug Baily, Anders Sandberg, Gustavo Alves, Max More, Holger Wagner, Natasha Vita-More, Eugene Leitl, Bernie Staring, David Pearce, Bill Fantegrossi, den Otter, Ralf Fletcher, Kathryn Aegis, Tom Morrow, Alexander Chislenko, Lee Daniel Crocker, Darren Reynolds, Keith Elis, Thom Quinn, Mikhail Sverdlov, Arjen Kamphuis, Shane Spaulding, and Nick Bostrom. Accessed September 13, 2017 on the website of Humanity+, an organization that advocates the ethical use of technology to expand human capacities. http://humanityplus.org/philosophy/transhumanist-declaration/.

wing its way efficiently through space. The physicality of our bodies enslaves us and is in marked contrast to the ethereality of God. Sukhovo-Kobylin writes:

> Flying horizontally on a bicycle, man is already moving toward the form of an angel, a higher being. By inventing these machines of horizontal flight man has moved toward an angelic state, toward an ideal humanity. Every thinking being understands that a bicycle is essentially mechanical wings, a step toward future organic wings, which man will undoubtedly use to tear free of the shackles binding him to the telluric world—and he will escape to the solar world surrounding him thanks to his mechanical inventions.[45]

Sukhovo-Kobylin acknowledged his extreme devotion to rationalism and considered his philosophy to be neo-Hegelian, "a synthesis of Hegelism and Darwinism," inasmuch as Hegel and Darwin "together created a philosophy of evolution or a philosophy of succession (*riadovanie*)."[46]

While Cosmists often dismissed occultism and mystical thinking, one can find points of convergence with theosophical thinking, specifically in Helena Blavatsky's *Isis Unveiled* (1877) and *The Secret Doctrine* (1888). Although differing on the specifics, Theosophy and Cosmism posit that human agency will transform the species to its advantage, which includes overcoming the limitations of the physical body. Theosophy holds that embodied humanity is the result of human monads (a monad is essentially a soul, a divine essence) descending into their material form.[47] This physical plane of existence is the crudest of all seven planes, and humanity must therefore work its way out of material entrapment to get back to its spiritual state.[48] Theosophists maintained that the current race of humans is inferior in all regards to the earlier Atlantean and Lemurian races, and our task is therefore to restore ourselves to

45 A. V. Sukhovo-Kobylin, *Uchenie Vsemir: Inzhenerno-filosofskie ozareniia* [The teaching of the allworld: engineering-philosophical epiphanies], ed. A. A. Karulin and I. V. Mirzalis (Moscow: S. E. T., 1995), 72.

46 A. A. Karulin and I. V. Mirzalis, "A.V. Sukhovo-Kobylin: Fragmenty filosofskoi biografii" [A.V. Sukhovo-Kobylin: fragments of a philosophical biography] in Sukhovo-Kobylin, 7.

47 Maria Carlson, *"No Religion Higher Than Truth": A History of the Theosophical Movement in Russia, 1875-1922* (Princeton, NJ: Princeton University Press, 1993), 116.

48 Just as man has seven aspects of being, so the planes of existence are seven. The planes are: physical, astral, mental, intuitional, spiritual, monadic, divine. Carlson, *"No Religion Higher Than Truth,"* 121.

our former mastery.[49] The first stage of development is the current one, when humans work toward mastering the physical plane: "The essential mission of this epoch of civilization is to adapt man to the physical plane to develop reason and practical logic, to immerse intelligence in physical matter so that matter may be understood and finally mastered."[50] Once current humans attain mastery of the physical plane, we can consider that "evolution has reached its acme of physical development, crowned its work with the perfect physical man, and from this point, begins its work spirit-ward."[51] Maria Carlson highlights the rational orientation of European Theosophy, pointing out that it "offered the possibility of reaching God 'scientifically,' with the rationalistic tools at hand, bypassing both 'narrow materialism' and 'traditional theology.'"[52] Born at least partially as a response to Europe's valorization of positivism, Theosophy emphasized the pursuit of higher (esoteric) knowledge to gain insight into metaphysical mysteries and ultimately attain spiritual advancement.[53]

With a worldview that privileged spirit over materiality and was informed partially by Buddhism (specifically, its doctrine of reincarnation), Theosophists favored a type of learning and cognition that was intuitive. Anthroposophy, an outgrowth of Theosophy articulated by the Austrian philosopher Rudolph Steiner, favored intuitive cognition enhanced by the power of intellectual cognition and a rigorous scientific methodology that would be based largely on observing personal experience. Steiner's devotion to empirical knowledge and reason echoed that of humanists and he was a champion of Enlightenment values. In fact, Steiner wished to name the Russian Anthroposophical Society in honor of Mikhail Lomonosov

49 Young, *The Russian Cosmists*, 189.

50 Rudolph Steiner, *An Esoteric Cosmology*, Published online January 15, 2001. http://wn.rsarchive.org/Lectures/GA094/English/SGP1978/19060614p01.html.

51 Carlson, "*No Religion Higher Than Truth*," 119. She is quoting Helena Blavatsky, *The Secret Doctrine*, vol. 1 (London: The Theosophical Publishing Co., 1888), 232.

52 Ibid., 12.

53 Theosophy explored the relationship between matter and spirit, the visible and the invisible, a project more broadly associated with phenomenology and the Kantian dichotomy of phenomena and noumena. Maria Carlson argues compellingly for the central role of Theosophy in shaping the literature and culture of the Silver Age. Symbolism's central premise of correspondences between images or symbols and transcendent, inexpressible ideas resonates with Theosophy's body/spirit cleavage. See Carlson, "*No Religion Higher Than Truth*." Also, George Young points to Scriabin's *Mysterium* as a Fedorovian artistic project: performers and audience members were to be part of a seven-day concert at the end of which there would be a "cosmic crescendo, signaling the end of the present human race and the beginning of a next, Blavatskian, higher race of superhumans" (181).

because, in his view, Lomonosov best represented the Enlightenment era's high esteem for intellect and reason.[54] However, the intellect was to be used in pursuit of spiritual research and overcoming the body. Carlson summarizes a central goal of Anthroposophy as bodily transformation in the name of esoteric knowledge: "By purifying and refashioning the astral body through meditation, concentration, and other exercises, thus enabling it to acquire higher organs of supersensible perception, trained spiritual researchers could participate actively in the spiritual world."[55] The active role imputed to man in mastering the material world, which hinges on his cultivation of the mind, recalls Fedorov and Cosmism, and again brings to the fore a convergence of humanism and transhumanism.[56] It is worth noting, though, one very critical difference. To Steiner, Christ offered an important model for man because Christ was an earthly embodiment of a Divine All: divine spirit had descended down to earth, where it found material form in Christ, and it can therefore return to its original spirit state. While Cosmists also viewed Christ as a model for man, they located Christ's importance in his own resurrection as well as that of Lazarus, which proved that a mere mortal could be raised from the dead.

Religious and political philosopher Nikolai Berdyaev proclaimed himself heir to the tradition of Dostoevsky, Fedorov, and Soloviev.[57] In *The Destiny of Man* Berdyaev hits a Fedorovian theme when he discusses man's ability to transcend himself. Berdyaev links this ability of humankind to its creativity and, in particular, its capacity for self-directed change (the same principle identified in Cosmism as "active evolution"). For Berdyaev, humanity's exceptionalism

---

54 Carlson, "*No Religion Higher Than Truth*," 100.

55 Ibid., 129–130.

56 The teachings of "Living Ethics," elaborated by Nikolai and Elena Roerich in the 1920s and 1930s, integrate theosophical, occultist ideas with a Cosmist vision of unity between humankind and the universe. See Anita Stasulane, "The Theosophy of the Roerichs: Agni Yoga or Living Ethics," in *The Handbook of the Theosophical Current*, eds. Olav Hammer and Mikael Rothstein (Leiden and Boston: Brill, 2013), 193–215.

57 Vladimir Soloviev shared Fedorov's ambition to outline a program for humanity to attain immortality, but his views hewed more closely to the traditional Christian idea of afterlife. He eschewed his mentor's embrace of science and technology as the instruments of resurrection in favor of beauty and erotic love. For Soloviev, aesthetics could counteract death. In his *Lectures on Divine Humanity* (delivered in 1880), he posited that man alone was capable of effecting the reintegration of the physical world with God and of attaining "all-unity" (*vseedinstvo*). For Soloviev, Christ's incarnation in human form was the most perfect expression of God; Christ was therefore a model of the Dostoevskian Godmanhood (the union of God and man wherein man remains subservient to God). To achieve this state of Godmanhood, Soloviev posited that the anthropocentric condition of mangodhood was a necessary stage, through which humanity had to pass. For more on Soloviev, see Irene Masing-Delic, *Abolishing Death*.

is a testament to the existence of a force even greater than humans: "The superhuman principle is a constituent element of man's nature. Man is discontented with himself and capable of outgrowing himself. The very fact of the existence of man is a break in the natural world and proves that nature cannot be self-sufficient but rests upon a supernatural reality."[58] Berdyaev's belief in a divine superpower upon which human exceptionalism depends is a variation on a theme expressed by Francis Fukuyama and noted earlier: Namely, human dignity stems from the fact that man is made in the image of God. Given Berdyaev's Christian anthropology, he posits that the goal of human life is to "put an end to the old world and to begin the new" at each moment of life, which echoes the eschatology of other Christian thinkers. Berdyaev writes: "He [man] is dependent upon his natural environment and at the same time he humanizes it and introduces a new principle into it. Man's creative activity has significance for the whole world and indicates a new stage of cosmic life. Man is a new departure in nature."[59] While identifying as Christian religious philosophers, Fedorov and Berdyaev nonetheless betray the imprint of humanism on their ideas by endowing man with free will and creative agency. As we see repeatedly, transhumanism is an intensified version of humanism; humanism on speed, if you will.

Religious philosopher Sergei Bulgakov also shared Fedorov's transhumanist concern with overcoming the forces of nature including death through human-directed action. However, instead of deploying technology as Fedorov advocated, Bulgakov saw caretaking or management (*khoziaistvo*) as key. He repudiated humanistic progress, which he thought was motivated "not by love, not by pity, but by a proud dream of earthly paradise, of the kingdom of mangodhood cut off from the other world."[60] In *Philosophy of Economy* (*Filosofiia khoziaistva*, 1912) he argued that humankind needs to control, care for, and ultimately humanize nature. By humanizing nature he meant that we need to endow matter with spirit, that is, transform non-living matter into living. Bulgakov had an organicist view that "the kingdom of life constantly intrudes on the kingdom of nonlife, seizes and carries away cold, lifeless matter with its warm tentacles, and transforms it into living material, organizes dead

58 Nicolas Berdyaev, *The Destiny of Man*, trans. Natalie Duddington (London: Geoffrey Bles, 1948), 45–46.

59 Berdyaev, *The Destiny of Man*, 46.

60 S. N. Bulgakov, *Svet nevechernii: sozertsaniia i umozreniia* [Ever-shining light: contemplations and speculations] (Moscow: Respublika, 1994), http://www.vehi.net/bulgakov/svet/003.html.

matter into a living body."[61] Consumption, or ingesting food—taking in dead matter and incorporating it into living matter—is a model of transformative synthesis and an affirmative act of human agency. The importance of consumption here is in vivid contrast to Fedorov's prognosis that our organs of digestion will wither away once we fulfill the task of resurrecting our forefathers.[62]

Scientific Cosmism

The realization of any posthuman future depends on the development of sophisticated scientific means, a point emphasized by Fedorov, who called for all scientists on earth to apply themselves to the common task of overcoming the blind forces of nature. The scholarly and speculative contributions of such scientists as Konstantin Tsiolkovsky, Vladimir Vernadsky, Aleksandr Chizhevsky, and Vasily Kuprevich recapitulate the Fedorovian principle of "active evolution," the need for humanity's intervention in its own development, and evince an organicist view of man's close relation to matter and other forms of life.[63]

Known by most as a pioneer of Russian rocketry, Tsiolkovsky saw space flight and habitation in space as means to save humanity from potential planetary crises (including overpopulation, should a Fedorovian resurrection of ancestors come to pass) and as the next stage in humanity's perpetual evolution. As an empirical scientist and engineer, Tsiolkovsky made calculations and designed spacecraft that would form the foundation of the Soviet space program. As a neo-materialist philosopher who sought existential meaning in his aeronautical work, he contemplated the shared organic basis of all material bodies, be they planetary or human. By recognizing the "atom-spirit" (*atom-dukh*) as the essence

61 Sergei Bulgakov, *Philosophy of Economy: The World as Household*, trans. and ed. Catherine Evtuhov (New Haven, CT. Yale University Press, 2000), 97.

62 Religious philosopher and polymath Pavel Florensky had a different philosophy regarding the role and fate of human organs in the species' development. George Young's summary of Florensky's 1919 article "Organ Projection" highlights the ability of a "projection of artificial organs, continuations of our bodies, to extend human capabilities throughout the cosmos. Projected organs and body parts can operate and act on the world beyond the limits of our present physical bodies." Young, *The Russian Cosmists*, 131.

63 Anindita Banerjee underscores the importance of Ernst Haeckel (1834-1919) for Russia's alternative approach to biological modernity. Haeckel made Darwinism compatible with a monistic view of evolution by embracing the latter's ideas from *The Descent of Man*, "in which humanity was conceived as part of organic nature's eternal movement toward self-perfection." Anindita Banerjee, *We Modern People: Science Fiction and the Making of Russian Modernity* (Middletown, CT: Wesleyan University Press, 2012), 125.

of matter, Tsiolkovsky held that the possibility of life inheres within all material and gaseous bodies, meaning that other, potentially higher forms of life could exist beyond our planet. Tsiolkovsky's atom-spirit prefigures the vital materialism of Jane Bennett discussed earlier in this Introduction. While Tsiolkovsky's concept of a universal atom-spirit that humans share with other matter implies a kind of immortality, it is one very different from Fedorov's. According to Tsiolkovsky, "Of course, every incarnation has its own form, unlike that which came before it. We have always lived and always will live, but each time in a new form and, naturally, without recollection of the previous one."[64] While Tsiolkovsky's concept of immortality is monistic and vitalist, he nonetheless preserves a hierarchy of forms and sees certain endowments of humanity as unique and determinative of a non-Darwinian kind of evolution. In "The Exploration of Outer Space by Means of Jet Propulsion Devices, 1911," he identifies reason and the capacity for self-perfection as the best aspects of humanity, which will ensure the immortality of that special essence that makes humans who they are. He wrote, "In all likelihood, the best part of humanity will never perish but rather will migrate from one Sun as it fades to another.... Thus, there is no end to life, to reason and the perfection of humanity. Its progress is eternal."[65]

While Tsiolkovsky envisioned an interplanetary future for humanity enabled by the technological development of spacecraft, his contemporary Vladimir Vernadsky proposed a restructuring of humanity for its life on a changing planet. An interdisciplinary scientist whose work brought together the fields of geology, biology, and chemistry, Vernadsky shared Tsiolkovsky's vitalist view on the interconnectedness of all matter. For Vernadsky, this took the form of the earth's interconnected layers, the geosphere, the biosphere, and the noosphere.[66] Vernadsky's research on the biosphere and humanity's dependency on other life forms for sustenance led him to worry about how humanity will survive on earth after we have depleted the planet's natural

64 K. E. Tsiolkovskii, "Kosmicheskaia filosofiia" [Cosmic philosophy] in Semenova and Gacheva, *Russkii kosmizm* [Russian cosmism], 282.

65 Konstantin Tsiolkovsky, "Issledovanie mirovykh prostanstv reaktivnymi priborami, 1911" [The exploration of outer space by means of jet propulsion devices, 1911] in *Sobranie sochinenii* [Collected Works] (Moscow, 1954), 139. For more on Tsiolkovsky and his relationship to Fedorov's ideas, see Julia Vaingurt, "The Anatomy of Spaceflight: Rockets and Other Mechanical Eggs in Russian Modernism," *Russian Literature* LXIX-II/III/IV (2011): 291–308.

66 Vernadsky is best known for his theorization of a third layer of the earth, the noosphere. This third, "thinking layer" of the earth has been developing in lockstep with the expansion of human consciousness and is co-extensive with the biosphere, meaning that the entire system of life on earth is influencing the field of thought and vice versa.

resources. He contemplated the possibility that humans could one day alter their physical and chemical makeup to become like plants and other autotrophic organisms (capable of self-nourishment, as by photosynthesis or chemosynthesis).[67] Vernadsky wrote in his article "The Autotrophism of Humanity":

> As soon as we discover how to synthesize food directly, without the help of organic substances, the future of man will change in a fundamental way. [...] To a large degree, the future of man is always made by man himself. The creation of a new, autotrophic being will give man opportunities, absent until now, to realize his eternal spiritual yearnings; it will effectively open the path to a better life before him.[68]

According to Vernadsky, it is the task of human scientists to discover how to effect such a physical transformation of the body, a position that illustrates his intellectual affinity with Fedorov and the twenty-first-century Transhumanists.

Less well known than Tsiolkovsky and Vernadsky, botanist Vasily Kuprevich used his insights into plant life to envision a strategy for humankind to extend life indefinitely. Joining Fedorov and other Cosmists in their intention to overcome death, Kuprevich maintained that since certain plants were able to live continuously for centuries through a mechanism of self-renewal, man should also have such potential. According to Semenova and Gacheva, Kuprevich insisted that "Having invented death, nature should show us the path for fighting it," meaning that the scientific study of the human genome could reveal the genes responsible for aging and death.[69]

Revolution: The Social and Economic Human

Cosmism's hubristic belief in man's ability to tame nature, including the human body, was also a hallmark of Leninist and Stalinist ideologies. Masing-Delic summarizes the Soviet will to power in terms that foreground the necessity of man's

---

67 Fedorov also envisioned humanity as autotrophic, a condition that would render our digestive organs obsolete and thus lead to their disappearance. Tsiolkovsky, too, imagined a new autotrophic humanity in his science fiction story "Dreams of Earth and Sky," which tells the story of a plant-man (*zhivotno-rastenie*) who has wings containing chlorophyll. See Banerjee, *We Modern People*, 137.

68 V. I. Vernadskii, "Avtotrofnost' chelovechestva" [Autotrophism in humanity], in Semenova and Gacheva, *Russkii kosmizm* [Russian cosmism], 305, 306–07.

69 Semenova and Gacheva, 349. Also see V. F. Kuprevich, "Dolgoletie: real'nost' mechty" [Longevity: the reality of a dream] (ibid., 350–54).

active participation in biology as well as history: "[N]atural evolution was slow and had perhaps run its course. Consequently, it had to be complemented and eventually replaced by man-initiated ameliorization, above all, cultural creativity, scientific research, and new forms of labor. The era of pure biology was gone, as was that of passive history."[70] Writing about Fedorov, Berdyaev observed the affinity between his priorities and those of communism. In addition to a shared admiration for positivist science and technology and collectivism, Fedorov and Marx viewed labor as a chief means to attain their respective utopian ends.[71] However, their attitudes toward labor as a means to an end differed: While Fedorov saw labor as a means of uniting humanity in pursuit of the "common task" of resurrection, Marx viewed humans in terms of their labor's economic value.[72] By conceiving of the human chiefly as a laborer, Marx instrumentalized the body; one must regulate the laborer's body in order to regulate economic output. While Marx oriented his philosophy around the control of labor and production, Fedorov concentrated his ideas on the control and abolition of sexual reproduction. They were thus united in the pursuit of biopolitical projects that variously promised mankind liberation from undesirable material conditions.

The biopolitical overtones inhering in the emancipatory utopias of Fedorov and Marx also resound in the Western models of production that were heralded by Lenin and his acolytes. Despite the overt connections of Taylorism and Fordism to capitalism, Lenin and Alexei Gastev ardently believed that such models of industrial organization would also suit an economy in transition to socialism. Gastev, who would go on to lead the Central Institute of Labor (founded in 1920), treated the human body as a machine and wished to control carefully its range of productive motion. In his 1924 tract *Literature and Revolution* Lev Trotsky famously called for a new type of person, a "higher social biological type." Trotsky predicted that such a new man would cultivate the ability to control himself—a transhumanist principle—while paradoxically insisting that man's intervention is "in accord with evolution":

> He will make it his business to achieve beauty by giving the movement of his own limbs the utmost precision, purposefulness and economy in his

70 Masing-Delic, *Abolishing Death*, 64.

71 Berdyaev, *The Russian Idea*, 209.

72 Fedorov professed a dislike for Marxism because of its earth-bound materialism (what he called its materiocracy) and its insistence on struggle as a necessity for historical progress. Fedorov also criticized socialism for fostering a false sense of brotherhood that lacked a spiritual dimension. The spiritual aspect of his agenda consisted in overcoming self-interest by concentrating on the resurrection of ancestors rather than the pursuit of self-perpetuation.

> work, his walk and his play. He will try to master first the semiconscious and then the subconscious processes in his own organism, such as breathing, the circulation of the blood, digestion, reproduction, and, within necessary limits, he will try to subordinate them to the control of reason and will. Even purely physiologic life will become subject to collective experiments. The human species, the coagulated *Homo sapiens*, will once more enter into a state of radical transformation, and, in his own hands, will become an object of the most complicated methods of artificial selection and psycho-physical training. This is entirely in accord with evolution.[73]

Gastev and Trotsky's intense conviction that the human body could be mastered and controlled like a machine is humanist in its reliance on reason and will. Also interested in the relationship of the body to problems of labor and economy, polymath Alexander Bogdanov advocated for humane machines instead of machinistic humans, effectively concurring with Berdyaev that humanitarianism is a central tenet of any Russian or socialist worldview.[74]

Bogdanov argued that socialism has different values than capitalism and therefore demands a different method for organizing labor. This belief put Bogdanov on a path to developing a universal system of organization, which he called tektology (*tektologiia*). Tektology was science of systems that could organize knowledge as well as organic and non-organic objects. Bogdanov insisted that all formations are comprised by interdependent parts, each of which carries an equal value in relation to the whole—a view not dissimilar from Latour's actor-network theory. Traumatized by the chaos ensuing after the Bolshevik Revolution, World War I, and the Civil War, he identified control and management as master tasks: "mankind has no other activity except organizational activity, there being no other problems except organizational problems."[75] Bogdanov's systemic thinking prompted him to seek out operational analogs across fields, a kind of metaphorical approach to organization. As scholar McKenzie Wark observed, "The word organ, from the Greek via the Latin *organum*, can mean a tool, but also a part of the body.

73 Leon Trotsky, *Literature and Revolution,* trans. Rose Strunsky (New York: Russell & Russell: 1957), https://www.marxists.org/archive/trotsky/1924/lit_revo/ch08.htm.

74 For more on Lenin, Gastev, and Bogdanov, see Julia Vaingurt, *Wonderlands of the Avant-Garde: Technology and the Arts in Russia of the 1920s* (Evanston, IL: Northwestern University Press, 2013).

75 Alexander Bogdanov, *Essays in Tektology,* trans. George Gorelik (Seaside, CA: Intersystems Publications, 1980), 3, https://monoskop.org/images/5/51/Bogdanov_Alexander_Essays_in_Tektology.pdf.

The seed of Bogdanov's thought is contained within the metaphorical leap of this primary term. A tool is an external organ of a body; an organ is an internal tool of a body."[76] The analogy of tools to organs illuminates Bogdanov's statement about the functional enmeshment of machines and bodies in the factory: "If several workers work at one machine, then as far as their system of collaboration is concerned, their relation to this machine, which binds them together, is an internal connection of the system, although this is a relation to a spatially external object."[77] By working together at a machine, the laborers are functionally bound together, as if by internally shared organs.

This parallel between a system of industrial production and the body's vital system points to another of Bogdanov's interests: blood transfusions. As a scientist and physician, he subjected himself and others to experiments, which he hoped would strengthen their immunity and combat old age.[78] In his science fiction novel *Red Star* the socialist Martians practice a type of restorative blood transfusion that "thoroughly rejuvenates all [one's] tissues."[79] The Martians have successfully doubled their life expectancy to two hundred years thanks to this hematological renewal. Anindita Banerjee insightfully explains that for Bogdanov sharing blood was an expression of his monist worldview and a route to brotherhood; mutual blood transfusions were a way to implement the socialist spirit of cooperation on a physiological level.[80] Harmonizing scientific progress with humanitarian concern, Bogdanov joined Fedorov and Marx in pursuing an emancipatory project.

Cosmism after 1917

Bogdanov's Martians are not only scientifically advanced, they are also socially progressive models of rational behavior and community orientation. They are,

---

76 McKenzie Wark, *Molecular Red: Theory for the Anthropocene* (London and Brooklyn: Verso, 2015). iBook.

77 Bogdanov, *Essays in Tektology*, 187.

78 Contemporaries of Bogdanov also working on rejuvenation included Ilya Mechnikov and Eugen Steinach; see Banerjee, *We Modern People*, 144. Mikhail Bulgakov satirized these attempts in works such as *The Heart of a Dog* and *Fatal Eggs* by depicting the ill consequences of attempting to modify human and animal nature.

79 Alexander Bogdanov, *Red Star: The First Bolshevik Utopia*, ed. Loren R. Graham and Richard Stites, trans. Charles Rougle (Bloomington: Indiana University Press, 1984), 85. For more on Bogdanov and blood, see Nikolai Krementsov, *A Martian Stranded on Earth: Alexander Bogdanov, Blood Transfusions, and Proletarian Science* (Chicago: University of Chicago Press, 2011).

80 Banerjee, *We Modern People*, 142.

in other words, a prototype of the New Soviet Man, that sociobiological innovation called for by Trotsky. While Marxist Leninism disdained all forms of mysticism and the false promise of divine miracles, it allowed for the pursuit of immortality by focusing on the physical body and mastering the scientific laws of nature. The embalmed body of Lenin housed in a glass sarcophagus emblematizes the early Soviet period's positivist devotion to the possibility of resurrection and immortality.[81] The early Soviet years also witnessed a continued aspiration toward liberation, with ideologues finding a parallel between the oppression of capitalism and nature. A group of twenty-six individuals known as the Biocosmists united under the emancipatory mantra of "Immortalism and Interplanetarianism" in the years 1920-1922. Under the leadership of anarchist and poet Aleksandr Agienko (also known as Sviatogor), the Biocosmists saw a continuity between the Bolshevik struggle against the bourgeoisie and humanity's struggle against death.[82] Recalling the Transhumanist Manifesto cited earlier, the Biocosmist Manifesto articulated two main human rights: "[T]he right to exist forever, and the right to unimpeded movement throughout interplanetary space."[83] A Moscow group of anarchist-biocosmists elaborated on those tenets in its Declaratory Resolution, asserting in the era's strident revolutionary language:

> Biocosmism is a new ideology, for which the cornerstone principle is the concept of personhood (*lichnost'*), growing in power and creativity to establish itself in immortality and in the cosmos. As real and essential rights of personhood, we consider the right to existence (immortality, resurrection, rejuvenation) and to freedom of movement throughout the cosmos.[84]

Makovets was another group in the early 1920s that united the revolutionary agenda with philosophical visions of a new man under the banner of defeating oppression. The most prominent members of the group were religious philosopher Pavel Florensky, Futurist poet Velimir Khlebnikov, and artist and

81 Masing-Delic, *Abolishing Death*, 14.

82 Young, *The Russian Cosmists*, 199.

83 Quoted in Young, 199. See Asif A. Siddiqi, *The Red Rockets' Glare: Spaceflight and the Soviet Imagination, 1857-1957* (New York: Cambridge University Press, 2010), 107–8.

84 Quoted in Young, 199. See I. Vishev, "'Filosofiia obshchego dela' Fedorova i biokosmizm" [Fedorov's 'Philosophy of the Common Task' and biocosmism], 180. In *Filosofiia bessmertiia i voskresheniia* [Philosophy of immortality and resurrection], eds. A. G. Gacheva, S. G. Semenova, and M. V. Skorokhodov (Moscow: Nasledie, 1996), 1:179–86.

poet Vasily Chekrygin.[85] Chekrygin followed Fedorov in wanting to effect a democratic resurrection of our ancestors and subscribed to the transformative power attributed to art (especially icon painting) by Fedorov. He planned to build a Cathedral of the Resurrecting Museum (*Sobor voskreshchaiushchego muzeia*), in which he would paint frescoes depicting the flight of resurrected bodies up to the cosmos. Chekrygin's artistic imagining of these rising bodies was, unfortunately, never realized visually, but he did compose a prose poem entitled "On the Cathedral of the Resurrecting Museum"[86] that contains unambiguous allusions to Fedorov's cosmic cathedral (architecture was his ideal union of science and art).[87]

Postrevolutionary utopian thinking about a new sociobiological type, the New Soviet Man, articulated a plan of active evolution that drew on both the hubristic humanism of the Enlightenment and Fedorovian projectivism (see the discussion of Trotsky above). Stalin's plan to restructure life comprehensively is a maximalist expression of the demiurgic spirit that characterized Cosmism, but it is buttressed by an unfaltering belief in the superior ability of Russians to realize this restructuring. Stalin-era production novels such as Nikolai Ostrovsky's *How the Steel Was Tempered* (1936) valorized the New Man as a socialist cyborg. Fortified by building socialism, the protagonist Pavka uses the force of his willpower to overcome his bodily limits.

Throughout the Soviet period, science fiction writers engaged with techno-political projects of human modification. Aleksandr Beliaev penned numerous works that touch on biomedical alterations to humankind, including

---

85 The early Soviet period and high Soviet period also witnessed writers engaging with Cosmist ideas, albeit without overtly evoking Fedorov or his philosophy. Fedorovian utopianism appealed to poet Nikolai Zabolotsky, known mostly as a founding member of the avant-garde writers' group Oberiu (Union of Real Art). As scholar Darra Goldstein puts it, Fedorov's "dreams of unity and harmony attracted Zabolotsky, finding reflection in his poetry," although it is unclear if the poet ever read the philosopher. See Darra Goldstein, *Nikolai Zabolotsky: Play for Mortal Stakes* (Cambridge: Cambridge University Press, 1994), 123. Mikhail Prishvin's diaries and prose reveal his conception of ideal brotherhood, which is not dissimilar from Fedorov's. Andrei Platonov's posthumanist perspective troubled the thresholds between human and animal, man and machine, and as Jonathan Platt argues in this volume, his writings continue to engage philosophers in emancipatory thinking.

86 Young, *The Russian Cosmists*, 215–17.

87 In "Kak mozhet byt' razresheno protivorechie mezhdu naukoiu i iskusstvom?" ["How can the contradiction between science and art be resolved?"] Fedorov likens the architectural cathedral to the universe (*mirozdanie*) in its ability to bring together art and science. In N. F. Fedorov, *Sobranie sochinenii v 4-kh tomakh* [Collected works in 4 volumes], ed. P. B. Shalimov, II:233–36 (Moscow: Progress, 1995), http://nffedorov.ru/texts/nff/2p.pdf.

induced anabiosis, organ transplants, genetic engineering, and changes in the endocrinology system. His novels *Amphibian Man* (1927) and *Ariel* (1941) feature humans with extraordinary physical abilities: a youth who can breathe underwater through surgically implanted gills and a youth who can fly thanks to experiments in Brownian movement, respectively. The works of another influential science fiction writer, Ivan Efremov, bear the imprint of Tsiolkovsky's monist ideas about the interconnectedness of all matter on earth and beyond. His 1957 novel *Andromeda Nebula* works out a communist-scientific vision of Cosmism in which there is a "harmonious realization of all natural and spiritual needs through a total transformation of the cosmos so that the human and the non-human are perfectly united in a perpetually life-giving process."[88] The Strugatsky brothers, too, engage in complex ways with Fedorov's ideas about restructuring the body with the help of technology, as Julia Vaingurt discusses elsewhere in this volume. Indeed, the chapters of this book are intended to pick up here and tell the story of posthumanism in late Soviet to post-Soviet Russian literature and culture.

C. OVERVIEW OF THE CONTRIBUTIONS

The enmeshment of the human body with various forms of technology is a phenomenon that characterizes lived and imagined experiences in Russian arts of the modernist and postmodernist eras. In contrast to the postrevolutionary fixation on mechanical engineering, industrial progress, and the body as a machine, the postmodern, post-industrial period probes the meaning of being human not only from a physical, bodily perspective, but also from the philosophical perspectives of subjectivity and consciousness. Galactic advances in cybernetic technologies have prompted humans to reconsider the definition of humanity's ontological essence. The essays in this volume address such questions as the following:

- what does it mean to be human as technological instruments and prostheses enhance the body, enabling it to transcend its physiological limits;
- how does artificially created sentience perform subjectivity and consciousness;

88 Vyatcheslav Bart, "Futurist, Decadent, and Pagan Influences in Transhumanism: The Dangers of Godlike Creativity," in *Science Fiction beyond Borders*, ed. Shawn Edrei and Danielle Gurevitch (Newcastle upon Tyne: Cambridge Scholars Publishing, 2016), 96–112, 102.

- to what extent did ideological and political particularities of the Soviet imperial experiment and its demise influence posthuman fantasies;
- what kind of empowering and emancipatory potential does posthumanist hybridity offer;
- what kind of ethical challenges do we confront with the attempts to overcome humanity;
- what happens to humanity's relationship to natural and built environments in the era of the Anthropocene and what do planetary changes mean for the future of the species;
- what possibilities for labor and play do new technologies offer and how do they transform human self-perception?

The contributors to this volume express and interrogate a broad spectrum of attitudes toward posthumanism, ranging from caution to celebration. Our role as editors is not to take sides but to illuminate different political orientations and lines of argumentation in order to do justice to the complexity of the issues. We've decided to focus on late Soviet and post-Soviet periods because up until now this period has remained relatively unexplored. The postrevolutionary project of creating a New Soviet Man has received ample attention, but the scholarly conversation stops with the end of Stalinism. Meanwhile, only in the 1950s did cybernetics and biotechnologies start developing rapidly. Scholars in the West have responded with a theoretical interest in the topic—alongside literary and popular culture explorations—in the subsequent decades. *The Human Reimagined* addresses the ways that posthumanist thought developed in the cultural sphere amidst the scientific discoveries and rapid technological advancement of the late Soviet period, as well as in the context of the post-Soviet cyber age.

The questions surrounding the posthuman are explored in an array of genres and media, including philosophy, speculative fiction (cybernetic fiction, science fiction, nanopunk, and intellectual thriller), autobiographical writing, performance art, film, video game, and design. Most people think of posthumanism as being futuristic and the provenance of science fiction, but these articles debunk this misperception.

In "Our Posthuman Past: Subjectivity, History, and Utopia in Late-Soviet Science Fiction," Elana Gomel demonstrates the influence of the early-Soviet project of human engineering on the ambivalent treatment of (post) humanism in the science fiction of later periods. Gomel explores the paradoxes of Soviet posthumanism, with the New Man embodying ongoing tension between humanist morality and posthumanist alterity. She points out that such writers as the Strugatskys and Gansovsky caution about the undesirable ends to which our experiments with humanity might lead: "[L]etting go of the human may mean letting go of all human ethics, not just the parts we personally find objectionable." In her discussion of the Strugatsky brothers, Julia Vaingurt focuses on the technological enhancement of the human in *The Kid, The Beetle in the Anthill,* and *Time Wanderers*. Her paper analyzes the Strugatskys' exploration of technology's role in fostering, qualifying, and transforming life through the prism of Fedorov's quest for immortality and the radical physical transformation of humanity it would entail. She demonstrates how the Strugatsky brothers question whether there is something in humanity that is worth salvaging and to what extent technology can assist in, rather than hinder, this task.

Colleen McQuillen picks up on the materialist thinking in Fedorov's work to frame her discussion of environmentalism in late Soviet science fiction. She demonstrates that the literary motif of human adaptation to new terrestrial and interplanetary environments is based in Cosmist-materialist views of the universe. The emphasis on the body's responsiveness to changes in its physical surroundings modulates the dominant Soviet discourse of Prometheanism and begins to suggest a more balanced network of agency. Diana Kurkovsky West complements McQuillen's treatment of the natural environment by focusing on the distribution of agency in the built domestic environment in "'Drilled Humans' or Automated Systems? Reconsidering Human-Machine Integration in Late-Soviet Design." West discusses how kitchen design evinces the changing relationship between humans and things over the course of Soviet socialism-building. The paper traces how plans for reconfiguring Soviet kitchens transformed the human's role from operating domestic technologies according to rote training to being part of a more complex assemblage of actors. In kitchen design there were impulses toward liberation and control, a tension that resonates with Gomel's observation about the contradiction between socialist humanist aspirations and Soviet dehumanization.

Jacob Emery's "Romantic Aesthetics and Cybernetic Fiction" picks up on a similar tension within cybernetic fantasies of Savchenko. Emery productively compares Savchenko's transmission of human personality by radio waves to earlier means of self-expression. On one hand, this vision embodies the Romantic aspiration toward self-discovery and self-creation via a technological medium such as writing. On the other, by externalizing all that is within, the artist becomes vulnerable to manipulation and exploitation by a nefarious other, and in the conditions of totalitarian control by state power. In "Writing and Technology: Writing the Self in 'Real Time,'" Kristina Toland likewise investigates the parallels between the technology of writing and newer technologies of recording and constructing the self. Her paper focuses on Lev Rubinstein's progression from writing autobiographical poetry in the 1960s to the song performances and social media presentations of self in the early twenty-first century. She views these changes as enabling communal, network-based interactions facilitated by shared memory and history. Ultimately, Toland refuses to get too concerned about our over-reliance on new media technologies, because she proposes that our humanity has been, is, and always will be "inescapably technological and prosthetic."

At the other end of the spectrum, Sofya Khagi adduces the threat of dehumanization (*raschelovechivanie*) brought about by the posthumanist reliance on technology. She uses Garros-Evdokimov's nanopunk novel *Gray Goo* and Ilichevskii's intellectual thriller *Matisse* to illustrate the anxiety in early twenty-first-century Russia over "freedom-suppressing, homogenizing, de-intellectualizing, and unethical forces of global contemporaneity." Khagi's writers treat the erasure of bodily and social boundaries as degenerative, while Trevor Wilson interprets posthumanist hybridity as liberatory. Influenced by feminist posthumanism, he reads hybridity as representing a way toward social inclusion for previously marginalized groups in "Nothing but Mammals: Post-Soviet Sexuality after the End of History." Wilson argues that the overwhelming presence of human-animal hybrids in post-Soviet fiction articulates current cultural anxieties over the emergence of sexual minorities, signaling the rupture of the collective social body of the Soviet citizenry. He compares Pelevin's satire of normative rules of society, which are ultimately left intact, with queer writer Mogutin's transgressive utilization of human animality.

Jonathan Brooks Platt's article looks for a way to reconcile Marxism and posthumanism by analyzing the critical reception of Platonov by such thinkers of the New Russian Left as Artemy Magun, Oxana Timofeeva, and Igor Chubarov. Platonov is useful for this task because his work bridges two seemingly irreconcilable worldviews: an earnest aspiration toward the goal of building communism (humanist in its affirmative and constructive potential) and an almost animal-like anxiety over one's physical inability to accomplish this tremendous task (posthumanist in its negativity, in its denigration of humanity to its basic animal nature, and its potential affiliation with neo-liberal *laissez-faire* attitude and passivity). The task that Platt sets for himself is to find what allows Platonov to be simultaneously active and doubtful; the hope is to locate "an emancipatory potential" in Platonov's posthumanist questioning.

Katerina Lakhmitko's "Modes of Perception in Transmodal Fiction: A New Russian Subjectivity" explores the creation of new subject positions through engagement with Glukhovsky's transmedial *Metro* franchise (which includes online multi-author fiction and a video game). Lakhmitko credits cybermedia with making irrelevant such traditional binary distinctions as artist vs. audience, reader vs. text, or active producer vs. passive consumer. She also interrogates the idea of collective consciousness and entertains the possibility of communal subjectivity. Unlike the articles that engage with others' artistic and philosophical responses to posthumanism, philosopher Keti Chukhrov shares her original ideas on the posthuman condition in an interview about her play *Love Machines,* which she adapted to film in 2013. *Love Machines* encapsulates the range of philosophical positions that challenge the basic premise of Western humanism, and it questions the collapse of the humanitarian ideals of compassion and collective sensitivity in the era of posthumanism. Artist Alex Anikina's contribution is also an original thought experiment related to her unfinished trilogy of films, the first two parts of which are *Aleph* and *Some Entropy in Your Tea.* Anikina imagines how Artificial General Intelligence would process the entirety of human-produced information in a post-apocalyptic world.

In Russia and among transhumanists worldwide, scholarly and amateur interest in Fedorov and Cosmism is experiencing a revival in the early twenty-first century thanks to radical advances in technology that promise to make immortality possible. This revitalized interest is not merely theoretical. For example, media entrepreneur and billionaire Dmitry Itskov is funding a group of scientists to develop "cybernetic immortality" by the year 2045. Following the fantasy of Hans Moravec, Itskov's Avatar Project proposes to download human consciousness to a non-biological carrier, thereby extending life forever.[89] According to the website of Itskov's *2045 Initiative,* the group seeks a new strategy for humanity's development, which will be informed by "the fields of neural interfaces, robotics, artificial organs and systems." The website explains:

> The main science mega-project of the *2045 Initiative* aims to create technologies enabling the transfer of a [sic] individual's personality to a more

89 Roboticist Hans Moravec's book *Mind Children: The Future of Robot and Human Intelligence* (Cambridge, MA: Harvard University Press, 1990) proposed that the organic body may become irrelevant as technology of the future will make disembodied consciousness possible.

> advanced non-biological carrier, and extending life, including to the point of immortality. We devote particular attention to enabling the fullest possible dialogue between the world's major spiritual traditions, science and society.[90]

Itskov's twenty-first-century program draws on the varied currents of emancipatory philosophical-religious thinking and scientific speculation that circulated in Russia during the nineteenth and twentieth centuries, from Fedorov and Sukhovo-Kobylin to Tsiolkovsky, Vernadsky, and the Biocosmists. Itskov outlines a path of active "evolutionary transhumanism" that will lead to neo-humanity and "the creation of a fundamentally new model for the existence of society: spiritual, humanistic, ethical and high-tech."[91] His reference to humanism reminds us that our capacity to control and direct our development according to free will and our creative application of intelligence is ultimately what will move us to a posthuman future.

In light of efforts like Itskov's, the discussion of posthumanism in Russia promises to be ongoing and provocative. While we attempted to include many different perspectives and to touch upon the cornerstones of posthumanism in Russia, this volume is not meant to be exhaustive. Rather, we envision it as the beginning of a conversation and are eager to see the continued exploration of questions that will remain of vital interest to us all as (post)human beings.

---

90 2045 Strategic Social Initiative (website), accessed October 19, 2017, http://2045.com/ideology/.

91 Dmitry Itskov, "The Path to Neo-humanity as the Foundation of the Ideology of the 'Evolution 2045' Party," last modified November 16, 2012, 2045 Strategic Social Initiative (website), accessed October 19, 2017, http://2045.com/articles/30869.html.

Part Two

Questions of Ethics and Alterity

CHAPTER 1

Our Posthuman Past: Subjectivity, History, and Utopia in Late-Soviet Science Fiction

Elana Gomel,
Tel Aviv University

The New Men in the Old Country

Maxim Gorky, enthroned in the Soviet Union as a classic of socialist realism, was quoted more often than he was actually read. Perhaps the most popular of his quotes was from the 1902 play *Na dne* (*The Lower Depths,* literally, *At the bottom*): "Chelovek—eto zvuchit gordo" ("Man—this has a proud sound"). Emblazoned on red banners, this quote graced Young Pioneers' parades and factory meetings alike, conveying what the regime saw as its defining characteristic—humanism. The Soviet ideology was proudly (and loudly) humanist, opposing itself to the inhumanity of capitalism whenever the opportunity presented itself. Especially after Stalin's death, socialist humanism was emphasized as the USSR's ideological mainstay:

> From Khrushchev's time, Marx's definition of humanism as an accomplishment of the humanization of humankind ... an abolition of human alienation by gaining full possession of the means of production under communism was declared to be achieved in the Soviet Union and nowhere else.[1]

So how can we even talk about Soviet posthumanism? The patron saints of philosophical posthumanism—Nietzsche, Heidegger, Kittler, and Foucault—were either unknown or disavowed in the Soviet Union. Technological and scientific advances were incorporated into the overall arc of the Marxist narrative of history. Adorno's postwar pessimism regarding the values of the Enlightenment found no purchase in the official Soviet discourse. Whatever utopian wonders awaited the future, they would surely enhance, rather than undermine, the essential humanity of the Soviet subject.

And yet, at the same time communism, along with Nazism and fascism, was one of the twentieth-century cluster of ideologies regarding the New Man, explicitly promising the reconstitution of human nature in the image of the "sublime" subject of ideology.[2] The Soviet utopian aspirations, articulated in official propaganda and more subtly, though equally insistently, in popular culture, offered human "prototypes of the new age."[3] Russian Constructivism, Futurism, and fascism were enchanted by the image of the man-machine. During high Stalinism (between the mid-30s and mid-50s), the man-machine became the preternaturally productive and ideologically pure Soviet subject: the "healthy, virile and handsome" inhabitant of the utopia in the making.[4] Indeed, the utopian thrust of the Soviet ideology is inextricable from posthumanism in the literal sense of post-humanism: that which comes after human. As Richard Stites points out, the "utopian begins with an ideal person and then

---

1 Jutta Scherrer, "'To Catch Up and Overtake' the West: Soviet Discourse on Socialist Competition," in *Competition in Socialist Society*, ed. Katalin Miklóssy and Melanie Ilic (London: Routledge, 2014), 18.

2 Slavoj Žižek, *The Sublime Object of Ideology* (London: Verso 1989), 5. See also Roger Griffin, *Fascism as a Totalitarian Movement* (Taylor and Francis, 2004) and Elana Gomel, *Science Fiction, Alien Encounters, and the Ethics of Posthumanism: Beyond the Golden Rule* (London: Palgrave/Macmillan, 2014).

3 Karl Schlögel, *Moscow 1937* (Cambridge: Polity Press, 2012), 253.

4 Lilya Kaganovsky, *How the Soviet Man was Unmade: Cultural Fantasy and Male Subjectivity Under Stalin* (Pittsburgh: University of Pittsburgh Press: 2008), 6.

constructs an ecology, an environment, and institutions" around this ideal.[5] Of course, an "ideal person" may be simply a better human being, but implicit in the idea of the New Man is such a radical revision of human nature that "better" slides into "different." The pejorative label of the *homo sovieticus*, devised by dissident writers to mock ideological purity, implies that the ultimate goal of the regime was indeed creation of a new type of human being. "Communism set out to transform consciousness," as Alexander Genis writes in his sketch of Soviet metaphysics.[6]

How could Soviet culture be simultaneously humanist and posthumanist, equal parts mundane and utopian? What paradox underlies the construction of the Soviet New Man? To answer these questions, I propose to consider Soviet science fiction (SF) as a preeminent textual site where the paradox of Soviet (post) humanism was explored and re-inscribed, though never resolved. In my other writings on the subject I focused on the specific nature of the Soviet utopia in its articulation of space and subjectivity.[7] But I have come to realize that this approach unnecessarily isolates both Soviet culture, in general, and Soviet SF, in particular, from the mainstream of postmodernity, and puts them in a political quarantine, as it were, thus implicitly representing the seventy-plus years of the Soviet Union as a sort of historical mistake. Nothing can be further from the truth. The USSR was "the twentieth century's first modernist state" and its legacy continues to shape the twenty-first century in innumerable and often unpredictable ways.[8]

In this article I propose to explore how the Soviet New Man reflects the basic contradiction within the project of posthumanism: the contradiction between the posthuman as better than, and the posthuman as different from, the human. Posthumanism may be seen as the fulfillment of the utopian promise of humanism, cleansed from the latter's historical legacy of exclusion, exploitation, and failure, in which case a posthuman subject is a better, more ethical human being. Or it may be seen as a denial of humanist morality and ethics, in which case a posthuman subject is Yeats's "rough beast," an entity so profoundly

---

5 Richard Stites, *Revolutionary Dreams: Utopian Vision and Experimental Life in the Russian Revolution* (Oxford: Oxford University Press, 1989), 14.

6 Alexander Genis, "Paradigms of Contemporary Culture," in *Russian Postmodernism: New Perspectives on Post-Soviet Culture*, ed. Alexander Genis, Mikhail Epstein, and Slobodanka M. Vladiv-Glover (New York: Berghahn Books, 1999), 416.

7 See Elana Gomel, *Narrative Space and Time: Representing Impossible Topologies in Literature* (London: Routledge, 2014); Elana Gomel, *Science Fiction, Alien Encounters, and the Ethics of Posthumanism.*

8 Brian Moynahan, *The Russian Century: A History of the Last Hundred Years.* (New York: Random House, 1994), 3.

different from our concept of good and evil as to amount to a different species. This contradiction is central to the theory and praxis of posthumanism today. On the one hand, the contemporary discourse of posthumanism arises out of the Nietzschean and Foucauldian critique of the Enlightenment and its notions of agency and freedom. Reinforced by evolutionary and cognitive science, posthumanism may be seen to deny everything liberalism holds dear: autonomy, equality, and human rights. On the other hand, theoretical posthumanism today strongly aligns itself with the progressive politics which seeks to expand the sphere of ethical consideration to previously marginalized groups but does not contest the nature of morality itself. This alignment, epitomized, for example, by Donna Haraway and Rosi Braidotti (about whom we will hear more later), creates both implicit and explicit trains of thought within the Western discourse of posthumanism and its spinoff, transhumanism.

The paradox of the Soviet New Man parallels this uneasy split within Western posthumanism, albeit in a striking and unique way: inflected by the vicissitudes of Soviet history. On the one hand, the putative "accomplishment of the humanization of humankind" in a socialist utopia presents the New Man as a perfected and purified exemplar of humanist moral aspirations.[9] On the other hand, hidden under his sunny exterior, lies a "sublime" subjectivity, which is strange, unfamiliar, and frightening in its radical alterity.

Through the lens of SF, I want to explore the tensions in the fictional representations of the Soviet subject between humanist morality and posthumanist alterity. I will argue that Soviet posthumanism should be seen as part of the mainstream of the posthumanist thought rather than its wayward and perverse tributary. And perhaps in taking Soviet SF seriously as a posthumanist discourse (rather than reducing it to the binary of ideological dissidence/compliance), we can reassess the philosophy and politics of Western posthumanism as well.

In what follows I will discuss the Soviet versions of the three iconic figures of posthumanism: the alien, the animal, and the cyborg. In each section, I will emphasize the unresolvable aporia between morality and alterity, humanism and posthumanism, that informs the Soviet SF's take on these figures. In the last section, I will briefly look at the crash of the Soviet New Man through the lens of Vladimir Sorokin's *Telluria* (2013) and consider what lessons this crash may hold for the Western posthuman subject.

---

9 Scherrer, "'To Catch Up and Overtake' the West," 18.

Beetles and Ants

Any discussion of Soviet and post-Soviet SF must begin with the Strugatsky brothers, whose towering presence shaped the genre in countless ways. Of course, there was a strong and interesting tradition of SF in the USSR before the Strugatskys (Platonov, Beliaev, Efremov) but apart from their unrivalled popularity, the brothers also became a bridge between the Thaw era of the '60s and the post-Soviet period, as their ideological and artistic influence has extended into the present day. The younger brother Boris's death in 2012 called forth a flood of touching testimonies from celebrities and common people alike, showing that the Strugatskys' utopian dreams and dystopian nightmares resonate with a generation who barely remember the Soviet empire. It seems that the collective imagination of post-Soviet Russia is still indelibly stamped with the Strugatskys' writings.

In the West, however, the Strugatskys' oeuvre is all too often reduced to the brothers' relation to the political regime. In his recent review of the new English translation of the Strugatskys' *The Dead Mountaineer Inn*, Ezra Glinter traces the arc of the brothers' career from utopia to dystopia as a response to the deterioration of the Soviet system and its ultimate collapse: "... their work did become critical and subversive over time. But at the beginning of their career, the Strugatsky brothers were the best socialist utopians in the game."[10]

Reading the Strugatskys exclusively in terms of the socialist/dissident dichotomy, however, is as reductive as reading Soviet culture exclusively in terms of political repression. While censorship and political dissidence were indeed a factor in the Strugatskys' writings, a far greater factor, I would argue, was the inherent contradiction in the concept of the New Man, a utopian/posthuman subject whose evolution the brothers' oeuvre traced from the 1950s to the 1990s. This contradiction can be summed up as the impossibility of disentangling the inhuman (morally evil) from the unhuman (radically Other).

In their novel *The Beetle in the Anthill* (*Zhuk v muraveinike*, 1979), the Strugatskys vividly represent this clash in the figure of Lev Abalkin, a space "changeling" developing out of an egg that was left behind by the mysterious alien Wanderers, who are an important component of the Strugatskys' universe. Abalkin does not know of his origin; he is a typical Soviet SF hero, kind, pure and somewhat naïve. He is a version of Anton/Rumata of

10 Ezra Glinter, "(Give Me That) Old-Time Socialist Utopia," *The Paris Review*, May 11, 2015, http://www.theparisreview.org/blog/2015/05/11/give-me-that-old-time-socialist-utopia/.

Hard to Be a God (*Trudno byt' bogom*, 1964), who dedicates his life to serving science and humanity. Abalkin's society, however, though still ostensibly communist, is shadowed by the darkness of the 1980s when the flaws of the system were becoming painfully obvious. He is being spied upon, and is ultimately murdered, by the futuristic version of the KGB whose head believes Abalkin is an alien impostor, a danger to humanity.

Besides the obvious critique of the paranoia of the security forces, the novel poses an interesting ontological question: can one be posthuman without knowing it? Abalkin believes himself to be a human being and behaves like one; why is he not a human being? And if he is, what is the meaning of his strange origin?

In *Alien Chic*, Neil Badmington describes how, in Western SF, "the line that once absolutely divided and distinguished human from alien has become blurred."[11] He sees the "contamination" of the human by the alien, expressed in stories of alien abduction, hybridization and so on, as one of the cultural symptoms of posthumanism becoming the cultural dominant. This contamination, however, takes a different form in Soviet SF where the definition of "the human" is not based on biology ("blood" or "genes") but on morality (socialist humanism). In *Hard to Be a God*, for example, the ostensibly alien inhabitants of the planet of Arkanar are sharply divided into Rumata's "brothers" and his enemies by their ethics rather than biology, which is treated as totally unimportant. Abalkin, however, is a different matter. He seems to be a thoroughly moral human being. But what if he is "programmed" by his alien progenitors to do—or be—evil? Or, far more frighteningly, what if his alien-ness renders the distinction of good and evil moot?

The specter of the totally Other, of the radical alterity beyond the strictures not just of humanist morality but of any moral system whatsoever, haunts the Strugatskys. The specter is conjured and confronted, but ultimately it cannot be exorcised, in their masterpiece *Roadside Picnic* (*Piknik na obochine*, 1972), arguably one of the best SF novels of the twentieth century. In his essay on the novel, Stanislaw Lem places it in the context of negative theology, which grapples with the nature of God as totally Other. His point is not that *Roadside Picnic* is a religious allegory but rather that it "transcend[s] the science-fiction tradition" as it attempts to represent the unhuman.[12] As he does in his own *Solaris*, Lem views the figure of the alien, "the reasonable, yet not human, being"

11 Neil Badmington, *Alien Chic: Posthumanism and the Other Within* (New York: Routledge, 2005), 30.

12 Stanislaw Lem, *Microworlds: Writings on Science Fiction and Fantasy* (San Diego: Harcourt, 1984), 253.

as a stand-in for the mystery of the universe outside the boundaries of human comprehension.[13] He commends the Strugatskys for preserving this mystery rather than succumbing to the reduction of the unhuman to the inhuman, alterity to evil. Like Lem's transcendent Ocean in *Solaris*, the alien Visitors of *Roadside Picnic* are beyond comprehension: Nothing at all is known about them except for the devastating consequences of the technology left behind on the sites of their Visitation. They are represented through paradoxes, omissions, evasions, and silences, as the novel develops a poetics of the alien sublime.

The protagonist's transformation at the end of the novel epitomizes this poetics. At the beginning, Red Schuhart is an ordinary guy: a small-time smuggler, not very bright, but a loving family man and a decent human being. At the end, he becomes either a murderer, or a saint, or both. He deliberately sacrifices the boy Arthur in order to reach the Golden Ball, which is supposed to grant every wish. Red wants to save his daughter from the creeping transformation into a monster, induced by the alien Zone. And yet, having reached the Ball, he asks not for his daughter's life but for what is impossible and unachievable—universal happiness: "HAPPINESS, FREE FOR EVERYONE, AND LET NO ONE GO AWAY UNSATISFIED!"[14] It is the emergence of this "impossible and inexplicable," as Fredric Jameson puts it, utopian desire that undermines the humanism on which the Soviet utopia was ostensibly predicated.[15]

The officer who shoots Abalkin in *The Beetle in the Anthill* operates within the parameters of this humanist ideology because he conflates the unhuman and the inhuman, alterity and evil. A similar conflation occurs in an earlier Strugatskys' novella *Malysh* (*The Kid*; also translated as *Space Mowgli*, 1971), in which an alien-raised child provokes a confrontation among the group of scientists who find him. Some of them are fascinated by the boy's strangeness, seeing him as a key to understanding the mysterious non-human entities that have raised him. The female technician, however, sabotages the "holy Contact" because she is repulsed by the boy's alien-ness and tries to salvage whatever human core he still retains. Not only has he been biologically modified, but he is also devoid of "normal" human emotions, imitating the deathly agony of his family with no sign of distress. The technician revolts against exploiting the "human tragedy" for scientific ends, implicitly casting the unhuman as the

13 Ibid., 244.

14 Capitals in the original. Arkadii Strugatskii and Boris Strugatskii, *Piknik na obochine* [*Roadside picnic*] (Moscow: Avrora, 1972), 193.

15 Fredric Jameson, *Archaeologies of the Future: The Desire Called Utopia and Other Science Fictions* (London & New York: Verso, 2005), 295.

inhuman. The novella ends inconclusively, as the Contact is not achieved but the child seems to be unable to shed his alien nature.

In discussing *Roadside Picnic*, Lem explicitly abjures any attempt to read the novel in sociopolitical terms, focusing instead on the poetics of representing the totally Other. Indeed, trying to fit the novel into the Procrustean bed of utopianism/dissidence misfires, as do, in different ways, its readings by Ursula Le Guin and Fredric Jameson. But *The Beetle in the Anthill* makes an explicit connection between its late-Soviet ambience and the problematic of the post- or non-human. This connection is articulated in the sequel called *The Time Wanderers* (*Volny gasiat veter*, 1985), in which it turns out that the Wanderers who have been present in the Strugatskys' universe from the early 1960s are not space aliens but rather the evolved descendants of humanity called *liudeny* (a pun on the Russian word for people), literally New Men. If humanity gives rise to the Other, does it mean that utopian humanism has failed or succeeded?

In her popular exposition of posthumanism, *The Posthuman*, Rosi Braidotti writes:

> A sustainable ethics for non-unitary subjects rests on an enlarged sense of inter-connection between self and others [...] by removing the obstacle of self-centered individualism on the one hand and the barriers of negativity on the other.
>
> In other words, to be posthuman does not mean to be indifferent to the humans or to be de-humanized. On the contrary, it rather implies a new way of combining ethical values with the well-being of an enlarged sense of community [...].[16]

This statement is not dissimilar from the ethics of Soviet humanism. Indeed, the left-wing politics that inform one branch of posthumanism (as opposed to transhumanism, about which more will be said later) have at least a historical connection with the twentieth-century utopian movements. But of course, the central paradox of this statement is the idea that "to be posthuman does not mean to be [...] de-humanized." If that is the case, what does it mean?

The problem with the New Man is precisely the irresolvable contradiction between "new" and "man." A utopian subject has to be so profoundly different from his/her humanist matrix as to push into the uncharted territory of the

16 Braidotti, *The Posthuman*, 120.

unhuman (Nietzsche's "bridge").[17] But in doing so, he/she inevitably slides into actions, which, from a humanist point of view, have to be classified as inhuman or evil. Lem dedicated most of his major novels to exploring this paradox. The actions of the alien "doublers" in Eden or of the Ocean in *Solaris* appear evil from the point of view of our "ethical values." And yet the protagonists of these novels refuse to condemn what looks like genocide or torture precisely because they try to transcend the boundaries of "human, all-too-human." At the end of *Solaris*, Kris Kelvin reaches out to the entity that has destroyed his lover hoping that "the age of atrocious miracles" has only begun.[18] Similarly, in *Roadside Picnic*, the "impossible and inexplicable" transformation of Red Schuhart points to such a radical remaking of human nature that the platitudes about the "well-being of an enlarged sense of community" fall flat in the face of the promise—and threat—of the unhuman.[19]

It may be rather surprising to those who see Soviet SF solely in terms of its relationship with the regime, but the topos of transformation, of the radical remaking of human nature through interaction with the unknown, is one of its central concerns. The wildly popular SF thriller *The Moon Rainbow* by Sergei Pavlov (*Lunnaia raduga*, 1978), followed by a sequel *Soft Mirrors* (*Miagkie zerkala*, 1983), and made into a film in 1984, deals with a group of astronauts who acquire miraculous abilities during a disastrous landing on Oberon, a moon of Uranus. Early in the novel two characters discuss the relationship between humans and space-generated posthumans whose existence at this point is only conjectured. One of the characters regards the transformation of humanity under the influence of the unhuman as an unmitigated catastrophe:

> We are losing because the process is irreversible. If the tempo of our penetration of the Far Space matches the tempo of the 'surprises,' we will be in danger of a biological catastrophe... we, the real humans of the Earth, we'll hardly be able to keep our natural essence.[20]

---

17 In *Thus Spoke Zarathustra* (1883), Friedrich Nietzsche famously describes man as a "bridge" or a "rope" between "animal and overman," a transitional stage on the way to becoming the Übermensch (15). See Friedrich Nietzsche, *Thus Spoke Zarathustra,* trans. Thomas Common, University of Adelaide Library, South Australia, 2016, https://ebooks.adelaide.edu.au/n/nietzsche/friedrich/n67a/.

18 *Solaris*, 204.

19 Braidotti, *The Posthuman*, 120.

20 Unless specified otherwise, all translations from Russian are mine. Sergei Pavlov, *Lunnaia raduga* (1978), http://www.e-reading.life/bookbyauthor.php?author=11927.

His interlocutor, chief of the International Bureau of Space Security, however, is surprisingly upbeat—not because he believes in the power of socialist humanism but because he dismisses it out of hand:

> You see, Poling, the difference between us is that you see the "space surprise" as a sword of Damocles hanging over humanity. And I believe that space surprises have accompanied man from his very origin. They have given birth, nurtured and educated our species.[21]

In other words, humanity is by definition Other than itself. Humanism is merely an ideological dam trying uselessly to stem the tide of historical and evolutionary change.

In his conservative discussion of biotechnology, *Our Posthuman Future* (2002), Francis Fukuyama argues, quite cogently, that our ethics derive from our human nature: in other words, that we consider certain actions and beliefs good and other evil because of the kind of biological and social creatures we are. Recent work in evolutionary psychology leaves no doubt that basic ethical templates are the product of our specific and contingent evolutionary history (this, of course, does not contradict the idea that these templates are culturally and ideologically malleable). But science, technology, and politics offer tools to modify, if not erase, these ethical constraints: to move from the familiar territory of the inhuman into the uncharted wilderness of the unhuman. Fukuyama views these tools with alarm, but he is honest enough to recognize that we can indeed become New Men, subjects remade in the shape of the unknown Other. And if we can, why shouldn't we? Precisely because Soviet culture confronted the notion of the utopian subject head-on from its very inception, Soviet SF illuminates the ethical paradox of posthumanism in a particularly striking way. If we can become beetles, alien supermen, what—if anything—do we owe to the morality of ants, ordinary humans?

The Red Bear

Animal studies are a significant and growing component of posthumanism. They offer a perfect vantage point from which to criticize "aesthetic and moral ideals based on white, masculine, heterosexual European civilization."[22]

---

21 Ibid.

22 Braidotti, *The Posthuman*, 68.

As opposed to aliens who may or may not exist, non-human animals are a palpable and material reality that may be studied, described, and analyzed. Moreover, our interaction with animals poses immediate ethical and political quandaries, especially in relation to industrial farming, meat consumption, and animal experimentation. As Cary Wolfe writes in his introduction to *Zoontologies: The Question of the Animal*, intersecting scientific and political developments have "led to a broad reopening of the question of the ethical status of animals in relation to the human."[23]

Considering the dismal ecological record of the USSR, it seems commonsensical to assume that such questions about animal rights did not bother Soviet culture very much. But such an assumption would be wrong. In fact, issues of cruelty to animals loomed large in the Soviet ethical discourse (and were the legacy of a traditional Russian attitude of pity and compassion for animals expressed in classic literary texts by Dostoyevsky, Turgenev, and Chekhov). And Soviet SF, especially in the perestroika years, responded to this attitude. In Ariadna Gromova's SF novel *We Are of the Same Blood* (*My odnoi krovi, ty i ia*, 1967), a young scientist's attempt to look for "animal geniuses" leads to his startled acknowledgment that his own cat is a speaking and thinking subject that deserves to be treated as an equal rather than a pet.

But the Soviet compassion for animals is mired in the same dilemma Wolfe diagnoses in the Western animal rights movement: "one of the central ironies of animal-rights philosophy [...] is that its philosophical frame remains an essentially humanist one [...] thus effacing the very difference of the animal other that animal rights sought to respect in the first place."[24] In Gromova's novel, the (not unreasonable) assumption that some animals are smarter than others leads to a redrawing of the ontological boundaries, in which talking cats and calculating parrots are subsumed into the enlarged domain of humanity, in opposition to their dumb brethren. As Wolfe points out, this division reinforces, rather than undermines, the humanist hierarchy of subject/object. But his suggestion that the reinforcement of humanism can be counteracted by "the emptying of the category of the subject" leads to its own problems, not least of which is the fact that there is no singular ontology of "the animal" but rather different, and differently constituted, branches of the evolutionary tree with different kinds and degrees of subjectivity and agency.[25]

23 Cary Wolfe, *Zoontologies: The Question of the Animal* (Minneapolis: University of Minnesota Press, 2003), xi-xii.

24 Ibid., xii.

25 Ibid.

The best exploration of these issues in Soviet SF is Sever Gansovsky's remarkable story "Dies Irae" (*Den' gneva,* 1964), made into a movie of the same title. Taking place in an unnamed Western country (a common ploy that enabled Soviet SF writers to engage politically sensitive issues), the story depicts the dismal consequences of a bioengineering experiment gone wrong. Bears have been artificially "uplifted" to give them a human-level intelligence. The resulting creatures called "otarks" are rational but devoid of any sense of ethics or morality. Having killed and devoured their creators, they escape from the lab and terrorize the human population of a remote rural district. Narrated from the point of view of Donald Betly, a correspondent sent to the district to investigate the situation, the story vividly depicts the fear and helplessness of the abandoned farmers who are forced to collaborate with the inhuman otarks to save their children from being eaten. The ethical issue of the relation between animals and humans is central to the story, but in a way intriguingly different from the Western versions of the same topos. From H. G. Wells's *The Island of Dr. Moreau* to David Brin's *Uplift* novels, intelligent animals have been depicted as victims of their human creators. In Gansovsky's story, on the contrary, otarks are the victimizers. And in contrast with the usual connotations of the animal in Western discourse, which center on passion and emotion, the otarks embody instrumental rationality. When Betly asks a local ranger why the farmers do not consider otarks human despite their speech and mathematical abilities, he replies: "Everybody asks the same thing: 'Is it true that they can learn geometry? Is it true that some otarks understand the relativity theory?' As if it made any difference! As if because of that they should not be exterminated!" Betly is shocked by the ranger's indifference to the question of intelligence but having witnessed the otarks' cannibalism and violence, he has the epiphany: "Man is not simply a creature capable of learning geometry." The beastly otarks represent "reason without kindness," while social humans are superior in spite, not because, of their intelligence.[26] Gansovsky's story thus preserves human superiority over animals, but this superiority is strikingly different from the typical iterations of Western anthropocentrism, which is based on what Braidotti calls the "aesthetic and moral ideals [of] white, masculine, heterosexual European

26 Sever Gansovskii, *Den' gneva* [*Dies irae*] (Moscow: Znanie, 2002), first published in 1964, http://lib.ru/RUFANT/GANSOWSKIJ/dg.txt.

civilization."[27] If these ideals privilege reason over empathy, Gansovsky insists in his story that empathy is the unique human characteristic that makes us different from, and superior to, animals. The story is posthumanist and humanist at the same time: Like much of Western posthumanism, it rejects the conflation between humanity and rationality, yet like traditional humanism, it still sees humanity as superior to other animals.

The peculiar inversion of the human-animal dichotomy can be read, like the Strugatskys' novels, within the context of the dissident movement (indeed, the movie is quite explicit in representing the otark-terrorized hinterlands as an allegory of the gulag). But it is more interesting to see it as an exploration of the ethical paradox of animal rights philosophy, which reifies the category of "animal" as a political tool against the humanism of the Enlightenment. However, in doing so, animal rights philosophy has to elide the fact that humans are animals as well, and that our exalted notions of kindness, inclusivity, rights and so on may be seen as a result of evolutionary adaptations specific to the kind of creatures we are. Bears are not social animals; if bears were intelligent, it is possible that they would resemble Gansovsky's otarks more than the creatures conjured up by the utopian dream of "progressive political and ethical agendas."[28]

The much-critiqued distinction at the heart of humanism is the dichotomy of "us" and "them." But it is hard to imagine a subject of any kind that does not make this distinction; in fact, studies of animal behavior (especially of chimpanzees and dolphins) show that the dialectic of social inclusion and exclusion exists in any animal grouping. In "Dies Irae," the dying Betly hallucinates a conversation with his seven-year son who says: "Dad, listen! We are what we are, right? And they are what they are. But they also think about themselves that they are what we are."[29] Otarks, who are capable of discussing theoretical physics with a man and then suddenly devouring their interlocutor, are a horrifying image of "reason without kindness." But by representing such reason as the product of a specific animal nature, Gansovsky highlights the same paradox at the heart of posthumanism as the Strugatskys do in their exploration of aliens' radical alterity: letting go of the human may mean letting go of all human ethics, not just the parts we personally find objectionable.

27 Braidotti, *The Posthuman*, 68.

28 Wolfe, *Zoontologies*, xiii.

29 Gansovskii, *Den' gneva*.

Socialist Cyborgs

In her celebrated work "A Cyborg Manifesto," Donna Haraway hailed the cyborg as an icon of a postmodern, posthuman, and progressive politics:

> The cyborg is resolutely committed to partiality, irony, intimacy, and perversity. It is oppositional, utopian, and completely without innocence. No longer structured by the polarity of public and private, the cyborg defines a technological polis based partly on a revolution of social relations in the *oikos*, the household. Nature and culture are reworked; the one can no longer be the resource for appropriation or incorporation by the other.[30]

Significantly, this politics was also socialist: the subtitle of "The Cyborg Manifesto" is "Science, Technology, and *Socialist-Feminism* in the Late Twentieth Century" (emphasis mine). But the socialism as practiced in the USSR looked at the cyborg with more mixed emotions. Even more so than the alien or the beast, the cyborg was a focus of the inherent contradiction between humanism and posthumanism, between "New" and "Man." On the one hand, early images of the New Man, especially in the Stalinist period, often emphasized his connection with technology in an unacknowledged echo of Futurism and Constructivism. In Nikolai Ostrovsky's *How The Steel Was Tempered* (1936), the disabled protagonist Pavka remakes himself into a true "man of steel" by overcoming his physical limitations by a sheer act of superhuman willpower. While technically not SF, Ostrovsky's iconic novel represented the New Man as an ideological cyborg for whom communism functions literally as a technology of subjectivity. Lilya Kaganovsky describes the protagonist Pavka as "a model subject, the new 'positive hero' of Stalinist art." According to her, Pavka "is waging a war against corporeality, in which ideology (the belief in progress, movement forward, in usefulness) can overcome material nature."[31]

This "war against corporeality" finds a strange echo in the contemporary discourse of transhumanism. The distinction between transhumanism and posthumanism is subtle yet important: while the latter is a philosophical, ethical, and political critique of humanism, the former is a techno-utopianism, which promulgates the physical and mental transformation of humanity

---

30 Donna Haraway, "A Cyborg Manifesto," in *Simians, Cyborgs, and Women: The Reinvention of Nature* (London: Routledge, 1991), 293.

31 Kaganovsky, *How the Soviet Man was Unmade*, 25.

through technological means. Central to transhumanism is the idea of the Singularity, in which the development of artificial intelligences will have created a breakthrough moment in history and generated a new cyborg subject. The idea has been given a popular expression by Ray Kurzweil, the founder of the Singularity University. Kurzweil's book *The Singularity is Near* (2005) suggests that the bodies of future transhuman cyborgs will be able to control their "physical manifestations at will."[32] And there are other similarities between the Soviet New Man and utopian transhumanism: they are alike in their breathless enthusiasm for technology (whether actual or imaginary) and their confident predictions of the future.

Transhumanism has been criticized for various reasons: its quasi-religious zeal, its disconnect from actual science, and its predilection for uncritically extrapolating contemporary trends into the future.[33] The same criticism, of course, applies to Soviet posthumanism, whose utopian and apocalyptic fervor was underpinned by the state apparatus of cultural control. But we would do an injustice to Soviet civilization by viewing characters like Pavka only in terms of propaganda. There was a corporeal vocabulary in Stalinist art that articulated a cyborg ideal of the "body as a physical site for spiritual transformation—the provenance of Fedorovian philosophy, the dreams of the futurist and the avant-garde."[34] Transhumanism and high Stalinism, while quite different in terms of their political philosophy (since transhumanism was inspired by libertarianism), converge on the notion of a cyborg transformation of the human body and mind as a road to utopia. And even though their social goals are not the same (libertarian thinkers, of course, abhor communism), the emphasis on the creation of a New Man, a utopian subject, unites these two very different cultural formations.

Post-Stalinist SF, however, views the cyborg with much greater suspicion. In the Strugatskys' novel *The Distant Rainbow* (*Dalekaia raduga*, 1967; not to be confused with Pavlov's *The Moon Rainbow* mentioned earlier), a character named Kamill is a cyborg, given virtual immortality by merging with an AI and thus fulfilling both the Fedorovian and the transhuman dream. But there

32 Ray Kurzweil, *The Singularity is Near* (New York: Viking, 2005), 310.

33 See, for example, the fellow computer scientist Paul Allen's critique of the idea that the Singularity is upon us. Paul Allen, "The Singularity Isn't Near," *MIT Technology Review*, Oct. 12, 2011, https://www.technologyreview.com/s/425733/paul-allen-the-singularity-isnt-near/. See also Francis Fukuyama, *Our Posthuman Future: Consequences of the Biotechnological Revolution*.

34 Kaganovsky, *How the Soviet Man was Unmade*, 5.

is nothing sublime about him: he is a cranky and disengaged observer of the human drama unfolding on the planet of Rainbow, where an unsuccessful physical experiment leads to a disaster. The ordinary humans face death with courage and dignity, while the posthuman Kamill is envious of their mortality.

The same dynamics play out in several stories by Igor Rosokhovatsky, which feature cyborgs (or, as he calls them, "sigoms"). Sigoms are synthetic New Men, physically perfect and endowed with super-powers. "Humans create us in the image of what they want to be themselves," a sigom explains in the short story titled "A Sigom and the Dictator."[35] But it turns out that sigoms long precisely for the human weaknesses that they lack. In this story the sigom sheds his arrogance by interacting with ordinary people whose emotions he is initially taught to despise by his creator (the Dictator of the title). The not-too-subtle political subtext of the story opposes the political transhumanism of the Stalinist era with the traditional humanism of the Russian literary tradition, which valorizes compassion, love, and mercy.

The final reckoning with the Stalinist cyborg occurs in Viktor Pelevin's 1992 biting satire *Omon Ra* in which the cadets of the Meres'ev Flying School (named after another ideological superman, whose semi-fictional biography is told in *A Story of a Real Man* [*Povest' o nastoiashchem cheloveke*, 1948]) amputate their feet to imitate the titular hero. Pelevin's novel is meta-SF, engaging all the clichés of Soviet utopia, from space flight to heroic self-sacrifice, only to smash them to pieces in a welter of black humor, absurdist reality games, and postmodernist pastiche. But as liberating as Pelevin's iconoclastic novel appears after the artificial heroism of Soviet SF, it is, in a sense, more limited than the genre it mocks. Pelevin reduces the cyborg problematic to an ideological falsification. There is no New Man, and there can never be one outside of the corrupt rhetoric of a failed system.

But while the New Man is dead, trans- and posthumanism are not. Despite its political limitations, Soviet SF took seriously the idea of the transformation of human nature and tried to explore the contradictions arising on the interface between the utopian aspirations of a progressive ideology and the limitless possibilities of technology. In this sense, it problematized the "socialist" component of Haraway's manifesto far more radically than any conservative critiques such as Fukuyama's. For Soviet SF showed that the cyborg's utopian potential is moot, not because the transformation of human nature fails inevitably, but because it just might succeed.

35 Igor' Rosokhovatskii "Sigom i Diktator" [A Sigom and the Dictator], in *Poniat' drugogo* [To understand the other] (Kiev: Radyans'kyi pys'mennyk, 1991), 23.

Nails in the Head

Twenty-five years after the end of the Soviet Union, the specter of communism is still haunting Putin's Russia and less conspicuously but equally insistently, the rest of the world. The apparition of the New Man periodically reappears in post-Soviet SF, no matter how often it is laid to rest. But his insistent return, whether in mockery, nostalgia, or anger, signifies that while the Soviet experiment is dead, the utopian hopes and dystopian fears it once unleashed are not. And the point at which these hopes and fears intersect is the posthuman remaking of human nature.

Vladimir Sorokin's *Telluria* (*Telluriia*, 2013) seems to have left the moral seriousness (or perhaps naiveté) of the Strugatskys far behind. Stylistically brilliant and wildly inventive, *Telluria* (which is the only imaginary country to have had a separate pavilion at the 2015 Venice Biennale) is the terrain of the future in which the world has fallen apart into self-contained cultural universes that refuse to have anything to do with each other. Globalization and cultural integration have been reversed: Now there are fifteen independent republics in place of the former Russia, some neo-communist, some neo-feudal; Muslim enclaves in Stockholm and Istanbul; and bio-engineered harems in Paris. There are giants and dwarves ("little people"); magic horses; talking penises; and the miraculous drug *tellur*, which is administered by driving a nail into the addict's skull.

The novel's form parallels the fragmentation of its fictional universe: it is composed of separate and independent sections which run in parallel without interacting with each other. In his excellent review of *Telluria* in *Public Books*, Bradley Gorski emphasizes this fragmentation as inherent in Sorokin's post-postmodern vision:

> Though this disjointed collage frustrates the reader's desire for a unified tapestry, it fits well with Sorokin's vision of the future. *Telluria* describes a time when comprehensive visions have failed. Heterogeneous societies have crumbled. The world no longer tolerates diversity. The very idea of grand unifying politics, an "end of history," seems ridiculous. Pluralism, as an ideal, or even as a concept, has disappeared.[36]

But if the present is broken, the past is monolithic. References to the USSR are obsessive, permeating even the most unlikely vignettes. From the Stalinist

36 Bradley Gorski, "Russia Is No More," *Public Books*, http://www.publicbooks.org/briefs/russia-is-no-more. Accessed June 1, 2014.

Soviet Socialist Republic (a pun on SSSR—the acronym of the USSR in Russian) to the pastiche of the Soviet propaganda doublespeak in the monologue of a soldier fighting for the United States of Ural, from the "Christian Communists" to "Stalin's Jewish commissars," the Soviet past is inescapable. And in the constant evocation of this past, Russia itself becomes the broken body of the stillborn New Man, haunted by the ghosts of dead utopias: "Moscow is the skull of the Russian empire, and its strange strangeness consists in those apparitions of the past that we call 'imperial dreams.'"[37] The drug *tellur* is literally the nail that Russia, unable to awake from its "dreams," drives through its own skull. The creepy corporeality of this surreal delivery system parallels all those images of mutilation and self-mutilation that have followed the New Man from his utopian inception to his inglorious end. But *Telluria*'s obsession with the dead utopia has something important to say to Western posthumanism as well.

In *The Posthuman*, Braidotti is at pains to distinguish the progressive politics of posthumanism from the totalitarian violence of communism. She does it by attacking the "implicit Humanism of Marxism, more specifically the humanistic arrogance of continuing to place Man at the center of world history."[38] But the Soviet subject at "the center of world history" was not just Man. He was the New Man. And while such a utopian subjectivity was never achieved in the USSR and arguably could have never been achieved, *Telluria* and many other post-Soviet SF texts demonstrate that dreams are as important in shaping history as actions. Moreover, they show that once a dream becomes part of history, it cannot be forgotten, even if its allure has turned into a recurring nightmare. Posthumanism is not an alternative to humanism but its twin, constantly challenging humanity to exceed or remake itself. The results of this remaking are not going to fit into the templates of progressive politics, whether of Marxist or green variety. The human subject may not be the center of history, but history, including the history of the bloody utopian experiments of the twentieth century, is at the center of any human—or posthuman—subjectivity.

---

37 Vladimir Sorokin, *Telluriia* [*Telluria*] (Moscow: Corpus, 2013), http://www.litmir.me/br/?b=178060.

38 Braidotti, *The Posthuman*, 23.

CHAPTER 2

Digressions in Progress: Posthuman Loneliness and the Will to Play in the Work of the Strugatsky Brothers

Julia Vaingurt,
University of Illinois at Chicago

Never overtly political, Soviet science fiction writers Arkady and Boris Strugatsky nevertheless found it increasingly difficult to publish in Soviet Russia, and the critical consensus today regards their work especially in terms of sociopolitical critique. It is, indeed, hard not to read their oeuvre as engaged with the political discourses of technologically driven competition and colonization that characterized the Cold War era, whether in the capitalist West or the socialist East.[1] Philosophical explorations in the Strugatskys' works, moreover, often appear to put rationalism and dialectical materialism—key Marxist-Leninist conceptualizations of history—to the test.

And yet, a central Strugatsky leitmotif, the technological enhancement of the human, evinces the influence of, and dialogues with, another philosophical

1 Their works frequently feature "Progressors" from an advanced communist planet who journey through space to rescue and/or "progress" underdeveloped alien populations.

The ethical dilemmas arising in the course of such operations echo the similarly problematic nature of the mission featured on NBC's *Star Trek* (1966–69). Here the Federation Starfleet, frequently inclined to render aid to the distressed and (per Federation mores) benighted, is at the same time enjoined by its own "prime directive" not to "interfere" with alien civilizations; this injunction is routinely agonized over and violated. This aspect of *Star Trek* and the Strugatskys' Progressor-ism would seem to allegorise competing U.S. and Soviet aspirations to self-portray as benefactors to the developing world, and the complicated nature of such aims.

system crucial to Soviet science fiction since its inception: namely, that of Russian Cosmism and its progenitor, Russian religious philosopher Nikolai Fedorov (1829–1903).[2] The Strugatskys never explicitly mention Fedorov, but their writing is so clearly indebted to the philosophical tradition he initiated that, as Sergei Nekrasov puts it, "outside of his semantic field, their work cannot be properly understood."[3] Here I will analyze the Strugatskys' exploration of technology's role in fostering, qualifying, and transforming life via the prism of Fedorov's quest for immortality and the radical physical transformation of humanity it would entail. With the techno-enhancement of humanity as their point of departure, the Strugatskys address, explicitly or otherwise, the following interrelated questions: What does the concept of human life include (or exclude)? What in humanity is worth salvaging, and how can technology be re-conceptualized such that it preserves rather than destroys this essence?

In the compilation of essays that compose Fedorov's *Philosophy of the Common Task*, technology is invested with a crucial role: to serve as a means of implementing the eponymous common task (also sometimes translated as "common cause"), the resurrection of ancestors, the unification of humanity, and the achievement of immortality. According to Fedorov, only the Christian doctrine of resurrection can equip and unite all scientific and technological activity with ethically meaningful purpose. Furthermore, reason itself demands that technology serve the abolishment of death and the resurrection of life, since dying makes any other technological and scientific goals and gains ultimately gratuitous. The restructuring of the body is thus of prime moral importance to Fedorov, who deprecates procreation in favor of artificial re-assemblage on the molecular or nano-level; implicit in this injunction is that natural reproduction represents a mere compulsive replacement of the old with the new, rendering us little more than contingent links in the chain of motion toward death. Reproducing sexually, we—unethically, egotistically—duplicate what *is*, rather than striving to create what *should be*. Instead of simply birthing other mortal beings, we could dedicate ourselves to the artificial resurrection of our forefathers, thereby learning to govern our own biology and becoming agents of a qualified life. The self-regulation of the human organism, according to Fedorov, would ensure functional immortality; the ability to resurrect life

2 See Leonid Geller, *Vselennaia za predelom dogmy* [The Universe beyond the boundary of dogma] (London: Overseas Publications, 1985), 63.

3 Sergei Nekrasov, "Kosmism N. F. Fedorova i tvorchestvo Strugatskikh" [The cosmism of N. F. Fedorov and the art of the Strugatskys], in Gacheva, Semenova, and Skorokhodov, 2:167. This and all other translations from the Russian in this chapter are mine, unless stated otherwise.

artificially renders sexual and digestive organs obsolete. Liberated from reliance on such physiological exigencies, we will become self-sufficient and self-renewing. Human interconnectedness will no longer be a matter of dependency, but of brotherhood (*bratstvo*). Moreover, as self-regulated organisms, people will be untethered from the planet Earth, able to travel cosmically. (Which will, indeed, be necessary, when the resurrection of all ancestors results in overpopulation.)

The technological overcoming of death proposed by Fedorov may, of course, be interpreted variously. The sheer remoteness of such an achievement might seem to render it little more than an object for contemplation. But, on the other hand, seen from a less indulgent point of view, Fedorov's quasi-ethical goal of transfiguration via technology might appear as the ultimate manifestation of what Giorgio Agamben pinpoints as the essence of modernity: the establishment of the state of exception as the norm.[4] To Agamben, this condition results from the interpolation of the simple state of living, or *zoē*, into the political (a particular, qualified way of living, *bios*), from the creation of a zone of indistinction between biological and political life. Biological life, due to its unqualified nature, its bareness, is banned from *bios* immediately upon its inclusion therein.[5]

Fedorov undertakes a similar synthesis of life as a whole with the body. He writes:

> Being born, a human being departs from totality and rejects life with all and for all; out of a lack of knowledge, this blind creature rejects what it should be doing with all the living and for all the dead. However, in the embryonic life an embryo acquired organs for the life with all and for all; while the stomach means life for the self and sexual organs means life for others, the chest and the head mean life with all the living and for all the dead. The chest is the repository of the heart, which is the organ of grief and empathy for all the dead and dying, while the head is the carrier of the project of resurrection.[6]

The spirit/body dualism prompting other Christian philosophers to talk of the former's overcoming of the latter does not exist for Fedorov; *sobornost'*

---

4 Giorgio Agamben, *Homo Sacer: Sovereign Power and Bare Life* (Stanford, CA: Stanford University Press, 1998), 170.

5 Ibid., 3-6.

6 N. F. Fedorov, *Sobranie sochinenii v chetyrekh tomakh* [Collected Works in Four Volumes] (Moscow: Progress, 2000), 2: 171.

[spiritual community] is hindered by the problematic materiality of the human body, which must be *transformed* if life is to be worth living. If we think of the "common task" as a kind of law, it follows that such legislation depends on what it bans; what it excludes, after all, is us as presently extant. If humanity unites in pursuit of the goal envisioned, total subordination of all aspects of life to the law of the common task will ensue, and what is not commensurate with Fedorov's conception of humanity transformed with the "brotherhood of sons who serve their fathers" will be eliminated as belonging to "blind, fallen nature."[7]

Fedorov makes a point to differentiate his own concept of super-humanity from Nietzsche's Übermensch. He sees the former's task as that of creation and the latter as that of negation and devastation. Nietzsche's superman separates himself from others and establishes his superiority over them, while Fedorov's transcendent human being wishes to unite himself with the rest.[8] However, what is excluded from the Fedorovian totality is the human life itself and human beings as biological creatures. The process of exclusion is evident in Fedorov's very language. It is no accident that when Fedorov describes the connectivity that humanity should attain through resurrection, he uses masculine "sons" and "fathers" (rather than neutral "children" and "parents"), while he calls that which needs to be overcome the "cult of woman that leads to degeneration and extinction."[9] It is, of course, clear that actual women will be included in the totality of immortal humanity only when they transfigure themselves, or stop being women. Will those who do not fit Fedorov's definition of properly human be excluded from the future unity? And if so, then by what means?

It is precisely through the demarcation of what constitutes proper from improper life that humanity's sovereign power over self, nature, life and death is asserted. Reading Fedorov through Agamben helps explain the ready amenability of the former's ethical ideals to totalitarian affiliation, especially to political discourse grounded in radical materialism. (Such a reading, for instance, amplifies the echoes between Fedorov's would-be transformation of unqualified biological life into *worthwhile* life, on the one hand, and Leninist enlightenment's trajectory of spontaneity-into-consciousness, on the other.)

7 N. F. Fedorov, *Sochineniia* [Works] (Moscow: Mysl', 1982), 181, 479.

8 Fedorov, *Sobranie sochinenii*, 2: 127. It is noteworthy that this transcendent picture of human synthesis is predicated on division. Supramoralism, the very idea of human synthesis, is, according to Fedorov, "an expression of the Slavic spirit" and is deeply inimical to anything Western. Fedorov, *Sobranie sochinenii,* 1: 429.

9 Ibid., 2: 145.

For Agamben, just as for Fedorov, biology is complicit in its own destruction: desirous of protection against death, it gives itself over to power—inevitably associated with technological reconditioning—thereby sowing the seeds of its own destruction. Ostensibly a tool for the mastering of life, technology devastates it in the process.

Reared on the ideals of Russian Cosmism, the Strugatskys inherit its task of discerning some ethical ends in the enormous power of technology. They are preoccupied, perhaps even obsessed, with the question of technology's role in the spiritual rather than material enhancement of humanity, and in the moral imperative of conquering death. But on the other hand, the authors inhabit a post-Holocaust, Cold War world, and are thus poignantly mindful of the potential ominousness of attempts at *mandating* radical biopolitical restructuring. Time and again, their texts seek out ways to disassociate technology from instrumentation, from the idea of mastery, and to imagine alternate conceptions of technology, especially such as to associate it with experimentation, play, and openness.

For example, in their novella *The Kid* (*Malysh*, 1971), Fedorov's biopolitical project becomes the political aspiration of a utopian communist state. Technology has rendered citizens of an idealized Earth futurity practically immortal. These new people aspire, moreover, to function as spreaders of enlightenment (in subsequent novels, the Committee for Contacts with Other Civilizations, or COMCON,[10] features agents, explicitly called Progressors), aiding underdeveloped species still mired in the constraints of biology and languishing on dying worlds. Specifically, the advanced humans seek out previously uninhabited planets and organize them as new homes for those less fortunate. On one such ostensibly barren candidate-world, the Earthlings find a human child (the sole survivor, it turns out, of an earlier shipwreck). Reared by this alien planet itself, and adapted to the conditions thereof, the boy has undergone radical physiological change. He is capable of almost metamorphosis-like mimicry, possesses extraordinary memory, and needs no food or other sustenance. He appears to be a self-sufficient organism, content with his life on the planet, where he believes himself to be completely alone. The boy's sovereignty is problematized, however, by the fact that the planet apparently controls him without his knowledge. Under the illusion of his at-homeness in this world, the boy is quite content until the arrival of the

10 There is a telling ambiguity in the abbreviation COMCON, since the last three letters begin not only the word "contact" but also the word "control."

newcomers from Earth. The planet had created surrogates of the boy for him to play with, but such virtual replicas cannot compare with actual humans, who introduce elements of unpredictability and newness. The boy's thirst for knowledge, seemingly his most human trait, induces him to seek out contact with humans. Play and curiosity thus outweighing his posthuman contentment, the boy becomes lonely, and torn between the pull of others of his kind—humanity—and his loyalty to the alien planet.

The planet, meanwhile, is slowly killing the boy for his betrayal, his association with humans, and it falls to the human interlopers to decide: to continue the project of enlightenment at the expense of the child's life or to abandon it in order to save him? This dilemma represents one of the numerous ethical obstacles the Strugatskys put before the Progressors in their novels, complicating the Progressors' righteous mission to spread the ideal of a life organized along rational and scientific parameters. Paradoxically, to insist in this case on the transformation of the planet along humanist ideals is to behave inhumanely toward the boy. In order to do right by him, the agents of progress must recognize the limitations of their techno-humanist project. The "kid" is the first to hint at this paradox in one of his conversations with the crew, when he is asked:

> "And why did you feel bad?"
> "Because there were people."
> "But people never harm anyone. They want everyone everywhere to feel good."
> "I know," said the kid. "Just like I said: people will leave, and it will be good."[11]

Furthermore, the Earthlings must reconfigure their relationship with the boy, from seeing him as an instrument of their plans to recognizing his autonomy and difference. For his part, the boy does not need humans; on the contrary, they cause him discontent, showing him he is not infinite and therefore not completely independent. And yet part of him desires their company. The humans must make a similar shift in attitude. Recognizing the imperative of coexistence with the Other, they must cease imposing themselves upon this alien world, and re-conceptualize technology from a facilitator of homogeneity to a mediator and enabler of difference. Unlike the will to power, which leads to the mastery and exploitation of the environment, the will to play drives

11 Arkadii Strugatskii and Boris Strugatskii, *Obitaemyi ostrov. Malysh* [Inhabited island. The kid] (Moscow: Tekst, 1993), 378.

exploration and curiosity. The would-be colonists need to abandon the dream of complete control and reconfigure their communication with the boy along the parameters of play and exploration.

When the team members decide in favor of *laissez-faire,* they leave one of their robots with the boy so that he can use it as a transmission device to keep in touch with them. The machine, originally conceived as an instrument of the transformation of the planet and one-sided control, thus becomes a means of mutuality and communication. Instead of being seized and shaped, the alien/unknown is now to be reached out to. Published in 1971, *The Kid* foregrounds the quest to use technology for purposes other than mastery of the Other; but by the late 1970s and early 1980s, the Strugatskys would revise such optimistic views.

The Beetle in the Anthill (written in 1979) offers an intriguing variation on the theme of the foundling. Whereas in *The Kid,* a human baby is left on an alien planet that rears and claims him as her own, in *The Beetle in the Anthill* the situation is reversed. Lev Abalkin, a Progressor, discovers, much to his despair, that he had been left on Earth as an embryo, with a batch of other foundlings, by some unidentified alien entity harboring some mysterious, hence ominous design.

These alien forces, whom humans have never seen but refer to as the Wanderers, appear to exist on a higher level of technological development; the instruments of their interference surpass humanity's capabilities and seem to be like magic. Humans find themselves in a difficult predicament: Cognizant of the Wanderers' advanced state, they are nevertheless more threatened than delighted by this interference. Even should the Wanderers' tampering prove beneficent or benign, this is ultimately of little importance if humanity must cede its agency. The Strugatskys set up the Wanderers' intrusion as a philosophical challenge for COMCON, the organization of Earth's Progressors. Faced with the prospect of the transformation of human life as they know it, these agents of progress perceive, in the face of being themselves "progressed," nothing but threat. They would rather grudgingly yield their belief in progress (the very foundation of their calling) than gamely imagine the ethical superiority of another life form:

> It is difficult, perhaps even impossible, to imagine a super-civilization capable of vulgar aggression or even just tactless experimentation with its younger intelligent brothers. According to the laws of the development of Reason/Mind, the pessimists' point of view looked, to put it mildly, artificial, far-fetched, and archaic. However, on the other hand, there was

> always the chance, even if a miniscule one, of some miscalculation. The general theory of progress might have been erroneous.[12]

The pessimists' point of view wins: COMCON treats Abalkin and the other foundlings as ticking bombs, carefully monitoring and controlling them throughout their childhood. When they become adults, they are trained as Progressors and sent out from the Earth. Abalkin is thus forced to become a Progressor, despite his obvious unsuitability and distaste for this occupation, in order to disburden COMCON of his presence. Ironically, then, the goal of Abalkin's Progressor-ism is to halt progress. COMCON leaders are made to realize that progress is not the objective, immutable category they had always held it to be. Now they are forced to treat it as subjective and relative, viable only to the extent their agency has control of it; beyond that control, progress is in fact destructive.

Mark Lipovetsky argues that the trope of Progressor epitomizes the self-conception of the Soviet technical intelligentsia of the 1960s: The Progressors' defining traits—exceptionalism, essentialism, and binarism— characterize the Soviet liberal mind-set, which was at once "anti-totalitarian and anti-democratic."[13] Members of the technical intelligentsia were essentialist in their unyielding belief in the idea of progress; binarist in their adherence to clear-cut distinctions, including the one between the enlightened "us" and the unenlightened "them," and in their general resistance to complexity; and, finally, exceptionalist in their self-image as standing apart from the corrupt, stagnant Soviet regime and the benumbed masses.[14] In their later fiction, the Strugatskys consistently explore the contradictions and challenges of the technical intelligentsia's self-positioning, and their hesitant, disoriented Progressors exhibit a crisis of identity to match the dissolution of the intelligentsia's former "essences"—progress, knowledge, and the like. In Lipovetsky's compelling interpretation, Abalkin, who is both a Progressor and an alien, a colonizer and subaltern, represents the inner contradictions of the Soviet intelligentsia.[15] In this identity crisis, we might further ask, what role does interrogating the foundations of the technical intelligentsia's sense of exceptionalism play? In other words, what part

---

12 Arkadii Strugatskii and Boris Strugatskii, *Zhuk v muraveinike* [The beetle in the anthill], in *Zhelanie strannogo* [A wish for strangeness] (Moscow: Astrel', 2012), 706.

13 Mark Lipovetsky, "The Poetics of ITR Discourse: In the 1960s and Today," *Ab Imperio*, 1 (2013): 121.

14 Ibid., 116–121.

15 Mark Lipovetsky, "The *Progressor* between the Imperial and the Colonial," in *Postcolonial Slavic Literatures after Communism*, ed. Klavdia Smola and Dirk Uffelmann (New York: Peter Lang, 2017), 29–57.

does questioning the techno-scientific means of societal betterment and the commensurability between knowledge and ethics play in this crisis?

In *The Kid,* humans are able to reprogram their technical tools toward less exploitative and more exploratory purposes. No such intervention is remotely achievable in *The Beetle in the Anthill,* since by now humans, including the Progressors, appear to have lost their agency. In fact, they themselves have become technical media: instruments rather than agents. Abalkin fervently desires agency and autonomy, but he is doubly deprived of these. First, he is dispossessed of agency by the alien forces who had planted him on Earth, defining him as a contingent implement of unknown provenance. Abalkin has an almost mystical connection with a strange device that bears the same mark as the one on his body (other foundlings die when their corresponding devices are destroyed). It is unclear whether this technical object is an appendage to Abalkin, or vice versa (a more grave scenario, from the standpoint of human agency). He has no power to reconfigure his relationship with the object, making him equal or even subordinate to it in their symbiosis. This inseparable connection to a machine makes Abalkin technically a cyborg—a status apparently most dismaying to him. (At one point Abalkin admits that his search for his origins was driven by the fear of being an android.[16]) Second, he is dispossessed of his freedom by the head of the COMCON agency, Rudolf Sikorski, who since Abalkin's birth has regarded him as a ticking bomb, an unaware infernal machine with the mysterious device as its detonator. Treating Abalkin accordingly as an object, Sikorski proceeded to mold him into a Progressor against his wishes, to exile him from Earth, and finally to neutralize him. In this scenario, however, Sikorski is as powerless, unknowing, and driven by fear as Abalkin himself.

The mysterious Wanderers, who turn agents of progress into its blind instruments, would seem to embody Heidegger's idea that, contrary to humanity's delusions of mastery, people are in fact themselves dominated by technology. In *The Question Concerning Technology,* Heidegger calls for an end to delusion and the adoption of a critical stance that would question techno-scientific instrumentality, or the idea that technology is simply a means to human ends. According to the philosopher, technology is not a tool for but a condition of living, and must be approached as such.[17]

Progressor Abalkin, having discovered his own instrumentality, attempts to break free of it, turning away from his professional duties, and toward the

16 Strugatskii and Strugatskii, *Zhuk v muraveinike,* 723.

17 Martin Heidegger, *The Question Concerning Technology, and Other Essays* (New York: Harper and Row, 1969), 3–36.

exploration of his own origins and identity. This questioning—essentially a form of technical malfunction—is his attempt to become a subject. The COMCON agency interprets this exit from their control not as an exercise of will but as evidence of subordination to other, alien objectives. COMCON agents are not permitted to ask questions; doing so is a sign of non-belonging. When Abalkin contacts past lovers, mentors, and friends, asking them questions and drawing portraits from memory, his every move is interpreted as part of some ominous strategy programmed by hostile aliens. Sikorski theorizes that Abalkin's behavior constitutes a form of "throwing rocks into bushes," which the former Progressor Maksim Kammerer, the story's narrator, explains thus: "Throwing rocks into bushes, to translate our jargon, means: leaving fake trails, placing false clues; in short, putting on an act."[18] While the head of COMCON interprets Abalkin's strange actions as moves in warfare, Kammerer disagrees: What looks like disobedience or even treachery is in fact a concerted effort on Abalkin's part to find out something about himself.

Abalkin's "playful" behavior is conditioned by his artistic personality; the psychiatric evaluations he underwent as a child report a predisposition toward theatricality, a quality manifest as he makes his contacts. He stuns his interlocutors and acts as if he is playing a role. His "psychic spasm," his abrupt abandonment of Progressor-ism, is also associated with his artistic, nervous nature.[19] The novel begins and ends with a poem Abalkin had composed as a child, which prophesies his attempt to exit, his being hunted and murdered: "Animals stood by the door. / They did not hide. / They were shot at. / And they died." The creative elements of Abalkin's personality offset his instrumentality. Read as a sign of his inhuman otherness by Sikorski, they, like the poem, in fact point to Abalkin's vulnerability, which humans share with animals. Sikorski succeeds in killing Abalkin, but Kammerer's vision of the latter as a machine attempting to prove its humanity triumphs in the end.

However, by the time the Strugatskys write *Waves Extinguish the Wind* (*Volny gasiat veter*)[20] in 1984, Sikorski's fears have come to fruition.

---

18 Strugatskii and Strugatskii, *Zhuk v muraveinike*, 673.

19 For example, upon meeting Abalkin, Doctor Goannek fails to recognize his professional affiliation. Later recounting his meeting with the ex-Progressor, Goannek is adamant that "the strange young man ... could never have been a Progressor; he did not have the proper nervous structure. No, he was not a Progressor but an artist, or a painter, who had experienced a huge creative failure." Ibid., 618.

20 The title of this novel in English translation is *The Time Wanderers*. (See Arkady and Boris Strugatsky, *The Time Wanderers*, trans. Antonina W. Bouis [New York: St. Martin's Press,1986].)

The concept of play has completely lost its association with humanness; now *super*human, it acquires a truly sinister tint. In the distant future, part of humanity has evolved to become immortals known as *liudeny* (an anagram of *ne liudi* [not people], as well as an allusion to *homo ludens*, "human the player"), perhaps because these "players" play *with* humans for the purposes of unnatural selection. The capacity to transcend biological limitations and ascend to the status of *liuden* is inherent in particular individuals, but a medical procedure is needed to activate it. Those who have the potential must be identified, entailing a complicated process of selection; technology is thus co-opted into this "game" of exclusion.

Here the Strugatskys question the very concept of the qualified life and its identification with goodness. On the one hand, *liudeny* seem qualitatively better than rank-and-file humans: the latter are xenophobic, afraid of the unknown, limited, whereas *liudeny* are open-minded and impeccably moral. However, either in spite of or because of this generous endowment, *liudeny* grow indifferent to humans. Ethically and physically superior, they lose all sense of affiliation with the ones they had apparently superseded. They sever ties with loved ones; after their transformation, human life appears to them as not worth living, as less than life. While they are Fedorovian in their ability to overcome indifferent nature, their feeling of brotherhood, of unity with all for all, does not extend to their forebears. Evolving beyond humanity renders them utterly inhuman. Since the novella is told from the perspective of one who is left behind, the state of mind enabling *liudeny* to abandon humanity remains alien. A former Progressor, Toivo Glumov, views his impending ascension to this higher state of being as an unavoidable tragedy, terrifying in its implications:

> Turning into a *liuden* means my death. It's much worse than death, because to those who love me, I will remain alive, but be repugnant beyond recognition. Arrogant, self-satisfied, self-assured. And what's more, probably eternal.[21]

Toivo is not wrong to imagine that his alien superiority will elicit repugnance in his loved ones. In the Strugatskys' universe, the more advanced beings such as Progressors are supposed to use reason to evaluate the worth of living entities, whereas the less advanced beings have their own mechanisms of establishing a

21 Arkadii Strugatskii and Boris Strugatskii, *Zhuk v muraveinike. Volny gasiat veter. Otiagoshchennye zlom* [The beetle in the anthill. Waves extinguish the wind. Burdened by evil] (Moscow: Tekst, 1994), 313.

protective distance: they inevitably experience feelings of disgust or revulsion toward superior forms of life. In *The Beetle in the Anthill,* Kammerer defines Progressor-ism as "the ability to decisively differentiate between self and other"[22]—precisely the quality that makes others "squeamishly wary" of Progressors.[23] Kammerer himself establishes his attitude toward the very profession and those who still practice it as a feeling: "I openly admit that I don't like Progressors, even though I was probably one of the very first ones, back when the term itself existed only in theoretical blueprints."[24]

Therefore, as not yet a *liuden,* Toivo is repelled by the inhumanity creeping into him. He perceives it as the cessation of his life with others, as abandonment and aloneness. In its sheer divorcement from any trace of origin, the state of being a *liuden* suggests indeterminacy, a fearsome play of possibilities. Afforded by technology, this play is not joyfully Derridean, but constitutes the eradication of humanity, a state of absence rather than presence.

In the Strugatskys' later works, former Progressors, disenchanted with the idea of unbounded progress toward perfection, attempt to forestall its deleterious effect on human life. They have failed to be agents of progress, they realize, all along having served as little more than this ideal's blunt instruments. Now that superior beings lay claim to the future of the qualified life, the question arises: is anything in humanity salvageable or worth salvaging? The Strugatskys seem to think so, nostalgically turning away from reason and toward finitude as the fundamental human trait, the one characteristic ensuring the existence of both disequilibrium and desire.

In connection with this viewpoint, we might cite an essay in Jean-François Lyotard's collection *The Inhuman* devoted to the highly Fedorovian question, "Can Thought go on without a Body?" Two possible responses are provided.

---

22 The original wording features an odd grammatical structure: *umenie razdelit' na svoikh i chuzhikh.* The verb *razdelit'* is transitive; but the lack of an object to go with it highlights the absence of a unifying concept of sentient life in the Progressors' perception. They see division where "regular Earthlings" see ethical equality: "I remember this vision of the world by which every sentient being is perceived as your ethical equal, *a priori,* and the very question of whether this being is better or worse than you, even if his morality is worse than yours, is simply impossible." Strugatskii and Strugatskii, *Zhuk v muraveinike*, in *Zhelanie strannogo,* 578.

23 The same squeamish wariness characterizes the narrator's attitude toward the mysterious, advanced Slimies in *Gadkie lebedi* [The ugly swans] (who, according to the doctor of the leprosy sanatorium where they reside, represent humanity's future—intellectually and morally superior beings, if by present standards unattractive ones). Arkadii Strugatskii and Boris Strugatskii, *Gadkie lebedi,* in *Zhelanie strannogo,* 144.

24 Strugatskii and Strugatskii, *Zhuk v muraveinike,* 578.

Much as Fedorov himself, the first speaker, a certain He, adduces the ultimate limitation on earthly endeavors—the death of the sun and with it the death of thought—as necessitating the direction of all human technologies toward finding ways for thought to exist beyond the hardware of the human body. Immortality in this view is reimagined as the perpetuation, not of the human species, but of disembodied thought, energies invested by human mind. The second speaker, called She, agrees in principle, but registers two objections. Firstly, thinking and suffering overlap, because thinking does not merely involve a selection of data, but an effortful suspension of ordinary intentions of the mind: the "soliciting of emptiness, this evacuation—very much the opposite of the overweening, selective, identificatory activity—does not take place without some suffering."[25] Secondly, the human body is gendered, hence incomplete, this incompleteness inducing the individual to desire another as a half complementary to the self. Lyotard's objection to the prospect of disembodiment, then, is that thinking machines will be too effortless, and too complete, to achieve the incredible complexity of human thought. Similarly, in an interview Boris Strugatsky expresses his worry that eventually human beings, having solved a multitude of social and scientific problems, will turn into carefree specimens of the *homo ludens*: too self-satisfied, too untroubled and freed from responsibility, to be properly human.[26] Moral choices are linked with human finitude, conditioned by the existence of the Other, by one's own limitations and lacks, and ultimately, by mortality. This doubting as to the viability or worthwhileness of the *homo ludens* stands as a double indictment of the Fedorovian project's conception of immortality as humanity's ultimate goal and of techno-reason as the route there. The Strugatskys wind up discrediting both the means and the end of this process, now read as inhuman, thus undesirable.

The Strugatskys are often read in terms of their political nonconformity. For example, Yvonne Howell, who was the first to trace the imprint of Fedorovian ideas on their writing, sees the Strugatskys as travestying Fedorov's style and thought starkly to reveal humanist scientific dreams as ineffectual under conditions of modernity and as inevitably neutralized

25 Jean-François Lyotard, *The Inhuman: Reflections on Time* (Stanford, CA: Stanford University Press, 1991), 18.

26 Arkadii Strugatskii and Boris Strugatskii, "Avtorskaia refleksiia" [Authorial reflections] in *Ulitka na sklone: opyt akademicheskogo izdaniia* [Snail on the slope: A first attempt at an academic compilation], ed. L. Ashkinazi and V. Efremov (Moscow: Novoe literaturnoe obozrenie, 2006), 529.

by the epoch's regnant powers of technology and the totalitarian state.[27] As compelling as this interpretation is, it suggests that the problem lies in the sociopolitical circumstances hindering the philosophy's flourishing rather than in the failure of the philosophy itself. My contention, by contrast, is that political reality has exposed not the ineffectuality of Fedorovian bioengineering, but rather its inherent inhumanity and the ominousness of its potential realization. In the end, the authors' political pessimism and disappointment with socialism might stem from their disillusionment with the possibility of finding an exit from the vicious circle of entrapment where our technological aspirations have led us.

---

27 Yvonne Howell, *Apocalyptic Realism: The Science Fiction of Arkady and Boris Strugatsky* (New York: Peter Lang, 1994), 122.

CHAPTER 3

Humans, Animals, Machines: Scenarios of *Raschelovechivanie* in *Gray Goo* and *Matisse*

Sofya Khagi,
University of Michigan

In Joseph Brodsky's sparkling, irreverent play *Democracy!* (*Demokratiia*, 1990–92), written on the heels of the failed 1991 coup and the collapse of the Soviet Union, the government of a newly independent East European country enjoys a luxurious meal in the presence of a stuffed bear that is loaded with a surveillance device and a robotic CNN feed. In the second act, a present arrives from London—a computer, "the state's brain"—with the country's future programmed into it, to be protected by a neutrino bomb. Next, Matilda, the ministers' sexy young secretary, enters the stage dressed in a leopard-like outfit, and proclaims her intent to become a wild animal. Whatever for, her bosses inquire? Matilda replies as follows:

> First of all, Mr. President, because history has ended. [...] When history ends, zoology begins. We've already got democracy, yet I am still young. Consequently, my future is nature. More precisely—the jungle. In the jungle it is either the strongest who survives or the one with the best mimicry. The leopard is the ideal combination of the former and the latter.[1]

1 Iosif Brodskii, *Sochineniia Iosifa Brodskogo* [Works of Joseph Brodsky] (St. Petersburg: Pushkinskii Fond, 1998), 7:279. Unless otherwise indicated, translations are my own.

To this, one of the officials retorts in a characteristic Brodskian manner:

> The strongest... the weakest... the law of the jungle.... No one survives, child, no one. And this is precisely the law of the jungle as well as of mixed forests, plains, mountains, and deserts. None survive.[2]

Lightheartedly, yet presciently, Brodsky points to the problematic of posthumanism, which has recently taken center stage in the West and in Russia alike. "When history ends..." echoes Francis Fukuyama's essay "The End of History?" (1989), in which he proclaims the final worldwide triumph of liberal democracy.[3] The stuffed bear is Brodsky's jocular rendition of the Orwellian telescreen that disseminates political propaganda while simultaneously spying on the country's government. The computer contains the country's future, scripted and handed down by the West, and is protected by an advanced weapon of destruction. The bear and the computer dramatize modern possibilities of technological control. What is particularly noteworthy for this analysis of posthumanism is Matilda's "transformation" into a female leopard, which satirizes the dehumanization resulting from the new conditions of society.[4]

In their charges against traditional humanism, thinkers such as Michel Foucault and Jean-François Lyotard and, following them, a number of other Western critics have called it both obsolete and insidious. Humanism has been problematized as an artificial construct that is used as a cover for capitalism, Western imperialism, patriarchy, and other concepts and entities. Not only the mutability of human nature but also the crimes committed in the name of humanism have prompted numerous thinkers to question its core foundations. As Foucault formulates it: "It is comforting, however, and a source of profound relief to think that man is only a recent invention, a figure not yet two centuries old, a new wrinkle in our knowledge, and that he will disappear again as soon as that knowledge has discovered a new form."[5]

---

2 Ibid., 7:279.

3 In "The End of History?" Fukuyama argues that the collapse of communism signaled the global victory of liberal democracy, after which no further major political changes would take place. See Francis Fukuyama, "The End of History?", *The National Interest* (Summer 1989): 3–18. On "When history ends..." as Brodsky's reaction to Fukuyama, see Lev Loseff, *Joseph Brodsky: A Literary Life* (New Haven: Yale University Press, 2012), 300. The essay "The End of History?" was later expanded into a book, *The End of History and the Last Man* (New York: Free Press, 1992).

4 Brodsky presents technological control (via the bear and the computer) and posthumanism (via Matilda) as co-existing (but not necessarily causally related) features of the new society.

5 Michel Foucault, *The Order of Things: An Archaeology of the Human Sciences*, trans.

Even though the accusations against humanism are weighty, from the vantage point examined here one finds an ethical necessity to save the concept of the human. In contrast to the post-Nietzschean and post-Foucauldian problematization of classic humanism and a strongly pronounced (though not unanimous) welcoming of posthumanism in the West, in the Russian context the latter tends to be conceptualized mainly in negative terms, as the dehumanization (*degumanizatsiia*) of humankind.[6] Contemporary Russian authors, in a variety of fictional and non-fictional genres, express acute concerns with the processes of dehumanization in the global community.

Raschelovechivanie (an equivalent of "dehumanization") is a term that has grown popular in recent Russian scholarly, journalistic, and literary discourses. Olga Sedakova's statement from 2012 is representative of the wider trend: "The West has moved away from the classical humanist interest" and "what happens to us in the present is called 'dehumanitarianization' [*degumanitarizatsiia*] [...] that means 'dehumanization' [*raschelovechivanie*]. Culture, as Y. M. Lotman said, is not transferred biologically".[7] The same key issue of *raschelovechivanie* is dramatized in post-Soviet fiction.

A. M. Sheridan Smith (New York: Pantheon, 1974), xviii. As Foucault argues, man, as the object of study, was born during the age of the Enlightenment, and is about to disappear: "If those arrangements were to disappear as they appeared [...] then one can certainly wager that man would be erased, like a face drawn in sand at the edge of the sea" (Foucault, 357). For post-Foucauldean and post-Lyotardian studies of posthumanism, see, for example, Hayles, *How We Became Posthuman;* Haraway, *Simians, Cyborgs, and Women*; and Wolfe, *Animal Rites.*

6 Not all Western critics have unequivocally welcomed posthumanism. Unlike his earlier works, Lyotard's *The Inhuman: Reflections on Time* (1991) considers both the pros and the cons of inhumanity taking over: "What else remains as 'politics' except resistance to this inhuman? And what is left to resist with but the debt which each soul has contracted with the miserable and admirable indetermination from which it was born and does not cease to be born?—which is to say, with the other inhuman?" See Lyotard, *The Inhuman,* 7. As Tony Davies points out: "It should no longer be possible to formulate phrases like 'the destiny of man' or 'the triumph of human reason' without an instant consciousness of the folly and brutality they drag behind them." Nevertheless, "it would be unwise to simply abandon the ground occupied by the historical humanisms" because "the freedom to speak and write, to organize and campaign in defense of individual or collective interests, to protect and disobey: all these can only be articulated in humanist terms." See Tony Davies, *Humanism: The New Critical Idiom* (London: Psychology Press, 1997), 131–32. As Elana Gomel writes: "Humanism has been philosophically demolished [...]. But it remains a default ethical position, especially when issues of fair treatment and universal rights are raised." See Gomel, *Science Fiction, Alien Encounters, and the Ethics of Posthumanism: Beyond the Golden Rule,* vix.

7 Svetlana Galaninskaia, "Babochka letaet i na nebo: Interv'iu s Ol'goi Sedakovoi" [The butterfly flies in the sky: Interview with Olga Sedakova], *Religare,* December 25, 2012, http://www.religare.ru/298818.html. "Dehumanitarianization" refers to the weakening of the

This study will examine the scenarios of *raschelovechivanie* in two prominent novels of the 2000s—Garros-Evdokimov's *Gray Goo* (*Seraia sliz'*, 2005) and Aleksandr Ilichevskii's *Matisse* (*Matiss*, 2007). I am intentionally bringing into dialogue writers who are very different: Garros-Evdokimov (the pen name of duo Aleksandr Garros and Alexei Evdokimov), effective practitioners of nanopunk and the intellectual thriller permeated by social satire, and Ilichevskii, a master of dense intellectual prose. Given their differences, it is all the more striking that their works zero in on the same problem and envision it rather consistently despite inevitable variations.[8] Since Garros-Evdokimov and Ilichevskii differ widely in their aesthetic as well as ideological agendas, the patterns discussed here do not exhibit typological parallels of marked intertextuality, but expose a more general zeitgeist—with the posthuman seen as the spirit or, rather, spiritlessness of our time.

As I will argue, in *Gray Goo* and *Matisse* posthumanism emerges as a form of biological and social degeneration. These novels enact two versions of dehumanization—animalistic (humans to beasts) and mechanistic (humans to machines). In so doing, Garros-Evdokimov and Ilichevskii raise probing questions about the quality of freedom in post-Soviet domains and in the globalized world at large. The human, understood in its traditional post-Enlightenment humanist gamut as an agent of individualism, reason, ethics, and, foremost, free will, is to be salvaged from the freedom-suppressing, homogenizing, de-intellectualizing, and unethical forces of global contemporaneity.[9] The novels under consideration, accordingly, do not so much probe the boundaries of what it means to be human as pinpoint what the writers perceive as a disturbing crisis of humanism and the endangered position of the human subject in today's world.

Garros-Evdokimov: Nano-Apocalypse in Riga

Alexei Evdokimov defines his chief preoccupation as "the *raschelovechivanie* of society as a result of the *raschelovechivanie* of individuals," that is, "the devaluation

---

status of the humanities in today's education while "dehumanization" designates making humans less than human. For Sedakova, it is important to continue teaching the humanities as a way to transfer culture (not acquired "automatically" at birth) to the next generations.

8 I am being purposefully selective here. Works by Victor Pelevin, Vladimir Sorokin, Tatyana Tolstaya, Olga Slavnikova, and Dmitry Bykov, among others, also treat the theme of *raschelovechivanie*. On Garros-Evdokimov and Ilichevskii in the context of the prose of the 2000s see, for example, Aleksandr Chantsev, "*Vita Nova* gadkikh lebedei" [*Vita Nova* of ugly swans], *Novoe literaturnoe obozrenie* 82.2 (April 2006): 425–26; and Inna Bulkina, "Proza 'nulevykh'" (The prose of the 2000s), *Znamia* 9 (Sept. 2010): 202–208.

9 For a detailed account of humanism, see, for example, Davies, *Humanism*.

of individual moral criteria under the conditions of social Darwinism [...] that saturates contemporary society with deadly pain, anger, and frustration."[10]

Russian Latvians Garros and Evdokimov entered the literary scene with their debut novel [*Head*]*crusher* ([*Golovo*]*lomka*, 2002), which won the National Bestseller award in 2003. Their other co-authored works include *Gray Goo*, *The Factor of the Wagon* (*Faktor fury*, 2006), and *The Juche: The Spirit of Self-Reliance: Russian version* (*Chuchkhe: Opora na sobstvennye sily*: *russkaia versiia*, 2006). All of these works were written in Russian and published in Russia, and investigate the phenomenon of *raschelovechivanie* on a global scale—including in Russia itself.[11]

Gray Goo, Garros-Evdokimov's second novel, takes place in Riga, Latvia, after the restitution of independence. Denis (Dan) Kamarin, a 24-year-old documentary filmmaker who has won an award at the Berlin Film Festival, learns about a series of murders and suicides taking place in his circle. More and more of his acquaintances from disparate walks of life, mostly young creative men and women opposed to the status quo, die violent deaths. He embarks on an independent investigation. In the course of the plot, several potential false solutions are offered, including the police suspecting that Dan himself is a serial killer, and the protagonist closing in on a childhood friend and role model, a rebellious character named Fed. Fed commits suicide. On the last page of the novel, Dan is left standing at the top of the as-yet-unfinished twenty-nine-story high-rise that is to house Hansabanka Headquarters.[12] He deliberates on whether to "grow up" and conform to the system, or throw himself into the river Daugava below.

As portrayed in the novel, Dan and his generation straddle the old Soviet and new techno-consumer ways of life. The capital of Riga, likewise, is poised precariously between its Soviet past and EU future. Sleek Euro-style plazas and glass and iron high-rises intermingle with abandoned factories and decaying Soviet apartment blocks. Garbage-strewn industrial zones, ruinous vestiges of

10 Aleksei Evdokimov, "Mne interesno raschelovechivanie obshchestva" ["I am interested in dehumanization of society"], *Vzgliad* (June 18, 2007), http://www.bigbook.ru/articles/detail.php?ID=2979.

11 Although Garros-Evdokimov's first two novels, [*Head*]*crusher* and *Gray Goo*, focus on the theme of the Russian diaspora in Latvia, they feature no pronounced Russian nationalist agenda. Their later works heavily criticize contemporary Russian society. In an interview, Evdokimov suggests that the Russian form of techno-consumerism is the worst of all. See Evdokimov, "Mne interesno raschelovechivanie obshchestva."

12 The Swedbank (formerly Hansabanka) main office building in Riga is the tallest skyscraper in Latvia. The name of the building is Saules akmens [Stone of the sun]. It was built in 2004.

the Soviet modernizing project, dominate the landscape: "At an angle there rises the seemingly endless, multi-storied façade of REZ in a depressing dirty mustard color [...]. Beyond an area that seems undecided about whether to become a carpool or a car dump [...] there is yet another burnt-out ruin."[13] This industrial wasteland is presented as an archaeological ruin, as if an immense historical distance separates the Soviet and the post-Soviet epochs.

Two equally valid, interrelated explanations for the mysterious deaths the novel offers might be schematically termed "realistic" and "fantastic." According to the former, Dan's friends die premature and violent deaths because they are unable to fit into the new system. Since all kinds of opposition are suppressed by the system that has established itself in Latvia and globally, Dan's non-conformist friends have no chance of faring well or, indeed, of surviving under these conditions: "Everyone dies—everyone who is worth something! With no exceptions. [...] Among our acquaintances not a single person is able to remain true to himself and survive. Just to survive, physically. [...] Either you die or you turn into complete shit. Into such shit that it is useless even to talk about it [...]. Into gray goo."[14]

A more SF-like plotline has the world transformed into "gray goo," a cemetery of nanobots replicating uncontrollably and turning everything around into identical matter that lacks individuating properties. As Dan researches nanotechnology online, he learns that industrial assembly on the atomic level will be performed by assemblers of nano-size. To create something suitable to humans, one needs a massive quantity of them. Experts propose solving this problem by creating nanobot replicators, that is, microscopic robots that create robots like themselves that, in their turn, create more of the same kinds of robots. What results is an avalanche of molecular self-replication.

Garros-Evdokimov here have in mind K. Eric Drexler's landmark *Engines of Creation: The Coming Era of Nanotechnology* (1986), a book that envisioned a world transformed by nanobots manipulating matter on the atomic level.[15]

---

13 Garros-Evdokimov, *Seraia sliz'* [Gray goo] (St. Petersburg: Limbus Press, 2005), 220–21. REZ—*Rizhskii Elektromashinostroitel'nyi zavod* [Riga Electric Machine Factory]—opened in 1946 to produce traction equipment for electrical trains, light railways and fork lifts, as well as lighting and power-supply equipment for passenger coaches.

14 Garros-Evdokimov, *Seraia sliz'*, 408–409.

15 Some of the better known SF works on nanotechnology are Neal Stephenson, *The Diamond Age: Or, A Young Lady's Illustrated Primer* (New York: Bantam Spectra, 1995); William Gibson, *Idoru* (New York: Viking Press, 1996); and Michael Crichton, *Prey* (New York: HarperCollins, 2002). Nanopunk, a daughter genre of cyberpunk, explores the pros and

Among the cognoscenti of nanotechnology, this threat has become known as the "gray goo problem." In Drexler's description, tiny self-replicating robots may exhibit exponential growth—the first replicator assembling a copy in one thousand seconds, the two replicators building two more in the next thousand seconds, the four building another four—until there are sixty eight billion replicators after ten hours. As Drexler warns, self-replicating nanobots could easily be too tough, small, and rapidly spreading to stop, and might reduce the biosphere to dust in a matter of days.[16]

Importantly, Drexler explains that the term "gray goo" does not refer to either color or texture so much as the pedestrian quality of replicators that could nevertheless beat the most evolutionarily advanced organisms including humans. Although masses of uncontrolled replicators need not be gray or gooey, the term "gray goo" "emphasizes that replicators able to obliterate life might be less inspiring than a single species of crabgrass."[17] Nanobots might be "superior" in an evolutionary sense, but this need not make them valuable: "We have evolved to love a world rich in living things, ideas, and diversity, so there is no reason to value gray goo merely because it could spread. Indeed, if we prevent it we will thereby prove *our* evolutionary superiority."[18]

Gray goo provides Garros-Evdokimov with a potent metaphor for what they see as contemporary humanity's de-individuation, de-intellectualization, and loss of free will and ethical principles.[19] The novel's "realistic" and

---

cons of nanotechnology. For Rafael Huereca, the "sinister ambiences created by cyberpunk" later extrapolated into its subgenres and appeared as a "speculation of the future in which technology would become oppressive, a method of surveillance and social control." See Rafael M. Huereca, "The Evolution of Cyberpunk into Postcyberpunk: The Role of Cognitive Cyberspaces, Wetware Networks and Nanotechnology in Science Fiction" (PhD diss., Universitat Autònoma de Barcelona, 2011), 4. Nevertheless, unlike the predominantly darker cyberpunk, nanopunk can deal with good as well as dystopian aspects of nanotechnology. On nanotechnology in Western SF, see Colin Milburn, *Nanovision: Engineering the Future* (Durham: Duke UP, 2008). Besides dystopian nanopunk, Garros-Evdokimov draw on the Western traditions of cyberpunk (Philip K. Dick, William Gibson, the Wachowskis, etc.) and "revolt of the clerk" novels as exemplified in particular by Chuck Palahniuk's *Fight Club* (New York: W. W. Norton & Company, 1996).

16 Drexler points out that nanomachines are limited in their growth by the quantity of raw material they have available for consumption.

17 K. Eric Drexler, *Engines of Creation: The Coming Era of Nanotechnology* (New York: Anchor, 1986), 173.

18 Ibid.

19 Unlike those SF scenarios that depict some literal nano-end-of-the-world, *Gray Goo* asks that we read its nano-apocalypse metaphorically. The authors state that "*Gray Goo* is not SF, it is an attempt to discuss what happens in reality, here and now." See Garros and Evdokimov,

"fantastic" motifs are essentially two takes on a single problem—that of corporate culture, advertising, movies, the internet, etc., turning individuals into "sludge":

> Nanobots begin to replicate unstoppably and endlessly, turning everything into themselves—until all earthly matter turns into a homogenous layer of identical molecules. [...] Not sure that the future needs us. This leaves for us a picture of an endlessly replicating primitive substance, dragging everything down to its level, disintegrating any complex, highly organized structures, conceptual systems, personalities, transforming the global intellectual field into an even layer of slimy gray senseless goo.[20]

Drexler's replicons are undifferentiated, unconscious (have no inner experience), and aggressive organisms that can do nothing but consume the world around them in order to proliferate.

As Dan meditates on the death of one more victim, his friend Dima Iakushev, he associates humanity with individuality and reason—and sees them both presently dwindling away:

> Novelty, not quantitative but qualitative. In this swift and powerful tele-radio-newspapers-movies-music-goods-tourists-computers torrent, details, nuances, and shades disappear. As if all the depths of psychologizing and all the artistic achievements of portraiture stream down, along a steep parabola, toward the most generic and therefore the most unerring—a stick figure. [...] The world is being homogenized [*niveliruetsia*] [...] standardized [*standartiziruetsia*] [...] simplified [*uproshchaetsia*] [...]. Such a familiar sensation. Likely familiar to any individual who thinks even a tiny bit [*malo mal'ski mysliashchemu individu*]. A sensation of total, all-suppressing, all-filling, all-replacing, unified obtuseness [*unifitsirovannoi tuposti*]. Of imbecilic plastic simplicity. Of the suffocating mind [*umstvennogo udush'ia*].[21]

"Literatura—eto tovar, no ne usluga" [Literature is a commodity but not service], http://www.gzt.ru/culture/2005/02/08/041900.html. Gray goo "is devoid of any characteristics," and everyone in the Garros-Evdokimov world "begins to replicate this substance." See Lev Danilkin, "'Seraia sliz'" [Gray goo], *Afisha* (January 26, 2005), http://www.afisha.ru/personalpage/191662/review/150083.

20 Garros-Evdokimov, *Seraia sliz'*, 427–28.

21 Ibid., 278. The first few lines of the passage quote Petr Vail', *Genii mesta* [Genius loci] (Moscow, 1999), 173.

Garros-Evdokimov oppose uniqueness to functionality, and place value on human individuality. The world of the present, as they envision it, is one in which reproducible schemes dominate, and in which humans are transformed into indistinguishable performers of functions.[22] Hence one of Dan's female acquaintances feels that she "is no longer herself but some kind of a machine [...] a biorobot [...] an ordinary work android, as in *Blade Runner*."[23] A properly functioning robot has a limited operating program that defines its purpose, and it cannot do anything that is not set by the program. Contrasting their post-Soviet posthumans to classic *Homo sapiens,* the authors claim that the former have weakened cognitive abilities. The intellect, in accordance with posthumanist ideology, is no longer regarded with certainty as having value. Humanity is rapidly devolving and will soon disappear "if not physically, then as the subject of collective reason."[24]

No less than the weakening of individuality and intellect, the suppression of ethics (via dwindling religious faith) makes men of contemporaneity less than human. Dan's meditation following Dima's death commences with reading Dima's poem, "It smells of sulfur. This is a smell of burnt-out faith [...]."[25] In his journal, Dan's friend laments the ousting of the miraculous from contemporary life: "The most terrible curses have lost their power. Spirits are now called forth for fun [...]. The world is swiftly becoming more and more primitive, losing its non-rational aspect."[26] The destabilizing of ethical principles, whether couched here from the point of view of weakening faith (as in Dima's journal) or, more frequently in this novel, in secular-humanist terms,

---

22 Cf. the characterization of contemporary stardom: "They are made into sex symbols precisely on account of their extreme ordinariness! Commonplaceness. They are the mathematical average of their fans. A composite identity kit of their million-sized audience" (Garros-Evdokimov, *Seraia sliz'*, 25). Cf. Garros on the "de-individuating movement of global consumer civilization." See Aleksandr Garros, "Kul'tura. Literatura. Mnogotochie sborki" [Culture. Literature. Ellipsis of construction], *Expert* (December 19, 2005): 89.

23 Garros-Evdokimov, *Seraia sliz'*, 80. Garros-Evdokimov refer here to Ridley Scott's movie *Blade Runner* (1982), based on Philip K. Dick's novel *Do Androids Dream of Electric Sheep?* (New York: Doubleday & Company, Inc., 1968). Although the central problem in Dick's and Scott's work is androids being in excess of their programming, Dan's friend considers herself to be a robot hardly in excess of its programming.

24 Garros-Evdokimov, *Seraia sliz'*, 214.

25 Ibid., 278.

26 Ibid., 276–77.

is seen as another distinct feature of the 2000s.[27] Modern humans know what they want to get, and do not care who or what gets smashed in the process.[28]

Most significantly perhaps, freedom of choice is also taken away from contemporary life. Dan's reflection on Iakushev's death ends with an attempt to reassure himself, "Well, it will go easier on me."[29] As Kamarin tries to tell himself (mistakenly, as the narrative later will demonstrate), he will not have to make the requisite hard choice between self-degradation and self-destruction, but will somehow be able to maintain both his social success and integrity. Yet, as it turns out, the only way to exercise freedom of choice in the world of *Gray Goo* is to die—or else live coerced, as most of the populace does.

Gray goo aptly captures the fundamental problem of unfreedom. Humans have no choice vis-à-vis nano-replicons: "What kind of a reaction can be there? [...] We just get sick and die."[30] As they devolve into gray goo, they lose agency altogether: "This is a process of utterly mechanical copying, lacking any kind of meaning and goal. Dust that turns into dust anything it

---

27 One may discern two different ways of addressing ethics in the text under consideration. The mentioning of "weakening faith" in Dima's diary makes *Gray Goo* sound borderline Dostoevskian. Elsewhere the novel connects ethics and reason. The latter line of thought is more prominent in the novel as a whole. Inasmuch as the biological constituent "dictates. Through instinct. Through emotions" (Garros-Evdokimov, *Seraia* sliz', 215), emotion, like instinct, is more often than not linked to unfreedom. It is reason, rather, that enables one to distinguish between good and evil as well as makes possible an independent choice between the two. The linkage of reason, free will, and ethics draws on post-Enlightenment and post-Kantian traditions. Under the Enlightenment-based principles (reactivated by Garros-Evdokimov's "fathers," the Soviet liberal intelligentsia), reason is coupled with free-mindedness and ethical behavior. In Kantian terms, the fundamental principle of morality is the law of an autonomous will, and moral requirement is based on a standard of rationality (the categorical imperative). Such a bonding of ethics and reason does not quite fall into the "anti-rationalist" strain of Russian thought that prefers to connect human ethics with faith, imagination, and feeling. Although Garros-Evdokimov's novel does not partake of the traditional Russian distrust of reason à la Dostoevsky or Tolstoy, it does echo Dostoevsky's conceptualization of free will as a human trait that is essential to the exercise of ethics. The destruction of reason (paradoxically) takes place in ultra-technologically-advanced societies along with the destruction of free will, individuality, and morals—highlighting the regressive nature of social Darwinism.

28 In *Chuchkhe*, post-Soviet children are characterized as ruthlessly efficient: "They know where all things are located in this world, and exactly how many bodily movements are required to grab what one wants." They are "some supermen, who are therefore not entirely men." See Garros-Evdokimov, *Chuchkhe* (Moscow: Vagrius, 2006), 136. For more on *Chuchkhe*, see Sofya Khagi, "One Billion Years after the End of the World: Historical Deadlock, Contemporary Dystopia, and the Continuing Legacy of the Strugatskii Brothers," *Slavic Review* 72. 2 (Summer 2013): 267–86.

29 Garros-Evdokimov, *Seraia sliz'*, 279.

30 Ibid., 441.

touches. With no goal. For no reason."[31] Dan is convinced that freedom of thought and action is the most valuable gift humans get at birth. As he sees it, the history of ninety-nine percent of humankind is the history of voluntary refusal of freedom because responsibility for a voluntary and conscious choice is exactly what the overwhelming majority fear most.[32]

Garros-Evdokimov's novel portrays the human being made less than human or liquidated altogether in order to build a new techno-consumer social order. As such, it suggests parallels with the postrevolutionary period when the Bolshevik state attempted to transform individuals into replicas of one another, countless little builders of socialist ideology.[33] As a more recent trope for mechanistic dehumanization, gray goo has a particularly rich metaphoric potential. It foregrounds standardization and absorption of the human subject by a system, as in the more conventional cog in the (socialist) machine but on a novel, all-encompassing scale. The subjects might pretend that they want to escape, but know for a fact that they do not. That is so because, unlike the crudely carceral collectivist states of old, the techno-consumer system, with its "gentler" modus operandi, regulates its subjects more efficiently. Although the status quo suppresses the populace efficiently, the subjects are content with their comfortable imprisonment.[34] Thus, the trope of gray goo aptly captures the totalizing effects of the global techno-consumer village.

While the motif of mechanistic dehumanization prevails in the novel, Garros-Evdokimov intertwine it with the imagery of animalistic *raschelovechivanie*.

---

31 Ibid.

32 In Garros-Evdokimov's description (resembling Dostoevsky's "Grand Inquisitor" scenario), humans are endowed with the freedom of choice but reject it because they fear responsibility. Having rejected freedom, "the majority of humans ipso facto stopped being human." See Garros-Evdokimov, *Seraia sliz'*, 214.

33 Julia Vaingurt points out that in postrevolutionary Russia "the whole universe of people, things, and the relations between them [was] rendered 'standing-reserve' for state goals." See Julia Vaingurt, *Wonderlands of the Avant-Garde: Technology and the Arts in Russia of the 1920s* (Evanston, IL: Northwestern University Press, 2013), 7. On "standing reserve," see Martin Heidegger, *The Question Concerning Technology and Other Essays* (New York: Harper Torchbooks, 1969), 17. As Elana Gomel asks: "In response to the horrors of the Holocaust, philosophers such as Adorno and Horkheimer blamed humanism and the Enlightenment. But insofar as the main project of both Nazism and Communism was to create a New Man, should they be not seen as varieties of posthumanism?" See Gomel, *Science Fiction, Alien Encounters, and the Ethics of Posthumanism*, 21.

34 Cf. [*Head*]*crusher*, in which the protagonist likens himself to a guinea pig in a jar: "The guinea pig pretended that it wanted to break out of the jar and escape. But everybody, including the guinea pig, knew for a fact that it did not really want to." See Garros-Evdokimov, [*Golovo*] *lomka* (Saint Petersburg, 2003), 24.

Gray goo itself suggests devolutionary reversal. Men-replicons are "superior" in an evolutionary sense due to their high reproductive ability and competitive success under capitalist conditions, but otherwise they are unthinking, aggressive, and thoroughly homogenized. The central trope that indicates nano-apocalypse and simultaneously suggests organic matter unifies both mechanistic and animalistic strands of the narrative. The novel's epigraph introduces gray goo, but in the context of biomorphic imagery: "The fish were processed, but the next day one fish was in really bad shape: its fins had disintegrated, its position was head down, and gray goo had spread all along its body."[35] The fish processed for consumption foreshadow the novel's critique of consumer society where humans are consuming and being consumed. Since the fish are already decomposing, it is darkly ironic that "one was in really bad shape."

As the novel unfolds, post-Soviet youth (people in their twenties in the 2000s) are portrayed as not just different from their older compatriots; rather, Garros-Evdokimov assign them an altogether different biological identity.[36] After reconnecting with a childhood buddy, a former rebel who has become a well-meaning member of the middle class, Dan characterizes him as someone who "has not changed but, rather, metamorphosed [*pererodilsia*] [...] in whom there remains nothing whatsoever of the former man." It was as if they now "communicated in divergent codes," with his friend "pressing 'delete' with automatic indifference."[37] In turn, another acquaintance pushing thirty perceives Dan's generation as "a different biological species [*drugoi biologicheskii vid*]"—"not merely completely ignorant but absolutely organic in their ignorance," no longer capable of doubt or critical analysis as befits *Homo sapiens*.[38] The transmogrified subjects do not notice that something has happened, and this is perhaps the worst change of all.

Concurrent with the weakening of cognitive powers, biological existence becomes accentuated. In the consumer realm, human consciousness functions

---

35 Garros-Evdokimov, *Seraia sliz'*, 6.

36 Cf. the description of young nouveaux riches as bio-robots in [*Head*]*crusher*: "Their startling social success is due to the fact that they are bio-robots, nurtured in the depths of super-secret Soviet research institutes to be deployed against the Western enemy. When the USSR collapsed, they switched on of their own accord and infiltrated the new world." See Garros-Evdokimov, [*Golovo*]*lomka*, 84. The robots are so successful because they are able to adapt ideally to the Darwinian social environment where the value of morals is trumped by the survival of the fittest. For more on [*Head*]*crusher*, see Khagi, "Garros-Evdokimov and Commodification of the Baltics," *Journal of Baltic Studies* 41.1 (2010): 119–37.

37 Garros-Evdokimov, *Seraia sliz'*, 74. The power of technology emerges through the consistent description of humans in computer terms.

38 Ibid., 82.

as an instrument for the satisfaction of needs, and thus in effect a reversion to an animal-like state:

> With countless sticky tentacles and toothy beak, pop culture and media reality climb into your brain to sheathe, latch onto and cut out the areas that are responsible for anything other than physical contentment and material prosperity, to connect you to the dynamo-machine of meaningless work and the anesthetic drip of meaningless entertainment, to transform you into chewing and breeding cattle.[39]

The "cattle" (*skot*) trope again helps drive forward the authors' critique of the techno-consumer paradigm. The media, portrayed as a predatory sea creature, degrades humans to the status of livestock caught in the purely physical processes of consumption and propagation, robbed of any will or understanding. Through social conditioning, the global community is reduced to biomass.

Like mechanistic *raschelovechivanie*, animalistic dehumanization helps Garros-Evdokimov examine the problems of degraded reason, individuality, ethics, and, most crucially, freedom in contemporary society. The devaluation of individual moral criteria takes place under social Darwinism, and biology ousts the freedom of choice. The biological constituent "by definition does not give you choice (choice is a category of reason anyway). It dictates—as it is supposed to. Through instinct. Through emotions. Including higher kinds of emotions, important emotions that mean so much to all of us. The stronger their dictate."[40] To exercise free will means to engage your rational rather than biological faculties.

As the authors attempt to elucidate the reasons for the civilizational deadlock portrayed in *Gray Goo*, they draw on the Strugatsky brothers' famous notion, "the Homeostatic Universe" (*gomeostaticheskoe mirozdanie*). Since humans, by virtue of the gift of reason, have a mass of physical and emotional energy not used up in the process of survival, "mother nature attacks the mind that is alien to it [...] through forced socialization."[41] But, unlike the

39 Ibid., 215.

40 Ibid., 252.

41 Ibid., 242. That is, all members of a given society are compelled to take part in social relationships and conform to the prevalent patterns of thought and behavior. The Strugatskys define The Homeostatic Universe as follows: "The gist of the Homeostasis of the Universe consists in maintaining the balance between the increase in entropy and the development of reason. [...] And what was happening to us now was nothing other than the first reaction

Strugatskys' blueprint, the Garros-Evdokimov world has no scientists trying to fight the forces of homeostasis. Indeed, it is no longer a question of scientific geniuses needing to be held in check because they might turn humanity into a super-civilization, but rather one of humanity devolving to the condition of the subhuman. And what are the implications of scientists in fact being present in this post-Soviet world?

Ilichevskii: Homeless Scientists Confront the Great Non-Living

Aleksandr Ilichevskii defines *raschelovechivanie* as "the process of the loss of form, of the constituent structure, that is, the removal of the human image from the subject." This can result "from some kind of a psychological or physical trauma—for instance, hunger, war or gradual degradation, a movement toward dementia [*umalishennost'*] or an extreme form of exhaustion, when human existence becomes devoid of moral content [*moral'nogo soderzhaniia*]."[42]

Matisse, the winner of the 2007 Russian Booker award, tells the story of physicist Leonid Korolev in early 1990s Moscow.[43] As the Soviet Union disintegrates, he attempts unsuccessfully to pursue his scientific career in Denmark. He returns to Moscow to move through a series of uninspiring jobs (working as an insurance agent, for example). He subsequently seeks a modicum of freedom from the rough and raw new reality, abandons his apartment, and becomes a homeless person (*bomzh*) on the streets of Moscow. Korolev roams the cluttered urban landscape, sleeps in its cellars and passageways, has a

---

of the Homeostatic Universe to the threat of humanity becoming a super-civilization. The universe was defending itself." See Arkadii Strugatskii and Boris Strugatskii, *Sobranie sochinenii (Collected works)* (Donetsk, 2001), 7:103. The Garros-Evdokimov heroes are confronted "not with some kind of universe (which could still be beautiful and even romantic) but an utter and universal non-entity because the world in which this non-entity lives cannot bear anything good." See Dmitrii Bykov, "Bykov-quickly: Vzgliad-73" [Bykov-quickly: a glance-73], March 21, 2005, http://old.russ.ru/columns/bikov/20050321-pr.html. In contrast to the Strugatskys, Garros-Evdokimov exhibit "a radical distrust of solidarity." See Chantsev, "*Vita Nova* gadkikh lebedei," 426.

42 Ilichevskii, e-mail message to author, September 4, 2015. Ilichevskii's formulation of *raschelovechivanie* (similar to Garros-Evdokimov's) posits the linkage of ethics and reason: under dementia, human existence becomes devoid of moral content. As a whole, *Matisse* suggests both ethics as a function of reason and ethics as a function of feeling/faith/intuition lines of thought. For the latter, see especially the Nadia line.

43 Together with *Matisse*, *The Persian* [*Pers*] (Moscow: AST, 2010), *The Mathematician* [*Matematik*] (Moscow: AST, 2011), and *The Anarchists* [*Anarkhisty*] (Moscow: AST, 2012) form a novelistic tetralogy.

prolonged sojourn underground in the secret Metro 2, and befriends a pair of vagabonds, Nadia and Vadia. In the latter part of the novel, Korolev, Nadia, and Vadia leave Moscow to travel the Russian countryside.

The book's opening introduces its leitmotifs: social and cultural degradation, the rampant brutality of post-Soviet experience, entrapment in the techno-consumer world, and the protagonist's inability to fit in and desire to escape to a freer world. As a group of teenagers attack the *bomzhi* Nadia and Vadia, Korolev, trapped in heavy traffic, witnesses the scene:

> Leonid Korolev, a man of about thirty-five, a small wholesale business agent, slowly crawling with traffic in the direction of Presnia [...] knew that for several winters the hoboes have been at war with the homeless children. He knew that teenagers gathering into groups sometimes killed the homeless to intimidate them, freeing the area of underground habitat from their competition. [...] Their herd cruelty knew no mercy. [...] The street was shackled by a soulless throng of vehicles. They roared with worn-out mufflers, whistled from weakened belts; the expensive motors purred, snow tires clanged, and the low frequencies of audio systems boomed; here and there they crossed into the opposite lane, quaked, burped, gave out special signals. The cars concealed clumps of human fatigue, self-importance, hatred, carelessness, indifference, concentration. The traffic looked like a disaster scene. [...] The structure of snowflakes flashing first, impeccably rigorous and pure, brought down from many kilometers high, raised him over the city. [...] Pushing the gearshift, Korolev thought with fury that the inanimate is more decent than the human, that in the rigorous structure of a tiny crystal there is more sense, beauty, something meaningful that would explain what he is living for than in the chasm of the human brimming over the city.[44]

In the passage above, Ilichevskii employs animalistic Darwinian tropes to characterize the violent and divisive transitions of the time. Street urchins kill tramps "to free [...] the area of habitat" (*osvobodit' areal obitaniia*); teenage "herd cruelty" [*stainaia zhestokost'*] knew no mercy"; as a boy assaults Vadia, he calls him an "ape" (*obez'ian*).[45] Equally, Ilichevskii presents Moscow as a sort of a technological Leviathan where people are enslaved and exhausted by machines. Cars encase human emotions of a predominantly negative kind.

44 Aleksandr Ilichevskii, *Matiss* [*Matisse*] (Moscow, Vremia, 2008), 6–7.

45 Ibid., 5.

In contrast, nature, the snowy expanse of the sky, suggests to the protagonist a potential escape from the suffocating urban domain.

In the story of the vagabonds Nadia and Vadia, animalistic dehumanization comes as a consequence of deprivation and oppression. With the country disintegrating, animals and humans ruthlessly compete for habitat and sustenance. In this competition, humans are brought to the same level as non-humans through hardship and struggle; their life is the only resource they have. Thus, tramps, street urchins, and canines that have been thrown out of their homes grow wild and wage war on the streets of Moscow. Analogously, during their imprisonment in a mountain village in the Caucasus, Vadia and his comrade are treated on par with livestock. They are fed animal food, live in a shed with goats, and have to fight with their cohabitants for their share of nourishment and living space.

That the value of life, human and non-human alike, falls during this disruptive period is illustrated in the 1993 attack on the Russian government building (White House) seen from the perspectives of Nadia and Vadia. The couple finds a warm attic on Presnia Street, and lives there among flapping, fussing pigeons. On October 4, 1993, something strange begins to happen: tanks drive up to the White House, and people run around with machine guns. On his way back to his temporary home, Vadia observes a poodle shot down in the ensuing chaos while its owner, an elderly foreigner frightened out of his wits, effects a narrow escape. Vadia is beaten by a soldier, and Nadia barely escapes being killed by a sniper who enters the attic to shoot across the street at the offices of the government on Krasnopresnenskaia. At night, the spooked pigeons finally return to the attic, and Nadia and Vadia resume their cohabitation there. Neither of the *bomzhi* understands or is indeed interested in the political implications of the whole affair. All they want is to survive and (at least in Nadia's case) are shocked by lives lost in the ensuing mess.

Whereas Vadia and the other hoboes relate to the non-human world mainly through a struggle for existence, Nadia's relationship with that world, although stemming from the same conditions of hardship, emphasizes closeness due to shared suffering. Degraded by poverty, oppression, and violence, Nadia grows closer to the non-human world. After she brings an injured bittern, a heron-like bird, to the Moscow Zoo, she starts looking after animals there. One of the animals she takes care of is a dying female bear:

> The bear looked like a naked old woman. She was gray-colored, like stone. She was not immediately discernible against the even expanse of concrete.

> Nadia took it upon herself to begin visiting the bear; no one asked her. It was a lean time, and predators in the zoo were fed soaked soybeans. It was suggested that the animals begin to be fed dog carcasses. Homeless people feared stray dogs like fire. Trash cans in the city were empty, and the stray dogs had grown fierce. There were rumors of packs that lived in the abandoned hangars of the South port. They surrounded and cornered passers-by. [...] When the bear grew completely weak, Nadia began to guide her to the back of her cage for the night, onto the shelf covered with hay. She put her coat over her and lay next to her. The bear also shifted around, moving closer. So together they warmed each other.[46]

The references to rampant stray dogs continue the Darwinian "nature red in tooth and claw" imagery of the book's opening as well as the sections that depict Vadia's travails in the Caucasus. In the Nadia-bear case, however, the notion that neither humans nor non-humans have sustenance to relieve their hunger brings on an unexpected prelapsarian condition. The bear dies, and the grieving Nadia forgets entirely about the badly needed money she has hidden in the animal's cage.

Nadia's regressive metamorphosis highlights how history's violence victimizes humans and non-humans alike, and points to the imminent danger of cognitive and spiritual decline lying in wait for humans. She and her mother are victimized in the dissolution of the USSR. The older woman dies of a stroke after they had run from civil unrest in Baku to Pskov and were unable to obtain either registration or employment there. The feeble-minded Nadia grows even more disabled now that she is on her own, and there is no longer anyone to "methodically claw her from non-being."[47] She loses most of her memories and feels her mind gradually slipping away. As her mind grows numb, she experiences it as a "big gray bird that has been crippled by a stick. The bird sits on a sturdy branch growing from her right temple and sighs hoarsely, pulling up its broken wing."[48] She thinks it is impossible to understand where the human ends and that she will not notice the boundary or, more precisely, that when she crosses it, she will no longer care. Yet Nadia is terrified by her utter helplessness to prevent this slippage or at least convey her fear to someone else. The dissolving subject will not mourn the loss since there will no longer be anyone

46 Ibid., 90–91.

47 Ibid., 77.

48 Ibid., 79.

to mourn. But while she still possesses some degree of self-consciousness, she struggles to slow down her cognitive decline by counting.

The Nadia-Vadia theme of poverty and social change leading to regression, devolution, and animalism in *Matisse* recalls writings of the postrevolutionary period by authors such as Yevgeny Zamyatin. In both postrevolutionary and post-Soviet contexts, the trope of *raschelovechivanie* is mobilized as a response to drastic social change. In Zamyatin's short story "The Cave" (*Peshchera,* 1922), Martin Martinych, a refined, Scriabin-loving member of the intelligentsia, steals wood from his neighbor to provide a day of warmth for his dying wife and himself. Overstepping his ethical barriers, Martin Martinych feels he is being degraded into an ape-like predatory creature who is forced to fight other animals for survival. Similarly, in *Matisse,* the vagabonds must steal and fight to survive. They are dehumanized due to their unbearable conditions of existence.[49]

Whereas in the case of the *bomzhi* couple, dehumanization implies primarily the weakening of reason and ethical capacity (Nadia and Vadia, respectively), the story of Korolev, "the living corpse," concerns the decline of these faculties as well as of individuality and, most emphatically, freedom.[50] In the novel's opening scene, Korolev, one of the countless people trapped in Moscow traffic, thirsts to escape from the techno-consumer machine. The worn-out protagonist dreams of tearing himself away from the sickening mass of men and machines and becoming an individual on his own terms, alone with himself and nature: "Slowly he was tearing away, rising higher and farther over the hilly caviar of urban lights, and this rise was his deep inhalation."[51]

---

49 Martin Martinych is "bifurcated by the extreme deprivation of his circumstances into a purely animal Mart, a 'caveman' who says only 'I must,' and another Mart 'clinging tenaciously in memory, a Mart who used to love the music of Scriabin and who now, standing before Obertyshev's ample woodpile, says 'I am not.'" See Timothy Langen, "Evgeny Zamyatin's 'The Cave,'" *Philosophy and Literature* 29, no. 1 (April 2005): 210. Regressive metamorphosis also features in the postrevolutionary writings of Andrei Platonov such as *The Foundation Pit* (*Kotlovan,* 1930) as well as in the Strugatskys' works such as *Roadside Picnic* (*Piknik na obochine,* 1971). In the latter, the protagonist's daughter mutates under the influence of the alien Zone.

50 Ilichevskii, *Matiss,* 94. As Ilichevskii comments to Pavel Basinskii, "Almost any man at least once in his life feels himself on the edge of the abyss—liberation from external circumstances." See Pavel Basinskii, "Matiss bez shtampa: Laureat premii 'Russkii Buker' Aleksandr Ilichevskii ne liubit odnoznachnykh smyslov," *Rossiiskaia gazeta* (December 14, 2007), http://www.rg.ru/2007/12/14/matiss.html. *Matisse* "expresses society's yearning after renewal and freedom that were realized so equivocally in the 1990s, and whose victim the hero perceives himself to be." See Valeriia Pustovaia, "Krupitsy tverdi. Aleksandr Ilichevskii" [Grains of the firmament: Aleksandr Ilichevskii], *Voprosy literatury* 4 (2010): 100.

51 Ilichevskii, *Matiss,* 7.

In contrast with Nadia and Vadia, Korolev does not wind up homeless due to external forces. Instead, he makes a conscious choice to become a *bomzh* because of his thirst for freedom: "Korolev reveled in his freedom. Liberated from the nonsense of work, for the first month he completely forgot about Gittis and the abandoned apartment. [...] Moscow was a greedy-grasping commercial cesspit—but threaded through and through with passages and burrows to the unknown."[52] Research institutes are being shut down and Korolev is unable to continue his work, but neither is he able to fit into the new techno-consumer system. His choice—a situation that can be appositely contrasted to Dan Kamarin's final indecision whether to become a well-functioning "nanobot" or to kill himself—is purposeful self-marginalization.[53]

The former physicist Korolev's last name coincides with that of brilliant Soviet spacecraft engineer Sergei Korolev, the lead designer of the Soviet space program.[54] *Matisse* evokes spacecraft as the Soviet Union's ultimate modernizing project. The novel offers ample imagery of decaying rockets and planes from Soviet times, as in the following depiction of the wooden-plank hangar of the Polar Air Fleet: It "still survived among the high-rises of Tushino, enclosed by an impenetrable makeshift fence of wire grills from beds, the backs of chairs, doors lifted off their hinges and tangles of barbed wire." Wild dogs roam around the hangar which, "according to rumor, still preserved intact the legendary ANT-25 RD aircraft."[55] The description of places like the Institute of Theoretical and Experimental Physics in Cheremushki and the Presidium of the Academy of Sciences emphasize the disintegration of science institutions after the collapse of the USSR.

Socialist ideology with its modernizing projects of technological development and social progress lies in ruins, both metaphorical and literal.

52 Ibid., 261–62. Sample translation by Andrew Bromfield, http://academia-rossica.org/en/literature/new-russian-classics/matisse-by-alexander-ilichevsky.

53 Dan Kamarin is not afforded self-marginalization because in the world of *Gray Goo* techno-consumerism enforces total homogeneity over the populace and either reabsorbs or eliminates anyone diverging from the norm.

54 Korolev oversaw the Sputnik and Vostok projects including launching Yuri Gagarin into orbit on April 12, 1961. The Russian space program's mission control center is in the suburban Moscow town of Korolev.

55 Ilichevskii, *Matiss*, 262. The Tupolev ANT-25 was constructed in 1933. From June 18 to July 20, 1937, the crew headed by Valerii Chkalov made a nonstop flight to the US. The 9,130-kilometer flight took sixty-three hours and twenty-five minutes. Cf. the description of the Michelson plant where Korolev visits the site of Fanny Kaplan's would-be assassination of Lenin, and finds old printed media from Soviet times (Ilichevskii, *Matiss*, 169–70).

The Moscow where Korolev wanders around as a homeless person, like the Riga of *Gray Goo*, bifurcates between the decaying Soviet past and the chaotic present. Everywhere are vestiges of the Soviet project: gargantuan factories abandoned in part or completely, empty research laboratories, aerodromes and military bases gradually falling into disuse, and the labyrinth of the underground. The authorial gaze lingers over the remnants of the Soviet world, what Ilichevskii terms the "masterpieces of the unknown" and the capital's hidden treasures.[56] They include such things as the huge locks on the Moscow-Volga canal, the plaster nymphs from the 1930s, and the grounds of Mosfil'm with an abandoned pavilion full of fairytale movie sets from Korolev's childhood. These are the protagonist's escape routes from the commercial cesspit. Once again, the "archaeological remnants" of an "ancient" empire do not reflect a real significant temporal lapse so much as the intense alienation Korolev and his peers feel toward the post-Soviet way of life.

Korolev and the other people of his generation that populate *Matisse*, as it were, fall through the cracks between two realms—of their Soviet childhood and youth and post-Soviet adulthood.[57] Besides Sergei Korolev, Leonid Korolev alludes to "Len'ka Korolev" (1957), a song by the Soviet bard Bulat Okudzhava in which a young boy goes to fight in the Great Patriotic War before he has a chance to mature and meet his "queen" (*korolevu*). Figuratively if not literally speaking, this is what happens to people of Korolev's age who were swept in their youth by the seismic events of the early nineties. As Ilichevskii suggests, people born circa 1970 differ from those who can be casually called their peers because they were affected like no one else by the dissolution of the USSR:

> They turned out on the top of the tsunami, crushing down you know what: they developed in parallel with the time of turbulence, they were the first babble of that Time. [...] In other words, they had a unique trajectory of movement—along the wave. Whether they wanted to or not, they projected

---

56 Ilichevskii, *Matiss*, 107.

57 "What motivated me to write this was an attempt to try to understand what happened with this generation of people in the early 1990s, when no one was certain of one's future." See John Varoli, "Ilichevskii's *Matisse* Wins Russian Booker Prize for Fiction," *Bloomberg*, December 6, 2007, http://www.bloomberg.com/apps/news?pid=newsarchive&sid=awqzxhHe2Ad8. "Each book tells the story of a man who overcomes a personal existential crisis by abandoning his 'normal' lifestyle to join a real or imaginary community of people choosing to exist outside of established social norms." See Mikhail Krutikov, "From Azerbaijan to Silicon Valley and Back: How Aleksandr Ilichevskii Became a Russian Literary Star," *Forverts*, August 7, 2012, http://forward.com/articles/160316/from-azerbaijan-to-silicon-valley-and-back/?p=all.

> the development/destruction of the surrounding environment onto their own development. [...] Precisely because of the natural destructiveness of the time that created them, he used to think that their generation was incapable of anything noteworthy. Korolev thought: in the best-case scenario, he was a good observer and conducting detailed phenological analysis would probably be his lot. But their tendency to self-destruction turned out on the whole to be as central as their creative potential.[58]

The formative years of those of Korolev's generation, when a vital acceleration of thoughts and impressions takes place, coincided with that period of major historical change. As much as they may have tried to ignore the changes, they could not help but reflect on them and, simultaneously, reflect about themselves. Attuned to the noise (babble) of time, they are able to simultaneously discern different temporal strata (past, present, future). At the same time—and here zoomorphic Darwinian language enters again—they themselves are adversely affected by the destructive qualities of the "surrounding environment" (*okruzhaiushchei sredy*). In Korolev's thinking, all he can do is study the life-cycle events of his species as they are influenced by climate and habitat factors.

Like *Gray Goo, Matisse* envisions the particular historical threshold of the late 1980s and early 1990s as a larger breaking point—not merely a replacement of one social system by another but a point after which humankind, and the relationship between the human and the non-human, might be altogether reconfigured. This is the case because the human is being ousted by the posthuman. Ilichevskii offers, via Korolev's musings, a sustained investigation of the nature of the radical transformation that takes place. For one thing, Korolev mentions the "final impossibility of the end of the world on which the older generation fed and which turned out to be nothing," and yet he observes the overwhelming fear that has gripped the populace.[59]

If no conventional "end of the world" scenario is imminent, what are the reasons for the terror holding people in its grip? Korolev uses the metaphor of a train falling into a chasm to convey the country's historical catastrophe: "The locomotive had already fallen into the abyss but the carriages were still flying, accelerated by the inertia of the free fall, hoping in vain to jump over the parabola of the crash."[60] He extends the train metaphor to draw a parallel between the

58 Ilichevskii, *Matiss,* 104.

59 Ibid., 105.

60 Ibid., 232.

Russians and the Jews: "The only nations whose mentality is pulled along by the traction" of messianism.[61] The brake lever that has been pulled in post-Soviet Russia indicates the annihilation of the country's historical potential and an abandonment of its messianic hopes. But something more drastic takes place. Korolev "feels no nostalgia for the empire" and is concerned "not about the belittling of royal functions but of simple human ones [*prostykh chelovecheskikh*]."[62]

Matisse's mid-sections delve more deeply into the problematic of *raschelovechivanie*, what the author terms "the belittling of simple human functions." The protagonist continues to reject conventional eschatological visions as unable to capture the catastrophe of the present:

> In the end, they [the people] have always been in denial, and will always be in denial until the final moment: No, this is still not the end; everything will soon move again. But the rope will nevertheless sooner or later recoil—and those lips will grasp at the precipice. No, no, that's not it at all, everything is worse. Imagine that there will never be any end, either good or bad, and no Judgment, nothing at all—only multicellular stupidity, grief, and cluttered emptiness. [...] None of the conventional pictures fit. Wheels of fire rolling across the sky, a naked headless woman, taller than the forest, stepping ahead of war, glass reapers, formless in blind fury, collecting tribute in a broad sweep—all these images were trifles compared to what arose in front of Korolev at the thought of the Great Non-Living. There, in this effort of logical imagination, there was something he caught that does not yield to historical, mythological, or humanistic interpretation.[63]

What makes reality worse is that, in contrast to traditional eschatology that mixes catastrophic premonitions and millenarian hopes, the present moment is utterly unredeemed by hope. Unlike "bookish" apocalypses, the present bodes neither the final destruction of the world nor a Judgment or Revelation that may be catastrophic yet is also decisive and redemptive. Instead, there is only a banal, evil, and thoroughly inhuman infinity. As Korolev comes to see

---

61 Ibid., 233.

62 Ibid., 237. In Korolev's thinking, "the abandonment of the country's messianic hopes" does not lead to the "belittling of simple human functions." The two trends, rather, coexist post-1991. The agency that causes these is not specified.

63 Ibid., 237–40. "*V kontse kontsov, vsegda otmakhivalis*'" is an impersonal sentence. The implied subject is humanity awaiting the end of times.

this, conventional eschatology, with all its scares, is simply too human-centered to capture the ousting of humanity.

Korolev's attempts to imagine the posthuman veer between mechanistic and animalistic images of dehumanization: primitive biological organisms, genes, proteins, inanimate matter, machines, and artificial intelligence. Precisely because the "Great Non-Living" (*Velikoe Nezhivoe*) is thoroughly inhuman, *Matisse*'s hero circles around it with a series of questions and images, hesitant to zero in on a single definition. One of these conceptions, "multicellular stupidity, grief, and cluttered emptiness" (*mnogokletochnaia glupost', gore i zakhlamlennaia pustota*), resonates with Garros-Evdokimov's central metaphor of gray goo, a world overrun by primitive, unselfconscious replicons. Any conception, even the most sophisticated, is eventually rejected as too humanistic to capture this ineffable Non-Living. Korolev probes further:

> What is it? A machine? But you can negotiate with the machine, it is created by machine language. Inanimate matter, an atom in a swoon? A gene whose entire storm-like set of elementary molecules tells of the challenge it throws down? A thinking protein? [...] What is to come? What new era will take its turn to settle accounts with the human? [...] The human has come up against his own metamorphosis—copulation with dead matter—and what was going to be born as a result: artificial intelligence? A nonentity humanized by mimics? An era of ephemeral essences that multiply, elusive and meaningful in the same measure that the death they give birth to will be meaningless and real. There is no way out.[64]

Mechanistic and animalistic images alike envision the posthuman as inhuman as well as inhumane. The non-living challenges man with its unassailable elemental properties (a gene with its "storm-like set of elementary molecules"). It possesses no consciousness ("an atom in a swoon"). If it is to appear in the guise of artificial intelligence, it will be a perversion and a degradation of human essence ("a nonentity humanized by mimics" [*ochelovechennoe mimikoi nichto*]).[65]

---

64 Ibid., 240–42.

65 Cf. *Pers* [The Persian]: "Artificial intelligence, even if it arises, will do so through the degradation of natural intelligence." See Ilichevskii, *Pers*, 149. Cf. "Bukva i slovo kak mertvoe i zhivoe" [Letter and word as the dead and the living], "There is a probability that, if artificial intelligence is not created, natural intelligence as such, degrading in the direction of the complete impossibility of keeping up the cognitive process, due to the more and more robotized sphere of intellectual activity, will soon approach the characteristic point of the artificial." Ilichevskii, *Dozhd' dlia Danai* [Rain for Danae] (Moscow: AST, 2011), 239.

Concurrent with his struggle to conceptualize the posthuman, *Matisse*'s hero tries to work out how and why this collapse of humankind comes about. In his thinking, humanity no longer possesses a future because it has lost its anchorage in traditional humanistic norms and values. Long-held values like allegiance to one's country have been weakened. Humans' self-definition is in turmoil. They have lost their prior model for themselves and are now doomed to wonder "outside of self-cognition, making up interrogation sheets: 'Who are you?'—'Where are you?'—'What kind of an intelligence do you have: artificial or natural?'"[66] Questions like these multiply but do not yield viable responses.

The loss of anchoring in traditional humanist values co-exists with the hyper-commodification of life. In Korolev's eyes, because humans no longer possess a workable model of themselves, they are neither able to understand their past nor envision a meaningful future. Humanity and history are being extinguished in part because "the pull of time is held only by an energy of desire, but the total setup does everything to satisfy desire as soon as possible, to hollow it out."[67] The consumer machine is set up to satisfy one's needs as promptly and efficiently as possible, and what results is an inflation of human emotion, and hence historical stagnation.[68] Social and cultural progress is stalled.

Korolev's response to this premonition of the posthuman is initially to draw closer to the non-living, and next, traditionally but no less compellingly, to embrace nature and his new comrades.[69] Growing closer to the non-living is perhaps a gesture of defeat or perhaps, as Korolev sees this himself, a way to defend the human against *Velikoe Nezhivoe*. Even before he retreats underground, he exhibits a peculiar fascination with death and various amorphous conditions approaching non-being, as when, for example, he enjoys the sunset in the suburbs of Rehovot that "tectonically dissolves his face and consciousness," or when he falls in love with a sculpture of a dead girl from an old German cemetery in Lefortovo.[70]

---

66 Ilichevskii, *Matiss,* 144–45.

67 Ibid., 238.

68 Human desires are channeled into the act of selling/buying (and quickly satisfied). This precludes other than consumerist pursuits (sciences, arts, etc).

69 *Matisse* engages the dichotomies of Russia vs. Europe, city vs. country, underground vs. above ground, and domiciled vs. homeless. Of these, the city-country juxtaposition strikes me as particularly important. Korolev suffers from claustrophobia in Moscow, and feels healthier and freer when traveling through the countryside. "The 'spasm of space' in *Matisse* is not physicist Korolev's hallucination, but a trap he is genuinely experiencing, the tightness of social relations." See Pustovaia, "Krupitsy tverdi," 100.

70 Ilichevskii, *Matiss,* 132.

Korolev's closeness to the non-living is at its maximum during his sojourn in Metro 2, a legendary secret subway system supposedly constructed in Stalin's time underneath the public metro system to provide private passages and escape routes for Soviet government officials.[71] There, in subterranean darkness, among machines, he slowly grows stupefied, worn down by proximity to the non-living: "A somnambulistic state of chronic lethargy, apathy, and indifference gradually subjugated him, drew him in, and dissolved his personality."[72] Not unlike Nadia, Korolev experiences cognitive decline, which is further augmented upon his emergence from the underground when he is persecuted and beaten on the streets of Moscow.

The narrative closes, however, not with Korolev as an idiosyncratic interlocutor of the non-living, but with the trio of Nadia, Vadia, and Korolev leaving Moscow to wander the countryside southward, in pursuit of the color and beauty Korolev perceives in Henri Matisse's art. The protagonist escapes the techno-consumer machine, experiences the devolution of the non-living in the underground, and is subsequently revived by his return to the natural world, walking "after the sun climbing toward the horizon. After the sun harnessed to the future."[73]

The novel *Matisse* ends with an homage to Korolev's (and Ilichevskii's) favorite painter. For the author, Matisse is most fascinating because of his masterful work with color, which opens up a vision of beauty Korolev has been yearning for all along. The French painter is particularly important for the novel the way he is presented in Henri Cartier-Bresson's photograph with bird cages (1941), and the painting most significant for the book is *Goldfish*

---

71 "Rumored to be longer than the official metro and up to 200 meters deep, Metro-2 has become the stuff of urban legend." See Phoebe Taplin, "From Moscow's Hidden Tunnels to Russia's Top Literary Prizes," *Russia Beyond the Headlines* (April 3, 2012), http://rbth.com/literature/2012/04/03/from moscows hidden tunnels to russias top literary prizes15239.html. "The underground is the closest analogue of hell. Korolev has not yet died, but is already privy to the other world." See Alla Latynina, "Retsenziia na roman Aleksandra Ilichevskogo *Matiss*," http://www.club366.ru/articles/latynina.shtml. For a more critically inclined review, see Andrei Nemzer, who claims that *Matisse* "poeticizes non-being." See Andrei Nemzer, "Snova nasha ne vziala" [Our side lost again], *Vremia novostei* (April 6, 2007), http://www.vremya.ru/2007/60/10/175648.html.

72 Ilichevskii, *Matiss*, 268.

73 Ibid., 438. In an interview with Lev Danilkin, Ilichevskii comments: "The novel's movement is an exodus from metaphysical slavery. First, Korolev approximates dying, he seems to have entered a metaphorical hell, in darkness, in blindness—the underground, but having gotten out, wakes up completely, prepares for the opening of his vision—and the vision opens up, when the trio at last leaves Moscow: He sees color, light, God." See Lev Danilkin, "Ploshchad' Ilichevskogo" (The Ilichevskii Square), *Afisha* (August 28, 2007), http://www.club366.ru/articles/ilichevskii.shtml.

Bowl (1912).[74] The photograph, unlike Matisse's vivid art work, is black and white. It features the old, disabled Matisse confined to a chair and surrounded by cages of pigeons. In the celebrated *Goldfish Bowl,* the very opposite of the grim photograph, Matisse paints an idyllic, color-suffused study of his fish tank, plants, and garden furniture in Issy-les-Moulineaux, away from the pressures of Parisian life. *Matisse* evokes both the photograph and the painting, but in a reversed, optimistic temporal move: from the black and white prison-like space of the novel's initial depictions of Moscow to Korolev's final escape into the countryside suffused by the sun.

Conclusion: Does the Future Need Us?

When Francis Fukuyama published *Our Posthuman Future: Consequences of the Biotechnology Revolution* (2002), he defined his objective as follows:

> The aim of this book is to argue that Huxley was right, that the most significant threat posed by contemporary biotechnology is the possibility that it will alter human nature and thereby move us into a "posthuman" stage of history. This is important, I will argue, because human nature exists, is a meaningful concept, and has provided a stable continuity to our experience as a species. Human nature shapes and constrains the possible kinds of political regimes, so a technology powerful enough to reshape what we are will have possibly malign consequences for liberal democracy and the nature of politics itself.[75]

---

74 Ilichevskii, e-mail message. Discussing his novel in an interview, Ilichevskii terms it "a story about color, light, the color that creates. You see—it means you create. [...] When I still didn't know how to talk, I opened my parents' Matisse album and had an impression that I was transformed into an artist, that I acquired a secret vision." See Danilkin, "Ploshchad' Ilichevskogo." Ilichevskii does not address Matisse's technique of presenting the human body as simplified two-dimensional cutouts or his flattening of the horizon line. For more on Matisse in *Matisse,* see Liudmila Galushkina, "Roman Ilichevskogo *Matiss*" [Ilichevskii's novel *Matisse*], (February 12, 2008), http://www.litsovet.ru/index.php./material.read?material_id=185593. A number of critics (for example, Pustovaia, "Krupitsy tverdi," 96) have suggested a "painterly" quality in Ilichevskii's prose.

75 Fukuyama, *Our Posthuman Future,* 6–7. By the time Fukuyama wrote *Our Posthuman Future,* he had reconsidered his earlier thesis (in *The End of History and the Last Man*) that no further political change would take place after the collapse of the socialist block and the victory of liberal democracy. In *Our Posthuman Future* he views the recent advances in the life sciences as capable of transforming humankind in fundamental ways: "In the course of thinking through the many critiques of that original piece that had been put forward, it seemed to

What swiftly ensued were charges of naturalistic fallacy, essentialism, human exceptionalism, and all-round obsoleteness. Why claim that there is an intrinsic human nature, with which biotechnology threatens to interfere, if this nature is culturally contingent and there are no such things as "musts" or "universals"?[76]

Like Fukuyama's book, the fictional texts I have examined display the humanist's fears regarding the posthuman.[77] Of strategic importance to *Gray Goo* and *Matisse*—two very different novels that nonetheless resonate with each other and thus reflect a wider cultural situation—is the problem of dehumanization/*raschelovechivanie*. The use of metamorphic tropes is a way for these writers to characterize the complex, often adverse, practices of the time.

The regressive metamorphosis, whether of humans into animals or of humans into machines, highlights the degrading effects of the global social system. These tropes allow Garros-Evdokimov and Ilichevskii to comment on the effects of techno-consumerism. If animalistic tropes emphasize the degradation of life to the physical, deprivation and oppression, and the brutality of history, mechanistic tropes explore the consequences of corporate culture, virtual reality, and information systems for the human subject. In the works considered here, technological progress paradoxically sends humankind into a devolutionary reversal. De-individuated men-machines, "a nonentity humanized by mimics" (Ilichevskii), disappear "as the subject of collective reason" (Garros-Evdokimov).

Regressive metamorphosis allows these authors to comment on the crucial issues of suppressed reason, individuality, ethics, and especially freedom in contemporaneity.[78] Biology dictates through instincts and the iron call of

---

me that the only one that was not possible to refute was the argument that there could be no end of history unless there was an end of science." See Fukuyama, *Our Posthuman Future*, xii.

76 For a characteristic response, see, for example, Selinger: "Why [...] [should we] accept the appeal to human nature as the legitimate bedrock of moral, social, and political freedom when, as Fukuyama well knows, the very definition he currently presents of human nature may very well become outdated?" See Evan Selinger, review of *Our Posthuman Future: Consequences of the Biotechnology Revolution, The Quarterly Review of Biology* 78:1 (March 2003): 76.

77 The degeneration/dystopia trope examined here resonates with other recent Russian writings (for example, by Pelevin and Sorokin) as well as with earlier works by Zamyatin and Platonov. Among Western works, Aldous Huxley's *Brave New World* (1932) is relevant. Ilichevskii cites J. M. Coetzee's *Life and Times of Michael K* (1983) as a work he kept in mind while working on *Matisse*. The process of dehumanization as Coetzee depicts it, in turn, evokes Franz Kafka's *The Trial* (1914–15).

78 Cf. Adorno: "In the immeasurably expanded world of experience and the infinitely numerous ramifications of the processes of socialization that this world of experience imposes on us, the possibility of freedom has sunk to such a minimal level that we can

adaptation to the environment. Machines are programmable, and, thus, predictable and controllable. Not only are men-machines emotionally desensitized and socially depersonalized, but if the human brain acts like a computer, it will have no choice but to comply with the controlling user's commands. The humanist's older fear was that technology might take over the decisions of free individuals. A more recent, equally potent worry addressed by these works is that contemporary dependence on technology and commodification might make humans more easily prone to societal manipulation.

How would these writers (hypothetically) address the charges against Fukuyama? Given Garros-Evdokimov's well-known devotion to the Strugatsky brothers, their objection may be formulated as follows: The value of human nature is to a large extent civilizational. In other words, "something unique about the human race that entitles every member of the species to a higher moral status than the rest of the natural world" is embodied in the pre-postmodern "well-brought-up person" (*Chelovek Vospitannyi*).[79] And, according to the writers, this "well-brought-up person," whether in its pre-1917 or pre-1991 hypostasis, should be safeguarded against the degrading forces of global postmodernity.

In contrast to Garros-Evdokimov, Ilichevskii is no devotee of the Strugatskys, but he hardly needs to be one to uphold their classic humanistic stance.[80] *Matisse* opens with Korolev suffocating in traffic and witnessing Vadia and Nadia being harassed by a group of homeless boys. The youngest of the boys is distracted from his pursuit by the fairy-tale-like appearance of the Timiriazev State Biological Museum. The building used to belong to the brother of the famous merchant and

---

or must ask ourselves very seriously whether any scope is left for our moral categories." Theodor W. Adorno, *Problems of Moral Philosophy* (Stanford: Stanford UP, 2002), 98–99.

79 Fukuyama, *Our Posthuman Future*, 160. As I see this, for the Strugatskys and Garros-Evdokimov, the move toward the important civilizational aspect of humanness does not imply a complete rejection of essentialism. Rather, they see the core human traits as both innate and (perhaps more importantly) in need of nurturing. As Garros-Evdokimov phrase this, "In completely different books, which [the Strugatskys] wrote at different times, there is one common thought. Namely, that man is an objective carrier of reason, and if something prevents him from being so, it is possible and necessary to remedy this. The foremost and in general the only means to accomplish this goal is through upbringing. They even have this term—a well-brought-up person [*Chelovek Vospitannyi*]." Garros-Evdokimov, *Chuchkhe*, 214. This passage again links reason and ethical behavior: "You [well-brought-up people] will make this country different" (214).

80 "I have no opinion about the Strugatskys since I have not read a single book they wrote." See Ilichevskii, "Literatura kak iskusstvo ubezhdat'" [Literature as an art of persuasion], *Polit.ru* (May 11, 2013), http://polit.ru/article/2013/05/11/Ilichevskii_books.

arts lover Sergei Shchukin, and in 1911 Matisse visited there.[81] And so, *Matisse*'s opening immediately opposes animalistic/mechanistic/social degradation, violence, and brutality to culture and beauty. Fittingly, the book ends with Korolev choosing a spiritual quest over technology and urbanity.

I would like to conclude by referring to *Gray Goo* once more. As Garros-Evdokimov explain, the term "gray goo," originally coined by Drexler, was subsequently popularized by Bill Joy, head scientist of the company Sun Microsystems, who "published an 'alarmist' article 'Does the future need us?' in the journal *Wired*."[82] The article's actual title is "Why the Future Does Not Need Us" (2000). May one view this mistranslation as a sign of hope?

81 Scriabin in Zamyatin's "The Cave" and Matisse in Ilichevskii's novel embody culture opposed to social barbarism. Both Scriabin and Matisse are representatives of modernism. In Svetlana Boym's argument, modernist art "allows for synchronicity, mediation, the coexistence of different temporalities and symbolic systems"—that is, for "more freedom of reflection." See Svetlana Boym, *Another Freedom: The Alternative History of an Idea* (Chicago: The University of Chicago Press, 2010), 93. Ilichevskii mentions the connection between the Timiriazev Museum, Shchukin, and Matisse in his interview with Lev Danilkin. See Danilkin, "Ploshchad' Ilichevskogo."

82 Joy's essay has been translated into Russian as "Pochemu budushchee ne nuzhdaetsia v nas." The mistranslation is in the novel, not in the published Russian version.

Part Three

Natural, Built, and Imagined Environments

CHAPTER 4

Human Adaptation in Late-Soviet Environmental Science Fiction

Colleen McQuillen,
University of Illinois at Chicago

Trotsky's proclamation in *Literature and Revolution* (1924) regarding humankind's anticipated use of mechanical technologies to transform the earth's topography evinces the Prometheanism that would characterize official Soviet environmental policies through the Stalinist era and beyond. He declared: "The present distribution of mountains and rivers, fields, meadows, steppes, forests, and seashores cannot be considered final. Man has already made changes in the map of nature that are neither few nor insignificant. But they are the mere practice of school children in comparison with what is coming."[1] To wit, Stalin's ambitious 1948 Plan for the Transformation of Nature called for the creation of ponds and reservoirs, irrigation systems, and afforestation; under this plan, Soviet geoengineers undertook a series of

1 Leon Trotsky, *Literature and Revolution*. Trans. Rose Strunsky (New York: Russell & Russell, 1957). Marxists Internet Archive, https://www.marxists.org/archive/trotsky/1924/lit_revo/ch08.htm.

projects that were intended to redefine humankind's relationship to its physical environment.[2] Even Leonid Brezhnev, who aspired to be the "environmental General Secretary," undertook massive public works projects, most notably the Siberian river diversion project, which aimed to redirect water flow to suit the needs of humankind.[3] Like Prometheus who stole fire from Zeus and empowered humans to influence their material conditions by giving it to them, Soviet engineers and policy makers set out to gain control of land and water in order to fortify the growing socialist state.

Well-known literary responses to Soviet environmental Prometheanism included celebratory socialist realist novels, such as Leonid Leonov's *Russian Forest* (*Russkii les*, 1953), which critiqued forest preservation efforts because they contradicted the interests of the lumber-consuming Soviet construction industry. Also prominent were works of Stagnation-era Village Prose, like Valentin Rasputin's *Farewell to Matyora* (*Proshchanie s Materoi*, 1979), which condemned the flooding of a fictional island in the Angara River in order to build a massive hydroelectric dam. A third literary reaction in the late Soviet period to the Promethean policies and practices that were shaping humanity's relationship to its natural environment complicates this pro-contra dichotomy of realisms: in the genre of science fiction, speculative visions of the future depict humanity using its demiurgic powers to adapt the body to external material conditions. Enabled by scientific and technological breakthroughs, fictional humans engineered themselves to change physiologically in response to foreign environments. While genetic engineering and the manufacture of prostheses are Promethean acts, in as much as humans are actively involved in enhancing our embodied selves, the move to privilege the natural environment as a determining factor in these adaptations de-centers the human. The leitmotif of human adaptation in the works of environmental science fiction considered in this chapter pairs Promethean powers with an ecological materialism, which modulates the radical anthropocentrism of socialist realist prose and begins to suggest a more balanced network of agency. While a truly egalitarian ecology of animate and inanimate matter is still far off, I wish to show that an eco-materialist reading opens up a complex vision of the posthuman as portrayed in late-Soviet science fiction. Drawing examples from stories by Pavel Amnuel' and Sergei Pavlov, among others, I will argue that their

2 William B. Meyer, *The Progressive Environmental Prometheans: Left-Wing Heralds of a "Good Anthropocene"* (Basingstoke: Palgrave Macmillan, 2016), 188.

3 Douglas R. Weiner, *A Little Corner of Freedom: Russian Nature Protection from Stalin to Gorbachev* (Berkeley: University of California Press, 1999), 402.

eco-materialist orientation resonates with earlier Russian Cosmist fantasies about humans becoming nutritionally self-sufficient (that is, autotrophic), which would fundamentally alter our relationship to terrestrial and interplanetary environments.

Contemporary discourses of new materialism and ecocriticism foreground the interconnectedness of human and non-human forms of life, as well as animate and inanimate matter. Bruno Latour's actor-network theory popularized the concept of non-human actants participating in networks of mutual influence, thereby toppling the dominant power vertical over which humans have long thought themselves to preside.[4] New theories of vital materialism (distinct from ancient animisms) advocate for a broader conceptualization of agency, a goal of which is to offer a similar de-centering of humanity in relation to other material bodies. Jane Bennett advocates a theory of "thing-power," wherein non-human actants (a term borrowed from Latour) exert influence on humans and each other.[5] Although Bennett sidelines the important questions of subjectivity and will in this radical rethinking of agency as a power or force inherent in all matter, her materialism reminds us of the subtle yet countless ways in which we humans are reactive to our physical environments. Ecocritics such as Timothy Morton challenge enduring assumptions about humanity's relationship to the material conditions on Earth, in particular the qualifying categories and self-aggrandizing hierarchies we have constructed.[6] Ecocriticism aims to de-center the human to produce a more egalitarian network of interconnectivity among all forms of life; in other words, it proposes that we think of ourselves as part of an ecological system, no more or less important than other parts. The works of science fiction that I discuss in this chapter illuminate

4 See Bruno Latour, *Reassembling the Social: An Introduction to Actor–Network–Theory* (Oxford: Oxford University Press, 2005).

5 See Jane Bennett, *Vibrant Matter: A Political Ecology of Things* (Durham: Duke University Press, 2010).

6 Emerging in the 1980s, ecocriticism addresses the relationship between man and nature as represented in various modes of cultural production. See Timothy Morton, *Ecology Without Nature: Rethinking Environmental Aesthetics* (Cambridge, MA: Harvard University Press, 2007); and Lawrence Buell, *The Future of Environmental Criticism: Environmental Crisis and Literary Imagination* (Oxford, UK: Wiley-Blackwell, 2005). Ecological liberation movements focus on reconciling the conflicting demands of development, sustainability, and social justice. See Michael Watts and Richard Peet, eds., *Liberation Ecologies: Environment, Development, and Social Movements* (London: Routledge, 2002). Also concerned with reconciling nature and culture, the ecofeminist movement of the 1970s saw connections among gender, race, class and environmental issues. See Val Plumwood, *Feminism and the Mastery of Nature* (London: Routledge, 1994).

the influence of non-human actants, specifically those comprising our physical environments, on the physiology and subjectivity of humans.

Late Soviet Environmentalism

Under Leonid Brezhnev, environmentally ruinous infrastructure projects such as the Baikal–Amur Mainline railroad perpetuated the Promethean practices of the Stalinist era. Concurrently, though, environmental activism grew in popularity among students and intellectuals. Following William Meyer, I use the term "environmentalism" to designate activism premised on "core beliefs" about humankind's relationship to earth: the "irreplaceability of the natural world, in its basic contours, as a human home and the danger that excessive human pressures will disrupt its essential functions."[7] In the Brezhnev era, student-run environmentalist organizations known as *druzhiny* advocated for the protection of nature, and journalists such as Vladimir Chivilikhin and Viktor Iaroshenko devoted their work to publicizing the environmental consequences of industrialization.[8] Internationally, growing concern for the environment's wellbeing spurred the establishment of watchdog organizations like Greenpeace (founded 1972). The Soviet Union, too, introduced official policies and legislation that purported to protect the country's natural resources and non-human forms of life. The 1977 Constitution (also called the Brezhnev Constitution) laid out a social contract that listed the environmental obligations of Soviet citizens, including the duty to protect nature and conserve its riches (Article 67). For its part, the state promised to pursue a "rational use of the land and its mineral and water resources, and the plant and animal kingdoms" (Article 18).[9] The years bracketing this new constitution and

---

7 Meyer, *The Progressive Environmental Prometheans*, 3.

8 The first *druzhina* was established at Tartu University in 1958 but the organization was most active from 1965-1986. See Douglas R. Weiner, *A Little Corner of Freedom*, 313, 406. Iaroshenko's "Living Water" [Zhivaia voda] field expeditions in the 1970s "began systematically to investigate the proposed dam sites, canal routes, and other facilities of the river diversion project" (see Weiner, 417).

9 "Konstitutsiia (osnovnoi zakon) Soiuza sovetskikh sotsialisticheskikh respublik. Priniata na vneocherednoi sed'moi sessii Verkhovnogo soveta SSSR. 7 oktiabria 1977." Trans. Novosti Press Agency (Moscow: Novosti Publishing House, 1985) [*Constitution (fundamental law) of the the Union of Soviet Socialist Republics. Adopted at the seventh special session of the Supreme Soviet of the USSR, ninth convocation on October 7, 1977*], http://www.departments.bucknell.edu/russian/const/77cons01.html.

its mandates on environmental stewardship witnessed at least seven new pieces of legislation designed to protect water, air quality, forest, and wildlife; as well as to regulate land use and the excavation of minerals.[10] These environmentalist directives comprised an aspirational blueprint, which was not consistently followed, as subsequent decades have shown.

Despite spotty compliance with and enforcement of these laws, official discourse about environmental protection in the Soviet Union became a tool for advancing a socialist agenda.[11] Ideologues praised socialism's responsible environmental management and discredited capitalism's rapacious consumption of Earth's natural resources. Typical propaganda ran along the lines of: "If the goal [in capitalist countries] in regard to the worker is to 'wring out the sweat,' then of course the goal in regard to nature is to 'wring out the resources.' As one commentator soothingly concluded in 1979, "In socialist countries, where nature is shared property, where it is protected by law, there are no reasons for panic or despair."[12]

While official discourse insisted that socialist countries were uniquely protective of the environment, writers forging a literary movement known as Village Prose exposed the state's hypocrisy. The critical realism of Village Prose paired environmental ruin with the destruction of so-called traditional Russian culture by ideologically driven industrial progress. Writers like Rasputin, Viktor Astaf'ev, and Vasilii Belov depicted Soviet assaults on Russian nature in the name of industrial and infrastructure development. Boris Groys has labeled the Village Prose writers' idealization of and nostalgia for village life and unspoiled nature part of an "ecological-nationalist utopia."[13] Indeed, their romanticized portraits perpetuate a naturalistic fallacy, which is premised on a misguided belief that the earth's ecosystems would be naturally balanced and harmonious were it not for human actions

10 Charles Ziegler, *Environmental Policy in the USSR* (Amherst: University of Massachusetts Press, 1987), 83.

11 For an in-depth treatment of the politicization of environmental policies, see Weiner, *A Little Corner of Freedom.* See also Paul Josephson et al., *An Environmental History of Russia* (Cambridge: Cambridge University Press, 2013).

12 Vl. Gakov, "Budem chutochku umnee... Ob avtorakh i temakh sbornika" [We'll be a little bit smarter... About the collection's authors and themes]. *Sbornik nauchnoi fantastiki* [Collection of science fiction] 21 (1979), http://publ.lib.ru/ARCHIVES/N/"NF"/_"NF". html#021.

13 Boris Groys, *The Total Art of Stalinism: Avant-garde, Aesthetic Dictatorship, and Beyond,* trans. Charles Rougle (Princeton, NJ: Princeton University Press, 1992), 79.

or inaction.[14] Groys's observation that the paradoxical Village Prose project of reviving "what they imagine to be the 'Russian' humanity and recast[ing] contemporary *homo sovieticus* in its image" foregrounds the interrelation between environmental protectionism and the shaping of an ethno-national subjectivity.[15] Groys also identifies the humanist outlook buttressing the Village Prose movement: namely, that the program of active intervention to halt progress was analogous to the projectivism of Soviet Prometheans. He points to the belief that, "by manipulating the natural human environment, [they would] change humanity itself, that is, transform the modernist and technological individual into an antimodernist and nationalistic ecologist."[16] If in Village Prose humans change themselves as subjects for the worse when they alter nature, the works of environmental science fiction that I examine below posit a belief in an enduring human essence, which is independent of environment and embodiment. While the human body may adapt physiologically to modified terrestrial and interplanetary environments, our human essence (an ethical, rational subjectivity) remains intact.

Ethically Human, Physiologically Posthuman

Late Soviet-era environmental science fiction was dominated by stories like Viacheslav Rybakov's "Great Drought" (*Velikaia sush'*, 1979) that glorify an anthropocentric universe and brash humanism. What distinguishes this story, however, is its exploration of Soviet subjectivity in a non-terrestrial environment and its suggestion that an ethical essence inheres in humanity regardless of its material conditions. Humanity, in the course of its interplanetary exploration, has understood that the stars are dead, the universe has nothing in it, and that life on other planets will not spontaneously emerge by itself. When scientists identify conditions on the planet Sola that are suitable for sustaining life, it inspires hope in the twenty-seven billion humans living in eight solar systems that humans will not remain alone in the universe. For thirty years, humanity has labored and expended resources for the purpose of cultivating the physical

---

14 On the naturalistic fallacy, see Stuart Pimm, *The Balance of Nature: Ecological Issues in the Conservation of Species and Communities* (Chicago: University of Chicago Press, 1991) and John Kricher, *The Balance of Nature: Ecology's Enduring Myth* (Princeton, NJ: Princeton University Press, 2009).

15 Groys, *The Total Art of Stalinism*, 79.

16 Ibid.

conditions necessary to generate life on Sola in the hope of curing its cosmic loneliness.

Ignoring Earth's abundant biome, Rybakov portrays humans as the only form of life and thus offers up a worldview that defines life in qualified, humanist terms. He demonstrates humanity's scientific-technological might, but his real interest is in our sense of ethical responsibility. The story consists largely of the conversations between the narrator and his interlocutor, who try to figure out what went wrong: In the process of constructing a shield to protect Sola from an imminent onslaught of cosmic radiation, humanity actually blocks the main thing necessary for life to emerge on Sola, exposure to a mutagen (in the form of radiation). Humanity thus destroys Sola's proto-life and its own accompanying hope for cosmic company. Did we do the right thing, Rybakov's characters ask?

The narrator argues that humanity had no other choice than to act, even if such actions were ultimately misguided. We are powerful, we are kind, and "humanity needs a grand objective" (*chelovechestvu nuzhna velikaia tsel'*).[17] The fulfillment of humankind's existential purpose and the imperative to "protect, save—not so much life on Sola as ourselves, our hope, and our love, in which we have no one to bathe" stand as the commanding tenets governing man's relationship to the surrounding cosmos. Not only is the human species portrayed as the sole form of life, it is ostensibly justified in its supremely selfish behavior because of an assumed ethical essence. The narrator declares: "As long as a human essence is alive inside us, we are going to propose, coerce, and force our help on each other. And the stars."[18] Rybakov highlights human agency and free will, and ambivalently codes our actions as compassionate and selfish. Our destructive intervention is "help," suggesting that it comes from a magnanimous concern for both animate (each other) and inanimate (the stars) cohabitants of the galaxies, but our actions are motivated by a need to satisfy our humanist imperative.

Although echoing the Christian doctrine of "love for thy neighbor," Rybakov amplifies this self-important stance of benevolence toward the needy and vulnerable that ultimately results in a ruinous outcome. The story, however, betrays no regret and thus cannot be read as a cautionary tale of environmental destruction arising from a misguided notion of compassion;

17 Rybakov's positing of a grand task unifying humanity calls to mind Fedorov's "common task" of regulating nature and resurrecting our ancestors.

18 Viacheslav Rybakov, "Velikaia sush'" [Great drought], *Sbornik nauchnoi fantastiki* [Collection of science fiction] 21 (1979): 181–196. publ.lib.ru/ARCHIVES/N/"NF"/_"NF".html#021.

because "powerlessness is torturous," "mankind cannot not help." The narrator concludes that the tragedy was useful because humanity can learn from it; moving forward with our techno-scientific endeavors, "we'll be a little bit smarter" (*budem chutochku umnee*).[19] The story's celebration of a human essence defined by reason (techno-scientific achievement) and cosmic benefaction (the duty to help) accords with classical humanism. It also extends the project of forging the Soviet subject, begun in the 1920s as the quest to cultivate the New Soviet Man and continuing in the advanced socialist society of the 1970s.

In contrast to Rybakov's environmental Prometheanism, which valorized Soviet man's assumed ethical imperative "to protect" Sola's atmosphere through active intervention, Pavel Amnuel"s "I'm on Course" (*Idu po trasse*, 1979). The Russian text should be in itals (please refer to the style sheet). focuses humanity's scientific-technological prowess on altering our physiology to respond to different conditions on other planets.[20] Amnuel"s story affirms a humanist conception of a knowable human essence and an unshakeable faith in progress. However, it also expresses a materialist worldview that harmonizes with certain strains of posthumanist thought. Neo-vitalist and ecological materialisms seek to inscribe the human in vast networks of actors, thereby de-centering the human and troubling his claim to exclusive agency.

Jane Bennett's vital materialism is particularly helpful in conceptualizing the complex interplay of bodies and environment in "I'm on Course," because it introduces a posthuman perspective in an otherwise Promethean-humanist narrative. Characters called "variators" are genetically engineered humans who can reconfigure their physical bodies in response to external stimuli. The story takes place on Venus, where a trio of variators participate in a trial experiment of their corporal adaptability to the planet's scalding lava rivers and brutal hurricanes.[21] The variators' bodies can change instantaneously in response

19 Ibid.

20 I first encountered these two stories in *Sbornik nauchnoi fantastiki* 21 (1979), which is devoted to the theme of environmental protection. While the stories may not be considered canonical today, they were published in a mainstream journal with wide circulation and a vast readership.

21 While such a proposition may seem fanciful, by 1960 Soviet researchers were studying human physiological systems with such a goal in mind. In their article "Cyborgs and Space," Manfred Clynes and Nathan Kline asserted in the first sentence: "Altering man's bodily functions to meet the requirements of extraterrestrial environments would be more logical than providing an earthly environment for him in space." The practice of making conditions on other planets hospitable to human life is known in Anglophone SF as terraforming. See Manfred Clynes and Nathan Kline, "Cyborgs and Space," *Astronautics*, vol. 5, September

to even extreme environmental conditions and threats. In order to traverse a treacherous ravine and its wind currents, one variator becomes ball-like so he can travel in air; another transforms his body into a gelatinous mass in order to enter narrow passageways. Despite their struggles with atavism and psychological stress, and their near-death experiences, two of the three come out of the experiment alive and remain enthusiastic about mankind's adaptability to the environmental conditions on other planets.

The variators' bodily responsiveness cedes a controlling power to the planetary stimuli, thereby imputing a form of agency to the environment as a non-human actant. The presence of magma, for example, exerts an influence on the variators' physiology, which complicates the power dynamic between them and their milieu. The variators on Venus are part of a new political ecology, comprising a system of mutually formative influences. Interplanetary materialism, and in particular the impact external conditions have on the human body, owes a debt to Russian Cosmists who envisioned a transformation of the human body in response to its environment.

Human Autotrophism as Environmental Adaptation

Amnuel"s model of radical genetic engineering recalls the adaptive projects of Cosmists Nikolai Fedorov, Konstantin Tsiolkovsky, and Vladimir Vernadsky. All three proposed that future man would be able to alter his composition physically and chemically, and Fedorov and Tsiolkovsky envisioned man thereby transforming himself into an interplanetary being, liberated from the material constraints of Earth. Fedorov scholars A. G. Gacheva and S. G. Semenova write that his overarching call to regulate the "blind forces of nature" was more radical than Soviet-era Promethean ambitions to modify Earth's topography because Fedorov's "highest goal was the transformation of the very status of natural and cosmic existence, the very nature of man."[22] He called upon scientists to conduct experiments in tissue and organ generation, not for the purpose of curing or replacing those that are diseased or worn out, but rather for constructing entirely new ones designed for immortality ("A radical cure of all organs and in

1960 (the article was reprinted with the permission of *Astronautics* as part of "The Cyborg as Warp-Speed Evolution," *New York Times*, February 26, 1997, https://partners.nytimes.com/library/cyber/surf/022697surf-cyborg.html).

22 A. G. Gacheva and S. G. Semenova, "Filosofiia voskresheniia N. F. Fedorova" [N. F. Fedorov's philosophy of resurrection] in N. F. Fedorov, *Sobranie sochinenii v 4-kh tomakh* [Collected works in 4 volumes], ed. M. A. Kolerov (Moscow: Progress, 1995), 1:19.

all organs is needed, which is to say, a full redesign [*vossozdanie*] is needed")[23]. Fedorov anticipated that our organs of digestion and reproduction would be rendered obsolete when humanity overcomes mortality (death being the most pernicious of nature's blind forces). He theorized that the "nourishment of this organism [the transformed human] is man's consciously creative process (*soznatel'no-tvorcheskii protsess*) of converting elementary, interstellar (*kosmicheskii*) elements into mineral, then plant, and finally, living tissues."[24] In other words, humanity will be capable of satisfying its own nutritional needs independently of Earth's plant and animal life.

Rocket engineer Konstantin Tsiolkovsky, too, imagined a new autotrophic humanity in his science fiction novella *Dreams of Earth and Sky and the Effects of Universal Gravity (Grezy o zemle i nebe i effekty vsemirnogo tiagoteniia,* 1895), which tells of a race of plant-men (*zhivotno-rasteniia*) who have wings containing chlorophyll.[25] Of these biologically engineered wings, Anindita Banerjee writes: "They serve not only as an extension of the body but also the vital organ that transforms the human being into a self-sufficient ecosystem. Broad wingspans, exposed to trap maximum sunlight, contain chlorophyll, and can manufacture food from the carbon dioxide emitted during respiration."[26] In Tsiolkovsky's fiction, autotrophy is a consequence and necessity of humanity becoming a cosmic species and mastering technological means of self-modification; like Fedorov, he imagined that our bodily adaptation to extraterrestrial environments would be self-wrought.[27]

---

23 N. F. Fedorov, "O dramakh Ibsena i o sverkhiskusstve" [On the dramas of Ibsen and on Super-art] in Fedorov, *Sobranie sochinenii v 4-kh tomakh* [Collected works in 4 volumes], ed. I. I. Blauberg (Moscow: Traditsiia, 1997), 3:522.

24 N. F. Fedorov, "Vopros o bratstve, ili rodstve, o prichinakh nebratskogo, nerodstvennogo, i.e., nemirnogo sostoianiia mira i o sredstvakh k vosstanovleniiu rodstva" [The question about brotherhood, or kinship, about the reasons for the unbrotherly, non-kindred, i.e., unpeaceful condition of the world and the means for reviving kinship] in N. F. Fedorov, *Sobranie sochinenii v 4-kh tomakh* [Collected works in 4 volumes], ed. M. A. Kolerov (Moscow: Progress, 1995), 1:281.

25 Konstantin Tsiolkovskii, "*Grezy o zemle i nebe i effekty vsemirnogo tiagoteniia*" [Dreams of earth and sky and the effects of universal gravity], ed. A. N. Goncharov (Moscow: Tipografiia M. G. Volchaninova, 1895).
https://ru.wikisource.org/wiki/Грёзы_о_Земле_и_небе_(Циолковский).

26 Banerjee, *We Modern People*, 137.

27 Tsiolkovsky conceived of all material bodies in the universe as sharing the same essential organic building block, which he called the "atom-spirit" (*atom-dukh*). Based on our common composition, he concluded that the possibility of life inheres within all matter, including gases. His concept of a material "atom-spirit" calls to mind the neo-vitalist worldviews proffered by contemporary theorists of an ecological posthumanism.

Geochemist Vladimir Vernadsky shared Tsiolkovsky's vitalist monist view and imagined how humanity might transform itself in response to the deteriorating biophysical conditions on Earth. In his article "The Autotrophism of Humanity" (1925) Vernadsky envisioned that nutritional self-sufficiency would "open the path to a better life" characterized by a focus on spiritual aspirations. The scientific work of transforming humanity into an autotrophic species would be undertaken for practical rather than emancipatory purposes in as much as humans, he believed, will continue to live on Earth. Vernadsky understood that humans and our environment are intimately connected and therefore mutually direct the changes each undergoes. He writes: "It is hard, maybe impossible, for us to imagine all of the geological consequences of this event [becoming autotrophic]; but, obviously, it would be the crowning of a long paleontological evolution, not an act of the free will of man but a manifestation of a natural process."[28] In contrast to the human-directed active evolution postulated by Fedorov and Tsiolkovsky, Vernadsky envisioned a path of mutual transformation co-determined by the interactions between humans and the earth.[29]

Human Adaptation in Soviet Science Fiction

The autotrophic strain of Cosmism is one of the most vivid examples of philosopher-scientists anticipating how human physiology might change in response to evolving conditions on earth or a new, interplanetary habitat. Like Tsiolkovsky, Soviet science fiction writers such as Aleksandr Beliaev, Sergei

---

28 V. I. Vernadskii, "Avtotrofnost' chelovechestva" [Autotrophism of humanity], in *Russkii kosmizm* [Russian cosmism], ed. Semenova and Gacheva, 305, 306–07.

29 Vernadsky asserted that the Earth has three layers, the second and third of which evolved into being naturally, without human intervention: the first phase or layer is the geosphere (comprising inanimate matter); second, the biosphere (all forms of animal and vegetal life); and the third, the noosphere, is the earth's "thinking layer" (education, religion, science, and ideology) which has been developing in lockstep with the expansion of human consciousness. The noosphere is co-extensive with the biosphere and the geosphere, meaning that the entire system of life on Earth, as well as the Earth itself, is influencing the field of thought and vice versa: "The noosphere is a new geological phenomenon on our planet. For the first time mankind is becoming the most significant geological force because of it. Mankind can and must restructure the scope of life using its labor and mind, fundamentally restructure life in comparison with what it was previously. Ever more creative possibilities are opening up before mankind." See Vernadskii, "Neskol'ko slov o noosfere" [Some words about the noosphere], in *Russkii kosmizm* [Russian cosmism], ed. Semenova and Gacheva, 313.

Pavlov, and Amnuel' thought about humanity adapting itself to the environment instead of modifying the environment to suit its needs. The protagonist of Beliaev's 1927 novel *Amphibian Man* (*Chelovek-amfibiia*) is a young man named Ichthyander, who has the unique ability to breath in water and on land. An Argentinian organ transplant surgeon Sal'vator replaced Ichthyander's failing lungs with gills, a medical intervention that saved the boy's life. Ichthyander's unique physiology requires that he spend half of his time in the water, a requirement that proves fateful when he falls in love with a woman on land. The tragedy of Beliaev's character lies in the fact that he alone has the physiological ability to extract oxygen from air and water: the surgical implant of gills transforms Ichthyander into a solitary amphibian man who can exist physically in water but who nonetheless retains his human need for requited romantic love in order to live truly.

Sergei Pavlov further developed the theme of man's bodily modification in response to aquatic conditions in *Aquanauts* (*Akvanavty*, 1968). Bio-engineers have invented a special type of permeable membrane that humans can don that allows them to "breathe" at extreme underwater depths. Worn like a scuba diving suit, the membrane acts as a second skin and temporarily transforms the wearer into a "human-fish" (*chelovek-ryba*): a being capable of swimming underwater for prolonged periods and at extraordinary depths without pulmonary breathing. The membrane acts like gills by taking oxygen from the water and transporting it across the skin and into the blood stream, and doing the opposite with carbon dioxide. Although this membrane is a prosthetic and not a corporal (genetic) enhancement, the effect is to adapt human physiology to an otherwise inhospitable physical environment.

Pavlov's *The Moon Rainbow* (*Lunnaia raduga*, 1978) likewise probes the relationship of man to his environment and imagines how different physical conditions might alter the human brain and with it, our sensory perceptions. Cosmonauts live through a natural catastrophe on Oberon, a moon of Uranus, and the environmental impact enhances their powers of apprehension so that they hear ultrasound and see radio waves. Their physiology is also altered: they can now go without breathing for extended periods. While the lunar conditions effect physical changes in the cosmonauts, they retain their human subjectivities: "You see, nature made the [human] brain in the conditions on Earth and for the conditions on Earth. For obvious reasons, she simply didn't think about interplanetary conditions. But we are thinking about them now. And we are thinking poorly, as experience has shown, because we can think only with our fundamentally earthly brains, which can make sense only of the domestic problems on our native planet."[30] Bodily transformation and enhanced sensory perception do not immediately alter human comprehension and therefore changes in subjectivity lag.

Amnuel' takes up a similar line of inquiry in "I'm on Course": cosmonauts visiting other planets undergo bodily changes, which evinces a materialist interest in the role of non-human actants in conditioning the human form. Amnuel', though, frames these changes as the consequence of the techno-scientific revolution in genetic engineering and insists on an inviolable human essence. While the variators' bodies undergo radical transformations in response to environmental stimuli, they retain the qualities that define human exceptionalism: reason and moral good. The director of the variator experiment is a skeptic named Goddard, who is uncomfortable with genetic manipulation because of its ontological implications.[31] Goddard asks one of the surviving variators, Manevich, "What would you do if… Stress, mortal danger. Something goes wrong… […] You can't transform yourself back into a human. You get stuck in the form of some slimy, vile creature and your world is now 100 times [earth's] gravitational force, a thousand degrees, carbon dioxide and energy rations." Manevich responds by avowing the invincible nature of a particular essence that would make him human no matter what form his body may take. As if in response to the question "Are variators still humans?" he states definitively: "Humans. Humans through and through. The same brain, thoughts, and feelings, albeit in some cases more refined and in others more vulgar. […] You're thinking about man and imagining his body—Apollo, Venus. […] But that's not what counts." Manevich preaches that the most important thing for humans is to find meaning in the experience of life, which consists in the drive "to know as much as possible, to go everywhere and be in all guises, to feel the world as a part of oneself."[32] Manevich's understanding of human essence acknowledges our perpetual quest for knowledge and mastery while also speaking to our feeling of universal kinship—an ecological worldview of interconnectedness. He asserts, "nature everywhere is the same" (*priroda vezde edina*) in terms of

30 Sergei Pavlov, "*Lunnaia raduga*" [Moon rainbow], Moscow: Molodaia gvardiia, 1978. http://www.e-reading.life/bookreader.php/97235/Pavlov_-_Lunnaya_raduga._Kniga_1._Nauchno-fantasticheskii_roman.html

31 This could be a disparaging reference to American Robert Goddard, the so-called father of modern rocket propulsion, after whom NASA's Goddard Space Flight Center in Greenbelt, Maryland, was established in 1959. The Soviets confer the honor for similar discoveries to Konstantin Tsiolkovsky, whose work preceded Goddard's by a couple decades.

32 Pavel Amnuel', "Idu po trasse" [I'm on course], *Sbornik nauchnoi fantastiki* [Collection of science fiction] 21 (1979), 76–100.

its elemental composition, the implication of which is that the human body is materially compatible with non-terrestrial environments.

Despite Goddard's pangs of conscience, he ultimately does not want to stand in the way of science, instead making recommendations for further precautions that should be taken to avert the kinds of life-threatening challenges that his three variators experienced. The story acknowledges anxieties about such a drastic form of active evolution wrought by genetic engineering but answers them by insisting on the incontrovertible imperative for scientific advancement stemming from mankind's most fundamental humanist qualities. These qualities include intellectual curiosity and the agency to act on it; and, importantly, man's ability to take risks, suffer defeat, and persevere by building new technologies.

Conclusion

The works of SF that I've considered in this chapter stimulate questions about the nexus of embodiment, environment, and subjectivity. Official discourse in the Soviet 1970s perpetuated the narrative of an ideal socialist subject, such as that portrayed by Rybakov. In the West, this type of humanist construct would soon be challenged by emerging philosophies that acknowledge the body and the environment as actants in forming human subjectivity. Feminist posthumanists like Donna Haraway and Rosi Braidotti have vociferously advocated for the importance of embodiment in shaping subjectivity and therefore oppose the notion of a single human essence, which is predicated on a universalized European, white, male subject. Encouraging respect for multiple, diverse subjectivities, both theorists challenge androcentrism as well as anthropocentrism. Haraway extends her thinking about subjectivity to other species, and Braidotti goes even further toward a bioegalitarianism that incorporates non-animal forms of life.[33] Braidotti's geo-centered subjectivity complements the ecocritical perspective of scholars like Morton, who attempts to chart a way out of the binary thinking that separates nature and culture. By undoing qualifying categories such as "nature," human thought and actions might become more holistic and ecologically integrative.

---

33 See Donna Haraway, *The Companion Species Manifesto: Dogs, People, and Significant Otherness* (Chicago: Prickly Paradigm Press, 2003); on the "bioegalitarian turn," see Braidotti, "Animals, Anomalies, and Inorganic Others." *PMLA* (2009) 124 (2): 526–32; on the "planetary, geo-centered perspective," see Braidotti, *The Posthuman*, 81.

This chapter has focused mainly on works of Soviet SF that disregard the influence of the body and environment on forming subjectivities because of dominant assumptions about human essence (*The Moon Rainbow* is the exception since it allows for delayed changes in comprehension as a response to new conditions). The writers' thinking about how the environment shapes the body goes beyond Darwinian evolution: they portray humans actively intervening in their corporal adaptation. Although such intentional bio-engineering is part of the extreme humanism that was Soviet Prometheanism, the realization that humans are imbricated in a complex material environment of mutual influence represents an important step forward toward a balanced, ecological worldview.

CHAPTER 5

"Drilled Humans" or Automated Systems? Reconsidering Human-Machine Integration in Late-Soviet Design

Diana Kurkovsky West,
Northwestern University

The figure of Daedalus—which for Bruno Latour embodies modernity's attitude toward anthropocentric domination of all aspects of nature—offers an apt embodiment of the Soviet view of science and technology. Scholars have long noted that Soviet "Prometheanism," with its inherent rhetoric of conquest, was present in much of the discourse around technology and the anticipated techno-scientific future. Soviet history is rife with massive projects for dams, irrigation canals, reversing rivers, drained wetlands, terraforming, countrywide planning efforts, and many other showpieces of "socialist construction" aimed at "illustrating the technological and organizational might of Marxist-Leninist societies as compared with the feebleness of Western capitalist ones."[1] This Daedalean approach was not only present in such engineering feats, but also in the Soviet attitudes toward technology at large: the insistence on the categories of science that dominated both the official rhetoric and much of popular culture, and its applications to issues as diverse as urban planning, biology, and even consumer product design.

---

1 William B. Meyer, *The Progressive Environmental Prometheans*, 187.

And yet we should not take the Soviet Prometheanist claims at face value. The metaphor of Daedalus is not a heroic one for Latour; the mythological trickster is profoundly deluded, mistaken about his ontological distinctiveness from the material world, which he tries to bend to his will. He is an embodiment of modernity, which, in its misguided humanist pursuits, "overlooks the simultaneous birth of 'non-humanity'—things, or objects, or beasts," all the while arising from the "masking of the conjoined birth and the separate treatment of these three communities."[2] Such a narrative results in the misplaced sense of power over things and technologies. Daedalus personifies the hubris of modern techno-science, its anthropocentric solipsism, and its utilitarian attitude toward nature. In contrast, contemporary scholars like Latour, Michel Callon, John Law, Annemarie Mol, Jane Bennett, and other adherents of the turn toward material ontology propose expanding our vision of social interactions among human and non-human actors.

In this article, I will bracket the typical story of Soviet techno-scientific Prometheanism in favor of a more nuanced reconsideration of human-machine relationships. My aim is to expose various modalities in the hybrid co-functioning of human and non-human agents in Soviet techno-science. I believe that the turn toward a re-examination of materiality sheds new light on the Soviet experience and allows researchers to avoid the trappings of ideology-based arguments so common in Soviet studies, which tend to result in a radically polarizing disconnect between the alleged ideals of the regime and the reality of the actual experience. The dangers of such claims are too numerous to list here, but among some of the problems resulting from this polarizing approach are a certain inevitable dichotomy between the lived experience of socialism and the macro-political perspective, the disjunction between intention and consequence, the bifurcation of so-called collaborators and dissidents, and, in all of this, almost a complete myopia with respect to things, machines, and objects that populated the USSR. Thus, in my effort to move away from the moralizing undertones of Soviet claims to Prometheanism, I aim to capture the continual negotiation, reassembling, stabilization, and re-conceptualization of the human-machine relationship, which, I argue, was proposed in much of Soviet techno-science.

To achieve this, I will focus specifically on Soviet discourse around the design of material objects as the critical component of social engineering

2 Bruno Latour, *We Have Never Been Modern* (Hemel Hempstead, Hertfordshire, England: Harvester Wheatsheaf, 1991), 13.

necessary to achieve a socialist world order. I will examine two instances of the late Soviet design program: the government campaign for good household design of the late '50s and '60s, and the implementation of a statewide program of scientific industrial design in the '70s and '80s. I will begin by examining a body of design literature produced between 1958 and 1964, which set out to improve the Soviet consumer through rational design of household interiors. These design manuals were concurrent with the launch of Khrushchev's mass housing construction program and were geared specifically at the prefabricated apartments popularly known as *khrushchevki.* I will discuss the appointments of *khrushchevki* as spaces where the scientific ordering of the objects of consumption was to be implemented on all levels of organization and design by the female inhabitants.[3] They were to rationalize the domicile, organizing their family space and leisure and thereby becoming the tools of scientific ordering of the domestic sphere. I argue that the relationship between household operators and technology in these design manuals could be understood as akin to John Law's notion of "drilled people." Law uses the term "drilled people" in reference to fifteenth-century Portuguese navigators who were educated in such a way as to exclude most human error. These drilled people were part of a system working in concert with navigational technologies of Portuguese vessels. [4]

Like the Portuguese navigators who "were given a recipe that dealt with all the possible combinations," Soviet female household administrators were "drilled" through the detailed, exhaustive manuals published by Soviet institutes. Encouraged to function as a kind of human technology, the

3 Recent scholarship has recognized an ambiguity in women's roles as socialist consumers. On the one hand, a series of liberalizing measures put in place by Khrushchev re-legalized abortion in 1955, instituted longer maternity leaves, and made divorces more acceptable. See Natasha Kolchevska, "Angels in the Home and at Work: Russian Women in the Khrushchev Years," *Women's Studies Quarterly* 33, no. 3/4 (2005): 114–37. On the other hand, as Susan Reid has argued, women were expected to participate in the production of state ideology through acts of consumption. See Susan Reid, "Cold War in the Kitchen: Gender and De-Stalinization of Consumer Taste in the Soviet Union under Khrushchev," *Slavic Review* 61, no. 2 (2002): 211–52. Moreover, Reid has observed that despite the measures to offer women equal professional opportunities, Khrushchev actually reinforced a more traditional role for women. See Susan Reid, "Women in the Home" in *Women in the Khrushchev Era,* ed. Melanie Ilič, Susan Emily Reid, and Lynne Attwood (Houndmills, England: Palgrave Macmillan, 2004), 149–76.

4 John Law, "On the Methods of Long-Distance Control: Vessels, Navigation, and the Portuguese Route to India," in *Power, Action and Belief: A New Sociology of Knowledge?,* ed. John Law (London: Routledge & Kegan Paul, 1986), 234–63.

female household administrators were to become the vehicles for the mass implementation of a rationalist design program.

At the same time, however, these projections for highly mechanized behavior proved to be flawed and unrealizable. Fickle consumer tastes required a shift toward a more complex system of human-machine hybridization. The second half of this paper treats a later period of system-wide design automation, where designers at the All-Union Institute of Technical Aesthetics (VNIITE) attempted to develop a more embedded approach to product design. At VNIITE, designers were tasked with creating a specifically Soviet, large-scale program of comprehensive design, which posited another relationship to technology and social engineering: Namely, it implied a socio-technical stabilization by the virtue of embedding the program of interaction into the designed objects. In other words, the design of the objects was supposed to compensate for the impossibility of fully programming people. Taking the responsibility for rational household administration away from the ostensibly "drilled" yet still not wholly predictable, domestic operators of the earlier years, VNIITE's programs aimed to hybridize the human-machine relationship at the level of technology. Or, to borrow a term from Michel Callon, designers at VNIITE aimed to "blackbox" the complex, hybrid assemblage of the human and the non-human into the structure of the design process itself.[5]

Tracing the changing role of the "drilled human's" agency in Soviet design is crucial for understanding the Cold War. As scholars have noted, household goods such as domestic appliances were important weapons of the Cold War, imbued heavily with ideological messages and national tactics. Scholarship on the Cold War and America's deployment of consumer culture has explored the link between consumer choice and democracy, highlighting the role

5 See Michel Callon, "The Sociology of an Actor-Network: The Case of the Electric Vehicle," in *Mapping the Dynamics of Science and Technology: Sociology of Science in the Real World*, ed. Michel Callon, John Law, and Arie Rip (Basingstoke: Macmillan, 1986), 29–30. Bruno Latour has identified blackboxing as a process of stabilizing the various components of the assemblage into a technological object. When the blackboxing happens successfully, the social and the technical elements achieve a kind of balanced relationship that is no longer visible until a break or an accident occurs. Latour writes: "When a machine runs efficiently, when a matter of fact is settled, one need focus only on its inputs and outputs and not on its internal complexity. Thus, paradoxically, the more science and technology succeed, the more opaque and obscure they become." See Bruno Latour, *Pandora's Hope: Essays on the Reality of Science Studies* (Cambridge, MA: Harvard University Press, 1999), 304.

of kitchens especially in steering the public clear of communism.[6] Exhibiting modern, streamlined kitchens, equipped with the latest fashions in appliances became an important part of the Marshall Plan, and various such kitchens were displayed across Europe, serving as "models of technological change, as metaphors for modernism, and as microcosms of new consumer regimes of the twentieth century."[7] Such was the case with the 1959 American National Exhibit in Moscow's Sokolniki Park, where the famous Kitchen Debate took place in the color-coordinated kitchen of a Long Island developer home, humorously dubbed as "splitnik" by American press. In a heated argument with Soviet Premier Nikita Khrushchev over the merits of domestic gadgetry, Richard Nixon, the vice president of the United States at the time, drew a parallel between American people's freedom to choose their appliances and their leaders: "We do not claim to astonish the Russian people. We hope to show our diversity and our right to choose. We do not wish to have decisions made at the top by government officials who say that all homes should be built in the same way."[8] Khrushchev questioned this connection, believing, like many at the time, that given the chance, the Soviets would be able to produce an abundance of consumer goods on par with what they saw in Sokolniki. Already in the mid-50s, Khrushchev had launched a massive housing construction campaign, part of which put emphasis on making household appliances and consumer goods widely available, thereby building his own army of technological soldiers.

In 1957, construction began on the new housing district in Moscow called Novye Cheremushki. Here, along with exploring cost-effective methods of prefabrication and standardization of housing, Soviet architects engaged in re-conceptualizing apartment interiors. The proliferation of new, ultra-compact (*malometrazhnye*) apartments required a reconsideration of interior

---

6 Ruth Oldenziel and Karin Zachmann, "Kitchens as Technology and Politics," in *Cold War Kitchen: Americanization, Technology, and European Users*, ed. Ruth Oldenziel and Karin Zachmann (Cambridge, MA: MIT Press, 2009), 10. Although numerous kitchens were exported to Europe under the Marshall Plan, of particular note here is the 1952 exhibit titled "We're Building a Better House" held in West Berlin, which featured a single-family two-bedroom suburban home. The kitchen of this house was an instant hit; a reporter from the *Neue Zeitung* described it as a "completely automatic, mechanized wonder kitchen [...] somehow reminiscent of the control panel of an airplane." (*Neue Zeitung*, September 20, 1952, quoted in Gregg Castillo, "The American 'Fat Kitchen' in Europe: Postwar Domestic Modernity and Marshall Plan Strategies of Enchantment," in Oldenziel and Zachmann, *Cold War Kitchen*, 45).

7 Over 40 percent of the visitors to the exhibit were from East Germany, further emphasizing the rift between socialist ideals and capitalist consumer culture. See Castillo, 47.

8 Transcript of "The Kitchen Debate" between Vice President Richard Nixon and Soviet Premier Nikita Khrushchev at the U.S. Embassy, Moscow, Soviet Union. July 24,1959, http://teachingamericanhistory.org/library/document/the-kitchen-debate/.

layouts and furnishings, and the kinds of domestic technology appropriate to this new mode of living. These apartments also became the focus of the Soviet media's concern with modernization and good taste: Because their compact size required all rooms to be flexible and multi-purpose, they needed appropriate appointments which had not been available on the Soviet consumer market. The very conception of a small-size apartment required a fundamental transformation of attitudes toward interior decoration, design, and use of space. This, however, was not merely an extension of an ideological program to the realm of domesticity. Rather, the new designs, propagated in the era's journals and design manuals, were intended to cultivate a new kind of a domestic operator: a "drilled human," the woman of the house. Her task was to settle in these new, ultra-compact apartments.

In the Novye Cheremushki development, architects and designers concerned themselves with testing a range of room configurations and surface finishes, keeping in mind the specific task of living in a *malometrazhnaia kvartira.* In the 1958 government publication on the neighborhood called *9yi kvartal* (*The 9th district*) in reference to the first constructed district, several chapters are dedicated to the topic of built-ins and furnishings. The authors explain: "... the *malometrazhnaia kvartira* will not have rooms with special designations, i.e., bedrooms, dining rooms, studies, etc. Every room, as a rule, will function both as a living room and as a bedroom."[9] Therefore, the publication explains, former types of furniture will no longer work in this space. The new type of furniture required to optimize the apartment will be made of flexible, easily reconfigurable pieces:

> New furniture, its character, form, size and composition are a radical departure from the outdated furniture types. The presence of built-in closets, dressing rooms, and built-in kitchen cabinetry in a *malometrazhnaia kvartira* has allowed us to eliminate the need for freestanding armoires for clothes and linens, cupboards for dishes, and buffets [...].
>
> The inhabitants of a *malometrazhnaia kvartira,* in which each room does not solely function as a bedroom, have the natural desire to replace regular beds with more attractive pieces which change size—like fold-out sofas and armchair-sleepers, or closets where a bed can be put away.[10]

9 *9yi kvartal: opytno-pokazatel'noe stroitel'stvo zhilogo kvartala v Moskve (raion Novye Cheremushki)* [The 9th district: a pilot-project construction of living quarters in Moscow (the Novye Cheremushki neighborhood)] (Moscow: Gos[udarstvennoe] iz[datel'st]vo litertatury po stroitel'stvu, arkhitekture i stroitel'nym materialam, 1959), 213.

10 Ibid., 214.

The 9th District was written to promote ideas regarding housing construction and as a manual containing sections on household design appropriate to this type of construction. The section dedicated to apartment interiors offered a number of pointers regarding optimal furniture arrangements within the apartments, correlating the number and size of rooms in an apartment to the types of pieces that are needed. Sample furnishing sets required for one-, two-, and three-room apartments, are said to be available for purchase through Mosmebel'torg—a central furniture distributor in Moscow.[11] Along with several pages of photographs of the model units in the Ninth District of Novye Cheremushki the publication also offers tips on proper decorating appropriate to the new unit types.

> The rooms have compact sizes, and thus, simplicity, minimalism, comfort, nothing extraneous—such should be the operative principle for creating interiors. One should not block up the room with unnecessary pieces of furniture, knickknacks, and the like, and the number of objects should be minimal. Every item in these interiors should be very carefully selected in order to harmonize in its size, form, and color, with the rest of the room.[12]

A distinct rejection of all old-style furniture and decoration in favor of compact, lightweight, multifunctional pieces, as well as an interest in the overall design of the space, have a futuristic ring since they suggest a radically new type of living where rationalism and modern aesthetics prevail.

The issue of the inhabitant, especially the female inhabitant, as the household operator and the design mastermind emerges here, and is echoed in other literature on household organization. The rational use of space is understood to be something that does not come naturally to the inhabitants, and thus, the hybrid household must be properly administered. An article in the popular journal *Ogonek* from January, 1959 illustrates this problem.[13] It offers as an example a new, "light and airy" apartment in Novye Cheremushki, designed with built-in closets and other modern features. And yet old-school furnishings ruin the careful work of Soviet architects:

> The apartment building is built, inhabited, and you are invited to a housewarming, you enter the apartment–and don't recognize it. What has it

11 Ibid. I was not able to confirm that these purchases were made, or how many furniture "sets" were purchased in this manner from Mosmebel'torg.

12 Ibid., 223.

13 N. Svetova, "Tvoi dom" [Your home], *Ogonek,* January 1959, 14–15.

> become! Cluttered with old furniture, the apartment became uncomfortable, has lost its contemporary appearance. The simplicity which the architect cultivated has disappeared, the light from the large windows is lost behind the heavy velvet drapes, and the door of the built-in closet is blocked by a chest propped up against it.[14]

To fix the situation, the author advocates educating the inhabitants with respect to tasteful design—a task to be taken on by media depictions of good style, propagated by the furniture builders. For instance, the article suggests that diagrams of how sectional furniture could be rearranged in a multitude of ways best suited for the new type of dwelling would help the inhabitants make the correct choice. And for more detailed instructions regarding proper decoration, the author points to the publication of a new book called *The Apartment and its Decor* (*Kvartira i ee ubranstvo*)—a manual created by the Scientific Research Institute of Housing due to be published that same year.

Here, the female inhabitant is endowed with a particular role: to become the rational agent of administering a tasteful, modern new household. She is to be "drilled" through the manuals and media portrayals of her new role to implement the ideology of new design appropriate to the new kind of socialist interior. Her education was the principal goal of the 1962 book *The Apartment and Its Decor*. Positioning the home as a space that solves a range of "comprehensive challenges," the very first paragraph of the manual places proper household organization and decoration as the fundamental features of the new socialist lifestyle.[15] Complete with diagrams, drawings, and illustrations, the manual offers tasteful solutions to furniture layout, interior color schemes, and functionalism. It opens with diagrams similar to those found four years earlier in *The 9th District*, asserting the need to create a comfortable space for work and rest for each family member, all the while remembering to leave sufficient space for comfortable circulation. Drawings documenting the amount of space needed for various types of activities, such as dining or working at one's desk, help one establish the appropriate amount of space for movement, especially in the kitchen.

The Apartment and Its Decor urges the reader to understand the apartment interior in a comprehensive, total manner, positioning the inhabitant-cum-decorator as the mastermind of this new space, keeping a watchful eye on the

---

14 Ibid., 15.

15 R. N. Blashkevich, O. G. Baiar, *Kvartira i ee ubranstvo* [The apartment and its decor] (Moscow: Gosudarstvennoe izdatel'stvo literatury po stroitel'stvu, arkhitekture i stroitel'nym materialam, 1962), 15.

slightest impact of objects. "Sometimes articles of furniture that are simple in form and upon first glance less-than-interesting create unity, once placed in a room," the authors suggest. "Any article of furniture, regardless of its size or purpose, must conform to the overall composition of the interior."[16] This composition can be achieved by creating various focal points and color harmonies, all the while keeping the number of items in a household to a minimum. A detailed, room-by-room account of desirable fabrics and colors follows, emphasizing hygiene not only as a state of cleanliness but also as an aesthetic element. Similarly, a kitchen must not only be hygienic and comfortable for work but should also look inviting and not too "hospital-like," which can be achieved with "one or two cans of paint, and some inexpensive cotton fabrics and colorful dishware."[17] In setting up the bathroom, "one should use finishes that are light and clean in tone," while double beds, once again, "for the purposes of hygiene," need to have access from both sides.[18]

The level of detail in regard to all elements of interior decoration is striking: the publication even comments on tasteful approaches to the choice of plants, decorative items, and paintings. For instance, if the inhabitant owns several decorative objects, the manual insists that they should not be on display at the same time. Art forgery is highly frowned upon, and the authors recommend photographs of nature and landscapes if one does not own original art. Doilies and embroidered napkins must be banished in order not to diminish the natural beauty of wood grain. Plants like aloe, ficus, and philodendrons can add natural color and texture to any room, although their placement needs to be precisely determined after observing the light and heat cycles of the apartment. Freshly cut flowers are "an indispensible part of every room in the summer," and in the fall and winter may be replaced with green branches of pine or fir trees. "Intricate contours of papyrus sedge stalks in a tall vase, ivy in a ceramic pitcher, branches of oak or birch without the leaves in a crystal glass all add to the composition of the interior."[19]

The streamlined, minimalist aesthetic choices put forth in the publications are not accidental. Just as architects under Khrushchev were explicitly forbidden to spend public money on decoration and embellishment, the sentiment seemed to have extended to the domestic realm. In a dramatic turn away from Stalin-era "status" objects, *The Apartment and Its Decor* propagated trading frills and large, expensive furniture for clean, light-filled and flexible space that was

16 Ibid.

17 Ibid., 40.

18 Ibid., 38–40.

19 Ibid.

understood as a single composition where functionality met unassuming aesthetics appropriate for socialism. The word *poshlost,'* which roughly translates as something that is at once vulgar and retrograde, became a grave insult at this time, indicating unwillingness to shed the old bourgeois sensibilities.[20] The word *meshchanin*, or *petit-bourgeois*, was employed to deride the taste that stood in opposition to the regime's new stipulations and the social mission of good design. As Iurii Gerchuk argues, "'Petit-bourgeois taste,' as the embodiment of unculturedness, stagnant conformism and coarse self-interest, became enemy number one of the new style."[21] Citizens were urged to embrace new directions in interior decoration to become more cultured, and even where new furniture could not be purchased, tips were given on how to rationalize domestic space. Soviet women were thus to think about tasteful design as their social responsibility. From window treatments to lighting, from plants to rugs, they were to use the various manuals to set their families on the right track by creating comfortable, rational, coordinated, but not overly austere living spaces necessitated by the new ideology and worldview.

The normative discourse of Khurshchev-era interior decoration manuals positioned the Soviet consumer as an inhabitant-designer, whose aesthetic sensibility was part of her moral obligation. Numerous manuals on household administration highlight this. For instance, *The Brief Encyclopedia of Home Economics* (*Kratkaia entsiklopediia domashnego khoziaistva*), published in 1959, epitomized this utilitarian understanding of the household as primarily a space to be organized, rationed, and arranged. From diagrams of proper calisthenics for men and women of different ages, to detailed discussions of different kitchen appliances, apartment decor, as well as different kinds of baby food produced by Soviet industry, the manual reviews alphabetically anything and everything related to the Soviet household.[22] Of particular interest here is the

20 Susan Reid, "Destalinization and Taste, 1953–1963," *Journal of Design History* 10, no. 2:190. For a thorough discussion of *poshlost'* and its role in Soviet society, see Svetlana Boym, *Common Places: Mythologies of Everyday Life in Russia* (Cambridge, MA: Harvard University Press, 1995), 41–66. Boym defines *poshlost'* as "the Russian version of banality, with a characteristic national flavoring of metaphysics and high morality, and a peculiar conjunction of the sexual and the spiritual" (41).

21 Iurii Gerchuk, "The Aesthetics of Everyday Life in the Khrushchev Thaw in the USSR (1954–64)" in *Style and Socialism: Modernity and Material Culture in Post-War Eastern Europe*, ed. Susan E. Reid and D. J. Crowley (Oxford: Berg, 2000), 90.

22 *Kratkaia entsiklopediia domashnego khoziaistva* [The brief encyclopedia of home economics], ed. A. Revin, 2 vols. (Moscow: Gosudarstvennoe nauchnoe iz[datel'st]vo "Bol'shaia Sovetskaia entsiklopediia," 1959).

role of household technology, which was seen as part of Khrushchev's promise to improve the lives of Soviet housewives.[23] Discussions of how to operate various gadgets include typologies and mechanical aspects of television sets, radios, and even vacuum cleaners.[24] Along with tips on household machinery, the *Encyclopedia* also contains articles on sectional furniture, wallpaper, and apartment appointments. Drawings depicting furniture arrangements illustrate the ideas of comprehensive and modern design propagated in the entry. The featured furniture pieces, positioned in perfectly coordinated spaces, can be folded, unfolded, moved, and rearranged into dozens of different combinations, all at the whim of the enlightened and modern female inhabitant. The interior is managed and administered by the meticulously trained person, who has been educated in the science of tasteful household management, and who is now ready to exert her will on the new domestic space.

While promising to improve the availability of consumer goods on the Soviet market, Khrushchev was faced with a problem. The notoriously shoddy quality of Soviet-produced items continually plagued the system. How does one ensure high-quality goods in a closed system of production, where no competing items exist to weed out the less successful products? To address this problem, in 1962 the Soviet government issued a decree requiring all industries to improve the quality of their production by implementing the methods of *khudozhestvennoe konstruirovanie*, or design engineering.[25] The decree stipulated the need to create positions for staff designers across all industries—a radical idea, for design education as such had not existed in the USSR since the closing of *Vysshie khudozhestvenno-technicheskie masterskie* (VKhUTEMAS, or The Higher Artistic-Teaching Studios) and *Vysshii khudozhestvennyi tekhnicheskii institut* (VKhUTEIN, or The Higher Artistic-Technical Institute), which were the sites of experimental and

23 This was famously articulated in the famous "Kitchen Debate" at the 1959 American National Exhibit in Moscow, where Khrushchev locked horns with the American Vice-President Richard Nixon on the topic of household appliances, variety of consumer goods, and kitchen gadgetry.

24 *Kratkaia entsiklopediia*, 1:508.

25 Decree No. 394 from April 28, 1962 by the USSR Soviet of Ministers "Ob uluchshenii kachestva produktsii mashinostroeniia i tovarov kul'turno-bytovogo naznacheniia putem vnedreniia metodov khudozhestvennogo konstruirovaniia" [Regarding improving the quality of the products of industrial machine-building and cultural and household products through the integration of methods of artistic construction], cited in Natalia A. Kovshennikova, *Istoriia dizaina: uchebnoe posobiie* [History of design: a textbook], (Moscow: Omega L, 2011), 194. As with many concepts borrowed from the West, the Soviets could not openly use the term "design" but instead implemented the term "artistic engineering," which was first coined in the 1920s by the Soviet avant-garde.

avant-garde projects in the late 1920s. Drawing inspiration both from the early Soviet era, as well as from a wide range of Western design establishments, such as Knoll in the United States, the German Deutsche Werkbund, and Ulm School of Design, which continued the avant-garde design mission of the Bauhaus, the Soviets were to create their own school of industrial design. However, while lessons from Western architects were important, there was to be a fundamental distinction from "bourgeois" designers: *khudozhestvennoe konstruirovanie* was to focus on optimizing the process of design in order to avoid creating the unnecessary variety of competing products typical of capitalist economies. The 1962 founding of VNIITE under the auspices of USSR State Committee on Science and Technology brought about the official emergence of Soviet industrial design. Soon thereafter, with Decree No. 394, the design education system was established, and thirteen institutions of higher education were created in order to teach design.[26] VNIITE also had branches in several large cities like Leningrad, Sverdlovsk, Baku, Riga, and Tbilisi, thus aiming to eventually establish a country-wide system for implementing design into industrial practices.

The new field, however, could not be simply called *dizain*—this term, while it came into use by the 1980s, was at the time still laden with denunciations of Western consumerism and fashion for the sake of fashion. In keeping with the vision of creating a specifically Soviet, scientific, and non-bourgeois design program, the term technical aesthetics (*tekhnicheskaia estetika*) offered more than design of industrial or consumer objects. It entailed a program and a methodology that would simultaneously examine a host of issues and develop scientifically sound solutions. Iurii Solov'ev, the first director of VNIITE, wrote the following description of the field for the Great Soviet Encyclopedia:

> Technical aesthetics [is] a scientific discipline that studies the sociocultural, technological, and aesthetic problems of designing a harmonious environment of objects. Comprising the theoretical basis of design, technical aesthetics examines its social nature and principles of development, the principles and methods of artistic form creation, and the problems of professional creativity and skill of the artist-engineer.[27]

26 Dmitry Azrikan, "VNIITE, Dinosaur of Totalitarianism or Plato's Academy of Design?" *Design Issues* 15, no. 3 (1982): 49.

27 Iurii Solov'iev, "Tekhnicheskaia estetika" [Technical aesthetics], in *Bol'shaia Sovetskaia entsiklopediia* [Big Soviet encyclopedia], ed. A.M. Prokhorov (Moscow), 527–28, quoted in Anatole Senkevich Jr. "Art, Architecture, and Design: A Commentary," *Slavic Review* 37, no. 4 (1978): 589.

Solov'ev compared technical aesthetics to other sciences, such as biochemistry and astronautics, arguing for the field's interdisciplinary character.[28] Its goal was to analyze "numerous sociological, economic, technical, psychological, physiological, hygienic and aesthetic factors," and, in the process, to discover the "principles that form the foundation for formulating its requirements for the environment and the world of objects."[29]

Through establishing a scientific, rather than market-driven, program for industrial design, the Soviet government tasked the field's practitioners with improving the quality of Soviet consumer goods on the industry level. As Soviet state leaders continued to call for improved quality control (for instance, in the 1968 decree "Ob uluchshenii ispol'zovaniia dostizhenii tekhnicheskoi estetiki v narodnom khoziastve RSFSR" (Regarding the improvement of using achievements in technical aesthetics in the economy of the RSFSR), design was seen as the solution to streamlining the production process while improving its output. This call continued through the 1970s and 80s. For instance, in 1976, the XXV Communist Party Congress declared the urgent need to "widely implement comprehensive systems of quality control of production."[30] The Department of Design Promotion at VNIITE worked to generate industry-wide standards as a means of implementing new design, and generate a new manual of standards called "Industrial Design Requirements for Mass-Manufactured Products."[31] The Department of Quality Control implemented a system under which all industrial and agricultural products strove to achieve the "Mark of Quality," and economic sanctions were placed on those products that could not attain such a mark.

Despite its specific task to transform Soviet production, however, VNIITE designers articulated their mission as focused on a joint study of humans and non-humans; technical aesthetics was understood to be an umbrella for rigorous research in social sciences, engineering, art theory, ergonomics, and other related fields. Moreover, management and administration became important foci of this research. The 1977 volume of *What's new in life, science, technology* [*Novoe v zhizni, nauke, tekhnike*]—a series of publications on

28 Yulia Karpova, "Accommodating 'Design': Introducing the Western Concept into Soviet Art Theory in the 1950s–60s," *European Review of History: Revue européenne d'histoire* 20, no. 4 (2013): 10. http://dx.doi.org/10.1080/13507486.2012.763160.

29 Iurii Solov'ev, "O tekhnicheskoi estetike" [On technical aesthetics], *Tekhnicheskaia Estetika* [Technical aesthetics] 1 (1964): 1, quoted in Karpova, 10.

30 *Materialy XXV s'ezda KPSS* (Moscow: Politizdat, 1976), 168.

31 Azrikan, "VNIITE," 53.

scientific management—was dedicated to the problem of quality control and technical aesthetics, and closely linked the field of design to the problem of large-scale management. In order to concretize the issue of quality, the publication first defined quality of production as something that is objective and intrinsic to the object: "Indicators of quality in any industrial products are determined through the classification of their functional attributes, fundamentally connected to their type and structural characteristics."[32] Achieving high quality also entails the optimization of labor and planning for the technological aspects of the product that can minimize material and labor costs, all the while maintaining its key functional attributes. Finally, from the point of view of distribution, the product must be "legible" and recognizable: its use must be clear even when placed along with hundreds of other retail products, and hence packaging and specific object features must help in this regard.[33]

Because quality is a very complex interplay of characteristics, simply improving the methods of industrial production was insufficient because it entailed meeting only the standard set by the producer. The publication therefore states that a more nuanced method of quality control was needed:

> Such a challenge is only achievable by creating of a closed system of continual quality control, where, in the planning and design of a product, one considers both the structure of existing demand [...] (including its future projection), and the level of satisfaction with the product [...] in other words, tracking its use which allows for introducing continual correctives.[34]

Essentially advocating for a large-scale self-correcting system that would correlate production to consumption, the publication envisions the creation of such a system as the only solution to ensuring quality control. Similar systems were implemented in certain Soviet production facilities; the comprehensive system of managing the quality of production, called *kompleksnaia sistema upravleniia kachestvom produktsii* (the complex system for managing the quality of production), or KSUKP, was developed in the early 1970s in L'vov (now L'viv, Ukraine) and was introduced in factories around the Soviet Union. A basic feedback mechanism, KSUKP was a means of quality control by introducing

32 L. B. Pereverzev, *Tekhnicheskaia estetika i upravleniie kachestvom* [Technical aesthetics and quality control] (Moscow: Iz[datel'st]vo "Znanie," 1977), 1:7.

33 Ibid., 1:9.

34 Ibid.

annual correctives to the production plan based on attained practical knowledge. In 1975, several factories in L'vov began implementing KSUKP, which was deemed successful by 1979, when KSUKP was approved for use in the State Standard (GOST) no. 23554.0 – 79.[35]

The mere creation of a feedback mechanism, however, was insufficient, the author argued. Consumers are always changing, and the "consumer of the '60s does not resemble the consumer of the '50s, or, especially, of the '40s, not only due to a rise in actual income but also because of certain changes in psychology influenced by cultural and technological improvements [...]."[36] Therefore, instead of constantly trying to stay ahead of consumer demand and shifting tastes, the designers were to take matters into their own hands by setting the trends through their scientific expertise. The philosopher Karl Kantor wrote, "There is no other way to keep track of the actual changing needs other than forming them."[37] Crafting products that the consumers will want, rather than continually remaining one step behind in adjusting for their need, was the role of *tekhnicheskaia estetika*. Instead of producing a variety of redundant goods and leaving the selection to the consumer, the author asserts that it is VNIITE's role to develop an "optimized assortment of goods" by analyzing existing needs and demands all the while keeping in mind the goal of "shaping" the consumer and the product to each other through careful design.[38] Under VNIITE's guidance, Soviet design was to perform the ultimate function of socio-technical engineering, using methods of comprehensive analysis and design in order to optimize the human and non-human interactions embedded in all consumer products. The resultant

---

35 The Central Committee of the Communist Party of the Soviet Union, "Ob opyte partiinykh organizatsii i kollektivov peredovykh predpriiatii L'vovskoi oblasti po razrabotke i vnedreniiu kompleksnoi sistemy upravleniia kachestvom produktsii" [On the experience of party organizations and collectives of leading enterprises in the L'vov region regarding the development and implementation of the complex system for managing the quality of production], 1975, quoted in Shavrov, E. N., "O pravilakh tekhnicheskoi ekspluatatsii elektricheskikh stantsii i setei v svete novogo zakonodatel'stva Rossiiskoi Federatsii (k 70i letiiu izdaniia PTE)" [On the rules of technical operation of electric stations and networks in light of the Russian Federation's new legislation (for the 70th anniversary of the publication of RTE), *Energetik* [Power engineer], no. 11 (2010), 2. The text of 1979 GOST no. 23554.0 – 79 can be found in a publication of the State Committee on Standards available online at https://rosexpert-pravo.ru/law/Data2/1/4294741/4294741906.pdf.

36 Ibid.

37 Karl M. Kantor, "K probleme obshchestvennoi prirody dizaina" [Regarding the problem of the social nature of design], *Voprosy tekhnicheskoi estetiki* [Questions of technical aesthetics] 2 (1970), 71, quoted in The Central Committee of the Communist Party of the Soviet Union's Decree "Ob opyte partiinykh organizatsii [...]" (see note above).

38 Ibid.

ensemble would be blackboxed in the process of design, creating "smart" objects that could automatically engage in processes that, in previous decades, were initiated by the domestic consumer under the instruction of manuals.

VNIITE grew rapidly, opening branches in all major Soviet cities, and so did the scope of its projects. In the late 1970s, a new trend took over Soviet design, persisting until the fall of the Soviet Union. *Dizain-programma*, roughly translated as design programming, was a method of design management geared at not only creating new prototypes, but also envisioning a wide range of aesthetically related objects. One of the first Soviet design programming commissions was "Soiuzelektropribor," created for the Ministry of Electronics and Technology. This massive project, called ElektroMera (Electric Measurement Instruments), required the unification of the design of all electronics produced by the industry, special uniforms, the standardization of the workplace for engineers and technicians, and of all graphics, as well as aesthetics of the production plant itself, forming a comprehensive system for the production of all Soviet electronics. Design programming relied on the integration of several modular systems: the devices themselves, the furniture, and the environment. It also aimed at establishing a "systemic approach to planning, self-financing, organization and automation of control and management."[39]

The project was immense in scale: ElektroMera comprised thirty-two factories nationwide, with a staff of roughly twenty thousand workers in each, and producing some 1,500 devices. It did not start out this big; initially, the project's goal was to coordinate the design of several factories, but the program was eventually extended to include not only design, but also extensive organizational restructuring.[40] Dmitry Azrikan, who, along with Dmitry Shchelkunov, was one of the leading designers of the project, remembers that the industries that were involved conducted significant market research for ElektroMera project:

> This vision was as market-oriented as possible at that time [...]. Intermediate concepts also were presented. Moscow headquarters and leading

39 D. A. Azrikan and D. N. Shchelkunov, "O kontseptsii firmennogo stilia VO 'Soiuzelektropribor'," *Tekhnicheskaia estetika* 2, 1976. Quoted in Margareta Tillberg, "Collaborative Design: The Electric Industry in Soviet Russia 1973–79" (paper presented at the 2008 Swiss Network Design Symposium, May 30-31, Mount Gurten, Berne, Switzerland), 234. http://5-10-20.ch/~sdn/SDN08_pdf_conference%20papers/13_Tillberg.pdf.

40 Tillberg, "Collaborative Design," 237. This information comes from an interview Tillberg conducted with one of the project's engineers Marina Mikheeva in April 2008, and has not been independently verified.

> branches developed concepts representing each style group, and each particular type of product, system, or set. Thus, a lot of innovative ideas were given to clients, including graphics and packaging.[41]

Besides the stated interest in the consumer, the program also engaged an integrated approach to factory and workspace design, improving the production site as well. An image from the VNIITE publication on ergonomics contained several solutions it offered to Soiuzelektropribor for color schemes in their production facilities.[42] Organizing the workspace was argued to not only improve labor conditions but also to improve the workers' health and efficiency significantly, thereby minimizing error.

ElektroMera engaged thousands of Soviet designers in branches across the country as they set out to explore user-centered design, ergonomics, graphic design, and to establish a nomenclature of objects. But it was hardly a project that involved only the integration of design into all corporate products; it was seen as a real, tangible product of what scientific socialism could be. As Azrikan put it: "A City of the Sun was to be built in one selected industrial branch, in the middle of a gray country that had turned into an enormous garbage dump."[43] Designers involved with the project imagined that finally, after decades of promises and repression, they could have a hand in the complete transformation of the nature of production, and by extension, of all objects, into a single "harmonious environment" of humans and our sociotechnical objects. Moreover, literature about the project makes no secret of its close affinity with systems theory, and references were made to the work of A. A. Malinovskii, the son of Alexander Bogdanov, who, in the 1920s developed a proto-cybernetic organizational science called *tektologiia*.[44] *Tektologiia* presented a holistic theory of the universe, wherein all aspects folded into a single "universal organizational process: endlessly dividing itself into parts, boundless and seamless

---

41 Ibid.

42 V. M. Munipov et al., *Ergonomika: printsipy i rekommendatsii* [Ergonomics: principles and recommendations] (Moscow: Gosudarstvennyi kommitet SSSR po nauke i tekhnike and Vsesoiuznyi nauchno-issledovatel'skii institut tekhnicheskoi estetiki, 1983), 72.

43 Dmitrii Azrikan, "O proekte 'Soiuzelektropribor'" [On the project 'Soiuzelektropribor'] (unpublished manuscript), quoted in "Collaborative Design: The Electric Industry in Soviet Russia 1973-79," 237.

44 In particular, see references to Malinovskii's essays "Basic Methods and Definition of Systems Theory in Connection to Biology" and "Theory of Structures and its Position in a Systems Approach," in Dmitry Azrikan, "Metodicheskaia model'," *Tekhnicheskaia estetika* 9.

in its wholeness."[45] Malinovskii, a biologist, advocated the holistic aspects of his father's doctrine, his ideas dovetailing strongly with information theory and the idea of feedback. After six years of research and design, numerous aspects of the program were implemented, setting new standards for the electronics industry, although the project was never executed in full.[46]

A genuine interest in the non-market mode of quality control remained the dominant theme of all publications on technical aesthetics and its related subfields such as ergonomics. Moreover, Western designers who served as inspiration for the Soviets were often those who treated design as a scientific process requiring a calibration of social, technological, and aesthetic features. For instance, the Soviets were especially enthralled with Tomás Maldonado, who travelled to Russia a number of times, attended the IX International Council of Societies of Industrial Design held in Moscow in 1975, and was widely published in Soviet journals. Maldonado, a key figure at Germany's famous Ulm School of Design (HfG, or Hochschule für Gestaltung, Ulm) between 1954 and 1967, saw the designer as an "integrator," able to bring to design a large number of specialties, disciplines, and manufacturing considerations.[47] Another figure from the Ulm School, the engineer and theorist Abraham Moles, became immensely popular in the Soviet Union, as his analysis of information theory and aesthetics in *Sociodynamics of Culture* was first translated into Russian in 1973. An interest in semiotics and structuralism, along with scientific management theories like cybernetics, further expanded VNIITE's canon to include a multidisciplinary range of Western thinkers. Although VNIITE was a government agency whose primary task involved implementing new methods of quality control through design, its agendas, interest in systems theory, and optimization of design opened up an exchange of ideas with the West in ways that few Soviet organizations could claim.

VNIITE's comprehensive approach to design and its roots in systems theory, despite its stated efforts at consumer analysis, nonetheless remained focused on the consumer object's transformative potential both in the realms of production and implementation. For instance, the Institute's 1983 theoretical

45 Aleksandr Bogdanov, *Tektologiia: vseobshchaia organizatsionnaia nauka* (Moscow: Ekonomika, 1989), 1:73.

46 Iurii Solov'ev, *Moia zhizn'*, 194. Cited in Margareta Tillberg, "Collaborative Design," 242. There exists no current documentation outside of Solov'ev's accounts and memoirs of the actual scale of the program's implementation.

47 See Tomás Maldonado, "New Developments in the Training Industry in Product Design," *Ulm*, (October 2, 1958): 31.

publication called *The methods of technical aesthetics. Design program (Metodika khudozhestvennogo konstruirovanniia. Dizain-programma)* offers a sample analysis of how one develops designs for a universal food processor, or UKM (*Universal'naia kukhonnaia mashina*, or universal kitchen machine). It posits that while in a traditional kitchen, the layout of the space gravitates toward accommodating the nuanced set of operations performed by a human, in the kitchens equipped with food processors, most operations occur "outside the human" in the space "of the machine's activity."[48] Culinary skill is made obsolete by the machine:

> With the integration of technology, the old concepts of patience, dexterity, mastery, and complex order, as well as various tricks of culinary art lose their former meaning [...]. Thus, new demands for the form of technological devices emerge: [the machines] must become one's own, domesticated, and obediently performing the consumer's commands.[49]

The publication argues that the solution to all problems that arise from human-machine interaction could be solved by large-scale automation and the development of a wide range of machines capable of meeting all demands. "Progress in this regard depends first and foremost on the development of new mechanisms and technological processes that would be capable of [...] continually performing a wide range of operations without human participation," as the role of the cook is replaced by that of the programmer.[50] While the book admits that design had not advanced this far, the picture of a fully automated, operator-less kitchen was something the designer must keep in mind while imagining the new line of universal food processors.

So what becomes of the Soviet consumer, who, just a decade earlier, was the strategic "fully trained" operator in charge of creating an appropriate household for socialism? Now, the consumer/inhabitant performs the function not of the enlightened designer but of an object of scientific study herself. The specialist in technical aesthetics is told to look beyond

48 M. Khasymskii, Iu. B. Solov'ev et al., eds., *Metodika khudozhestvennogo konstruirovaniia* (Moscow: Vsesoiuznyi nauchno-issledovatel'skii institut tekhnicheskoi estetiki, 1983), 111.

49 Ibid.

50 Ibid.

the material realm of objects to penetrate the consumer's spiritual realm, though this is in no way a metaphysical undertaking. Instead, one uncovers the semiotic function of consumer objects and purchases: "for a person, in essence, purchases not things but solutions to a problem: not china, but a culture of table serving, not a rug but spatial intimacy, etc."[51] Thus, the technical aesthetician must not only fulfill a functional need but also consider the "ideologically value-based perspective"[52] by seeing into the essence of things through a set of binary oppositions such as "labor and rest, everyday and holiday, production and consumption."[53] The true meaning of a thing for any given person is only uncovered in the complex of oppositions, "at the intersection of at least two forms of vital activity."[54] Clearly taking inspiration from semiotics, a popular philosophical and methodological trend in the Soviet Union during the 1970s, *Methods of Technical Aesthetics* capitalizes on the notion of binary pairs, which, when examined in tandem, reveal the true function of consumer needs as a series of signs and symbols.

The technical aesthetician, then, not only discerns the needs of consumers but is also a scientist-semiotician who can understand the underlying cause of the specific need and its function. To demonstrate this in practice, *Methods* gives the example of a young family living in a room of a communal apartment. While the family waits to receive its own private apartment, its status is epitomized by transience and ultimate compactness of living in a single room, and in this case, it is the designer's role to develop a system of furnishings that fit this condition:

> The conditions of this lifestyle set against mass housing construction are perceived as temporary, which lessens the interest in [the apartment's] technological outfitting. In looking for a parallel to this model [of living] among the various spheres of life, one may see it in camping (to take one example). Here one gets the idea for the project: to replace the wardrobe, shelves, dresser, and other storage with machine-stiched equipment.... A tent (the future wardrobe), an awning (possible armchair), and pockets will be used as the basis of design. The pockets are bags and laundry

---

51 Ibid., 91.

52 Ibid. A more literal translation of the Russian phrase "*ideino-tsennostnaia tochka zreniia na veshch*'" would be "idea-and-value based perspective on matter."

53 Ibid., 93.

54 Ibid.

> reservoirs, and paper storage bins. Pockets can be on walls, on stands. A possible pocket screen (to make a child's special space), a pocket that is expandable and is fillable with granules (for softness). This kind of equipment is easy to personalize, change according to one's need, and repair.[55]

Methods argues that the essence of the family's living condition needs to be reflected in all elements of design. It also departs from the principal field of focus for technical aesthetics—namely, the technological object—to perceive the whole living environment as a kind of mechanical extension of a specific human condition best captured through flexible, portable, and non-permanent modules. In this case, the interior constructed of camping fabrics transforms the room in a communal apartment into a totality of experience, with all components of the space underscoring the fundamental premise of transience.

To summarize, in its quest for the underlying cause of need or desire, technical aesthetics posits a new relationship between the consumer and the domestic interior, and seeks to embed this hybrid relationship into the new culture of Soviet design. Simply put, the system no longer requires a trained human to run its kitchens as it did in Khrushchev-era design manuals; the kitchen has become hybrid by design, its intricate nexus of social and technical actors blackboxed into a specific program. The new arrangement redistributed agency more evenly between human and non-human actors. The posthuman kitchen's ultimate goal is complete human-machine hybridity at the level of full automation: The optimally designed system, envisioned through a thorough analysis of human form and activity, will cook, clean, and organize space. The establishment of comprehensive design programs, systematizing thousands of objects, would solve the problem of the Khrushchev-era's unpredictable "drilled" operator who might not heed advice from the manuals and could adorn her living room with a crystal chandelier.

The shifting notion of hybridity in Soviet design does not, of course, suggest that the designers imagined their roles to be anything other than Daedalean or truly considered the kind of ontological blending that Latour, Haraway, and others have argued to be endemic to modernity. In order to trace the significance of the shift from "drilled people" to sociotechnical blackboxing

---

55 Ibid.

through the objects of design that I have outlined in this essay, it is essential to consider the human-machine relationship posited by the various design programs. Although both the Khrushchev-era household design campaign and the programs implemented by VNIITE were ideologically designed to attain a material world appropriate for socialism, they also demonstrate the different ways in which the Daedalus-engineer-designer is imagined to deploy his powers as the manipulator of the world of things. Nonetheless, VNIITE's articulation of design, technical aesthetics, and the role of the designer in crafting a socialist collective of humans and non-humans cannot be overlooked.

Part Four

Technologies of the Self

CHAPTER 6

Romantic Aesthetics and Cybernetic Fiction

Jacob Emery,
Indiana University

Living Information

The driving conceit of Vladimir Savchenko's 1980 story "Mixed Up" (*Pereputannyi*) is that the human personality can be converted into information and beamed from place to place as a packet of radio waves. This potential is unique to human beings, and not even all of them—people "submit to the process only with difficulty," and some cannot do it or are destroyed in the process.[1] To encode one's self as information in this alien medium explicitly recalls the work of an artist encoding his or her self in the medium of the artwork. It requires, indeed, something like genius. "They couldn't do this with experimental dogs or monkeys: Only creatures with intelligence, consciousness, and free will can be 'read.' You must not only not fear the transition into radio-wave form, you must want it, must long for it, must invest the whole of

1 Vladimir Savchenko, "Mixed Up," in *Red Star Tales: A Century of Russian and Soviet Science Fiction*, ed. Yvonne Howell, trans. Kevin Reese (Montpelier, VT: RIS Publications, 2015), 360. All translations are mine unless otherwise indicated.

your soul—with no exaggeration—into the process."[2] This futurist technology can in fact be read as an allegory of the artistic impulse to create an object in which the artist "recognizes his own self," as Hegel puts it, and "in this reduplication of himself" turns his internal state "into knowledge for his own mind and for those of others."[3] By undergoing a transformation into a packet of information that can be broadcast into the universe, Savchenko does not just describe a fantasy of a future technology but articulates a definition of the aesthetic dating back to the early nineteenth century and expresses the hope that informatics technology can hyperbolize and empower it.

The relationship between "psy-transmission" and aesthetics, and the technology's association with touchstones of historical romanticism, is emphasized throughout the story. After his consciousness returns to his body from a transmission to a satellite, the narrator experiences that recovery of his self as a transformative shock, expressed through a quotation from a paradigmatic poem about artistic inspiration, Pushkin's "The Prophet."

> With fingers light as a dream
> He touched my eyes
> My prophetic eyes opened
> Like a frightened mother eagle's.
> He touched my ears:
> And noise and ringing filled them ...[4]

This technologically mediated self-discovery—the title of another and thematically related Savchenko work, the 1967 novel *Self-Discovery* (*Otkrytie sebia*)—is thus explicitly a breakthrough in aesthetic experience that opens up new possibilities, articulated through reference to canonical works of historical romanticism. Something has changed, however, since in Savchenko's story the alien race that communicates this technology to the human species is a part of the background. Rather than a Pushkinian visitation of a transcendent power that transforms the poet and empowers him to articulate a divine knowledge, the moment of aesthetic transformation that sets in motion the story's plot is the recovery of the self, or at least the biological human's transformative confrontation with its encoding as information. The encounter is literally

2 Ibid.

3 Georg Wilhelm Friedrich Hegel, *Introductory Lectures on Aesthetics*, trans. Bernard Bosanquet (London: Penguin, 2004), 36.

4 Savchenko, "Mixed Up," 353–54.

transformative: because the narrator's physical brain has partially liquefied during the absence of its governing genius—the flight into interplanetary space of its soul—the narrator becomes synesthetic. He begins to hear light and see sounds. The conceit that the human personality can be transcoded without loss from a biological to an electronic medium sets in motion a vertiginous problematic of encoding between media of all kinds, and, ultimately, the dream that all information can be fluidly transferred into any medium at all though the joint projects of self-knowledge and self-perfection.

Some elements of this fascination with the transposability of information, and especially of personal identity understood as information, are directly relatable to Savchenko's longstanding interest in cybernetics. Even more specifically, they reflect his status as a bilingual writer always conscious of the translation or transcoding of his work between Russian and Ukrainian.[5] Indeed, this same story was first published in Ukrainian, with the wry note that it was translated from Russian by someone named "Teslenko" (probably a pseudonym of Savchenko himself that alludes to the pioneer of electrical transmission, Nikolai Tesla).[6] What interests me here, however, is the larger phenomenon of which Savchenko's story is symptomatic—how the medium of self-expression, and the dream of an identity encoded without loss in a series of alien media, are persistently put, by science fiction of the last fifty years or so, in terms inherited from historical romanticism.

It is a commonplace of informatics that every copy degrades the information value of the original. Savchenko's answer to this problem is, effectively, genius. "Solving the problem of just what information you need to broadcast so that the carrying radio signal doesn't dissipate turned out to be simple: you have to broadcast *yourself*. You have to broadcast the whole of your make-up, as expressed in biocurrents and psy-potentials, your individual distinctiveness, your motivation, your life activity, the depths of your understanding of the world."[7] This "live"—as opposed to "dead"—information is impervious to entropy.

The closest thing to it, evidently, is the legacy of romantic art, which carries the essence of its creator forward into perpetuity. The plot of the story is a kind of *Bildung* or aesthetic education of the narrator, who learns to process

5 I am grateful to a comment given by Sibelan Forrester at the "Radiant Futures" conference held at NYU for bringing out this element of Savchenko's inspiration. "Radiant Futures: Russian Fantasy and Science Fiction," New York University Jordan Center for the Advanced Study of Russia, New York, NY, April 8, 2016.

6 As suggested by Kevin Reese's notes to "Mixed Up," 352.

7 Savchenko, "Mixed Up," 359.

visible sound and audible color by experiencing romantic artworks; implausibly, he even learns to understand human speech as a signifying palette of colors. In the process, he discovers his apparent disability to be a source of aesthetic potential, which he hopes to share with all humanity and other intelligent species of the galaxy. Listening to a composition by Chopin, the narrator somehow recognizes the piece by the visual impressions it imparts ("semitransparent, with shifting outlines, permeating one another") and compares it to another shift in medium that invokes a famously synesthetic artist by name. "I've seen something like this in the paintings of Čiurlionis: now it's like I'm watching an abstract film based on his work."[8] Beethoven also generates "Čiurlionis-esque visions," the "grief of a strong person."[9] Listening to Tchaikovsky, the narrator comes to the realization that art, like psy-transmission, is "live" rather than "dead" information and is, in cybernetic terms, impervious to entropy. "That music *lived* there, lived in its primary essence. And I was going to its creator, who, having died an age ago, also lived, more soundly and more fully than many thriving today."[10] The narrator's synesthesia, which seems at first to be a disability, is in fact the condition of art to survive its creator's physical body in a different informatic medium. And far from being a fantasy of a transformed future, Savchenko's story is at the same time the centuries-old fantasy of the expressive, immortal artwork in which the romantic genius is to live on forever.

The Archive of the Self

In this article, I want to approach Savchenko's work as symptomatic of a wide body of science fiction that, centered as it is on technologies like cloning, psy-transmission, and other means of encoding human identity in some informatics medium, also enters into debates about the aesthetic legacy of romanticism in a changing landscape of information technology. A wide variety of authors writing in Russian as well as in other languages turn to informatic duplication of human individuals not just as a science fiction conceit but as one that reflects upon the aesthetic functions of self-representation and self-knowledge.

Often, as in Savchenko, this is put in purely informatic terms. Perhaps the most widely spread science fiction trope of this kind is cloning, which becomes implicated in aesthetic activity whenever genetic duplicates enter the text as

8 Ibid., 382.

9 Ibid., 382–83.

10 Ibid., 385.

narrators and artist figures. Because this move is widespread in traditions as distinct as hard science fiction (John Varley), baroque Nabokovian labyrinths (Gene Wolfe), and the descendants of the Russian avant-garde (Vladimir Sorokin), I take the common techniques and preoccupations of such texts as diagnostic of a problematic in aesthetics. Most striking is how such texts invoke the legacy of romanticism. For example, the clone heroine of Varley's "The Phantom of Kansas" is a "weather artist" whose medium is the pathetic fallacy and who is called "the last Romantic" in an admiring review; Wolfe's most prominent clone text, the 1972 *Fifth Head of Cerberus*, is a pastiche of Coleridge's "The Rime of the Ancient Mariner" that transposes its narrative repetition into a genetic medium; and Sorokin actually populates his work with the clones of romantic writers and composers.[11] His novel *Blue Fat* (*Goluboe salo*, 1999) describes cloned writers as secreting a substance, blue fat, which is impervious to entropy and emblematizes the "immortality" of art through the vagaries of history.

Clones in contemporary art have inherited something of the uncanny doubles of romantic fiction, of course, but there are important differences too. For example, the ontological status of doppelgängers is open to doubt (as in Dostoevsky, Poe, Hoffmann, and others), whereas the clone is a basic premise of the book's world. Then, too, doppelgänger texts are associated with moral allegories of the individual, whereas clone narratives "are explicitly political, in the sense that they represent the ways in which communities of (genetically identical) individuals are formed and governed."[12] I want to argue that texts in which self-identity is expressed as reproducible in an alien medium essentially consisting of data—of which the DNA of clone narratives is one instance and the radio transmissions of Savchenko's story is another—recall the aesthetic canons of romanticism more fundamentally, in addressing three central constituent categories of romantic aesthetics: the ideal of self-expression; the concept of the interesting; and the aesthetic goal of freedom, that is, an artwork's organic development into its own form. Taken together, such texts sketch out adaptations in the romantic aesthetic paradigm, whose valorization of originality and self-expression remains a touchstone of art in the early twenty-first century, to the shifts in information and mass reproduction technology that have transformed society since its inception.

---

11 John Varley, *The Persistence of Vision* (New York: Berkley, 1978), 19.

12 Amit Marcus, "Telling the Difference: Clones, Doubles and What's in Between," *Connotations* 21.2-3 (2011/2012): 371.

A compact example from Wolfe's *The Fifth Head of Cerberus* stages these crucially interrelated concepts of the expressive, the interesting, and the free. Unbeknownst to himself, the narrator is a clone of his "father," one in a long series of duplicates of a geneticist who originally cloned himself in the spirit of scientific inquiry; the duplicate killed the original and, in the effort to discover why he committed the murder, started the fatal cycle of self-knowledge over. The genetic duplication is also a linguistic duplication, since they share a name that is never given to us directly. The semiotic and the genetic occur in parallel throughout the text. As a child, our narrator is taken to a library whose dome, "drawing up with it a spiraling walkway lined with the library's main collection," is both an archive of information and a representation of the helical structure of the DNA molecule. In this symbolic architecture of books and genes, the narrator races ahead of his tutor looking for the hundreds of books he has been told his father has authored. The story thus frames itself in the early pages as a bibliographic search for the genetic original and his original text, of which our narrator and his account are an unwitting copy:

> When I was still quite young it would often occur to me that, since my father had written (on the testimony of the lady in pink) a roomful of books, some of them should be here; and I would climb resolutely until I had almost reached the dome, and there rummage. [...] The upper shelves were, if anything, in worse disorder than those more conveniently located, and one glorious day when I attained the highest of all I found occupying that lofty, dusty position (besides a misplaced astronautics text, *The Mile-Long Spaceship*, by some German) only a lone copy of *Monday or Tuesday* leaning against a book about the assassination of Trotsky, and a crumbling volume of Vernor Vinge's short stories that owed its presence, or so I suspect, to some long-dead librarian's mistaking the faded *V. Vinge* on the spine for "Winge."[13]

Although the narrator seems not to find what he is looking for, we can deduce some things from the neighborhood where he looks. These books by Kate Wilhelm, Virginia Woolf, David Bertram Wolfe, and Vernor Vinge are all collections of thematically unified narratives—like Wolfe's own trilogy, a collection whose title, *The Fifth Head of Cerberus,* is also that of our unnamed narrator's literary effort. To judge by the company, our narrator's name (and therefore

13 Gene Wolfe, *The Fifth Head of Cerberus* (New York: Ace, 1976), 9.

the name of his genetic original) must begin with W.[14] Because the narrator is raised in a brothel called Cave Canem or *maison du chien*, with a statue of a canid on the front lawn alluding to the proprietor, we can conclude that the narrator's family name is Wolfe.[15] In the same stroke we decipher a great number of puns, opposing the "cathouse" of female sexuality and biological birth from a "pussy" to the punningly anal "Cave Canem" that is the "doghouse" of all-male technological reproduction, as well as a metaphorical underworld guarded by a metaphorical Cerberus. Furthermore, the great helix of the library on which the narrator carries out his literary or genetic researches—a search for the text of his genetic original—is, in this tale of genetic technology, a rebus whose solution is "gene." The clone, like the biological and the literary author of his being, is hence apparently named Gene Wolfe—a puzzle whose solution is arrived at through the intersection of literary and genetic information. The genre of science fiction, which shows us alien planets and futurist technologies, is thereby aligned with the genre of autobiography, which represents the inner self. At the same time, the project of deciphering the human genome is aligned with the project of cataloging literary history.

What do we gain by discovering the book's curious autobiographical claim? Like autobiography, the clone in this novella is supposed to render its maker knowable. We "seek self-knowledge," the geneticist explains his project. "We wish to discover why we fail, why others rise and change and we remain here."[16] However, this world of all-male technocratic rationality does not render the Oedipal complex obsolete but merely allegorizes it.[17] The genetic

---

14 *The Mile-Long Spaceship* is by Kate Wilhelm, also the author of several works of clone fiction (New York: Berkeley, 1963); Bertram David Wolfe is the author of *Three Who Made a Revolution* (New York: Dial, 1948); *Monday or Tuesday* is a short story collection by Virginia Woolf (London: Hogarth, 1921); no collection of short stories by Vernor Vinge yet existed in 1972, so this can be identified as a "future" text by one of Wolfe's contemporaries.

15 Much of this evidence comes from Robert Borski, "Je m'appelle Jean Loup" [My name is Jean Loup], WolfeWiki, last modified January 25, 2008, http://www.wolfewiki.com/pmwiki/pmwiki.php?n=CaveCanem.Number5.

16 Wolfe, *The Fifth Head of Cerberus*, 74.

17 The male technocratic rationality that excludes women from the life cycle is thematized along the same lines throughout. Compare Sorokin, for whom cloning is associated with non-reproductive sexuality and especially homosexuality; compare also Ursula K. Le Guin's "Nine Lives," whose feminized planet Libra revolts against and destroys the clone-miners that penetrate her surface in an allegorical rape. See Marleen S. Barr, "'We're at the Start of a New Ball Game and That's Why We're All Real Nervous': or, Cloning-Technological Cognition Reflects Estrangement from Women," in *Learning from Other Worlds: Estrangement, Cognition, and the Politics of Science Fiction and Utopia*, ed. Patrick Parrinder (Durham, NC: Duke University Press, 2001), 193–207.

redundancy that is the fruit of Enlightenment reasoning generates a cul-de-sac in the scientific project of accumulating information. The "hundreds of books" the narrator's father has supposedly written are the hundreds of self-investigations written across the various iterations of the clones, one of which we are reading. Without knowing it, the narrator in his story is looking for his own autobiography in someone else's words, as in his genetic research he looks for his own identity in someone else's genes.

What he finds are cycles of narratives. The reader's effort to collate series of interlinked literary texts is thereby compared to other efforts, notably genetic ones, to come to grips with an underlying phenomenon by comparing its different iterations. In the late 1700s, Friedrich Schlegel suggested that we read modern, or "interesting," literature by this comparative method.[18] The fate of "Gene Wolfe," however, suggests that the tactic may trap the reader in the same vicious circle of self-knowledge: not a permanent revolution, as the bibliographic reference to Trotsky would have it, but an eternal return à la Nietzsche. In Wolfe's information economy, literary and genetic media are themselves iterations, in different codes, of a single message about the authorial self. Self-knowledge through duplication yields overdetermination instead of the transformative "becoming" valorized by theorists of romanticism.[19] In this conspiratorial plot, even an apparent aberration from the rules, like V. Vinges's misfiled collection, becomes an allegory of the repetition of the self: the "double V" is misread as a "double you," legible, in the French-speaking colony where the novella takes place, as a *double vie* or double life.

Tyranny of History and Tyranny of Form

Aestheticians of the romantic period powerfully identify the epistemological urge for self-knowledge with the aesthetic impulse to create an object in which the artist "recognizes his own self," as Hegel puts it, and "in this reduplication of himself" turns his internal state "into knowledge for his own mind and for those of others."[20] Within Russian theory we might add claims like Batiushkov's "words are the mirror of the soul" ("slog est' zerkalo dushi") or Kroneberg's aphorisms that insist art is the materialization of the artistic

---

18 The reader searches for a "*common element* in that thorough anarchy evident throughout the entirety of modern poetry, a *characteristic train* that could not exist if there were no *common inner foundation*." Friedrich von Schlegel, *On the Study of Greek Poetry*, trans. Stuart Barnett (Albany, NY: SUNY, 2001), 22.

19 See Anne Mellor, *English Romantic Irony* (Cambridge, MA: Harvard University Press), 24–25.

20 Hegel, *Introductory Lectures on Aesthetics*, 36.

conception.[21] In an essay on Mary Shelley's *Frankenstein,* Barbara Johnson has described uncanny doubles in the romantic canon as stemming from this impulse: "The desire to create a being like oneself—which is the autobiographical desire par excellence—is also the central transgression in Mary Shelley's novel. [...] Frankenstein's monster can thus be seen as a figure for autobiography as such."[22] For Johnson, *Frankenstein* stages autobiography's monstrosity and the repression of autobiography that constitutes plot.

In both historical romanticism and in Wolfe's novella, the technologically produced double allegorizes an expressive aesthetic related to Enlightenment reason; like any artwork, it represents its creator in a sensible medium. For Shelley, the Promethean overreach of human knowledge annihilates its own process, as the monster in the novel's final lines intends to "collect my funeral pile and consume to ashes this miserable frame, that its remains may afford no light to any curious and unhallowed wretch who would create such another as I have been."[23] This simulacrum engenders no successor. In its failure, it ends itself, its narrative, and the project of imitation; it testifies to a humanity beyond the reach of mimetic technologies. The failure of "Gene Wolfe," on the other hand, is embedded in a narrative loop that repeats itself generation after generation as each clone participates in the fruitless cycle of self-production and self-destruction that is the Freudian master plot and our aesthetic text. This feature is shared by other clone texts by Wolfe, as well as works by Varley and Sorokin that unfold within narrative loops.[24] Furthermore, for all those authors this narrative cycle is associated with the succession of cultural history, something Wolfe makes present in the library, and which is at least embryonically present in Savchenko's aesthetic education as well.

21 Konstantin Batiushkov, *Sochineniia v dvukh tomakh* [Works in two volumes] (Moscow, 1989) 2:71; compare I. Y. Kroneberg's aphorism, "proizvedenie isskustva ne inoe chto, kak otelesevshaiasia ideia," *Russkie esteticheskie traktaty pervoi treti XIX veka* [Russian aesthetic tracts of the first third of the nineteenth century], ed. Z. A. Kamenskii (Moscow: Isskustvo, 1974), 290.

22 Barbara Johnson, *A World of Difference* (Baltimore: Johns Hopkins University Press, 1989), 146.

23 Mary Shelley, *Frankenstein* (New York: Signet, 1965), 210.

24 The clone in Varley's *Golden Globe* is an actor who is made to memorize the entirety of Shakespeare by his genetic original, making the replication of genetic information homologous with the passing down of textual information. See John Varley, *The Golden Globe* (New York: Ace, 1999); in *Blue Fat* it is canonical Russian writers themselves who are cloned, writing recognizably if parodically in the style of Nabokov, Dostoevsky, Tolstoy, etc.; in the process, they produce the iridescent "blue fat" that incarnates the immortal, time-transcending quality of art, and makes possible the time-travel loop through an alternative history populated by grotesque versions of Akhmatova, Brodsky, and other literary figures. See Vladimir Sorokin, *Goluboe salo [Blue fat]* (Moscow: Ad Marginem, 1999).

The shift from romantic simulacra that bring the plot to crisis and genetic copies that engender overdetermined narrative loops has to do with both literary and biological media, both of which have latterly become legible as information.[25] Whereas the simulacrum Frankenstein is annihilated together with his namesake in the mutually destructive confrontation that ends the plot, "Gene Wolfe's" murder of his namesake subsists, generation after generation, in a process of repetition that analogizes mass reproduction and information media. Like doppelgängers, clones figure genius as genesis, self-expression as self-replication—but historically conditioned by developments in biological as in other informatic media. In his short story "NRZB" (the title is an editorial abbreviation for "nerazborchivyi tekst," indicating an illegible original), whose conceit is that a work of literary genius is so rich in meaning that it encodes its creator, Aleksandr Zholkovskii recycles de Botton's 1753 quip "style is the man" to suggest that an ideal reading is therefore a resurrection.[26]

> The latest sensation here is a program to resurrect geniuses. It's been confirmed that a true artist is immortal. A poem of genius contains such a wealth of information that by referring to it, it becomes possible to return to life an author in his entirety, moreover with absolutely unitary meaning. That is, each text of a given poet always produces one and the same person. [...] The resurrection is produced not according to molecules, but according to bytes of information.[27]

"Perfect verses work like a self-reproducing genetic imprint," continues Zholkovskii, extending the metaphorical identification of textual and biological media, and "thus with the help of a semiotic program we have managed to obtain an almost perfect clone of the verses 'I remember a wonderful moment' [Ia pomniu chudnoe mgnoven'e]."[28] According to this conceit, an ideal algorithm of reading makes of every work an autobiographical expression so complete that it can be translated back from the literary into the genetic idiom—realizing the romantic trope of art's immortality through a fantasy of an information technology impervious to entropy, in which remembrance of a wondrous moment is its recreation in the flesh.

---

25 "As repositories of information," writes Marilyn Strathern of genetic science's impact on popular notions of kinship, persons related by family ties "are replicas of one another." Marilyn Strathern, *Kinship, Law and the Unexpected: Relatives Are Always a Surprise* (Cambridge: Cambridge University Press, 2005), 73.

26 Aleksandr Zholkovskii, *NRZB* [NRZB] (Moscow: Vesy, 1991), 138.

27 Ibid., 140.

28 Ibid., 141.

In this scenario, perfected information technologies supersede Nelson Goodman's distinction between autographic and allographic media. Goodman proposes that we "speak of a work of art as *autographic* if and only if the distinction between original and forgery of it is significant," and allographic if "to verify the spelling or to spell correctly is all that is required to identify an instance of the work"—"an art seems to be allographic just insofar as it is amenable to notation," he concludes.[29] Thus a photocopy of a Pushkin poem is the poem, but even the most exact copy of a Rembrandt painting is an imitation or forgery. The authors I have mentioned in this essay imagine a historical moment at which the unique human genius expressing its inner self—the ground of romantic aesthetics—becomes information, susceptible to reproduction in some notational medium. In this ultimate alienation, the mimetic project of the artist sets in motion an endlessly reproduced series.

As Friedrich Schlegel elaborates the "interesting" as an aesthetic category, its fundamental manifestation is "comparative individuality," a succession of unique but comparable entities; the interesting implies a series even etymologically, since *inter esse* means to be between. For Schlegel, such a series brings into view the small differences that justify critical attention and generates ironic play between its members. Because a series of comparable variants kindles the critical impulse for analysis and abstraction, to be interesting is also to be self-reflexive (think of romantic irony as used by Pushkin and others) by producing metafictional, critical doubles. In her development of these ideas, Sianne Ngai shows how the interesting in romanticism derives from the contemporary explosion of print culture and professional criticism. She argues that this aesthetic mode has become increasingly central to contemporary information society, which utilizes cookie-cutter cultural forms even as it commodifies novelty. Building on work by Philip Fisher, she describes how the seriality of the interesting becomes adopted as a strategy by artworks that seek to define themselves as autonomous aesthetic objects. The series of works—Monet's haystacks, Malevich's numbered compositions, Cindy Sherman's film stills—creates a context that remains in force even when one of its members is appropriated into the institutional frame of a museum gallery or syllabus. "In this manner," Ngai concludes,

> [T]he artist in the modern culture of museums (and, we might add, university syllabi and literary anthologies) finds a way of controlling the

29 Nelson Goodman, *Languages of Art: An Approach to a Theory of Symbols* (Indianapolis: Bobbs-Merrill, 1968), 112–13, 121.

> implicit commentary externally conferred by the work's anticipated 'neighbors' by supplying it with its own internal logic of betweenness. [...] Serial and/or interesting art [...] thus comes to prevail in cultures in which the artist routinely 'finds himself face to face with an intellectual world within which he is forced to see himself as an episode.'[30]

The literary analogue to Monet's haystacks is the cycle of interlinked and mutually reflecting tales—the form of clone fictions by Wolfe, Varley, and Sorokin.[31] This artificial context, Ngai argues, defends the work's integrity against critical vicissitudes and the vagaries of literary history. Here the clone theme reflects a tactic for situating the individual author and her artwork within a cultural history that incorporates art as information within a historical series. When the clone-narrator "Gene Wolfe" goes looking for the original Gene Wolfe's writing at the end of the alphabet, he is looking for the place of *The Fifth Head of Cerberus* in literary history, where it will keep company with notable 1970s science fiction authors, canonical modernists like Virginia Woolf, and histories of revolutionary thought; perhaps all these could be synthesized into a single genre of narrative preoccupied with aesthetic utopia. Albeit in a more naïve fashion, Savchenko's narrator, in learning to make sense of the world again through an interaction with works of romantic art, is also inscribing the story "Mixed Up" within that cultural history.

Alongside the metaphoric mode in which the clone represents the artwork and the artwork represents the artist's inner life, evoking questions of simulacrum, mimesis, and expression, there is thus a metonymic mode in which phenomena line up into series: of clones, of narratives, of literary and historical events. The three novellas in Wolfe's trilogy evoke the clone problematic in three different styles—the autobiography, the exotic tale, and the police dossier. Sorokin's 1999 novel *Blue Fat* too progresses through three distinct and stylistically differentiated dystopian visions—technocratic hypercapitalism, theocratic nationalism, and Stalinism. Their common element is the "blue fat" produced by clones of Akhmatova, Pasternak, and others, an anthology of whose parodic

30 Sianne Ngai, *Our Aesthetic Categories: Zany, Cute, Interesting* (Cambridge, MA: Harvard University Press, 2015), 36.

31 In the three interlinked novellas of *The Fifth Head of Cerberus*, even all the library books named by the child-narrator are cycles of stories or of biographies; in *Blue Fat*, the residue of the creative literary process is the element that links together the initial technocratic hypercapitalism, the subsequent narrative set in a nationalist theocracy, and the Stalinist totalitarianism that loops us back to the beginning.

writings make up much of the first third of the book. In this fashion, the "clone" that figures normative identity and repetition actually becomes associated with pastiche, a genre Fredric Jameson has called "blank parody" that voids style of historical content.[32] Here pastiche becomes a tool to reconfigure literary history around the artwork, which thereby contrives a context for itself. In Wolfe's helical library, the recurrent clone narrator traverses the alphabet looking for what turns out to be his own story; in Sorokin's futuristic Siberian laboratory, the clones of six canonical authors show their contributions to the Russian tradition and hence to Sorokin's own work. Because both texts exist within fixed narrative loops dealing with colonialism and totalitarianism, both Wolfe and Sorokin force us also to project political history onto their assemblages of artworks and authors. In the clone, the metaphoric axis of self-expression intersects with the metonymic axis of historical succession.[33] The clone unites both tactics of self-commentary in a single figure—the text's mimetic relationship to the original ideal image in the author's inner life, and its status within the institutional series of repetitions that makes up cultural history.

We are already dealing with problems of self-definition: the author's efforts to defend her artistic legacy and the aesthetic text's efforts to guard the integrity of its form, if only as an overdetermined narrative loop. The informatics double thus becomes a figure marking the precarious independent status of the aesthetic vis-à-vis history and institutions. In some strains of historical romanticism, the organic and integral form of the expressive artwork augurs a political utopia. For Schiller, the artist "subjugates the manifold variety of the world to the unity of his own self," so that the chaos and diversity of phenomena become a series of repetitions of the self that "annul time."[34] In this reading, the atemporal beauty of the artwork is a formal allegory of a social structure similarly characterized by play, harmony, symmetry, and fairness; the artwork's audience is invited to make this harmonious structure real in social life by imitating it. Many recent clone texts seem to act out the failure of Schiller's scheme. Wolfe's

32 Fredric Jameson, *Postmodernism, or, The Cultural Logic of Late Capitalism* (Durham, NC: Duke University Press, 1991), 17.

33 Both are critical strategies by which artworks represent themselves. On the one hand, the clone resonates with that aspect of modernism Steven Kellman has called the "self-begetting novel," in which the dream of an autonomous art is manifested as a novel's pretension to having authored itself and being a reflection of its own ideal image; on the other hand, the clone attempts to situate his text, the words we are reading, somewhere in the series of words that is the literary archive. Steven Kellman, *The Self-Begetting Novel* (New York: Columbia University Press, 1980), 1.

34 Friedrich Schiller, *Essays* (New York: Continuum, 2005), 118.

and Sorokin's narrative loops "annul time," but their overdetermination is not a utopia but a trap.

In alienating the artistic self who is the source of affect and expression in the form of information, clone fictions track the aesthetic and economic history of the twentieth century. In his famous critique of mechanical reproduction and cinema, Walter Benjamin suggests that the film actor offers the market "not only his labor but his whole self, his heart and soul."[35] More recent descriptions of the "affective labor" performed by flight attendants or customer service representatives analyze how empathic communication, both within and without the aesthetic sphere, becomes a commodity. However, Benjamin also saw a utopian potential in reproductive media. In Soviet fiction particularly futuristic genetics could be associated with technology's actualizing potential. Leon Trotsky's *Literature and Revolution* projects that a united and rationally organized humanity will refuse "the dark laws of heredity" and "create a higher, social biologic type" through new reproductive technologies.[36] This aesthetic of life-creation [*zhiznetvorchestvo*] remains explicit into the 1960s. "Feedback, that's what I want!" insists "Adam," the clone-hero of Savchenko's 1967 novel *Self-Discovery*.

> That's why the effect of art information is so low—there is no feedback between the source and the receptor. [...] There has to be direct, technical feedback, so that the information from art that is being introduced into a person can be changed to suit his individuality, character, memory, abilities, even appearance and biography. In that way his own behavior in critical situations can be played for him during synthesis [...] he can be displayed to himself—instead of an invented hero—with his spiritual world, abilities, qualities, and flaws. He can help him find himself [...] and then that great information will *become* his life experience. It will take on the universal force of truth that comes from scientific information. This will be a new kind of art—not written, not acted, not musical—everything together, expressed in biopotentials and chemical reactions. The art of synthesizing man![37]

As for Hegel, for Schiller, or for Wolfe's geneticist, the apotheosis of the aesthetic is here the feedback loop that makes humanity apprehensible to itself

35 Walter Benjamin, *Illuminations* (New York: Schocken, 1969), 231.

36 Leon Trotsky, *Literature and Revolution*, trans. Rose Strunsky (Chicago: Haymarket Books, 2005), 207.

37 Vladimir Savchenko, *Self-Discovery* (New York: McMillan, 1979), 239–40.

in the form of information.[38] But the belief in perfectibility through feedback loops can generate a dismal cul-de-sac as well as the triumphal progress of *zhiznetvorchestvo* or Schiller's atemporal utopia. In Wolfe's colonial allegory or Sorokin's depiction of Stalin as the master of history, the materialization of the artist's self in the world as it occurs in contemporary clone fictions creates an eddy within historical time. The single narrative form that proliferates from this temporal loop becomes, in its ineluctable return, identified with tyranny as well as with the integrity of the autonomous artwork, proliferating itself in endless series according to its own law of form.

Romantic Doubles and Postmodern Clones

Mimetic reproduction of the artist's inner self, the interesting artwork in a landscape of information media, narrative overdetermination—the science fiction conceit of the self reproduced in an informatics medium bundles together a set of related aesthetic preoccupations from historical romanticism and revises them in important ways. A brief consideration of Dostoevsky's 1846 *The Double* [*Dvoinik*]—perhaps the most canonical double text in the Russian tradition—shows how these problematics occur in a coherent complex, if not a single figure, within historical romanticism. The double is apparently summoned to Golyadkin's workplace by the clerk's desire to "resolve" his self-doubt ("on nachal zhelat', chtob khot' bog znaet kak, da tol'ko razreshilos' by vse poskoree").[39] "Fate" takes him at his word ("sud'ba poimala gospodina Goliadkina") and manifests a simulacrum in which Golyadkin sees himself.

> This was a different Mr. Golyadkin, quite different but at the same time identical with the first—the same height, same build, dressed the same, bald in the same place; in short, the resemblance was perfect; nothing, absolutely nothing had been omitted, so that had they stood side by side, not a soul would have undertaken to say who was the real

38 Ibid., 250. Adam's fantasy of self-perfection through biogenetic information technologies looks much like the final pages of *Literature and Revolution*: the perfectibility of human beings, now adaptable to disease resistance, winged flight, hostile alien planets, and "the blue ocean depths, where he will go without diving gear." Trotsky, *Literature and Revolution*, 207.

39 F. M. Dostoevskii, *Polnoe sobranie sochinenii v tridtsati tomakh* [Complete collection of works in thirty volumes] (Leningrad: Nauka, 1972), 1.146; Fyodor Dostoevsky, *The Double*, trans. George Bird (Bloomington: Illinois University Press, 1958), 86.

> Mr. Golyadkin, and who the counterfeit, who the old, and who the new, who the original, and who the copy.[40]

As is a commonplace of the criticism, this simulacrum is also the revelation of suppressed self-knowledge.[41] Golyadkin Senior's attitude of meekness and forthrightness is itself a mask hiding the characteristics that Golyadkin Junior embodies for him—ambition, sensual appetites, social manipulation, et cetera. This interesting situation of comparison between the two Golyadkins, the effort to distinguish the "autographic" original from the counterfeit, is immediately blended into Golyadkin's work as a copy clerk. Hoping to resolve this new doubt over his own existence aroused by his comparison to the double("on [...] zhelal, chtob khot' kakim-nibud' obrazom razreshilis' ego somneniia"),[42] he recovers from his shock to find himself "automatically and unconsciously guiding his pen over the paper. Not trusting himself, he began checking what he had written, but could make nothing of it."[43] Thus Golyadkin's self-doubts call into being the double to which he compares himself, but his relationship to the double leads to a new vertigo of doubt that culminates in a comparison of his scrivening with the original text. This text too becomes reduced to confusion as Golyadkin's copying becomes "automatic and unconscious" ("mashinal'no i bessoznatel'no") and apparently illegible. The mysterious "fate" that drives the plot seems related to this unconscious, mechanical force that takes over Golyadkin's pen, a force of predetermination that persists even in the book's last lines: "Alas! He had felt this coming for a long time!" ("Uvy! on eto davno uzhe predchustvoval!").[44]

"The bureaucrat is the parody of the Poet," remarks Friedrich Kittler of Hoffmann's 1814 "The Golden Pot," another tale of doubles and copy clerks, in which the writer achieves an image of his own individuality through the "unconscious dexterity" with which he takes dictation from his mysterious inner self.[45] The mechanical power that exerts a determinate power on Golyadkin's pen is Dostoevsky's artistic vision. Here and throughout the plot, Golyadkin traces that literary destiny, which he can apprehend only as a "fate" that becomes

---

40 Dostoevsky, *The Double*, 89.

41 For a summary, see, for example, Julian W. Connolly, "The Ethical Implications of Narrative Point of View in Dostoevsky's *The Double*," *Dostoevsky Studies* vol. 17 (2013): 99.

42 Dostoevskii, *Polnoe sobranie*, 1:147.

43 Dostoevsky, *The Double*, 90.

44 Ibid., 254; Dostoevskii, 1:228.

45 Friedrich Kittler, *Discourse Networks 1800/1900* (Stanford, CA: Stanford University Press, 1990), 98–99.

realized in the narrative. In a compact cluster, though not in a single figure, we have here issues of expression and identity; issues of information media; and issues of overdetermination. Although the doppelgänger is heavily implicated in all of these, it is not sufficient to constitute them. As we saw in the case of Shelley, the appearance of the simulacrum in Dostoevsky leads to a breakdown of mimetic meaning rather than a fixed system of information; the framing plot too ends in a crisis rather than cycling into a structure of eternal return. We could extend this observation into a wide range of texts—in "The Golden Pot" too it is an uncanny simulacrum, a bewitched mirror, that interrupts Anselmus's copying and triggers the denouement.

I hope to have shown that the continuity between clones and romantic literature does not come from uncanny doubles precisely, but from a larger complex of tropes, focused on a coherent constellation of aesthetic concerns. From this perspective a study of the romantic doppelgänger goes hand in hand with the equally key but understudied figure of the copy clerk. They appear together in Hoffmann's "The Golden Pot," "The Doubles," and *The Life and Opinions of the Tomcat Murr*; in Gogol's tales of scrivening errors and hallucinatory doubles; in Flaubert's twin copyists Bouvard and Pécuchet; and in Melville's Bartleby, who one day preferred not to check his copy against the original. In the twentieth century, technological shifts in the reproduction of written text begin to develop these motifs in the informatics direction described above. For instance, the mirror images and fatalistic plots that thematize Clarice Lispector's *The Hour of the Star* and Nabokov's *Bend Sinister* go hand in hand with the typewriter at which Lispector's heroine labors at dictation, and with Nabokov's villainous, uncanny "padograph," which reproduces handwriting and affords "one purchaser after another [...] the luxury of seeing the essence of his incomplex personality distilled by the magic of an elaborate instrument."[46] In this literary genealogy of doubles and copy clerks we start to see how the alienation of the artist or producer of text creeps, by way of increasingly powerful techniques of notation and technologies of reproduction, into the artistic process of reproducing inner genius in an information medium.

Perhaps no contemporary artist in any language so self-consciously stages this shift as Vladimir Sorokin, who has written clone texts including his 1999 novel *Blue Fat*, his screenplay for the 2004 film *4*, the 2005 opera libretto *Rozental's Children* (*Deti Rozentalia*), and the 2013 *Telluria* (*Telluriia*). Sorokin is arguably motivated in his drift toward science fiction by issues of reproductive

46 Vladimir Nabokov, *Bend Sinister* (New York: Time, 1964), 61.

media. Nariman Skakov observes that in *Blue Fat*, Sorokin's first clone text and his first piece to be composed on a computer, "the trope of cloning—a variation on the theme of the computer operation of cutting and pasting—possesses a determining structural function."[47] Indeed, in Russian as in English, "cloning" (*klonirovanie*) has the meaning in informatics of a duplicated complex system of code. Sorokin's longstanding interest in technological media appears above all in his clone texts, where authors or "machines for writing" are themselves mass produced by genetic technologies.[48] His first major clone text, *Blue Fat*, wears its clones proudly as a metaphor for literary production and commodification. Our initial narrator, a "biophilologist," sends the works of genetic duplicates of famous authors by clone-pigeon-post (*golub'*) to his homosexual lover (*goluboi*) along with his own erotic epistles. The conceit of the cloned author figures and motivates Sorokin's parodic stylizations; it also represents the autonomous immortality of art insofar as in the act of writing the clones produce a subcutaneous substance, blue fat, which is impervious to entropy, i.e. is "timeless." The very first of Sorokin's interpolated clone texts, a garbled parody of Dostoevsky, brings out precisely the elements we stressed in our reading of *The Double*. The clone in Dostoevsky's prose is characterized by a nervous tic of repetition, associated with a foreshadowing or reproductive power articulated here by "Count Rashetovsky":

> In all my life I have not been led to experience such a, not so much a presentiment, as a—*predestination* of events, as today today today! [...] Imagine, gentlemen, I had not yet drunk my coffee, when Misha [...] swiftly swiftly swiftly hands me the envelope, and I already precisely foreknow the contents of the letter, the plot, so to speak![49]

The count's foreknowledge of the "plot" and of the contents of this letter seems actually to apply to the framing narrative, which ends with the delivery of a letter whose text began the novel; indeed, one of such letters contains the transcription of the clone-Dostoevsky's prose. The count's intuition, expressed

---

47 Nariman Skakov, "Slovo v 'Romane'" [*Word/Discourse in "Roman"*], *Novoe literaturnoe obozrenie* 119 (2013): 84.

48 For a fuller reading, see Jacob Emery, "A Clone Playing Craps Will Never Abolish Change: Randomness and Fatality in Vladimir Sorokin's Clone Fictions," *Science Fiction Studies*, vol. 41 (July 2014): 413–15, 422–29.

49 Vladimir Sorokin, *Sobranie sochinenii v trekh tomakh* [*Collected works in three volumes*] (Moscow: Ad Marginem, 2002), 3:36.

through stammering repetition, thus figures the reader's knowledge, at the end of the book, of the contents of the letter that Stalin—who has attempted to appropriate art's immortality by hypodermically injecting the blue fat into his brain, which causes his cerebrum to expand and fill the universe, from which apocalypse he reemerges as the slave of the biophilologist's lover—surgically extracts from the body of a clone-carrier-pigeon on the last page. The *mise en abyme* of the pseudo-Dostoevsky narrative is rendered a double of the larger text, and the system of circularity and repetition that makes it a stable and self-contained unit within which all knowledge is foreknowledge. A kind of triumph of the romantic artist's aim to overcome time by patterning the material of the world after the genius of the artistic personality, this result is at the same time identified with uncanny developments that parallel those in Gene Wolfe's *The Fifth Head of Cerberus*—an all-male homosexual technocratic rationality that eliminates biological reproduction, associated with political tyranny and with a hellish afterlife in an infernal underworld.

Aesthetic Essence

Savchenko is less sophisticated as a literary artist than Wolfe or Sorokin, and the complication of the romantic categories is not part of his central project, which has rather to do with the utopian potential of cybernetic technology. This technology is however strongly marked as aesthetic potential. *Self-Discovery*, which imagines a means for "synthesizing information into a person" and whose plot centers on the production of multiple genetic copies of a scientist in an amniotic cybernetic vat, makes explicit the link between informatics, identity, and the imagined apotheosis of a romantic art of self-creation and self-discovery, basically as we encounter it in "Mixed Up." Here too the "computer-womb" that gives birth to duplicates and confronts human individuals with themselves is part of a project of perfection of the species. Although identified with "a new kind of art. [...] The art of synthesizing man!" the terms of this art are familiar from the utopian proclamations of aesthetic theorists from Trotsky to Schiller.[50] As in "Mixed Up," the duplicating technology invokes the coherence of the human genius it cybernetically encodes; it cannot be fully exploited with experimental rabbits, since "they have no consciousness, no will, no satisfaction with self."[51] The strength of the subject's personality is the condition

50 Savchenko, *Self-Discovery*, 304.

51 Ibid., 250.

of the duplication. Both works can be contextualized in Russian literature with cybernetic laboratory experiments like the one in the Zholkovskii story alluded to above or Zinovii Iur'ev's 1978 "Black Box" (*Chernyi Iasha*), in which artificial intelligence research leaves the narrator-scientist with a cybernetic duplicate of his own self.

The subject matter of Savchenko's utopian novel reappears, however, in his 1987 *Kidnappers of Essences* (*Pokhititeli sutei*), in darker terms—as if the author has been forced to come to terms with the historical and technological developments that shift the ground of romantic idealism, or as if the utopian potential of this technology cannot survive a plot that sets it free from the laboratory to enter into social practice. In this text, cybernetic duplication of the personality has been implemented as an interplanetary transportation technology; the personality can be alienated from the body and beamed from planet to planet, or stored on "cassettes" and transported physically. Once again, this technology is unique to intelligent beings, since the transmitted self is a special kind of information that can hold itself together. Yet offering to this medium "one's whole self, one's heart and soul" (as Benjamin writes of the film actor in the essay quoted above) does not in this case wholly safeguard and realize the potential of the self, but rather renders it vulnerable.

Kidnappers of Essences is a detective novel in which the best qualities of human beings—their self-control, courage, brilliance, and so on—are purloined in transit and sold on the black market for cash. The alienation of the self for the market is bitterly compared to the reduced condition of art, which dreams of great genius but is only a meager piece of the self offered to the market: "I give you a poem, you give me pennies ... Art for sale."[52] To rail against worldliness in the name of art is a familiar stance, of course; what interests me here is how the diminishment of the artist stems from the aesthetic technology's passage from the laboratory into an economic, political, and institutional context. Savchenko's terms strikingly parallel those we have seen in texts by Wolfe and Sorokin. Although the technology is supposed to provide proof of the entropy-resistant integrity of the human self, it also makes the self vulnerable, potentially alienable; it makes evident the need for a political and state apparatus to protect, and ultimately to define, the same self that was supposed to generate a field of control over the material in which it would be manifested without loss. Those same definitions set the market

52 Vladimir Savchenko, *Pokhititeli sutei* [Kidnappers of essences] (Kiev: Radians'kii pis'mennik, 1988), 273.

value of personal qualities, and are compared even to the institutions that set the terms of literary value: the black marketeers who sell human essences are likened to Dante scholars exploiting and parasitizing the genius of the poet for their own academic careers.[53] Indeed, the transportation hub where the recording and transmission of personalities takes place is architecturally a series of circles, alluding to the geography of Dante's inferno. The paradise of aesthetic freedom—self-discovery and self-production—thus yields a hellish world of police surveillance, alienation in the marketplace, and institutional exploitation of culture. The "living information" of the personality becomes encoded, as in Wolfe or Sorokin, as a nightmarish land of the dead.

I have suggested in this essay that the replication of the self as information is broadly implicated, for writers of genre fiction as for self-consciously postmodern authors who aim at academic audiences, in a set of aesthetic concerns and even a set of aesthetic strategies that defend the independence and integrity of the expressive artwork, more or less successfully, through overdetermining repetitions. These repetitions are ambiguously identified with the ideal of the autarchic and self-sustaining work of genius grounded in the creative self, as well as with the horror of institutional control that limits cultural life. Some years ago I had a long argument, lasting late into the night, with a scholar who had suggested that the amount of information in any artwork could be quantified precisely; this led to discussions of how to compare disparate sensory media, how to account for information brought to the table by the reader, and so on, and ultimately resolved into a dispute over whether a copy of *War and Peace* contains the exact same amount of information as a block of stone of the same weight. Digital technologies, which convert into quantities of bytes artworks of all media—to say nothing of non-aesthetic objects and increasingly detailed data on human behavior—seem to provide the common measure that makes perfect duplication and perfect conversion possible. In the same stroke, they force us to ask hard questions about the special category of the aesthetic—about the degree to which the aesthetic persists as a special category in the terms we have inherited from historical romanticism, at a time when the human self whose expression and discovery grounds aesthetic experience has become imagined as alienable and reproducible information. There is no entity that has a larger stake in this discussion than artworks themselves, and the science fiction discourses of cloning and cybernetics make major statements on the point.

---

53 Ibid., 273.

CHAPTER 7

Writing and Technology: Writing the Self in "Real Time"

Kristina Toland,
Bowdoin College

Today, we need to understand the process of technical evolution given that we are experiencing the deep opacity of contemporary technics; we do not immediately understand what is being played out in technics, nor what is being profoundly transformed therein, even though we unceasingly have to make decisions regarding technics, the consequences of which are felt to escape us more and more. And in day to day technical reality, we cannot spontaneously distinguish the long-term processes of transformation from spectacular but fleeting technical innovations.

Bernard Stiegler[1]

Electronic circuitry is an extension of the central nervous system.

Marshall McLuhan[2]

Machines create my past. Machines create melancholy. [. . .] Machines control our memories, they own the fundamental materials that shape us, and they manage the structures that generate human meaning and perspective. We long for our humanity.

Ollivier Dyens[3]

Our Technological Being

Technology is an inescapable condition of human life, and today it defines much of what has traditionally been thought of as "human nature." This fact

1 Bernard Stiegler, *Technics and Time, 1: The Fault of Epimetheus* (Stanford, CA: Stanford University Press, 1998), 21.

2 Marshall McLuhan and Quentin Fiore, *The Medium is the Message: An Inventory of Effects* (New York: Random House, 1967), 40.

3 Ollivier Dyens, "The Sadness of the Machine," in *Memory, Documents of Contemporary Art*, ed. Ian Farr (Cambridge, MA: The MIT Press, 2012), 78–79.

urges a radical reimagining of posthuman subjectivity. While we engage in the tasks of self-conceptualization and self-creation, the perceptions of ourselves in time are shaped by our environment and tools that continue to blur the boundaries between nature, technology, and humanity. Our use of language, as a technical structure, is just one instance of this tool dependency.[4] Today, we cannot imagine our lives without technology, and technology seems increasingly to have become the inseparable extension of ourselves, enhancing our abilities to think, communicate, and remember. Cognition itself is essentially prosthetic—meaning that we use technology to articulate our perceptions of the world and of ourselves, and because of this, our evolution is grounded in *technics*.

Underscoring our thinking as essentially techno-logical, Bernard Stiegler, a contemporary French philosopher who expounded on the idea of *technics* in his multi-volume *Technics and Time*,[5] demonstrates how *technics*—the conceptual amalgamation of technology, techniques, and the technical[6]—mediates the perception of the self in time, and thus, invents our memory. Stiegler emphasizes the constitutive role of *technics* in the genesis of temporality and the emergence of the human as a temporal being. Hence, central to his philosophical ideas is the relationship between *technics* and time, as well as *technics*-as-time, where temporality is related to the act of writing as both supplementary and

---

4 Walter Ong, in his 1982 book *Orality and Literacy: The Technologizing of the Word*, wrote that literate human beings are "beings whose thought processes do not grow out of simply natural powers but out of these powers as structured, directly or indirectly, by the technology of writing. Without writing, the literate mind would not and could not think as it does, not only when engaged in writing, but normally even when it is composing its thoughts in oral form." In other words, he argues that even when one is expressing oneself orally, the literate human being is reading himself and interpreting himself *to the letter*—that is, he is "literally" in the process of writing himself. See Walter J. Ong, *Orality and Literacy: The Technologizing of the Word* (London: Methuen, 1982), 77.

5 A philosopher of science and technology, Stiegler is the founder and head of the *Institut de recherche et d'Innovation* (Institute of Research and Innovation) (IRI). He has authored numerous texts on the subject. His most important contributions include *Technics and Time, 1: The Fault of Epimetheus* (1998), *Technics and Time, 2: Disorientation* (2009), *Technics and Time, 3: Cinematic Time and the Question of Malaise* (2010)—all published by Stanford, CA: Stanford University Press—and *Symbolic Misery*, Volumes 1 & 2, published, respectively, in 2014 and 2015, by Polity Press (Cambridge, MA).

6 *Technics*, as an essentially originary prosthetic supplementation of the human, is defined by mobilizing the Derridean idea of *différance*—a concept based on the interplay of two terms, difference (spatial) and deferral (temporal)—as a mode of composition, mechanization, and techno-logical exteriorization of our experiences. See Stiegler, *Technics and Time, 2*, 3-5. For the original explanation of *différance*, see Jacques Derrida, *Margins of Philosophy* (Chicago: University of Chicago Press, 1982), 3-27. Stiegler pushes Derrida's argument for *différance* further, placing it in relation to *tekhnè* by connecting it back to life or *physis*.

originary. Writing, as the process and product of technology and as a prosthetic communicative medium, can thus be compared to "a language machine, producing a language of synthesis."[7] Furthermore, because writing is always "the time of invention," and the past is always a form of projection that exists in an already historical present, writing appears as a materialized trace—the expression of interiority. The present-ness of the past in the moment of remembering and writing relates to the idea of memory as a product of writing technology. The moment of writing, which can also be seen as a moment determined *by* writing, marks the appearance of the concepts of "historiality" and "history."[8] It creates our sense of self in time. It is this technologically-mediated memory that is at the core of autobiographical writing.[9]

Changes in modes of communication—writing is just one of these modes—force us to adjust to those new forms in order to continue to fulfill our essential desire to comprehend our existence in time. This is also the central theme of "life-writing"—a term that signals the oceanic nature of autobiographic writings. In this paper, I will be using "life-writing" and autobiography interchangeably. Life-writing is the projection of the past onto the present using various communicative forms of text and image. As it concerns questions about who we are, as well as who we were, life-writing is reliant on the technical conditions of its belated appearance.

We live in an electronically dominated, multimedia, multiuser, interconnected reality, one where we create, select, and remake ourselves and our memories using the currently available technologies of inscription and communication. Embroiled in what has been keenly termed a "paroxysm of personal

---

7 Stiegler, *Technics and Time, 1*, 205.

8 Stiegler, *Technics and Time, 2*, 30. In the first volume, Stiegler explains: "If the already-there is what constitutes temporality in that it opens me out to my historiality, must not this already-there also be constitutive in its positive facticity [...] in the sense that its material organization in form constitutes historicity itself, prior and beyond history?" See Stiegler, *Technics and Time, 1*, 240.

9 Autobiographical subjectivity is articulated and exteriorized, and thus, also prosthetic. To use Stiegler's idea of the term, "prosthetic" here does not operate in the sense of compensation for a loss or insufficiency, but rather as a means of putting a thing in front—*pros-thesis*. In other words, set in front, and in advance of. Thus, it functions as a technique for spatialization and temporilization (foresight), which are processes essential to cognition. Furthermore, Stiegler states, "a pros-thesis is what is placed in front, that is, what is outside, outside what it is placed in front of. However, if what is outside constitutes the very being of what it lies outside of, then this being is *outside itself*. The being of humankind is to be outside itself." See Stiegler, *Technics and Time, 1*, 193.

culture,"[10] living in the "dot com" era, we have come to document and project ourselves through "selfies," wikis, social network profiles, blogs, tweets, Instagram images, personal pages, online diaries, and archives, all of which are generated via computers. Our "I" is conditioned by personalized iClouds, iTunes, and other i-prefixed digital tools and devices. Our memories—a mass of virtual memorabilia that encompass photos, videos, and other documents—are stored online, in file hosting cloud storage services, on external drives, and via other digital memory extensions. As our virtual lives become more complex and consuming, our media literacy shapes the ways in which the literature of the self—life-writing —is constructed. The processes of creating an "identity"—unsettled in the nature of autobiographical subjectivity—is part of an ongoing, but also coinciding, transformation. The technology of writing is an inseparable constituent part of this process, continually manifested through new technologies, even if the consequences of *technics* in our lives increasingly escape us.

While scholars of both technophile and technophobe schools make pertinent claims about the aftereffects of media on our cognitive and corporeal habits or, at least, of their development alongside the progress of new media, following Stiegler, I propose that our interdependency with technology and the inherent prosthetic nature of our existence remains essentially stable, even when manifested differently. Autobiography, as a genre dealing with the questions of self-perception, bears out this argument.

Yet the speed at which exponentially expanding technology transforms our capacity to grasp its workings as well as its ensuing implications can often be quite disorienting. In considering how technology structures our concept of the self, this article seeks to answer the following question: How does this technology-dictated shift affect the genre of autobiography?[11]

While exploring alternative modes of experiencing the self by utilizing recent autobiographical projects by Lev Rubinstein (b. 1947), this essay underscores the vital interdependence of the human and the technical in the writing self, and it demonstrates how *technics is* a means of mediating

10 Nancy K. Miller, "But Enough About Me, What Do You Think of My Memoir?," *The Yale Journal of Criticism* 13, no. 2 (2000): 421.

11 In fact, it is important to question whether this virtual form of life is qualitatively different from the preceding era of the analog (such as home-film footage, scrapbooks, handwritten diaries, letters, postcards, books, etc.). After all, the concept of "I" is an image that exists at a distance from lived experiences: cast into narrative linguistic conventions, it always exceeds them. See John Zuern, "Online Lives: Introduction," special issue, *Biography* 26, no. 1 (2003): xi.

phenomenological consciousness. The concept of *technics* is particularly valuable in analyzing life-writing experiments, as it explores the idea of the self as a remembering and self-documenting being vis-à-vis a text. Thus, autobiography offers particularly fertile ground for exploring man's prosthetic nature; as one faces the questions of time, memory, authenticity, and amnesia, the autobiographer—in our case, Rubinstein—looks for new means to be re-embodied. Here, I demonstrate how the autobiographer is constituted through his relationship with *technics*, by which he gains the ability to view and exteriorize himself as a remembering being, one who "invents himself in the technical by inventing the tool."[12]

Writing, especially autobiographical writing, forms a complex cultural response to the technological impacts on our perceptual systems—specifically, the systems of memory keeping and self-reflection. It is a process by which life "proceeds by other means than life."[13] In writing, we perceive ourselves in the process of exteriorizing the self. This relationship of one's self to self-representation is the "techno-logical" dynamic of co-individuation and negotiation, where "the writer is affected in writing."[14] More than just a means of creating a record, writing constitutes the *who* of the autobiographical subject. As I demonstrate later, this "auto-effect" is central to Rubinstein's interactive, multimedia, life-writing experiments. Rubinstein's social media postings and live performances constitute new, posthumanist manifestations of subjectivity, enhanced by *technics*.

While grappling with the impossibility of an "authentic" written record (meaning: original, truthful, accurate) in the post-postmodern era, Rubinstein's autobiographical projects from 1985 to the present illustrate a shift away from the logocentric paradigm of typical linear, written narratives. Instead, they gesture toward the auto-bio-graphing act that extends into technologically enhanced and articulated sentience. Moving away from his earlier, mostly textual—although already experimentally conceptualist—formats to new forms that are driven by images, multimedia, and interactive textualities, and then culminating in his live performances and online publishing, such an iterative textual economy draws our attention to alternative genre possibilities. Thus, this article also underscores the role of new media, which creates the

12 Stiegler, *Technics and Time, 1*, 141.

13 Stiegler, *Technics and Time, 2*, 6–7. See the outline of Stiegler's argument in "Introduction" of the second volume of *Technics and Time, 2*.

14 Ibid., 37.

conditions for the existence of posthuman autobiographical identities shaped primarily by virtual, network-based interactions and mediations.

Ways of Writing the Self

To reiterate briefly, we comprehend ourselves in time through exteriorization, which is constituted through our use of tools and external aids—our prostheses—where writing is but one example. Additionally, the modalities of mediation available at any given present moment determine our past as technical specificities, as "media or grounds for recording the past," conditioned by the modes of expression that are unique to each period.[15] In the process of life-writing, the autobiographer anticipates himself—specifically, his current sense of self—by returning to his past; yet, the past he constructs is not, in fact, *his actual* past. Instead, it is an invented, recollected past. Hence, this entire process is a prosthetic return.

Here, it is important to extend our understanding of life-writing to other forms of documentation, such as "light-writing," known as photography, and its sister art, cinematography.[16] These alternative forms of recording, constituting different visual textualities, have played a significant role in the development of the autobiography genre. They have provided some unusual, "unliterary" solutions to the problems of autobiographical self-representation, both by supplying new aids for remembering and by offering new contingencies of seeing and telling. Faltering or suppressed memories, and their resulting generated falsehoods, have been among autobiographers' chief anxieties. Yet, endowed with a unique referential capacity, photography, the so-called "mirror with memory," came to corroborate life-writing as a guarantor of "natural"[17]

15 Ibid., 5.

16 Increasingly, light, as the means to "write" photography, is being replaced by electromagnetic radiation, which is used to create digital images.

17 According to Louis-Jacques-Mandé Daguerre's characterization of his invention, "a chemical process gave [Nature] the power to reproduce herself." Louis-Jacques-Mandé Daguerre, "Daguerreotype," c. 1838, as quoted in Helmut Gernsheim and Alison Gernsheim, *L. J. M. Daguerre: The History of the Diorama and the Daguerreotype* (New York: Dover Publications, 1968), 81. And as André Bazin, one the early theoreticians of photography, famously wrote: "The objective nature of photography confers on it a credibility absent from all other picture making. In spite of any objections our critical spirit may offer, we are forced to accept as real the existence of the object reproduced, actually *re*-presented, set before us, that is to say, in time and space." André Bazin, *What is Cinema?*, vol. 1, trans. Hugh Gray (London: University of California Press, LTD, 1967), 13, as quoted in Scott McQuire, *Visions of Modernity: Representation, Memory, Time and Space in the Age of the Camera* (London: Sage,

representation: existing outside of the inherent "self-other" and "author-subject-object" dilemmas. Ostensibly, these tools provided physical evidence, independent from an author's subjective self-perception.

In his continuous effort to elucidate the concept of *technics*-as-time, existing via writing and other means of recording, Stiegler returns to the idea of technics as a "surface of *différance*, an instrumental mirror that reflects time as differentiation, as differing, as deferred," now vis-à-vis photography. Yet he also interrogates this connection. Using the "mirror" analogy, he calls *technics* a reflective "instrumental mirror," which tests the photographic "gaze."[18] Indeed, the photographic technique is a tempting, but thorny metaphor for the autobiographical process of looking at oneself from a variety of vantage points and at specific time-instances. Autobiographic and photographic "truths" [19] need to be, and have been, questioned by both autobiographers and their readers, most especially, by literary and visual art scholars. In any case, Stiegler's inviting evocation of writing as an "instrumental mirror reflecting time" is well suited to the discussion of autobiographical subjectivity, where the text is the surface upon which a life is auto-bio-graphed—fixed through the act of inscription. To build on this metaphor in relation to memory, writing as *technics* is the mirror by which the autobiographer, while looking at his past, finds his reflection (and that of the world around him), thus allowing him to form a perception of himself.[20]

1998), 13. The *indexical* nature of photography has been at the center of a rich discourse by scholars ranging from Charles Sanders Peirce and Roland Barthes to contemporary media theorists and art historians.

18 See Stiegler, *Technics and Time, 2*, 41.

19 One of the key concerns in autobiographical self-exposés, from St. Augustine's to Jean-Jacques Rousseau's *Confessions*, and even to Nabokov's *Speak, Memory* (1951), was to create an authentic account of oneself. As Marcus Moseley suggests, Rousseau sets the key for the genre themes—namely, sincerity, truthfulness, and the importance of childhood—as the genre fundamentals. See the introduction to Marcus Moseley's book, *Being for Myself Alone: Origins of Jewish Autobiography* (Stanford, CA: Stanford University Press, 2006). Rousseau set out to present himself as "painted from nature and in all its truth" in his 1769 *Confessions*. Using the *camera obscura* as a metaphor for truthfulness, he foretold the future relationship between the photographic camera and the genre. See Jean-Jacques Rousseau, "The Neuchâtel Preface to The Confessions of J.-J. Rousseau," in *The Confessions; and Correspondence, Including the Letters to Malesherbes* (Hanover, NH: University Press of New England, 1995), 589.

20 Stiegler discusses the idea of memory in Chapters 3 and 4 of *Technics and Time, 2*.

Contemporary memory enhancements and instruments for writing—electronic communication devices, our "companions"[21]—are the current forms of our prosthetic selves. The promise of truth once held by a photographic likeness is now given over to another image-centered regime—video communication, which is now often broadcast in "real time." Escaping the flawed nature of the photograph, ideally, the video image is no longer stored, manipulated, and transmitted, but is now experienced as the reproducing event occurs simultaneously—at least, supposedly. In the early twenty-first century, life-writing also takes place in "real time," in a temporality made possible by the internet. Here, life-writing becomes the live writing of blogs, tweets, and social media posts. Such an intimate, immediate presence is recorded to be shared while, simultaneously, the author's identity itself is continuously being shaped through his or her virtual life. While this provides the benefits of immediacy, accessibility, and a superior means of data capture, storage, transmission, and connectedness, we should ask what is lost when our lives, identities, personas, and memories are entrusted to a machine.

Live Life-Writing

One example of the new forms of life-writing is Rubinstein's combination of performances and performative textualities, which constitute a part of his online identity. Rubinstein, a contemporary writer, essayist, conceptualist artist, journalist, cultural critic, columnist, blogger, and performer, is best known as a celebrated *maître* of the Moscow Conceptualist School, as well as a staunch political activist.[22] Borne out of the high-tech viscera of the internet

---

21 For a discussion of the "Companions" project, led by the University of Sheffield and fourteen other partners in the US and UK, see the article by Paul Longley Arthur, "Digital Biography: Capturing Lives Online," *a/b: Auto/Biography Studies* 24, no. 1 (2009).

22 A librarian by training, Rubinstein developed his index card catalog poetry style in the early-to-mid-seventies. His poem "That's me" (1995) was the "closing statement" of his conceptualist card-catalog phase. Since the mid-nineties, as a contributor to a number of periodicals, Rubinstein has been writing journalistic prose (more specifically, *publitsistika*), only performing his already-famous card-poems. These poems bear a strong autobiographical tone. Rubinstein's life story can be assembled from utterances scattered throughout, as many of Rubinstein's lyrical heroes speak to his personal experiences, using the narrating first person "I." For instance, Rubinstein uses the first person in the poems "S chetverga na piatnitsu" ["From Thursday to Friday"] (1985), "Poiavlenie geroia" ["The emergence of the hero"] (1986), "Mama myla ramu" ["Mother was washing the windowsill"] (1987), and "I vot ia zdes'" ["Here I am"] (1994), to name a few.

and refracted through the prism of current events, his activities today are anchored in recollections of the Soviet past. Specifically, Rubinstein's online publishing and video-recorded performances represent a new dimension in multimedia experimentation within the autobiographical genre. Addressing enduring autobiographer's concerns, the media-besotted Rubinstein continuously returns to the theme of childhood and the ideas of authenticity and originality while simultaneously deconstructing narrative conventions and questioning the status of the text through live performances and online posts. Here, I first address Rubinstein's social media life before moving on to discuss what I call his "nostalgia performances."

Rubinstein's current auto-bio-graphing project is more than a return to the significant times of his earlier life. The greater project is a way to re-experience the past self in the present moment. It is about collecting pieces of the self and recomposing them, accomplished by using unexpected documents and sources, as well as a minimalist, postmodern textual pastiche of, as he calls them, "linguistic instances."[23] Rubinstein also continues to produce writings that essentially carry on his card-poetry experiments, formulated in the period between the mid-seventies and the mid-nineties. Containing mostly "linguistic ready-mades,"[24] mirroring diverse generic conventions, composed of short sequential phrases written on index cards, these poems are recomposed, each time anew, in the act of reading. Underscoring the performative function of the text, his card catalog (*kartoteka*) is an enduring metaphor for textuality itself, where, as he explains, "the process of reading is more important than the text

---

Continuing with the author-centrism of his poetry and the theme of the Soviet past, Rubinstein's essays, collected in *Reguliarnoe pis'mo* [Regular writing] (1996) and *Sluchai iz iazyka* [Linguistic instances] (1998), are also sharply focused on the personal perspective. His more recent collections, entitled *Domashnee muzitsirovanie* [Domestic music-making] (2000), *Pogonia za shliapoi* [Chasing after the hat] (2004), *Dukhi vremeni* [Spirits of time] (2007), and *Znaki vnimaniia* [Signs of attention] (2012), among others, are likewise solipsistic and pronouncedly nostalgic. Covering current issues (such as nationalism, xenophobia, religion, advertising, politics, culture, and art), in his contributions to online forums like stengazeta.net (*Stengazeta*), polit.ru (*Polit.Ru*), grani.ru (*Grani*), and bg.ru (*Bol'shoi gorod*), and before these, in ej.ru (*Ezhenedel'nyi zhurnal*), itogi.ru (*Itogi*), and politburo.ru (*Politbiuro*), Rubinstein has remained autobiographically focused.

23 "Linguistic instances" or "episodes from language" (*sluchai iz iazyka*) is a phrase from Rubinstein's eponymous essay, which also became a title of his 1998 book *Sluchai iz iazyka* [Linguistic instances] (Saint Petersburg: Limbakh, 1998).

24 I borrow this term "linguistic ready-mades" from Gerald Janecek. See Gerald Janecek, "Citationality in Lev Rubinstein's 'Šestikrylyj Serafim,'" *Russian, Croatian and Serbian, Czech and Slovak, Polish Literature* 66, no. 1 (2009): 37–50.

itself because it creates the text" ("*vazhen ne stol'ko sam text, skol'ko protsess chteniia, kotoryi, sobstvenno, etot text i sozdaet*").[25]

Rather than as an outlet for political activism or an educational mission, Rubinstein considers his involvement in online communities such as Facebook[26] and LiveJournal, as well as other social media sites he has joined, as a personal experiment and "continuation of his card-style life in a different technological situation" ("*prodolzhenie kartotechnoi zhizni v drugoi tekhnologicheskoi situatsii*").[27] He likens his "status updates" and posts on Facebook to his notecard statements—both are meant to be simultaneously concise and eloquent. Another important similarity to his earlier work is the quality of its autobiographical nature: Similar to his poetry and essays, his updates and posts often refer to his childhood and his life in the USSR. For example, a typical timeline post from July 24, 2015 starts: "During my childhood, I happened to read various terrible stories and the most authentic and heart-chilling testimonials about the horrors of the capitalist world in general, and America in particular."[28] In another post, regarding the word étagère (*etazherka*) and its etymology, he again draws on his childhood recollections, writing: "We lived in a rather overcrowded situation. In one communal apartment, in one room, [there were] five of us."[29] On his Facebook wall, Rubinstein's clever one-liners alternate with longer musings, conversations, Moscow style *stiob*, plentiful photographs, self-promotion ads, and links to longer pieces found in various online media outlets.

Importantly, as a way to chronicle his day-by-day existence, Rubinstein's Facebook timeline continues his experiments with self-reflection. The posts

---

25 All translations of Rubinstein are mine unless otherwise noted. Lev Rubinstein, "Dana ustanovka na nerazlichenie dobra i zla" (An order is given for non-discrimination between good and evil), interview by Kirill Golovastikov, *Meduza*, June 25, 2015, https://meduza.io/feature/2015/07/25/dana-ustanovka-na-nerazlichenie-dobra-i-zla. For a discussion of the performative function in literature, see Lev Rubinstein, "Voprosy literatury," [Literary questions] interview by Zara Abdyllaeva, *Druzhba Narodov*, June 6, 1997, http://magazines.russ.ru/druzhba/1997/6/rubin.html.

26 In his latest interview for *Radio Svoboda* Rubinstein comments on Facebook as a new dynamic literary genre, stating that, "currently, Facebook is the most interesting literary text. I think of it as the most contemporary, dynamic, and promising literary genre." Lev Rubinstein, "Rubinshtein raduetsia melocham" (Rubinstein delights in the trivia), interview by Roman Super, *Radio Svoboda*, June 10, 2015, http://www.svoboda.org/content/article/27291064.html.

27 Rubinstein, "An Order is Given."

28 Lev Rubinstein's Facebook page, entry dated July 24, 2015, 11:16 PM, accessed September 6, 2017, https://www.facebook.com/profile.php?id=100000022518126&fref=ts.

29 Ibid., entry dated July 22, 2015, 9:43 PM, accessed September 6, 2017, https://www.facebook.com/profile.php?id=100000022518126&fref=ts.

often have a chatty tone, replete with colloquialisms, verbal puns, and the presence of marginalia emphasizing the daily and the insignificant. This creates the sense that he is addressing a friend while sharing his life's minutia. For example, in one post, he writes: "Today, I stood near the Park Kul'tury subway station waiting for a complete stranger—a young woman that I'd never met; I had to pass a book from another young woman, but one I knew, to this woman… Anyway, this is not so important…."[30] However, Rubinstein's self-referential texts are hardly instances of omphaloskepsis or navel-gazing; such an opening remark usually precedes a profoundly political and unabashedly individualistic, passionate text addressing political and social problems. As in Soviet times, Rubinstein opposes the ruling regime in Putin's Russia. Like his Facebook timeline, his LiveJournal profile serves variously as a means of self-reflection, outreach initiative, political mouthpiece, and venue for conversation with both real and virtual friends.

Yet, even though posted online, and thus very public, his writing still retains aspects of the form of private introspection, more closely approximating conventional autobiographical writing—chronologically unfolding texts—because of the temporal aspect inherent in the diary-like social media format. The flow of time is recorded in concrete terms via time stamps that register his posts and comments. Thus, while Rubinstein's writings remain focused on enduring autobiographical themes, formal changes are dictated by the dynamic nature of the medium. Rubinstein's new stylistic developments are a product of the ongoing process of reevaluating the author's role, as well as a return to the value of subjectivity, currently fueled by new media.

Thus, the autobiographical focus of his writings, evident in his poems and book-form essay collections, is continued in his online publishing activities and through his Facebook and LiveJournal posts and updates. No longer limited by self-expression in the form of discrete printed and performed events, and now liberated from time constraints and the cost of book publishing, Rubinstein can exist and write in "real time."

To return to Rubinstein's card poetry, the self-reflective performative subjectivity continues to evolve, as do the tools for mediating it. Cognizant of the interdependency between his artistic output and his current tools, especially social media, Rubinstein accentuates, and even celebrates the role Facebook

30 Ibid., entry dated July 13, 2015, 12:26 AM, accessed September 6, 2017, https://www.facebook.com/profile.php?id=100000022518126&fref=ts. For a general discussion of contemporary diary practices, see Chapter 3 in Philippe Lejeune, Jeremy D. Popkin, Julie Rak, and Katherine Durnin, eds., *On Diary* (Honolulu, HI: University of Hawai'i Press, 2009).

plays in his poetics: "Forty-six thousand subscribers exactly! Every anniversary must be celebrated, I reckon. Yay, comrades! The responsibility for the confabulation is increasing. I will do my best to kowtow! I love practically everyone. Well, well, not everyone—[but] many," as he posts on March 28, 2017.[31]

Due to the emergence of new inscription technologies, Rubinstein's textuality enters into new relationships of co-participating and co-authorship with neural machine translation engines, social media interfaces, and live audiences. Rubinstein's fondness for "linguistic instances" and accidents is now also supplied by the texts generated by neural machine translation (NMT) engines and multilingual Facebook composer tools. Each of Rubinstein's posts in Russian is followed by an automatic translation, and these posts change depending on the designated language he chooses for his postings, as well as the locale specified in his account settings. In a Facebook post from April 1, 2017, in the spirit of the April Fools' Day, Rubinstein invites a discussion on the machine's aesthetic capacity to translate. The post showcases an automatic translation that rivals the Futurists' transrational poetry.[32]

Life-writing has long been central to Rubinstein's poetics. The autobiographically inclined Rubinstein insists that the life of any artist "is, of course, a text. The text created in front of everybody."[33] The interactive interface text, as it is being created in the presence of all using posts and photos, references Rubinstein's body of work, life anecdotes, and jokes, but presents a different aesthetic task. After all, as Rubinstein explains in an interview for *Current Times*, "The artist must be capable of selecting something valuable, meaningful, important, [and] beneficial from the chaos of the landfills: that is, social media."[34]

---

31 Lev Rubinstein's Facebook page, entry dated March 28, 2017, 10:54 AM, accessed September 6, 2017, https://www.facebook.com/search/top/?q=%20Сорок%20шесть%20тысяч%20подписчиков%20ровно!%20Всякий%20юбилей%20надо%20праздновать%2Cя%20считаю.%20Ура%2C%20товарищи!.

32 Lev Rubinstein's Facebook page, entry dated April 1, 2017, 6:58 PM, accessed September 6, 2017, https://www.facebook.com/profile.php?id=100000022518126.

33 Lev Rubinstein's Facebook page, entry dated April 2, 2017, 10:53 AM, accessed September 6, 2017, https://www.facebook.com/search/str/Жизнь+поэта%2C+как+и+жизнь+любого+артиста+это%2C+разумеется%2C+текст.+Текст%2C+творимый+на+виду+у+всех./keywords_top.

34 "Strictly speaking, this is an artistic task. An artist is one who pulls out of the chaos something valuable, meaningful, consequential, beneficial. Social networks, in a sense, are a city dump." Lev Rubinstein, "Rubinshtein: 'Intellektual'nye kukhni 60-70 gg. priuchali liudei derzhat' vorotniki zastegnutymi, a feisbuk zastavil nas resdevat'sa'" (Lev Rubinstein: "intellectual kitchens of the 1960s–70s taught people to keep their collars buttoned up, and Facebook [*sic*] forced us

Rubinstein's level of comfort with this new technology is refreshing, especially when so many writers have difficulty parting with their more habitual textualities. In his tongue-in-cheek dealings with the technological and generational divides, when answering a somewhat misguided question about the role of the internet in the creation of his card-poetry genre, Rubinstein claims that, in fact, it is he who "preceded and influenced the internet." [*Internet na menia ne povliial, eto ia na nego povliial. Eto, konechno, shutka, no—no.*][35] It is telling that at the end of this statement, he emphasizes the final phrasing, "It is, of course, a joke, but—but." As Rubinstein's work is self-professedly about proto-texts, genre memory, and context, his essays, like his genre-mirroring cards, have the capacity to reflect—or even assume—new generic forms when grouped and contextualized differently.

The Hypertrophy of Memory

In an ongoing debate among media theorists, some warn that the technical forms of inscription and media that have emerged in the current stage of the technological evolution appear to be autonomous; or, at least, that the process "lays claim" to some sort of qualified autonomy from man.[36] As Mark Hansen, a scholar of cultural theory and media studies, phenomenology, and cognitive science, tells us, technology today is "no longer pre-adapted to or constrained by the sensory and perceptual threshold of human experience."[37] In fact, according to Hansen, for the first time in history, "the technical infrastructure of media is no longer homologous with its surface appearance."[38] Taking stock of the expansive role that computation processes play in creating experience, he points out how "difficult [it is] to ignore the reality that we depend on regimes of technical mediation—what geographer Nigel Thrift called the 'technological unconscious,'—that not only exceed our attention but also remain fundamentally

---

to undress"), interview by Andrei Korolev, *Current Time* [*Nastoiashchee Vremia*], December 8, 2016, accessed September 6, 2017. http://www.currenttime.tv/a/28146021.html.

35 Rubinstein, "An Order is Given."

36 In Continental philosophy, this debate was spearheaded by Paul Virilio, a French philosopher, cultural theorist, and media scholar, and by Friedrich Kittler, a media philosopher and a literary scholar, both of whom have written extensively about technology and its history. A Canadian philosopher of communication theory, Marshall McLuhan, was another notable figure in this debate.

37 W. J. T. Mitchell and Mark B. N. Hansen, eds., *Critical Terms for Media Studies* (Chicago: The University of Chicago Press, 2010), 178.

38 Ibid., 179–80.

unfathomable by us."[39] The computer—broadly defined by desktops, smartphones, tablets, laptops, and so on—underlines "a certain apparent dissociation of media from technics."[40]

The seemingly excessive—but increasingly inevitable—dependency on the machine and on technological autonomy leads one to question the authenticity and value of self-knowledge and the quality of memory gained through this excessive reliance. Comparing "traditional memory" to today's technologized model, Pierre Nora, a French historian, points out the flaw of this type of remembering: "Memory has begun to keep records: delegating the responsibility for remembering to the archive, it deposits its signs as the snake deposits shed skin."[41] He also observes:

> What we call memory is in fact a gigantic and breathtaking effort to store the material vestiges of what we cannot possibly remember, thereby amassing an unfathomable collection of things that we might someday need to recall [...] fragments, records, documents, images and speeches—any tangible sign of what was—as if this expanding dossier might someday be subject to subpoena as evidence before who know what tribunal of history.[42]

Nora's own verdict is that "[t]he realm of the memorable has expanded without reason: we suffer from hypertrophy of memory, which is inextricably intertwined with our sense of memory's loss and concomitant industrialization."[43] Yet it is important here to ask if this "industrialization" of memory is, qualitatively speaking, a truly novel development. Indeed, do we need to oppose notions of memory and technology as antagonistic forces, ultimately leading to

---

39 Ibid., 179. See also Nigel Thrift, "Remembering the Technological Unconscious by Foregrounding Knowledges of Position," *Environment and Planning D: Society and Space* 22, no. 1 (2004): 175–90.

40 Following Kittler, Hansen explains: "As distinct from phonography, where the grooves of a record graphically reproduce the frequency ranges of humanly perceivable sound, and from film, where the inscription of light on a sensitive surface reproduces what is visible to the human eye, computation media involve no direct correlation between technical storage and human sense perception. What we see on the computer screen (or other interface) and hear on the digital player is not related by visible or sonic analogy to the data that is processed in the computer or a digital device." Mitchell and Hansen, *Critical Terms for Media Studies*, 178-9.

41 Pierre Nora, "Realms of Memory" in Farr, *Memory*, 62.

42 Ibid., 62–63.

43 Ibid.

so-called "hypertrophy?" Helping to reconcile the remembering, thinking, and writing humans with their technological nature, Stiegler insists that a "tool is, before anything else, memory [...]. The tool refers in principle to an already-there, to a fore-having of something that the *who* has not itself necessarily lived."[44] Our memory has always been exactly that—a tool.

Nonetheless, some find this hypertrophy of technological memory and resultant atrophy of human memory worrisome. Do we lose our capacity to remember when we entrust this task to a machine? Joining the chorus of nostalgic mourning for the loss of memory and humanity, Ollivier Dyens, a writer whose work examines twenty-first-century cultural and technological evolutions, emotes: "The memories that we now have are ahuman, created and manipulated events, preserved outside ourselves." Further, he states, "machines control our memories, they own the fundamental materials that shape us," while also "manag[ing] the structures that generate human meaning and perspective."[45] The consequence of this situation, where "machines, technologies, institutions and commercial phenomena are so fertile with memories and emotion (and human beings have offloaded onto machines so many of them)," is that "sociological meaning must come from their interplay."[46] Dyens connects this development with a postmodern epistemological crisis. Indeed, this idea is the central premise of the concept of *technics*—the notion that machines create our past. However, as Stiegler makes clear, this is neither a new nor a negative thought. As much as some may regret—or even resent—the machine's involvement in our memory management, there exists an "irreducible link between thought as memory and the technical dimension of memorization."[47] As Stiegler underscores, "the modern modalities of archivization" affect all relations with the future, where "this prodigious change augments not only the size, the quantitative economy of this memory labeled artificial, but its qualitative structure as well."[48] Instead of avoiding, rejecting, or devaluing this connection, it is important to acknowledge and accept the inevitability of this change. Rubinstein's somewhat anachronistic relationship with the internet serves as evidence of this essential connection.

---

44 Stiegler, *Technics and Time, 1*, 254.

45 Ollivier Dyens, "The Sadness of the Machine" in Farr, *Memory*, 78-79.

46 Ibid.

47 Stiegler, *Technics and Time, 2*, 31. Here, Stiegler quotes Derrida's *Memoires for Paul de Man* (1989).

48 Ibid.

When considering new media, particularly the digital regime, media theory scholar Mark Poster correctly points out that the "material infrastructure of the sign"—both the relations between the signifier and the signified and the relation between the sign and the referent—has been "drastically reconfigured" by new media without bemoaning or celebrating the loss of some aboriginal materiality.[49] To extend this comment to the concerns of this essay, we may propose that, in fact, there has been no "authentic" relationship between humans and their memories—between the autobiographer and his representations—even though autobiographers since Jean-Jacques Rousseau have viewed such authenticity as an ideal. As textual representation augments our abilities to know, remember, and represent ourselves, it continues the established dynamic that has long existed between man and his technologically-mediated writing self, as well as the bond between man and technology. Of course, it is true that there will be new forms, and even new genres, of self-documentation, as dictated by future technological innovations, but the nature of this dependency will continue to remain fundamentally unchanged, based on differentiation and deferral through technologized writing, which establishes a horizon of belated and mediated self-awareness.

Contemporary authors working in new, digitally-born media recognize this interaction, and many make this the focus of their life-writing projects by exploiting the rich possibilities of interconnectedness—the author with the responsive, dynamically changing world of information, and the actively engaged audience offered up by technology. The composite, changeable nature of autobiographical subjectivity is matched by the characteristics of our current communication media. As the linguist Jukka Tyrkkö writes, "Digital media rely on a new understanding of texts not as definitive objects, but as networks of relations and meaning which by their very nature are relative, transitory, and subject to change at any moment." In this way, he states that they suggest a "new, more fluid concept of digital coherence."[50] Yet the dissociation borne from our present technological complexity, which alarms some, actually liberates us from worries about becoming mechanical by providing new creative opportunities and freedoms, thus giving rise to a new era of self-expression that is interactive, performative, and participatory.

---

49 Quoted in Bill Brown, "Materiality," in Mitchell and Hansen, *Critical Terms for Media Studies*, 55.

50 Jukka Tyrkkö, "Making Sense of Digital Textuality," *European Journal of English Studies* 11, no. 2 (2007): 147.

Self-perception is a dynamic process, where gaining a sense of identity is doubled with forgetfulness and erasure. Likewise, life-writing is a generative, imaginative, and selective process, and as such, it is a distorting practice. Our identities are always changeable and pluralistic—they are never static, even when solidified in the form of a text.[51] This dynamic relationship often takes place in the virtual space of the internet, which serves as the forum for exchanges between self and other, as well as between self and projected self. An autobiographical statement will always remain a composite image, with only a small degree of fidelity to what we, naively, hope to know as "true" life. Similar to the self-mythologizing undertaken by Rousseau or Leo Tolstoy[52]—the celebrities of their times—the identity management we perform by selecting and presenting information to the public virtually, is, in principle, the same as that from years past; namely, it is self-mythologizing. It is the search for compelling, "accurate" forms of documentation to support the perceptions of ourselves, just as it is our conscious attempt at controlling our own self-perceptions.

Rubinstein: The Orphan Memories of Anyone's Past, or, Performing Nostalgia

Against this theoretical backdrop, we can once again focus our attention on Rubinstein's work, which uses the internet to connect him with his audience via social media and online press. He also uses singing performances, along with his more expected poetry recitals, as aesthetic practices to negotiate his Soviet past in the present moment. Even though Rubinstein's now classic card poetry had already evoked dramatic acting, this form of scripting was still limited in terms of reflecting the performance aspect. Earlier, the physical event of Rubinstein's public reading was the ultimate realization of the poems' content.[53] His work in the last decade, however, has added important

51 Here, I gesture toward reader-response theory. See Jane P. Tompkins, *Reader-Response Criticism: From Formalism to Post-Structuralism* (Baltimore: Johns Hopkins University Press, 1980).

52 Visual representation played a significant role in Rousseau's self-documenting project, offering both metaphoric and formal solutions in his search for adequate forms of literary self-portrayal. His experiments served as a foil for Leo Tolstoy's lifelong self-documentation project. Popular perception forced both authors to continuously recreate themselves in response to their mediated images.

53 In his essay "The Last Flowers of Lev Rubinstein: Bibliography," Mikhail Berg explains that Rubinstein's work was not nominated for the prestigious "Northern Palmyra" literary prize because the committee could not easily classify Rubinstein's poetry books. Although disqualifying him from the impressive nomination, Rubinstein's acting-reading style stands

layers. Next to the singular reading act itself, the video and audio recordings of Rubinstein's recitals,[54] which capture the author's physical presence—his voice, intonations, looks, and choices in sequencing the cards—function as a more complete realization of his card-poetry genre. The multiple media also serve to underscore the author's uniqueness, as well as his present-ness. Rubinstein insists on the importance of the context, saying that each of his texts now "sound" anew, whether in the setting of a book, a website, or a reading; furthermore, he states, each text will acquire an individual meaning for a particular reader.[55]

In addition to the web-based journalism and online journaling that I discussed above, Rubinstein recently began expressing a certain wistfulness for the Soviet past by performing on stage—an act that I call "performing" nostalgia. He sings popular songs as a new form of autobiographical mediation. In his "nostalgia performances," Rubinstein turns to Soviet-era songs, the popular music associated with the period of the late 1940s,[56] where he engages a network of collective memories and nostalgic associations, thus emphasizing the aural and visual senses, and using his body as something of an open archive, accessible to all.

Rubinstein's current singing repertoire is limited only to Soviet songs that were popular during his early childhood. Before he begins singing, Rubinstein typically makes brief remarks regarding his choice of music. These songs, he explains, entered his blood, "where they now circulate together with [his] childhood memories" (*prakticheski voshli v sostav moei krovi i tam tsirkuliruiut vmeste s detskimi vospominaniiami*).[57] In a 2005 interview, Rubinstein explained:

---

as the essential genre-defining element in his autobiographical self-presentation. See Mikhail Berg, "Poslednie tsvety L'va Rubinshteina: Bibliograhiia" [The last flowers of Lev Rubinstein: bibliography], *NLO* 30 (1998), accessed September 6, 2017, http://magazines.russ.ru/nlo/1998/30/rubin.html.

54 Rubinstein has long been documented by others in the form of amateur or professional video-recordings, which now abound on various internet sites with video clips showing Rubinstein in action.

55 See Lev Rubinstein, "An Order is Given."

56 Heard on the radio, played at home, performed by popular street orchestras and during ubiquitous official celebrations, or sung during informal communal festivities, the "Soviet lyric" formed a typical daily soundtrack. Raised in a Moscow *kommunalka* or communal apartment, Rubinstein identifies and connects with this "singing generation."

57 Rubinstein gives his performances the title *Pesni detstva, voshedshie v moiu krov' na skorosti 78 oborotov v minutu* [*Songs of childhood, which have entered into my blood stream at the speed*

> When we'd get together, it was customary to sing a bit when we were in a certain condition [meaning inebriation—KT] at the table. Generally speaking, I belong to a generation that sings rather than listening. These songs form a sound background of my early childhood. I grew up listening to the radio—I lived in communal apartments where the radio was on all day long. It's not that I loved or did not love these songs; they just became a part of my blood. It was a given—like a cloud or the view from my window.[58]

By singing, Rubinstein reconnects with his past through the medium of period-specific music. Possessing no musical training (in Rubinstein's own words, he "does not even know the notes"), he is now commonly dubbed a *chansonnier* in the popular press. He performs in clubs and restaurants, as well as at more expected venues, such as literary gatherings. Usually, he sings with his eyes closed. Immersed in his thoughts, he seems removed from the places where he stands, often surrounded by the cacophony of restaurant noise. He also teams up with various musicians, such as the Klezmasters orchestra. His raspy voice recalls those of Leonid Utesov and Mark Naumovich Bernes, two extremely popular singers in the 1940s, whose performances are still imprinted onto Soviet cultural memory. The audience—generally Rubinstein's contemporaries, but sometimes his seniors—often close their eyes along with Rubinstein, as if suspended in a trance-like state, induced by his unsophisticated, but heartrending delivery of Soviet classics. They hum or silently move their lips, rocking in rhythm to the sound of his voice, while some even stand to dance to the waltz-like tunes.

The audience's capacity to identify with the performer opens up potentially non-exhaustive creative interpretations, where the past refuses to be fixed as a singular text-event. Instead, the past is released into the present to be actualized in myriad possible viewing experiences. In this gesture of collective mediation, each member of the listening community goes back to his or her familiar trove of personal memories. Thus, Rubinstein's singing serves as an instrument of remembering and, so aided, the audience enacts nostalgic identification with both Rubinstein's own specific past and their own. In other words, the sing-

---

of 78 revolutions per minute]. Audio file formatted as YouTube video, June 3, 2007, http://booknik.ru/today/show/lev-rubinshteyin-s-pesnyami-voshedshimi-v-krov/.

58 Lev Rubinstein, "Lev Rubinshtein, Prezumptsiia modnosti i est' ofitsial'naia kul'tura" [Lev Rubinstein, Presumption of trendiness, indeed, is the official culture], interview for *Polit.Ru,* June 17, 2005, http://polit.ru/article/2005/06/17/rubinshtein/.

er's body functions as a medium for exploring an archive of shared memory. Rubinstein's body is also his tool for accessing private memories, where the embodied sensorial affectivity is made possible by sharing his "nostalgic" imagination with his audience. Each iteration is an event that allows recollections to be embodied differently in an attempt at the recovery of one's singular past. The insistence on replaying allows for a subjective shift from the supposedly "unique" author, with his singular, authentic memories, to that of a community sharing memories, of which he is but one member. Captured by technology on videos, then viewed, bookmarked, and contextualized by being embedded in online posts and exchanged as links, Rubinstein's acts participate in an endless network of associations and pasts.

This corporal meditation on the experience of time and memory becomes an instance of constitutive self-affection[59] through which the autobiographer comes to an originary sense of self. The shift to performance directs the focus from an "authentic memory" to the problem of temporality itself—the present-ness, the present, and the past. By reanimating habitual sounds and customs, Rubinstein dramatizes the notions of time and memory. This allows for a more intense experience of autobiographical subjectivity in its constitutive incompleteness and performative potentiality. His memories, while prosthetic and originary in a Stieglerian sense, are part of the shared collective, where, to quote Henri Bergson, the past "might act and will act by inserting itself into a present sensation from which it borrows the vitality."[60] This act of inserting the past into the present is also the act of life-writing, the manifestation of *technics*, whereby the author is "affected in writing—encountering and reflecting on the writerly self."[61]

---

59 Self-affection, or auto-affection, is a phenomenological concept dealing with the foundational conditions of human experience. Following Aristotle's definition of God as "thought thinking itself," but also Husserl's idea of auto-affection as lived-experience (*Erlebnis*)—as hearing oneself-speaking, and even as absolute subjectivity—this idea was further questioned by Derrida, and subsequently, by Stiegler, among others. (Michel Henry's work on the subject is not considered here.) It is particularly relevant to the considerations of autobiography as a form of auto-affection or self-relation, where the dynamic experience of the present is filtered through the memories of the past as well as the anticipation of the future, thus creating the distance from the self that is essential for the emergence of self-consciousness. For a discussion of Derrida, see: Leonard Lawlor, "Jacques Derrida," in *The Stanford Encyclopedia of Philosophy* (Spring 2014 Edition), ed. Edward N. Zalta, http://plato.stanford.edu/archives/spr2014/entries/derrida/.

60 Henri Bergson, *Matter and Memory*, trans. Nancy Margaret Paul and William Scott Palmer (London: G. Allen & Co.; New York: The Macmillan Co., 1912), 320.

61 Stiegler, *Technics and Time*, 2, 37.

Rubinstein's body of online work and his "nostalgia performances" raise the question of how one can make an adequate record of such work, now demanding new extra-literary modes of inscription.[62] As if to underscore the *technics*-based nature of his methods, whereby he engages in the process of cultivating greater self-awareness, his performances are structured as mechanical "readings"—articulating and translating into sound-form the encryptions that, as Rubinstein suggests, have been inscribed onto him and have become a part of his physical makeup. As a canonical conceptualist poet moves beyond the boundaries of literary discourse and into the popular culture of websites, blogs, and YouTube videos, his earlier autobiographical writings can no longer be fully comprehended without looking at his current multimedia self-expression. His project brings the complexity of the interactions between man and technology into sharp focus, showing how social media has inaugurated new modes of articulating one's identity.

Conclusion

As we try to find our bearings in this accelerated and increasingly technological world, the new media accentuate the fluid, contested status of concepts such as truth, singularity, and authenticity, thus bringing the inherent problem of linear periodization and temporal definition to the fore. Distinctions between the "new" and the "old" become blurred, as such seemingly idiosyncratic, anachronistic developments in Rubinstein's proto-digital card poetry, as well as his current technologically-inspired sentience, invite us to come to terms with our humanity as inescapably technological and prosthetic. New technologies provide us with possibilities to reimagine and re-image ourselves vis-à-vis *technics*. We gain greater self-awareness as technological prosthetic, posthuman beings. In our day-to-day technical reality, we, as Stiegler heeds, "cannot spontaneously distinguish the long-term processes of transformation from spectacular but fleeting technical innovations."[63]

As material and digital cultures evolve, offering new techniques for self-documentation, autobiographers will continue to react by inflecting their

62 Rubinstein no longer uses the textual conventions of life-writing or photographs—those unreliable visual correlates of memory. For a discussion of Rubinstein's critical approach to photography and cinema in his autobiographical poems and essays, see my work: Kristina Toland, "Picturing the Self: The Changing Medium of Russian Autobiography" (PhD diss., Northwestern University, 2010).

63 Stiegler, *Technics and Time, 1*, 21.

work with technologically-mediated conceptions of memory, time, and, self. Extra-literary types of evidence, offered by the digital regimes of new media, structure the processes of substantiating and legitimizing an author's life-record. The "graphing" part of the "auto-bio-graphing" project has been increasingly entrusted to non-literary—and even non-textual—forms of machine-based documentation and communication. The forms of memories also evolve: Each historical moment is affected by the progress of time, and in each period, memories form new relations with the notions of "self" and "truth."

In the moment of writing—in the broadest sense of the term—we create a sense of time; the remembered past becomes fixed as historical while our sense of selves (our past selves) become exteriorized and articulated. Our past lives and actions shape our perpetually evolving perceptions of who we are. These articulated memories make us who we are in the present—we *become properly historical through our acts as they are conceptualized and recorded. Technics,* then, is thus both the method and the message of life-writing; the reflected and refracted message goes on indefinitely.

CHAPTER 8

Modes of Perception in Transmodal Fiction: New Russian Subjectivity

Katerina Lakhmitko,
University of Illinois at Urbana-Champaign

During the first decade of the twenty-first century, digital technology, Web 2.0, and transmedial fictions have transformed the relationship between labor and leisure in post-Soviet Russia. Digital networks have created communities and subjectivities that participate in virtual "immaterial labor"[1] and content production.[2] When we consider the potentialities for creativity and subjectivity unlocked by cybertext media, the traditional binary dynamics between artist and audience, or reader and text cease to be relevant. Scholars of the literary sciences must find new ways to study creative cultural processes and artifacts. This article analyzes how the formerly discrete disciplines of ludology, humanities, psychology, and neuroscience mingle and coalesce through new modes of social and cultural production in the post-post-Soviet virtual space. In what follows, I argue that new strategies of information production and media processes facilitate user creativity through the direct networking of a communal consciousness or intersubjectivity. Recent studies in neuroscience and philosophical challenges to conventional phenomenology have suggested that human subjectivity takes shape as a result of object-related perception, which is activated by bodily

1 Philosopher Maurizio Lazzarato coined the term "immaterial labor" to describe affective and cognitive work that exists outside the traditional material-commodity labor model.

2 For an informative summary of the origins of Runet and the evolution of online Russian literature since 1994, see Henrike Schmidt, "Russian Literature on the Internet: From Hypertext to Fairy Tale," in *Digital Russia: The Language, Culture and Politics of New Media Communication*, eds. Michael Gorham, Ingunn Lunde, and Martin Paulsen (New York: Routledge, 2014), 177–97.

responses that are embedded in a cultural environment or stem from inherited dispositions. I also argue that user engagement with virtual objects in the virtual environment has unlocked a matrix of discursive and configurative practices that factor into how we perceive ourselves and the world.

This case study of Dmitrii Glukhovskii's transmedial fiction syndicate *Metro* demonstrates the ways in which cybertext[3] allows for modifications in audience interaction with the text as an immersive environment and promotes engaging its readers as users, players, and/or *prosumers* of a virtual world. By way of the embodied user experience, I look at the issues of creativity, perception, and subjectivity in the wake of *prosumerism*, transmedia, and digital environments (I will discuss prosumerism later in this article). I want to be clear that the user's engagement with virtual objects is weaker than the engagement she has with physically present material objects. Nonetheless, building on the work of neuroscientist Antonio Damasio, I argue that in both cases the processes of mapping, feeling, and recall looping have an impact on the organizing mechanism of the self. Damasio represents a recent psychoanalytical turn among neuroscientists[4] toward the study of self and consciousness and provides a nuanced framework for navigating the space between various layers of explicit and implicit, perceived, recalled, and simulated images and objects. In this article, I take a transdisciplinary interactive approach to examining texts, games, performance, and other cultural phenomena. In the process of researching Glukhovskii's enterprise, I read the *Metro* texts and played the *Metro* games. Thus, when I speak about the referent reader, player, or user, I am referring to my own lived experience. Consciousness and understanding of the processes that govern sociocultural behaviors start with awareness of the self.

The frame for looking at the relationship between gaming and embodied experience in this article is informed by Damasio's arguments in the book *Self Comes to Mind: Constructing the Conscious Brain*. Damasio approaches subjectivity as a composite of three selves: the pre-conscious protoself; the conscious, object-related, active core self; and the defined individual autobiographical self, which comprises consciousness and memory. He suggests that the protoself is the physical and emotional base for the activation of the core self. The core

3 I use the definition of cybertext proposed by Espen J. Aarseth in *Cybertext: Perspectives on Ergodic Literature* (Baltimore: Johns Hopkins University Press, 1997), 3.

4 See also Joseph LeDoux's *Synaptic Self: How Our Brains Become Who We Are* (New York: Penguin, 2002); Jaak Panksepp and Lucy Biven's *The Archaeology of Mind: Neuroevolutionary Origins of Human Emotions* (New York: W. W. Norton, 2012); Adrian Johnston and Catherine Malabou's *Self and Emotional Life: Philosophy, Psychoanalysis, and Neuroscience* (New York: Columbia University Press, 2013).

self's mechanism of perception triggers bodily feelings and maps the organism through engagement with object-related images.[5] Inquiry, response, and reflection initiate motor interactions, elicit changes in the protoself, and shape the topography of the mind. This form of engagement not only applies to objects perceived in real time, but also to objects that are recalled or imagined. While I do want to highlight the importance of imaginary and simulated experience in the construction of subjectivity, it is crucial to remember that there are other layers of engagement that structure our embodied experience. But even relatively simple feelings and neurochemical processes can lay the groundwork for the evolution of complex conscious selves. According to Damasio,

> First, distinct levels of processing—mind, conscious mind, and conscious mind capable of producing culture—emerged in sequence. That should not leave the impression, however, that when minds acquired selves, they stopped evolving as minds or that selves eventually stopped evolving. On the contrary, the evolutionary process continued (and continues), possibly enriched and accelerated by the pressures created by self-knowledge, and there is no end in sight. The ongoing digital revolution, the globalization of cultural information, and the coming of the age of empathy are pressures likely to lead to structural modifications of mind and self, by which I mean modifications of the very brain processes that shape the mind and self.[6]

The conscious self is comprised of the mind and body states that incorporate sociocultural aspects like religion, art, mythology, politics, technology, environment, and other components. Damasio claims that since our "autobiographical selves can operate on the basis of knowledge etched in brain circuits and in external records of stone, clay, or paper, humans become capable of hitching their individual biological needs to the accumulated sapience."[7] Ritual, storytelling, and art are only some of the ways we have found to transmit cultural knowledge, morals, survival traits, and dispositions. Neurobiological and cultural evolution complement each other.

In his essay "Transaesthetics" in *The Transparency of Evil: Essays on Extreme Phenomena,* Jean Baudrillard suggests that we are currently in an age of transaesthetics, where art has been assimilated and incorporated into all other

5 Antonio Damasio, *Self Comes to Mind: Constructing the Conscious Brain* (New York: Vintage, 2012), 109.

6 Ibid., 193.

7 Ibid., 308.

aspects of life. Politics, finance, media, and culture interact with each other in such a way that it is impossible to separate any one element from the others. He writes:

> By its liberation of form, line, colour, and aesthetic notions—as by its mixing up of all cultures, all styles—our society has given rise to a general aestheticization: all forms of culture—not excluding anti-cultural ones—are promoted and all models of representation and anti-representation are taken on board. Whereas art was once essentially a utopia—that is to say, ultimately unrealizable—today this utopia has been realized: thanks to the media, computer science and video technology, everyone is now potentially a creator.[8]

Indeed, the concept of art's autonomy is contrary to how cultural processes originated. The knowledge and feelings transmitted in art derived from lived experience. There is no reason to believe that art should, or can, remain separate from other cultural forms. Furthermore, creative production processes may be collaborative. Imaging, emoting, and storytelling are implicit cognitive functions that each of us performs every day. It is more likely that media and technology have accelerated the potential of art, so that creation of a multifaceted sociocultural perspective, which could have taken millennia, has been dramatically condensed.

In the span between Ted Nelson's 1963 introduction of the hypertext[9] model and Espen Aarseth's 1997 cybertext theory,[10] the field of cybernetics awakened the awareness of scholars and philosophers to the potentialities of digital technology for use in communication and cultural production. N. Katherine Hayles' book *How We Became Posthuman* provides a succinct summary of the ways in which cybernetic concepts like "reflexivity" and "feedback loop" entered the humanities. Irrespective of trends, classification, or theoretical applicability, the digital media in their various manifestations have revitalized the interactive potentiality of texts globally. In Russia, transmodalities, first introduced by writers like Sergei Luk'ianenko in the 1990s, created

8 Jean Baudrillard, *The Transparency of Evil: Essays on Extreme Phenomena*, trans. James Benedict (London: Verso, 1993), 16.

9 Hypertext is text that contains embedded links to provisional text and media materials.

10 Aarseth's cybertext theory designates the technological medium and user function as important elements in textual communication.

an alternative to the single author-subject mode of production[11] in the 2000s. Transmodal fictions and cybertexts problematize narrative studies and expand literary possibilities. A prominent example of such digital cultural production is Roman Leibov's 1995 collectively authored hypertext *Novel* (*Roman*). Henrike Schmidt suggests that the variety of online literary forms and processes was born in the unregulated creative spaces of the internet.[12] By 2002, when Glukhovskii founded his transmedial *Metro* franchise, online novel publishing and universe building were well-established practices. What sets Glukhovskii apart is, that unlike other novel-to-game online worlds such as *S.T.A.L.K.E.R.* and *Night Watch*, his was conceived and orchestrated in accordance with his own vision.

Initially, Glukhovskii sent out a manuscript of his post-apocalyptic science-fiction thriller titled *Metro* to several Russian publishers. The young Glukhovskii received less than stellar responses from publishers, who deemed the novel uninteresting and reacted negatively to the ending, which featured the death of the protagonist.[13] Undeterred, Glukhovskii drew upon available resources, set up his own domain m-e-t-r-o.boom.ru, and self-published the nascent thirteen-chapter text online. The novel's online success resulted in the release of a best-selling print version of *Metro 2033* (Metro 2033) by Eksmo Press in 2005.

Despite its unorthodox genesis online, the print version of *Metro 2033* generated a lot of traditional, narrative-centered criticisms. In a non-ergodic novel the narrative is the dominant organizing principle and supports the interpretative functions of the text. However, Glukhovskii's novel is ergodic, a quality that, according to Aarseth, "require[s] non-trivial reader effort to traverse the text."[14] *Metro 2033* belongs to the post-apocalyptic dystopian subgenre, as it is set in a razed future world that is the outcome of an imagined 2013 nuclear war. According to the story, a portion of the Moscow population escapes underground into the Metro (or subway) tunnels, as nuclear fallout leaves the surface uninhabitable. The escapees settle in communities at various

11 See the example of Andrei D'iakov and other writers who publish novels set in the *Universe of Metro 2033* in an interview by Anna Popova, "Monolog pisatelia" [Monologue of a writer], *Kul'tura Moskvy* (April 21, 2015), https://cult.mos.ru/reviews/monolog-pisatelya-dmitriy-glukhovskiy/.

12 Schmidt, "Russian Literature on the Internet," 178.

13 Glukhovskii began writing the novel in high school. See Jure Aleksič and Borut Peterlin, "Dmitrii Glukhovskii: Ruski Post-Apokalipticni Klasik in Pionir Pisateljskega Spletnega Marketinga" [Dmitrii Glukhovskii: Russian post-apocalyptic classic and pioneer of online marketing], *Mladina*, 33 (August 17, 2012): 63, http://www.mladina.si/115019/dmitry-glukhovsky-metro-ni-tisto-kar-se-zdi/.

14 Aarseth, *Cybertext*, 1.

metro stations. The action of the novel takes place in 2033, as the 20-year-old protagonist Artem, resident of the *Vystavka Dostizhenii Narodnogo Khoziaistva* (from here on abbreviated as VDNKh) station, sets off on a mission to ask the Polis—the central Metro station—for help in fighting the Dark Ones. These creatures are telepathically killing the residents of his station and seem to be trying to find a way into the VDNKh station from the surface. As he traverses the Metro map, Artem observes different communities and ideologies of the underground factions like the Red Line Communists, the Fourth Reich Nazis, and the Great Worm Cult. Mark Griffiths reads *Metro 2033* as commentary on Putinism and the "splintering urbanism"[15] of the post-Soviet Moscow. Glukhovskii admits that he borrowed the ideological and political tendencies he saw around him and placed them in an underground post-apocalyptic scenario.[16] Glukhovskii insists that he foresaw some of the future xenophobic and antagonistic propensities that would characterize Vladimir Putin's administration while he was writing the text in the late 1990s. Griffiths argues that *Metro 2033* adheres to the dystopian novel genre conventions and depicts an exaggerated form of the political world outside Glukhovskii's window.

In spite of surviving a nuclear holocaust and facing the threat of mutant monsters called demons, the remaining humans that populate the underground tunnels continue to foster ideological prejudices and slaughter each other. As the reader interprets the text, she draws associations between the text and reality of her society, recalls her own perceptions, and thus composes a moral subjectivity. Once she reaches the end of the novel and looks at the back cover, a new outlet opens to her as she scans the web address printed there. If she chooses to visit the website, the reader can find herself within a sociocultural network of creative possibilities.

The Universe of Metro 2033 comprises over sixty novellas, a magazine, artwork, movies, and short stories written by various individual authors who contribute to Glukhovskii's website. Readers who have become immersed in the Metro universe can create and contribute their own media content. The *Metro* transmodal fiction coalesces in the space between the novels, video games, portals, and forums: in the experiences and performances of its user.

The online versions of the novel *Metro 2033* developed an interactive hypertext experience that included links to music and art, which Glukhovskii

15 Mark Griffiths, "Moscow after the Apocalypse." *Slavic Review* 72:3 (2013): 501.

16 Aleksei Alekhin, "Apokalipsis dlia shou-biznesa" [Apocalypse for show business]. *Ekspert* (December 15, 2008), http://www.expert.ru/expert/2008/49/apokalipsis_dlya_shoubiznesa.

intended for the reader to consult in conjunction with each chapter. At this point we can begin to see the transmedial and intermedial qualities of the *Metro* texts. In her article "Intermediality, Intertextuality, and Remediation: A Literary Perspective on Intermediality," Irina Rajewsky broadly defines intermedial phenomena as those that "cross borders between media," while transmedial phenomena "share motifs, aesthetics or discourses across media."[17] Glukhovskii employed a film- and television-inspired discursive style to create a "live," "immersive" experience of the *Metro* world for his readers.[18] We can see the presence of both intermedial and transmedial phenomena in the *Metro* project. He readily engaged his audience through online links and social media, and shortly thereafter established a core base of followers and collaborators who served as his test group. Early critics found transmedial parallels between Glukhovskii's narrative and Arkadii and Boris Strugatsky's cult science fiction novels *Roadside Picnic*[19] (*Piknik na obochine,* 1971) and *The Doomed City* (*Grad obrechennyi,* 1975). Furthermore, the association with the S.T.A.L.K.E.R. gaming universe was actually beneficial to Glukhovskii's brand. The temporal setting of the *Metro* text, as well as its subject matter, were allusions to the post-apocalyptic fantasy world and appealed to several existing online communities of gaming experts and science-fiction fans.[20] In Rajewsky's view, intermedial products can be identified using one or several of the following three functional criteria: medial transposition, media combination, and intermedial references. In Glukhovskii's case, the functional criteria are less noticeable due to the character of the digital medium. According to Rajewsky, digital technology produces a "virtual" intermediality that can flawlessly simulate and merge analog media. Thus, Glukhovskii's digital novel or hypertext was more than a novel in the classic sense, because it combined, referenced, and facilitated several different modes of creative expression. Glukhovskii's online text displayed virtual intermediality through its combination of music, art, narrative, and arguably the online forum. At the same time, the logic of the text continued to cross media boundaries by enacting a video-game-like quest narrative, where

---

17 Irina O. Rajewsky, "Intermediality, Intertextuality, and Remediation: A Literary Perspective on Intermediality," *Intermédialités: Histoire et théorie des arts, des lettres et des techniques* 6 (Autumn 2005): 46.

18 See interview by Aleks Pevchev, "Literatura—eto virus, i moia zadacha im zarazit'" [Literature is a virus and my goal is to infect], *Izvestiia* (June 21, 2013), http://izvestia.ru/news/552427.

19 Adapted in 1979 into the film *Stalker*, directed by Andrei Tarkovsky.

20 Paul E. Richardson, "Underground Novelist," *Russian Life* 51, no. 6 (November/December 2008): 40.

the protagonist moved from station to station along a virtual map. Although literary critics saw the video game logic as a stylistic flaw, Glukhovskii viewed this transmediality as a viable continuation of the *Metro* franchise. In March of 2006, Glukhovskii partnered with 4A Games in Ukraine and began developing a first-person shooter video game *Metro 2033*, which was released in March of 2010. His involvement in the design process and participation in video game conventions and trade shows demonstrate Glukhovskii's commitment to the transmodal functions of his text and to the video game medium as an art form.[21]

Glukhovskii continued to run his online novel production models, releasing the novel *Metro 2034* one chapter at a time on his website, where users could again influence the text with their discussions and suggestions. The print version of the *Metro 2034* novel was published in 2009 and was considered a sequel to the first novel, despite featuring an entirely new cast of characters. This storyline follows several of the inhabitants of Sevastopol'skaia station, who are fighting for survival against such threats as biological weapons and disease. Glukhovskii has exploited the intermodal growth potential of his text by cultivating and nourishing his fan culture on portals and domains and through interactive texts like video games and phone apps. For example, in response to his fans' requests Glukhovskii continued Artem's storyline in a video-game sequel *Metro: Last Light*, released by Deep Silver in May of 2013. In the midst of developing the storyline for *Metro: Last Light*, Glukhovskii decided to transpose the video game and write *Metro 2035*.

Despite the presence of plot in both the *Metro 2033* and *Metro: Last Light*, video games should be viewed not as adaptations but, rather, as altogether qualitatively new experiences in an altogether new medium.[22] Video games call on the mapping processes and somatosensing regions in our minds, thereby expanding the user's involvement. The somatic system is a network of sensory neurons that receive and relay haptic information about the surface, position, and movement of the body. In his *Cybertext Poetics*, Markku Eskelinen applies

21 Glukhovskii contends that well-written and well-designed video games are the art of the new generation. See interview by Svetlana Rakhmanova, "Na menia rabotal nastoiashchii kollektivnyi razum" [The real collective intelligence worked for me], *Novye Izvestiia* (March 29, 2013), http://www.newizv.ru/culture/2013-03-29/180145-pisatel-dmitrij-gluhovskij.html.

22 Note that there is an ongoing debate in game studies, where scholars Henry Jenkins and Marie-Laure Ryan argue that narrative is an important organizing feature of games, while ludologists Gonzalo Frasca and Jesper Juul argue that games are not narratives and do not share the defining features or functions of stories. Markku Eskelinen pushes the debate further by suggesting that video games complicate the standard definition of medium, as each unique gaming system could be labeled a new medium.

ludology and Aarseth's cybertext theory to the field of poetics, including in it new forms of ergodic cybertexts. Eskelinen develops Aarseth's ideas regarding game ontology and promotes the fledgling field of ludology (a field of cultural studies dealing with games). He stresses the importance of studying medium behavior, suggesting that scholars should study what a medium does rather than what it is. Eskelinen argues that video games are ergodic texts, where the users' configurative practices predominate over traditional interpretive practices.[23] By viewing *Metro 2033* and *Metro: Last Light* as cybertexts, we are able to plug them into the *Metro* transmodal fiction while preserving the integrity of the dominant functions and processes of each text. Glukhovskii's various text types and modes offer distinctive entry points to the transmedial *Metro* syndicate and virtual community. Thanks to such innovations, scholars can think about texts in new ways: as immersive and interactive sociocultural practices or perhaps rituals.

In their paper "Gaming and the Limits of Digital Embodiment," Robert Farrow and Ioanna Iacovides follow Merleau-Ponty in suggesting that human subjectivity is shaped by physical interaction with the environment.[24] They argue that the digital game environment also simulates an embodied experience, which, though mediated through an avatar, is instrumental in shaping human subjectivity. For Merleau-Ponty, human subjectivity, or consciousness, is perceptual and is grounded in our physical being. Merleau-Ponty explains that the body experiences a variety of phenomena in terms of movement, depth, and sensation, but must learn and "reorganize the body schema" to perform behaviors like seeing colors or playing piano.[25] According to Merleau-Ponty, objects and technologies (for example, glasses or game controllers) that remain long enough on the surface of the body become incorporated into the body image and turn into areas of sensitivity. In the same way, in his book *Play Redux: The Form of Computer Games*, David Myers suggests, "Computer game structures reflect our natural senses and those cognitive properties that interpret and value the natural senses, and this reflection is, once engaged, trapped within its embodiment."[26]

---

23 Markku Eskelinen, *Cybertext Poetics: The Critical Landscape of New Media Literary Theory* (New York: Continuum, 2012).

24 Robert Farrow and Ioanna Iacovides, "Gaming and the Limits of Digital Embodiment," *Philosophy & Technology* 27, 2 (2014): 221–33.

25 Maurice Merleau-Ponty, *Phenomenology of Perception*, trans. Donald A. Landes (London: Routledge, 2012), 155.

26 David Myers, *Play Redux: The Form of Computer Games* (Ann Arbor: The University of Michigan Press, 2010), 160.

Myers posits that computer and video games capitalize on habitualized and repetitive behaviors, and substitute real referents and values to provide us with a visceral confirmation of our virtual selves. Imagine spending hours mapping and remapping some immersive "live" world, as well as the properties of the avatar body, to achieve some task or goal. The same kind of engagement that usually serves to form associations in reality is used to navigate the virtual space. Damasio points out that "the process of repeated practice that results in mastering a *performing skill*" is a ritual, and has long been used as a way to program conscious systems of action into the unconscious functions of the mind.[27] In his book *In-Game*, Gordon Calleja suggests that the video game player undergoes the simultaneous processes of incorporating the virtual environment into her mind and the body reacts to its perception of the virtual environment of the game.[28] According to Calleja, "the avatar aids the player in incorporating her consciousness into the game environment and serves as a digital manifestation of self."[29] These considerations should change the way we see traditional texts and narratives. Damasio contends that storytelling—the type that structures perception, image-feeling recall, and the construction of the self—is an implicit brain activity that prevails in all forms of sociocultural narrative.

Both Merleau-Ponty and Damasio suggest that certain paradigms of perception and organization are implicit and a result of evolutionary knowledge. Damasio does not cite video games in his book; however, his ideas help to resolve the difficult dynamic between digital simulation and real-life experience. According to Damasio, both real and simulated images activate emotions and motor involvement. He explains that, "the brain can *simulate*, within somatosensing regions, certain body states, *as if* they were occurring; and because our perception of any body state is rooted in the body maps of the somatosensing regions, we perceive the body state as actually occurring even if it is not."[30] The perception of a friend walking in a particular way can simultaneously trigger a variety of emotions, recall of the physical movement, and recall of other memories of that individual. The way in which the mind enacts storytelling is through simulation, convergence-divergence feedforward-feedback loops, and engagement, rather than a simple narrative or order of events.[31]

27 Damasio, *Self Comes to Mind*, 298.

28 Gordon Calleja, *In Game: From Immersion to Incorporation* (Cambridge, MA: MIT Press, 2011), 169.

29 Ibid., 181.

30 Damasio, *Self Comes to Mind*, 109.

31 Ibid., 154.

In simple terms, the subject simulates the environment and the processes of the story, reacting emotionally to elements that converge or diverge from expectations, and, at times, commanding and at other times, adjusting his reactions to the story. Subjectivity is the organization and concentration of bodily feelings and cognitive maps that are continually looping and converging with memories and predispositions. Physical sensations motivate action, morality, and decision-making, and serve as the only means for authenticating information about the world.

My analysis suggests that the way in which we perceive simulated worlds and their objects is similar to the way in which we perceive real objects. Our engagement through feeling and action is always mediated through the system of feedback loops that comprise the mechanism of the self and the body as a whole.[32] It follows that games fitting the cybertext criteria facilitate the construction of self through engagement by activating the sensory and mapping regions of our brains. On a large scale, Damasio suggests that the imaginative potential of the mind, as seen in mythology, is capable of improving the transfer of knowledge and morals in a society and accelerating the pace of cultural evolution. On a smaller scale pertinent to my analysis, immersive electronic games promote the creative user/player encounter with intermediality and transmediality, influencing social behavior and generating images of the living body.

In the *Metro 2033* video game, players experience different outcomes as a consequence of their in-game karma. Accordingly, the play-through of the game provides a simulation of the real world and reveals characteristics of each individual player. At the end of his quest, Artem finds himself on an aboveground tower ready to give his cohorts the coordinates for a missile attack on the Dark Ones. Shortly after he relays the coordinates, Artem experiences a telepathic communication from the Dark Ones, who, as it turns out, want to help the human race by saving it from itself. In the 2005-version ending of the novel Artem dies, but in the 2007-version ending he is merely disenchanted. In the computer-game-version ending of *Metro 2033,* depending on the players' karma rating based on altruism during game-play, the Artem avatar is presented with the choice of whether to kill the Dark Ones or not: an option which, according to Glukhovskii, was unlocked by less than 3% of the players that were able to earn enough good karma. This choice simulates real-life matrices and a new realm of game potential, one that brings it closer to the

32 A feedback loop is a recursive, self-regulating system, in which the output affects the subsequent input.

ideal immersive cybertext. The contemporary video game market is permeated with shooters that suspend the moral and social responsibility of the player, the bouts of shooting oftentimes interrupted by storylines that conceal the loading screen. In contrast to other games in the genre of first-person shooters, this game is extremely immersive, with a carefully crafted storyline and an interface that includes haptic and auditory events. As the player traverses the tunnels and post-apocalyptic wasteland, snow, mist, muck, and splattered blood obscure and complicate her vision, while the voices of the Dark Ones intensify and crowd out all other sounds with their telepathic pleas. The action of the video game *Metro: Last Light* takes place one year after the events of *Metro 2033* game and features an ending in which Artem carries out a missile strike against the Dark Ones. In the game Artem is now an official Ranger of the Polis, as the Red Line and The Reich fight and maneuver to gain control over the D6 section and the weapons stored there. Artem's missions are motivated by guilt as he escorts the "last" remaining Dark One to the Polis in a final effort to save humanity. The two possible endings conclude with Artem dying while destroying D6, or with the Dark Ones destroying the Red Line army.

The virtual environment, whether platform, portal, or game, shapes the user/player's experiences of being. The case of the *Metro* games' virtual space is based on the actual architectural system and mythologies of the Moscow Metro. The temporal setting is marked as post-Soviet with images and sound artifacts. Knowledge of the actual architectural space, the novel, and the post-Soviet sociocultural climate is useful to players in mapping their environment and planning their actions. The most striking form of engagement with the game is, of course, the feeling of fear that is triggered by the mutants who populate the metro tunnels, waters, the destroyed city above, and even the sky. Their appearance and screams are difficult to get used to, and luckily one can turn the sound down as one battles with mutant creatures that once were animals or perhaps humans. As the player activates her imaging and mapping knowledge and motor actions, fear is replaced by concentration, sensitivity, and a sense of control. The game provides enough time to train for combat and learn how to inflict the most damage on one's adversary. In essence, like many others, the game simulates the fight for survival and although the weapons and environment may change, the technique is always the same: maintain life, locate ammunition, expose the opponent's weakness, repeat. Whether in response to the simulated images, physical stimuli, or emotional triggers, the processes of the self are activated during game play. The depth of this engagement is supplemented by the virtual universe and culture surrounding the cybertext.

The *Metro* video games have enjoyed successive re-releases with downloadable content packages. As Glukhovskii continues to use interactive models to create, promote, and publish his works[33] on social media platforms like Twitter and VKontakte,[34] the model seems to be gaining popularity around the globe. Glukhovskii's bestseller status suggests that it is possible that his transmodal model can inspire many more writers in the future. While I am familiar with examples of adaptations of novels and films into games and vice versa, the instances of the author having any creative control over all the aspects of the franchise are rare.[35] In interviews at gaming conventions, Glukhovskii serves as a legitimizing asset to the multibillion-dollar gaming industry, highlighting the artistry of code in creating rich virtual environments and profound digital experiences. Glukhovskii states in an interview that he was happy to adapt the novel to a gaming format because, unlike a film adaptation, the game development process allowed him more creative freedom and influence.[36] The *Metro* franchise appears to have made a lasting impact due to both inventive marketing strategies and prosumer effort.

In an interview Glukhovskii explains that with the *Metro* video games he focused on creating a "living world," not a "product" or "brand."[37] The Russian voices and music create a multi-chronotopic atmosphere of hyperreal nostalgia, populated with expats, Communists, Nazis, and mutants. The in-game world resembles a post-Soviet alternate reality. This world and its components are the result of a collective sociocultural storytelling and image-making—or more succinctly, art. Video games register, simulate, and communicate the experience of embodied being in a virtual format, which makes them a form of art. In summary, video games are more than interactive stories or entertainment; games simulate real-world values and human behavior in a way that causes players to incorporate game play and game environment into their perception of the self. I am not suggesting that game play and real life are synonymous, but

33 These books include *Sumerki* [*Twilight*] (http://s-u-m-e-r-k-i.ru/index_old.html, Moscow: AST, 2007), *Rasskazy o rodine* [*Tales of the motherland*] (http://www.glukhovsky.ru/#motherland-read, Moscow: AST, 2010), and *Budushchee* [*Future*] (http://www.futu.re/, Moscow: AST, 2013).

34 *Future* was first published on the social network site VKontakte.

35 Author Tom Clancy is an atypical example of a US author who seems to have an active role in the game development of his novels.

36 See interview by Boris Nevskii, "Kontakt: Dmitrii Glukhovskii" [Contact: Dmitrii Glukhovskii], *Mir fantastiki* [World of fantasy], April 2010, http://mirf.ru/Articles/art4016.htm.

37 Alekhin, "Apokalipsis dlia shou-biznesa."

virtual images can activate the mirror neurons responsible for how we adopt and perceive states of our bodies. In this way video games supplement the individual player's lived experience,[38] support her creative and homeostatic impulses, and inform the mechanisms of her subjectivity. Furthermore, these virtual experiences and images initiate a chain of events that modify sociocultural group behavior.

In her article "Co-opting Transmedia Consumers: User Content as Entertainment or 'Free Labour'? The Cases of *S.T.A.L.K.E.R.* and *Metro 2033*," Natalia Sokolova outlines the conditions of the information economy that problematize traditional consumer and producer roles in the wake of transmedia and prosumerism.[39] The term "prosumer," coined by Christian Fuchs, is a portmanteau of producer and consumer and is meant to signify the conflation of the two roles. Sokolova argues that the internet has brought about "the implosion of production and consumption, labour and free time, work and entertainment, the author and the audience, the professional and the amateur."[40] Sokolova explains consumer function in relation to transmedia as follows: "[T]ransmedia is the creation of new cultural practices and experiences for their audiences. Transmedia involves interactive feedback inviting consumers to participate in 'co-production' of a topical fictional 'world' or 'universe'."[41]

According to Sokolova, rather than passively experiencing data, transmedia consumers are asked to view themselves as content creators. If the audience members passively scan without engaging or providing feedback, the transmedia project fails to produce consumers for its brand.[42] Sokolova emphasizes

---

38 For example, see Ortiz de Gortari, Angelica B., Karin Aronsson, and Mark Griffiths, "Game Transfer Phenomena in Video Game Playing," in *Evolving Psychological and Educational Perspectives on Cyber Behavior*, ed. Robert Zheng (Hershey, PA: Information Science Reference, 2013), 172.

39 For more on prosumerism, see Christian Fuchs, "Labor in Informational Capitalism and on the Internet," *The Information Society*, 26, no. 3 (2010): 179–96.

40 Natalia Sokolova, "Co-opting Transmedia Consumers: User Content as Entertainment or 'Free Labour'? The Cases of *S.T.A.L.K.E.R.* and *Metro 2033*," *Europe-Asia Studies* 64, no. 8 (October 2012): 1566.

41 Ibid., 1568.

42 Sokolova writes: "The communicative activities of consumers play an increasing role in product promotion and dissemination within transmedial projects, especially with the advent of widespread 'social media' in Russia. Glukhovskii claims that he even has nothing against a pirate version of his book. In his opinion, the text distributed free of charge is an opportunity to advertise the product. However, here the point is not about creating a product proper, though fans, modders and others do create virtual artifacts, widely adopted by the media industry, or which contribute to product dissemination. This issue should be considered in a broader sense: prosumers are crucial in the production of a special commodity—the transmedial project brand." Ibid., 1576.

that a new and effective marketing practice is based on creating a "communicative-informational environment around the brand" and providing consumers with opportunities for "maximum creativity."[43] Indeed, Glukhovskii's first website hosted a forum where users could post impressions and criticism of the narrative flow, character types or various technical details. In an interview Glukhovskii explains how the details he gleaned from the forums pertained only to small changes like the accurate depiction of metro infrastructure and firearm capabilities.[44] Nevertheless, in response to his fans' feedback Glukhovskii rewrote the novel (including making changes to the ending) and released the new twenty-chapter version in 2005 on a new website m-e-t-r-o.ru. Glukhovskii muses that it would be interesting to see the video game world expanded and set in other parts of the globe, citing the thriving and ripe content of *The Universe of Metro 2033* portal and fiction series. Consequently, *The Universe of Metro 2033* portal, as well as the other official sites associated with the syndicate, function essentially as content farms for Glukhovskii and AST.[45] Glukhovskii owns the rights to *The Universe of Metro 2033*, including all likenesses and characters associated with *Metro*, and as a result receives a share of royalties every time other authors publish a novel set in the universe of Metro 2033. In her article Sokolova explores the dynamics of prosumer creativity and brand marketing and speculates about the ethics of prosumer exploitation and consumer rights. She concludes that new patterns of media production permit transmedial franchises to employ co-creation strategies as part of the consumer participation model of brand life-style marketing. Sokolova suggests that Glukhovskii calculated the prosumer potential of his transmedial franchise and capitalized on the creative output of the *Metro* fans turned prosumers.[46]

Sokolova uses Henry Jenkins' concept of transmedia storytelling to argue that the *Metro 2034* transmedial franchise structure is "based on the further development of the story world through each new medium, and ideally each medium makes its own unique contribution to the unfolding of the story, the purpose being to create a unified and coordinated entertainment experience."[47] For Jenkins, transmedia is an assemblage of media united in the service of a

---

43 Ibid., 1576–77.

44 Alekhin, "Apokalipsis dlia shou-biznesa."

45 AST is the *Metro* series publisher.

46 Sokolova, "Co-opting Transmedia Consumers," 1572. Sokolova goes on to state, "Glukhovskii, who acts not only as the author but also as the project's producer, employed the strategy of 'co-creation' with the reader, which has since become popular among Russian writers."

47 Ibid., 1567–68.

story or narrative. Because they privilege the narrative function regardless of medium, Jenkins and, following him, Sokolova put all the value on the final product and don't foreground the creation of new subjectivities. It is for this reason that Sokolova concludes her paper with this paradox, "—on the one hand, consumers receive opportunities for creativity and self-expression, unavailable before, but on the other hand, we witness total commodification of their creativity; moreover, it is implied by the new business model and encouraged by it."[48] Eskelinen attacks Jenkins' foregrounding of narrativity and storytelling in his discussion of video games. According to Eskelinen, Jenkins subsumes games and other media under the "transmedia story-telling" economy, and studies the market and media practices surrounding transmedial products, rather than the inherent properties of each medium. Eskelinen points out that transmedial practices are not limited to storytelling or narrative structures, and that transmedial fictions share events and existents rather than the narrative mode of story.[49]

However, Rajewsky and Eskelinen both purport that transmedial practices have been part of human creativity for centuries. Eskelinen explains that, "Narrativist similarity studies too often either ignore or misunderstand that when bits and pieces of content move across 'media' they often change context, function and position, which may affect and usually also affects the modal status of these moving parts."[50] For Eskelinen digital games are "dynamic configurative systems of feedback loops,"[51] which combine explorative and constructive action, communication and interpretation, with the dominant configurative action.[52] When considering the atmosphere of ergodic texts and transmedial phenomena, we find that the creative and configurative user behaviors are closer to performance and rule-based structured play than to labor.

According to Baudrillard, communication technology and the information economy have changed the ways in which individuals encounter the world and themselves. Baudrillard proclaims: "There is no longer any system of objects. [...] But today the scene and mirror no longer exist; instead, there is a screen and network."[53] In his essay *The Ecstasy of Communication*, Baudrillard describes

48 Ibid., 1581.
49 Eskelinen, *Cybertext Poetics*, 334.
50 Ibid., 338.
51 Ibid., 309.
52 Ibid., 278.
53 Jean Baudrillard, *The Ecstasy of Communication*, ed. Sylvere Lotringer, trans. Bernard and Caroline Schütze (Brooklyn: Semiotext (e), 1988), 126.

the ways in which advertising monopolizes public and private life, making everything obscene. Baudrillard suggests, "Obscenity begins precisely when there is no more spectacle, no more scene, when all becomes transparence and immediate visibility, when everything is exposed to the harsh and inexorable light of information and communication. We are no longer a part of the drama of alienation: we live in the ecstasy of communication."[54] In his view each individual is a control center or satellite streaming an abundance of information but rarely communicating. I would suggest, however, that the user of the cybertext has many more options (besides production and consumption), because she is not just interpreting the data—she is making decisions and configuring her virtual experience. Changes in cultural production models point to constructive developments of cybertext-user modes and engagements, such as affirmative feedback loops. All of this prompts the unsettling question: is human subjectivity the product of one individual or of many individuals? Considering evidence examined in Glukhovskii's transmedial franchise *Metro*, one may conclude that the world and its things exist through the collective perspective of multiple subjectivities and their intersubjectivity.

---

54 Ibid., 130.

Part Five

Politics and Social Action

CHAPTER 9

Nothing but Mammals: Post-Soviet Sexuality after the End of History

Trevor Wilson,
University of Pittsburgh

And thus he spent his wretched age,
Neither beast nor man...

Alexander Pushkin, *The Bronze Horseman*[1]

Persecution and torment by no means require persecutors and tormentors. They need only ordinary us, as long as we are faced with someone not like us: a blackamoor,
a wild animal, a Martian, a poet, or a phantom. Those not like us
are born to be persecuted.

Marina Tsvetaeva, *Contemporary Sketches*[2]

---

1 Alexander Pushkin, *Mednyi vsadnik* [The bronze horseman], https://ru.wikisource.org/wiki/Медный_всадник_(Пушкин).

2 Marina Tsvetaeva, *Sovremennye zapiski* [Contemporary sketches], http://rulibrary.ru/tsvetaeva/memuarnaya_proza/162.

In an added footnote to his *Introduction to the Reading of Hegel* (*Introduction à la lecture de Hegel*), Alexandre Kojève attempts to address the problem of man's relationship to his animality at the infamous Hegelian end of History. He writes:

> If Man becomes animal again, his arts, his loves, and his games must also become purely "natural." It would be necessary then to admit that after the end of History, mankind would construct its edifices and its works of art like birds build their nests and spiders weave their webs, would perform its musical concerts in the manner of frogs and cicadas, would play like young animals play and would give itself to love like adult beasts.[3]

Kojève sees the end of History as the moment of man's reconciliation of the modernist splitting of nature and culture. If through his industry he has mastered, but also estranged himself, from his nature, in the end man can hope for a peaceful return to the base, if powerful and "spontaneous," conditions of the natural world and his animal-like atavistic condition.[4] Kojève wrote and delivered his lectures at a moment of a unique convergence of humanity and animality, as the Soviet project struggled to make sense of its socialist society as both an industrialized population, which dominated the natural world, and an autochthonous, animal-like force with its own inherent vitality. Soviet culture simultaneously sought to conquer "savage life" and to naturalize its industrialization: if the rhetoric surrounding the Five Year Plans attempted to seize upon man's raw, "natural" spontaneity in an effort to establish an organized social totality, an image of a natural machinality dialectically emerged as a result.[5]

---

3 Alexandre Kojève, *Introduction à la lecture de Hegel* [Introduction to the Reading of Hegel] (Paris: Gallimard, 1947), 436; all translations are mine unless indicated otherwise.

4 Of course, this paradigm of nature vs. culture, naive vs. sentimental, savage vs. civilized, etc., is a frequent and familiar modernist dichotomy. Its relevance to Soviet culture is most saliently expressed in the opposition of spontaneity and consciousness. See Katerina Clark, *The Soviet Novel: History as Ritual* (Bloomington: Indiana University Press, 2000 [1981]), 15–24. I am suggesting here a correlation of the spontaneity of rural peasant life as animalistic and the consciousness of urbanity and the proletariat as indicative of man's estranged industrial labor.

5 Describing the Russian avant-garde and later Stalinist utopian project, Boris Groys invokes this synthesis: "If such work succeeds in creating an artificial unconscious, an artificial context, and new and as yet unseen machines of desire called, say, 'Soviet people,' then these persons will suddenly be able to lead lives and generate texts that do not differ from natural ones, rendering irrelevant both the distinction between natural and artificial and all the effort expended upon it." Boris Groys, *The Total Art of Stalinism: Avant-Garde, Aesthetic Dictatorship, and Beyond*, trans. Charles Rougle (Princeton: Princeton University Press, 1992), 120.

According to Kojève, that which estranges man from nature and the animal, namely, his labor, will become reintegrated into the natural world at the end of History. In the final analysis, the Soviet man was formed at the "critical threshold, at which the difference between animal and human, which is so decisive for our culture, threatens to vanish."[6]

What happens, then, at the end of the end of History? After the collapse of the Soviet Union, cultural depictions of the human body fracture at the juncture of animal and non-animal. This crisis in representation seems to arise precisely in conjunction with the emergence of socially (here, sexually) deviant subjects who trouble an easier, earlier imagination of the Soviet totality. Werewolves, foxy prostitutes, and zoophilic queers haunt the pages and screens of the post-Soviet cultural imaginary. These depictions of the socially abject as part animal or driven by animal instinct mark a disruption in the past Soviet reconciliation of culture and nature. In its transition from Soviet to post-Soviet, therefore, representation of sexuality moved from a place of social function, tied to collectivity and use value through its reconciliation of natural and social needs, to an exiled place of individual expression and exchange value, something which at its best was successfully sequenced into the family and at its worst threatened a stable definition of "human" through its gesturing toward an essential, "true" self beyond socially derived norms for identity. By suggesting a new, free-market-driven subjectivity in post-Soviet Russia, in particular the chaotic years of the 1990s, the human-animal articulates a larger cultural anxiety surrounding individual, newly expressive desires that provoke difference rather than singularity, chaos rather than order. This anxiety seems to be the product of a larger crisis in biopolitical control over the post-Soviet collective. This crisis has transformed in the twenty-first century, as Putin's Russia has seized upon anxiety over individual desires in order to justify his solidification of state power. It is no accident that the sanctioning of imported Western foods in 2014 mirrors the ongoing criminalization of sexual content deemed "propaganda to minors" as well as the recent blocking of popular pornographic sites Pornhub and YouPorn in 2016. These steps underscore Putin's rejection of consumerist individuality, and with it, the idea of non-normative sexuality, in a steady march toward illiberal collective traditionalism.

Previously, before the collapse of the Soviet Union, Soviet sexuality could be seen as permeating the social fabric of everyday, communitarian life. This

6 Giorgio Agamben, *The Open: Man and Animal*, trans. Kevin Attell (Stanford, CA: Stanford University Press, 2004), 21.

imbrication was at odds with the sexuality of bourgeois individualism, which remained isolated from the social collective. Eric Naiman suggests that nascent Soviet society's "status as a single entity [...] had transformed the link between sexual activity and the depletion of energy into a phenomenon that affected all areas of social and economic interaction."[7] He cites in particular Evgenii Poletaev and Nikolai Punin's 1918 manifesto *Against Civilization* (*Protiv tsivilizatsii*), in which the two imagine a communist future where "cultured society will not reject pleasures and will fear neither their qualitative nor quantitative use. But this use will be regulated by a [state] apparatus so that a simple means of relaxation does not become the goal of vital individual and societal efforts."[8] Their words presage Andrei Platonov's parodic pamphlet "Antisexus" (*Antiseksus*), which advertised an imagined masturbation device said to "regulate the field of sexuality and, thanks to this, bring out the highest function of man: his spirit, his concealed divinity, which needs to be made more visible and widely used as one of the most important goods of civilization."[9] This universal sex toy, the narrator claims, makes it possible to "achieve pleasure of any duration, ranging from a couple of seconds to a number of days" and "to regulate the amount of sperm in order to achieve spiritual balance, that is, not allow for a needless exhaustion of the organism and reduction in the vitality of life functions."[10] Platonov's piece suggests that Soviet culture and its command economy had begun to approach sexuality as a social need demanding satisfaction, thereby implicitly opposing, for example, Sigmund Freud's theory of sexuality and civilization, where the animalistic impulses of the libido are suppressed or sublimated in order to enact civilized society. Instead, Platonov (as well as Poletaev and Punin) offer a utopian Soviet culture, which can in fact incorporate sexual behavior (even sexual deviancy) into society through commerce and industry.

This is not to suggest, of course, that sexual diversity was somehow championed in Soviet Russia. Canonical narratives of Soviet sexual mores describe a retreat from the early experimentation of the 1910s and 1920s back into a traditionalist understanding of the family as a social unit, this transition most commonly dated to the 1936 law banning abortion.[11] Any evaluation of Soviet

---

7 Eric Naiman, *Sex in Public: The Incarnation of Early Soviet Ideology* (Princeton, NJ: Princeton University Press, 1997), 74–75.

8 Evgenii Poletaev and Nikolai Punin, *Protiv tsivilizatsii* [Against civilization] (St. Petersburg: 4-aia Gosudarstvennaia tipografiia, 1918), 44.

9 Andrei Platonov, "Antiseksus" [Antisexus] in *Sochineniia* [Works] (Moscow: IMLIRAN, 2004), 128.

10 Ibid., 129.

11 Wendy Z. Goldman, *Women, the State, and Revolution: Soviet Family Policy and Social Life, 1917–1936* (Cambridge: Cambridge University Press, 1993), 331.

sexuality must necessarily take this conservative turn in mind, for it helps to explain the near absence of public discussions of sexual experience until perestroika. Sexual normativity and traditionalism were enforced starting with the conservative turn under Stalin through the late-Soviet period, as the forced obscurity and state persecution of dissident LGBT authors like Evgenii Kharitonov and Gennadii Trifonov clearly indicate. Juxtaposing Soviet and post-Soviet discourses on sexuality reveals, more generally, the deficiencies of the political systems in both periods. Contemporary radical sexual politics harken back to the experimentation of the early Soviet period, and it is through an examination of this revival, that, to quote Jonathan Brooks Platt, "we recognize the impulse to preserve the revolution's utopian potential to imagine new forms of proletarian sensuousness."[12]

Keti Chukhrov, arguing that "under the conditions of an economy aimed at use value, desire stops being libidinal," identifies in commodity-free culture an attempt to incorporate sex and sexuality within the larger framework of everyday Soviet sociality:

> Sexual intercourse is of course present, but it becomes one of the modes of communication within the framework of existential necessity—be it love, friendship, or even just physiological need. That is, it is inscribed into the more general framework, so that the elements of sexuality do not acquire any surplus value that would make them seductive in a specific way [...]. It is inscribed into the collective Eros, presupposing joy rather than enjoyment (*jouissance*).[13]

What is important here is the Soviet emphasis on *collective* Eros. Sexuality's inscription into the social body concomitantly rendered the individual sexualized human body un-visible. This, of course, is not to suggest the absence of expressive individual experiences of sexuality; these experiences, however, assumed secondary signification in a modeling system that sequenced the social before the individual. The result is an imagined reconciliation of nature/animal desire and human culture.

For example, Chukhrov cites Lev Vygotsky and his *Thought and Language* (1934) as an example within psychology where the social predicates the

---

12 Jonathan Brooks Platt, "Queer-Militancy and Post-Soviet Russia," in *Sex of the Oppressed*, ed. Nikolay Oleynikov (Guelph, ON: Publication Studio, 2016), 15.

13 Keti Chukhrov, "Sexuality in a Non-Libidinal Economy," *e-flux*, no. 54 (2014), http://www.e-flux.com/journal/sexuality-in-a-non-libidinal-economy/.

individual. In his critique of Jean Piaget's theory of child development, Vygotsky rejects the Swiss psychologist's borrowing from Freud not only the claim "that the pleasure principle precedes the reality principle [...] but also with it the entire metaphysics of the pleasure principle, which transforms from a subordinate and biologically auxiliary moment into some kind of self-sustained vital source, into a *primum movens*, into the primary mover of all psychological development."[14] On the contrary, Vygotsky's work emphasizes the influence that surroundings and social activity have on the production of a child's intellect. Chukhrov is correct to interpret this re-sequencing as subordinating pleasure to the child's larger adaptation to a social reality, so that the social prefigures the individual. It also implies that "natural" sexuality cannot be differentiated from its cultural socialization.

Furthermore, this subordination of instinct to social reality implicates the position of the animal in social structuring. In his attempt to discover the "roots" of thought and speech, Vygotsky approaches the question of primitive cognition amongst animals, and in particular fellow primates. Citing Engels, he concludes that both small children and animals develop along similar lines in terms of speech and intellect: "It is clear on its own that we do not intend to deprive animals of the capacity for planned and premeditated action."[15] The true moment of the divergence of humans from animals arrives with the emergence of verbal thought (*rechevoe myshlenie*), which is contingent upon the child mastering the social means of thinking, that is, language.[16] It is important to stress this Soviet paradigm, by which socio-historical development acts concomitantly with instinctual, animalistic life, inducing their reconciliation.[17]

From the mid-1980s onward, however, the massive wave of cultural, economic, and political transformations that swept across Russian society produced a new popular imagination driven by the consumption of foreign products.[18] In particular, sex and sexuality flooded Russian markets, televisions, literature, and films, filling a discursive void in post-Soviet society once so aptly summarized in the *krylataia fraza* (adage) "*v SSSR seksa net* [there is no sex in

14 Lev Vygotskii, *Myshlenie i rech'* [Thought and language] (Moscow: Labirint, 1999 [1934]), 55.

15 Ibid., 103.

16 Ibid., 108.

17 The scientifically questionable approach to biology advocated by Trofim Lysenko provides another example of the interaction of historical materialism and nature. See Dominique Lecourt, *Lyssenko: Histoire réelle d'une "science prolétarienne"* [Lysenko: the real story of a "proletarian science"] (Paris: François Maspero, 1976); see also David Joravsky, *The Lysenko Affair* (Cambridge, MA: Harvard University Press, 1970).

18 See Adele Marie Barker, ed. *Consuming Russia: Popular Culture, Sex, and Society Since Gorbachev* (Durham, NC: Duke University Press, 1999).

the USSR]."[19] The phrase was coined on the joint television broadcast in 1986 with hosts Vladimir Pozner and Phil Donahue, where Soviet and American audiences had the chance to ask one another questions about their respective cultures. When asked by an American about the publicity of sex in the Soviet Union, Liudmila Ivanova, a member of the Soviet Women's Committee, demurred that sex didn't exist in the USSR and that they were categorically against it. This, however, was quickly changing: Whereas previously Soviet sexuality figured predominantly within a utilitarian, public discourse, popular culture suddenly offered an unprecedented view into the most private quarters of Russian life. Sex shops dotted the streets of Moscow and prostitution became a possible profession for women across the Soviet Union. Films like *Intergirl* (*Interdevochka,* Petr Todorovskii, 1989) and *Little Vera* (*Malen'kaia Vera,* Vasilii Pichul, 1988) introduced female sexual agency into the culture of perestroika. Furthermore, homosexuality was decriminalized in 1993, resulting in an onslaught of LGBT oriented publications, notably Dmitry Kuzmin's almanac *RISK.* Also, Glagol Press made headlines mostly for being the first to publish James Baldwin's *Giovanni's Room* and William Burroughs's *Naked Lunch* in Russia.[20]

Public organizations dedicated to distributing information about sex education also emerged in the late 1980s and early 1990s. Groups like the Association for Health and the Family, the Association for Combating AIDS, the Center for Shaping Adolescent Sexual Culture, the Russian Family Planning Association, and the "sexological" association Culture and Health all formed at this time with the intention of jumpstarting a conversation in Russian society about healthy sexual behavior. In contrast to the previous control of sexuality in Soviet times, the appearance of the wide variety of public organizations signaled the recognition that sexuality is multifaceted. Here, the influence of Igor' Kon, often considered the founder of Russian sexology, cannot be overstated.[21] These markers of a renovated Russian sexuality had particular consequences for the conceptualization of the human body, encouraging, amongst other things, an endorsement of the sexual body through information on masturbation, safe

19 For a fuller account of the cultural shift within popular culture, see Eliot Borenstein, *Overkill: Sex and Violence in Contemporary Russian Popular Culture* (Ithaca: Cornell University Press, 2008).

20 See Laurie Essig, *Queer in Russia: A Story of Sex, Self, and the Other* (Durham, NC: Duke University Press, 1999), 94–97.

21 For his most groundbreaking work, see Igor' Kon, *Klubnichka na berezke. Seksual'naia kul'tura v Rossii* [Sex culture in Russia. Strawberries on the birch] (Moscow: OGI, 1997); Igor' Kon, *Vkus zapretnogo ploda. Seksologiia dlia vsekh* [The taste of the forbidden fruit. Sexology for all] (Moscow: Sem'ia i shkola, 1997).

sex practices, family planning, and so on. This re-discovery of the body, as I hope to illustrate, fundamentally troubled the previously sealed juncture of the human-animal in Soviet ideology, undoing the Soviet modernist nature/culture reconciliation and producing instead monstrous pariahs in the shape of hybrids.

Retrospectively, the experience of individual embodiment, be it gendered, sexualized, or generally "othered," can be seen to presage or pave the way to a cultural trend that would become full blown in the immediate post-Soviet period. This cultural change emerged vividly in women's prose.[22] In the words of Helena Goscilo, female writers of the post-glasnost era documented their bodies' suffering: "they bruise, hemorrhage, and break; they endure rape, childbirth, abortion, beating, and disease; they succumb to substance addiction, incontinence, and sundry dehumanizing processes—all painstakingly detailed in slow motion."[23] The general increased attention to *byt* (everyday life) and the lived physical experience of being a woman in post-Soviet Russia produced a phenomenological split: women became at once human and inhuman. Women's experiences as represented in literature reveal the irreconcilable conflict between one's social and embodied lives: The body "refuses to undergo the procedures of becoming human," that is, it refuses to subsume instinct to social life. Instead, the subject fights a "tug-of-war between the social and the psychical channels of bodily inscription."[24]

While this tug-of-war most visibly plays out within gendered bodily experience, the frequent denigration of sexuality as "animalistic" and "savage" suggests that sexually embodied alterity plays a foundational role in the process of determining who and what becomes a human in post-communist Russia, and that it is far more deeply implicated in establishing subjectivity beyond the frame of the "woman question." Indeed, it seems that sexuality's signifying potential as a base and instinctual force of nature (specifically, that which is animal and non-human) threatens to upend the social cohesion, and nature/

---

22 While the corporality of women's prose is outside of the scope of this study, the demarcation of women's bodies in post-Soviet fiction is important to any study on sexuality, corporality, and social cohesion. See Benjamin M. Sutcliffe, *The Prose of Life: Russian Women Writers from Khrushchev to Putin* (Madison: University of Wisconsin Press, 2009); see also Helena Goscilo, "Speaking Bodies: Erotic Zones Rhetoricized," in *Fruits of Her Plume: Essays on Contemporary Russian Women's Culture,* ed. Helena Goscilo (New York: M. E. Sharpe, 1993): 135–64.

23 Helena Goscilo, *Dehexing Sex: Russian Womanhood During and After Glasnost* (Ann Arbor: University of Michigan Press, 1996), 89.

24 Vitaly Chernetsky, *Mapping Postcommunist Cultures: Russia and Ukraine in the Context of Globalization* (Montreal: McGill-Queen's University Press, 2007), 118.

culture synthesis, of the post-Soviet sphere. Take, for example, the protagonist's speech at the conclusion of *Sad Detective* (*Pechal'nyi detektiv*, 1986) by Viktor Astaf'ev:

> It is not the male and female, copulating according to the will of nature in order to propagate the species, but a human with another human, united in order to help one another and the society in which they live and improve themselves, as from one heart to another they transfuse their blood and with it everything that is good in them. By their parents they were given their life, their habits and their characteristics, and from all kinds of raw material they must produce solid material, fashion a cell in the centuries-old building called Family, as if again emerging in this world and, having reached the grave, separating from one another with an unrepeatable suffering and pain that no one can hope to know.
>
> What a great enigma! Millennia have been carelessly wasted in an attempt at comprehension, yet, much like death, the family enigma is still not understood, still not solved. Dynasties, societies, empires have crumbled to dust if the family began to disintegrate, if he and she lost their way, unable to find one another. [...] [W]ith the downfall of the family comes the downfall of harmony, evil begins to overcome good, the earth opens up beneath our feet in order to swallow up *the rabble who already have no reason to call themselves people.*[25]

It is precisely these people who do not deserve to be called people that emerge once the sexually embodied subject enters the field of visibility. Of course, the frequent rhetorical claim that sexual minorities threaten civilization is by no means unique to post-Soviet Russia, yet it is remarkable how quickly the relatively new visibility in Russia of homosexuality has mobilized scapegoat politics that actively dehumanize and exclude certain individuals from the social consensus: "[O]nce sexuality may be read and interpreted in light of homosexuality, all sexuality is subject to a hermeneutics of suspicion."[26]

Furthermore, it is through their status as social pariahs that these minorities become culturally coded as animalistic. Much like Giorgio Agamben's

---

25 V. P. Astaf'ev, *Pechal'nyi detektiv* [Sad detective], in *Zhizn' prozhit'* [To live your life] (Moscow: Sovetskii pisatel', 1986), 121–22 (emphasis added).

26 Lee Edelman, *Homographesis: Essays in Gay Literary and Cultural Theory* (New York: Routledge, 1994), 7; see also "The Other within Us," in Brian James Baer, *Other Russias: Homosexuality and the Crisis of Post-Soviet Identity* (New York: Palgrave Macmillan, 2009), 71–89.

homo sacer, they emerge at the threshold of indistinction between political and biological life, their biological (and sexual) bodies the constant object of state control.[27] Similarly, Agamben's metaphorical werewolf occupies a liminal zone between man and animal:

> What had to remain in the collective unconscious as a monstrous hybrid of human and animal, divided between the forest and the city—the werewolf—is, therefore, in its origin the figure of the man who has been banned from the city. That such a man is defined as a wolf-man and not simply as a wolf [...] is decisive here. The life of the bandit, like that of the sacred man, is not a piece of animal nature without any relation to law and the city. It is, rather, a threshold of indistinction and of passage between animal and man, *physis* and *nomos*, exclusion and inclusion: the life of the bandit is the life of the *loup garou*, the werewolf, who is precisely *neither man nor beast*, and who dwells paradoxically within both while belonging to neither.[28]

The post-Soviet period provides an interesting response to Agamben's formulation of biopolitics, having borne witness to the post-post-historical rupture of a claimed reconciliation between political and biological life. I would like to turn, then, to two examples in post-Soviet fiction in which sexuality becomes animalistic, triggering social exclusion and the transfiguration of subjectivity into the human-animal hybrid pariah. I have chosen two authors, Viktor Pelevin and Iaroslav "Slava" Mogutin, in order to approach the subject of human-animal sexuality from both universalizing and minoritizing perspectives.[29] On the one hand, sexuality's splitting of the body into its social and corporeal components resonates dramatically across sexual and gender orientations. But on the other hand, prostitutes or "sexual deviants" are simultaneously excluded from and interpellated by Russian society. Pelevin's work demonstrates this process through the transfiguration of characters from human to animal and vice versa. Unlike for Vygotsky, for Pelevin sexuality moves from biological life toward

---

27 Giorgio Agamben, *Homo Sacer: Sovereign Power and Bare Life*, trans. Daniel Heller-Roazen (Stanford, CA: Stanford University Press, 1998).

28 Ibid., 105.

29 I am referring here to Sedgwick's bifurcated hermeneutic, well known to queer theory, whereby "minoritizing" interpretative frameworks privilege homosexuality as uniquely important to LGBT groups, whereas "universalizing" approaches instead interpret LGBT culture and texts as indicative of larger social trends in sexuality, thereby re-instating homosexuality's larger significance within predominantly heterosexual culture. See Eve Kosofsky Sedgwick, *Epistemology of the Closet* (Berkeley: University of California Press, 1990), 1–2.

socialization and facilitates commentary on the problematic state of social cohesion in post-Soviet Russia. Despite its satire, however, Pelevin's work leaves the normative rules of social life and biopolitical control intact. While his novels address relatively explicitly the aforementioned "hermeneutics of suspicion" toward newly visible sexuality, he ultimately allows his plots to conclude with a return to social coercion. Pelevin is more concerned with what pariah figures (prostitutes, queers, werewolves) share with acceptable members of society (government officers, who are also queers and werewolves). Mogutin, on the other hand, illustrates how one's own experience of this division produces a more defiantly transgressive aesthetic of human animality. Through a reclamation of the abject, Agamben's *loup garou,* Slava Mogutin's writing attempts to reclaim the experience of social exclusion by embracing his status as social pariah and by becoming zoomorphic. His sexual perversions in this regard function much like the corporeal experience of female bodies in women's prose, openly challenging the normative rules that define who and what counts as human. The result is a firm challenge to biopolitical control: Mogutin rejects the return of the formerly excluded sexual minorities to society and embraces his abject status.

Pelevin's relationship with sexuality and cultural alterity in his works shares a common conceptual origin with writers such as Viktor Erofeev and Vladimir Sorokin, whose employment of homosexuality's non-reproductive nature frequently pairs with the grotesque and "underscores the rejection of the social burden traditionally foisted on Russian writers and artists to contribute to the 'production' of good Russian and Soviet citizens."[30] In their attempts to rid themselves of the realist-driven literary style of the Soviet period, these authors grapple instead with extreme bodily experience. Hence, for example, Sorokin's use of homosexuality coupled with dark humor and graphic violence in works like "A Business Proposal" (*Delovoe predlozhenie*).[31] Sorokin claims, in an interview with *Moskovskie novosti,* that he wanted simply "to compensate for the absence of corporeality in Russian literature."[32] Pelevin's works likewise position the marked individual in opposition to communally ascribed life, often explicitly invoking animality and sexuality in order to do so.[33]

30 Baer, *Other Russias,* 123.

31 Vladimir Sorokin, "Delovoe predlozhenie" [A business proposal] in *Utro snaipera* [The sniper's morning] (Moscow: Ad Marginem, 2002), 24-32.

32 Vladimir Sorokin, "Provintsial'nyi 'roman' Vladimira Sorokina" [Vladimir Sorokin's provincial "novel"], *Moskovskie novosti,* Dec. 18–25, 1994, 19.

33 My argument that zoomorphic depictions in Pelevin's work are indicative of a disruption in Soviet social cohesion is indebted to Sofya Khagi's article on biopolitics and the works of

Beginning as early as his story "Hermit and Six-Toes" (*Zatvornik i shestipalyi*, 1990), Pelevin and his writing interrogate the relationship between biopolitical social control and an individual's sexual alterity.[34] The story follows two chickens at a factory in their messianic countdown to slaughter. Their universe, the Lunacharskii Chicken Factory, obviously suggests that of the Soviet "social organism"[35], and their names, Hermit and Six-Toes, suggest two possible reasons for expulsion from the social: religious, spiritual wandering and corporeal abnormality. A passing conversation about love, however, reveals that sexual and romantic mores are equally cause for banishment. Six-Toes tells Hermit: "[W]hen they drove me out of the community, they asked me if I loved the things that should be loved. I said I didn't know."[36] The conversation doesn't go anywhere, perhaps because of the chickens' mutual incomprehension of what love is, yet it will set a precedent of marginalized, grotesque, and abnormal characters reflecting on love in Pelevin's writing.

Pelevin's "Nika" (*Nika*) further develops the theme of sexualized animality, here pushing ever so slightly into the taboo realm of bestiality. The narrator describes at length his relationship with Nika, who possesses "swarthy southern charm" and a spontaneous drive for pleasure.[37] The slow realization that Nika is in fact the narrator's cat obfuscates the boundary between girlfriend and pet, thereby suggesting sexuality as something perversely un-socialized—Nika has a tense relationship with his friends and family. In her search for comfort and pleasure, Nika approaches objects "only as long as she was using them, and then they disappeared, probably because she had practically nothing of her own at all. I sometimes thought that she was the exact type the old-style communists had attempted to breed, without the slightest idea of what their results might look like."[38] Pelevin here presents a very

---

Viktor Pelevin. See Sofya Khagi, "The Monstrous Aggregate of the Social: Toward Biopolitics in Victor Pelevin's Work," *The Slavic and East European Journal* 55, 3(2011): 439–459.

34 Viktor Pelevin, "Zatvornik i shestipalyi" [Hermit and six-toes], in *Vse povesti i esse* [Complete novellas and essays] (Moscow: Eksmo, 2005), 7–63.

35 Anatolii Lunacharskii was the first head of the People's Commissariat for Education (Narkompros), formed in the early years of the Soviet Union to accelerate public education and cultural production. Lunacharskii and the organization played a major role in establishing connections between the proletariat and the intelligentsia.

36 Ibid., 41.

37 Viktor Pelevin, "Nika" [Nika], in *Vse rasskazy* [Complete short stories] (Moscow: Eksmo, 2005), 319.

38 Ibid., 321.

provocative distinction between Nika's Soviet-era utilitarian relationship to material objects and his own as post-Soviet. For Nika, the lack of property and libidinal investment in objects reduces her pleasure (and sexuality) to mere use value, whereas for the narrator these objects are invested with sentimental value:

> For Nika the sugar bowl was nothing more than a shiny truncated cone, stuffed full of papers. For me it was a kind of storehouse for all the proofs of the reality of existence which I had gathered through life: a page from a long-destroyed address book with a telephone number which I had never dialed; a ticket to the Illusion movie theater with the stub still intact; a small photo; and several prescriptions that had never been filled.[39]

Like most animals, her needs are "purely physiological: a full belly, a good sleep, and enough physical affection to maintain a sound digestion."[40] The narrator's envy of Nika's "wholeness" implies a reversion back to the romantic trope of gazing from the outside upon a simpler life: "We see then in irrational nature only a happier sister who remained behind in the parental home from which we rushed forth to foreign climes, in the arrogant high spirits of our freedom. [...] As long as we were mere children of nature, we were happy and perfect; we have become free and have lost both."[41] The return of the opposition between culture and nature suggests that the Soviet project of synthesizing the two, and therefore eliminating the human/animal distinction, has collapsed. What remains is a precarious biopolitical subject who must instead oscillate between the two yet belong to neither.

Nearly all of Pelevin's writings employ similar interspecies motifs, yet it is in his two works devoted to animal shapeshifters ("A Werewolf Problem in Central Russia" [*Problema vervolka v srednei polose*, 1991] and *The Sacred Book of the Werewolf* [*Sviashchennaia kniga oborotnia*, 2004]) that one sees most clearly the paradox of social coercion and exclusion. In "A Werewolf Problem in Central Russia," a lone man named Sasha stumbles upon a meeting of werewolves in the woods just as they are about to undergo the rites of transformation.[42]

39 Ibid.

40 Ibid., 322.

41 Friedrich Schiller, *On the Naïve and Sentimental in Literature*, trans. Helen Watanabe-O'Kelly (Manchester: Carcanet New Press, 1981), 30.

42 Pelevin, *Problema vervolka v srednei polose* [A werewolf problem in Central Russia], in *Vse povesti i esse* [Complete novellas and essays] (Moscow: Eksmo, 2010): 64–112.

The protagonist's own transformation into a werewolf signals his entrance into the social group. The pack leaves for Kon'kovo and with it the Michurin Kolkhoz (like the Lunacharskii Chicken Farm, another clear indication of a return to a Soviet symbolic). There, Sasha and his pack confront Nikolai, another elderly werewolf who has been exiled from the pack. According to Nikolai, they are upset because he breaks the laws of the werewolves:

> If I am bound by laws, they are of my own making, and I believe that is my right—to choose which authority to submit to and in what way. You are not strong enough to allow yourselves that, but in order not to seem like idiots in your own eyes, you convince yourselves that the existence of individuals like me can harm you.[43]

Nikolai, "not a wolf but a pig," eating garbage and living with "a mongrel bitch," has become the figure of the *homo sacer* through his transgression, for it is at his expense that the social collective, the werewolf pack, is formed.[44] Agamben argues that *homo sacer*'s exclusion is necessary for the authority of the sovereign over social life.[45] In order to join the pack officially, Sasha must therefore fight and kill Nikolai in a kind of initiation rite. Only this will allow him equal status as a member of the group. Looking at the shadows of different werewolves, Sasha notes that everyone has a human shadow except him, for he has a wolf one. While the wolf shadow for a (were)wolf might seem to suggest coherence, it is fitting that members of the collective are simultaneously both wolf and human. Sasha is an outsider as long as he refuses to make this transition—he remains purely animal and therefore out of the realm of the social.

The work blurs, however, any true distinction between "insiders" and "outsiders." Both groups are capable and even guilty of the same perversions (here understood as the monstrous transformation between man and wolf). Former comrade Nikolai could have been former pariah Sasha, and Sasha or any other werewolf runs the risk of one day becoming excluded like Nikolai. Pelevin's more recent *The Sacred Book of the Werewolf* continues this ambiguity and places sexuality at the very center of the human/animal, collective/outcast divide.[46] A sequel of sorts to "A Werewolf Problem," the novel describes a race

---

43 Ibid., 94.

44 Viktor Pelevin, *A Werewolf Problem in Central Russia and Other Stories*, trans. Andrew Bromfield (New York: New Directions, 1998), 22.

45 Agamben, *Homo Sacer*, 84.

46 Viktor Pelevin, *Sviashchennaia kniga oborotnia: Roman* [The sacred book of the werewolf: A novel] (Moscow: Eksmo, 2004).

of ancient foxes, human-like except for a tail, who live on the fringes of human society, vampirically feeding off the sexual energy of humans. The foxes have neither biological sex nor mortality. They also do not necessarily express sexuality in the "normal" way humans do: "although we don't have any sex in the sense of the ability to reproduce, all of its external signs are present."[47] All foxes have a tail that grows erect (pun intended) in order to cast an illusion on their target. Whoever is under the spell will imagine himself/herself copulating with the fox, yet the fox simply projects the illusion onto the victim and "assimilates" sexual energy in order to maintain her powers.

Animality is the prime mover of this queer sexuality in the novel. It is telling that this sexuality always emerges from a peripheral place: A Hu-Li, the aptly-named protagonist of the novel,[48] works as a prostitute with Lolita-tinged pedophilic insinuations. Although legal (and ageless), the fox is often asked to prove her age, and her clients request a wide buffet of sexual favors, from anal sex to group play. The place of non-normative sexual identity is at first located not only at the fringe of sociability but also at the fringe of humanity and animality. This changes when A Hu-Li meets Sasha, the protagonist from "A Werewolf Problem," who is now working as a government officer and using his werewolf services to howl at the moon in the Arctic north in an occult ritual to help Russia's oil extraction (the logistics of this are never explained). A Hu-Li teaches Sasha how to have sex in their unique, shapeshifter way, using their hypnotic tails to imagine sexual scenarios instead of physically copulating. Sasha, however, recoils at joining A Hu-Li in her perverse sexual practices and fringe lifestyle living away from Muscovite society in a drainage pipe in Bitsevskii Park. He eventually returns with "enhanced" werewolf powers to serve the greater good of Mother Russia with a heavy dose of Nietzschean superman undertones. His coworkers in his particular agency are also werewolves, some of which requires massive amounts of amphetamines to transform into a wolf (or "get it up").[49] The novel concludes with the suggestion that while A Hu-Li remains an outsider and Sasha a crucial figure for the machinations of the state, both ultimately are similarly abject characters with zoomorphic and sexual perversions. This results in an absurdist unveiling of the hypocrisies of

47 Ibid., 23. The distinction between (re)productive and non-(re)productive sex echoes the previous distinction made by Astaf'ev regarding heteronormative, reproductive sex and its role in supporting social stability.

48 A Hu-Li is a reference to the vulgar phrase "a khuli," meaning roughly "what the f*ck."

49 Sorokin similarly satirizes the sexual hypocrisies of the state apparatus in his *Den' oprichnika* [The day of the oprichnik] (Moscow: Zakharov, 2006), which famously imagines the social bonding of the *oprichniki,* the thuggish arm of the Russian state, as a drug-fueled gay orgy.

social conformity in post-Soviet Russia, where the only difference between an underage prostitute and an FSB officer is a state of mind.

If Pelevin dabbles in anthropomorphism in order to comment on the chaotic implications of individualism, where we are all guilty of sexual incongruities after the collapse of the Soviet resolution of our "animal" needs, for queer writers like Slava Mogutin the zoomorphic position represents a more political declaration of independence. Mogutin led a prolific career in the 1990s, both in and outside of queer politics. He rose to fame through journalism and essays in mainstream Russian newspapers, eventually becoming named the best critic of the year in 1994 by *Nezavisimaia gazeta.*[50] Beyond journalism, Mogutin has had and continues to have an incredibly diverse career: from poetry to pornography to translation and visual arts, his professional pursuits have unfolded across both the United States and Russia, with several stops in between. According to Vitaly Chernetsky,

> Similarly to many other contemporary writers exploring marginal subject positions, Mogutin's work testifies to the fact that the erosion of the author function is far from a universal phenomenon in contemporary culture. [...] His project can be seen as a post-modernist update of the Russian Symbolist notion of "life creation" [...] combined with tireless (post)-avant-gardist "self-fashioning," continuous reinvention, and modification of subjectivity.[51]

His queer-oriented journalism and literature is his legacy in Russian cultural politics of the 1990s. In 1993 Mogutin had charges first brought against him for his publication of the article "The Communist Youth League members' dirty peckers" (*Griaznye kontsy komsomol'tsev*), in which he openly discussed Boris Moiseev's homosexuality and his sexual dalliances with Komsomol elite. Later, Mogutin made international headlines when he attempted to marry his American partner, Robert Filippini, in Moscow. These press scandals helped shape Mogutin into something of a *bête noire* of Russian counterculture.[52] While there are several affinities in the ways that Pelevin and Mogutin fashion queer subjectivities, Mogutin politicizes those marginal subject positions in order to find an escape from social coercion. Just like Pelevin's texts, Mogutin's transgressive writings touch upon bestiality, rape, fascism, and masochistic

50 Chernetsky, *Mapping Postcommunist Cultures*, 171.

51 Ibid.

52 For an account of both of these scandals, see Essig, *Queer in Russia*, 17–21.

violence, and in doing so question what constitutes "humanity" proper in post-Soviet Russia.

In his novella *Romance with a German* (*Roman s nemtsem*, 1997), Mogutin reworks the postwar rapprochement between Germany and the Soviet Union in the framework of a love affair between an unnamed Russian (who is heavily implied to be Mogutin himself) and a German named Peter.[53] In a stream of consciousness, Mogutin fantasizes about Peter in a Nazi uniform, Peter forcing him to smell his dirty sneakers, Peter forcing Mogutin into sexual slavery: "Look! I have dirty boots, Peter says in my fantasies, why don't you lick them clean like the slave you are? Well, go on! Faster, faster, Russian pig!"[54] Mogutin's sexual proclivity for being dominated reveals his acute awareness of his marginal subjectivity and his attempt to reclaim his abject position: "Already in my childhood I dreamt that I was a child-slave to the beautiful son, my age, of rich slave owners in ancient Rome. He would be in total control of my body and my life. I would sleep, like a dog, at his feet."[55] He actively desires the subordinated position of the sexualized animal. When the pair, accompanied by another queer couple Vitalii and Dzhozefina, spots seals from their car outside of San Francisco, they strike up a conversation on what animals they would like to be:

> "If I were an animal, least of all would I want to look like one of these fatty, sagging shiny carcasses!," I shouted to Vitalii, trying to drown out the noise of the motor.
> "It'd be nice being a seal, or a dog! I could piss and fuck wherever I wanted!" He quipped in response.[56]

The ability to "fuck wherever I want" is a privilege enjoyed by the subject who lives outside of society and its preordained values. When Peter excitedly professes his love for seals, Vitalii teases Mogutin: "You've got yourself a zoophile! [ ] He loves these smelly wineskins more than you!"[57] This is a telling statement, for later it becomes clear that Mogutin has all along preferred the *idea* of Peter as a fascist, sadistic German master rather than the reality that Peter is a relatively well-adjusted German gay man. To the point of bestiality, the figure of the animal here symbolizes Mogutin's fantasy of living outside of

53 Iaroslav Mogutin, *Roman s nemtsem* [Romance with a German] (Tver': Kolonna, 2000).
54 Ibid., 30.
55 Ibid., 47.
56 Ibid., 17.
57 Ibid., 18.

social law. The theme of bestiality continues in his reworking of Chekhov's "Lady with a Lapdog," where the sexual tryst between the two eponymous protagonists insists upon taking Pelevin's "Nika" romance literally.[58]

Citing the influence of Nietzsche and Jean Genet, Jean-Claude Marcade remarks that in Mogutin's work "there is an evident desire in sexual activity to make the flesh cry out, to return it to an original unity with the plant and animal worlds full of eternal breath."[59] Mogutin's position as an already marginalized subject in post-Soviet Russia is the image of the savage figure gazing upon itself, unlike Pelevin's parodic image of a desire to return to the romantic schism of the civilized man gazing longingly upon his savage and free past nature. Mogutin's protagonists must either reject themselves, their embodied lived experience as gay men, women, Others, and so on, in order to achieve social legibility, or embrace their abject status and live on the social periphery. The former requires a denial of one's animality, the latter suggests its embrace.

The Soviet organicist model attempted to bridge this divide: by denying Freud's pleasure principle, this organicist model suggested nothing natural outside of the social.[60] In post-Soviet culture, on the contrary, individuality thrives on the allocation of desire, that is, sexuality, to the realm of the natural, outside of the collective and driven by commodification.[61] Mogutin's work is keenly aware of this paradox for those bodies marked by their sexual alterity:

> In Lisbon on the square before the station
> I saw an elephant man
> A pile of folds and warts for a face
> He was selling his disfigurations two steps from the sex shop
> What a joker! I thought, what a trickster!
> It's not for nothing that those Yankees say:
> "there's a market for everything"
> for everything a market
> a market for everything
> well
> everyone wants to fuck:

58 See Iaroslav Mogutin, "Dama s sobachkoi" [Lady with a lapdog], in *Amerika v moikh shtanakh* [America in my pants] (Tver': Kolonna, 1999).

59 Jean-Claude Marcade, introduction to Iaroslav Mogutin, *Termoiadernyi muskul* [Thermonuclear muscle] (Moscow: Novoe literaturnoe obozrenie, 2001), 13.

60 See note 8.

61 For more on prostitution and post-Soviet economics, see Borenstein, 87–93.

taxi drivers and tax inspectors
lawyers and mountain skiers
ballerinas and night receptionists
even elephant-men [62]

There is a clear sense of camaraderie between A Hu-Li, the magic fox-*cum*-prostitute, the elephant-man salesman, and the abject queer life offered by Mogutin. For each of them, their sense of individuality exists outside of the realm of the socially accepted and is therefore at the whim of the market. Driven by supply and demand, sexuality is a commodity and thus not quite human. Note, for example, Kon's remark on the unexpected inflection of post-Soviet Russian sex culture: "[i]nstead of sexuality becoming individualized—more private and intimate—it is being deromanticized, commercialized, and trivialized."[63] As Mogutin describes in his poem "Centaurs" (*Kentavry*): "they tell themselves: / yes I can be successful in my career / but for this I need thick, young sperm / its streams should run continuously down my lips and cheeks."[64] The poem's title is intriguing, and not only for the obvious, human/animal divide of the centaur. According to several slang dictionaries, *kentavr* can mean both a strong powerful person and a homosexual that has both active and passive anal sex.[65] It finds a loose counterpart in the common use of the Russian word *natural* to denote heterosexuals. The poem describes a group of centaurs that manage to achieve both financial success and existential satisfaction through the use of their grotesque bodies: "they tell themselves: / yes I could quite simply have become influential and popular / but that can't be done without a pair of young tight thighs / and a gripped, bulging ass for which I would exude optimism and confidence in tomorrow."[66] Mogutin's work expresses the inability of the marginalized to escape their commodification given that the collective, which could otherwise imbue them with use value, has chosen to exile them. It is a particular free-market paranoia, in that individualism can be granted

62 Iaroslav Mogutin, *Chelovek-slon* [Elephant-man], in *Deklaratsiia nezavisimosti* [Declaration of independence] (Tver': Kolonna, 2004), 63.

63 Igor S. Kon, *The Sexual Revolution in Russia: From the Age of the Czars to Today* (New York: New Press, 1995), 267.

64 Mogutin, *Deklaratsiia*, 105.

65 I have been unable to verify this usage amongst native (LGBT) Russian friends, who claim to have never heard the term. It is included in several dictionaries, however, including V. M. Mokienko and T. G. Nikitina, *Slovar' russkoi brani* [Dictionary of Russian profanities] (Saint-Petersburg: Norint, 2003), 167.

66 Mogutin, *Deklaratsiia*, 105.

only at the expense of one's profitability. In describing the marketing tactics of heterosexual pornography, Goscilo writes that "[c]leverly packaged, manipulative ads that play and prey upon 'illicit' wish-fulfillment fantasies have sold the public, in fact, on a pseudonormative sexuality shared by those marked for success."[67] For those *not* marked for success, cultural representations of non-normative sexuality, in pornography and other cultural media, are rife with what Dan Healey calls a "dilemma of the self," or "the question of how publicly to express that [same-sex] desire while still being considered a good citizen."[68] Russian LGBT cultural representation is, simultaneously, increasingly visible and subjected to normative methods of social surveillance.[69]

In the years following the first publication of his notes on the human and animal at the end of history, Kojève remarked that he miscalculated the timeline of his predictions and that the United States was perhaps in fact the final stage of communism:

> I understood a little later (1948) that the Hegelian-Marxist end of History was not to come but was already here and present. [...] One could even say that from a certain point of view, the United States has already reached the final stage of Marxist "communism," given that, practically, all the members of a "society without classes" can take advantage of everything which seems good to them, without working much more than their heart tells them to [...] I was inclined to conclude that the *American way of life* [sic] was the way of living proper to the post-historical period, the current presence of the United States in the World prefiguring the "eternal present" of all of humanity. In this way, the return of Man to animality seems no longer a possibility to come but an already present certitude.[70]

Certain interpretations of Kojève's claim to the end of History, namely Francis Fukuyama's *The End of History and the Last Man*, have sought to imagine this shift as Kojève's admission that it is not Stalinist Russia but instead Fordist America, and liberal democracy, that will constitute the "post-historical"

---

67 Goscilo, *Dehexing Sex*, 140.

68 Dan Healey, "Active, Passive, and Russian: The National Idea in Gay Men's Pornography," *Russian Review* 69, no. 2 (2010): 229–30.

69 For an extended take on this paradox of LGBT visibility, see Baer's chapter "Making a Spectacle of Homosexuality" in *Other Russias*.

70 Kojève, *Introduction*, 436.

condition.[71] While it is deeply erroneous to imply that the United States, then or now, or post-Soviet Russia are somehow "societies without classes," neoliberalism imagines individuals as possessing the means to satisfy their own needs and wants, suggesting that this satisfaction resolves what Kojève described as the relationship between our humanity and our animal urges. The post-Soviet authors described here, however, suggest otherwise. Post-Soviet sexuality remains a divisive factor by which the social collective decides who deserves a place in it, privileging individuals based on reproductive and normative sexual behaviors. If the subject cannot reproduce, or at least reproduce a norm, its place is either in the zoo or on the market.

Given that Putin's era has witnessed an ever-increasing biopolitical scrutiny in regard to an individual's sexuality, the depiction of individualism in the midst of a transformation from Soviet to post-Soviet social organization illustrates that "free love" comes with fine print. Instead of sexuality's inscription into the general framework of a useful, collective life, reproductive or otherwise, sexuality now glistens in the marketplace, selling itself beside freak shows and general lawlessness, and packaged as a pleasurable commodity under the guise of individual liberty. As Nikolay Oleynikov and Oxana Timofeeva put it, "all potential Soviet sexuality was quickly absorbed by the market and put on completely explicable and generally accepted economic rails."[72] Those marginalized by their sexuality have little choice but to oscillate between bare animality and ossified humanity, their own individuality neither here nor there. History, then, continues. In the words of Pelevin's Sasha, "history may have ended in Belarus, but in Russia there is no sign of any break with it."[73] While the early Soviet dream of sexual liberation was never truly realized, one cannot help but feel a nostalgia for a lost community and the utopian possibility of reconciliation in the zoomorphic sexuality found on the pages of Pelevin and Mogutin's works. A feeling of incompleteness haunts the disjuncture of human and animal in post-Soviet fiction, as though despite the increased visibility of sexuality, sexual politics still waits for a renewed political call to arms, one which will once more unite diverse sexual expression with social affirmation and utility. This may be the greatest takeaway from the posthuman portrayal of the man-animal: better to be a politically offensive animal than disingenuously human.

---

71 Francis Fukuyama, *The End of History and the Last Man* (New York: Free Press, 1992).

72 Nikolay Oleynikov and Oxana Timofeeva, "Six Letters about Hair and Fur, Secretions and Protests, the Female Orgasm and Slavoj Žižek, and Also about Margarita, Budulai, and the Black Swan," in *Sex of the Oppressed*, 81.

73 Pelevin, *Sviashchennaia kniga oborotnia*, 188.

CHAPTER 10

Postsocialist Platonov: The Question of Humanism and the New Russian Left

Jonathan Brooks Platt,
Higher School of Economics, Saint Petersburg

The reception of Andrei Platonov has undergone a distinct turn since the first post-Soviet decades. After the full extent of his oeuvre became known in the late 1980s and early 1990s, Platonov was most typically read as a forgotten dissident, rescued from oblivion by the Soviet collapse. Today, however, his doubts and anxieties about the construction of socialism appear in a very different light. Leftist intellectuals in Russia (and increasingly abroad[1]) now look to Platonov as a visionary who mapped the flows of revolutionary desire with unmatched sophistication and feeling. Instead of treating his works as documents of oppression and despair, many leftist readers of Platonov are

This essay reflects the state of my thinking on Platonov and the New Russian Left in 2013–2014. While I remain faithful to the arguments, I would update them, mostly in the final section, where I am too vehement (not sufficiently dialectical) in my rejection of affirmative posthumanism.

1 The central Western theoretical text on Platonov remains Part Two of Fredric Jameson, *The Seeds of Time* (New York: Columbia University Press, 1994). A more recent text is chapter 5 of Jonathan Flatley, *Affective Mapping: Melancholia and the Politics of Modernism* (Cambridge, MA: Harvard University Press, 2008). Slavoj Žižek includes a brief discussion of Platonov (and Jameson) in a number of recent works. The most extensive version is the foreword to Oxana Timofeeva, *History of Animals: An Essay on Negativity, Immanence and Freedom* (Maastricht: Jan van Eyck Academie, 2012), 6–10. Another text worth mentioning is Aaron Schuster, "One or Many Antisexes?: Introduction to Andrei Platonov's 'The Anti-Sexus'," *Stasis* 4.1 (2016): 20–35. In his 2015 *Molecular Red: Theory for the Anthropocene*, "hacker theorist" McKenzie Wark attempts to deploy Platonov's thought in a discussion of anthropogenic climate change and possibilities for building a new world.

reclaiming his legacy, pushing the emancipatory potential of his thought and imagery in new directions.

In this essay I will examine the place of Platonov in the writings of three Russian leftist philosophers: Artemy Magun, Oxana Timofeeva, and Igor Chubarov. Both Magun and Timofeeva are members of the *Chto Delat* collective and have been very active in the development of new intellectual institutions in Russia. Timofeeva was a former editor at the *New Literary Observer* (NLO), and she has now joined Magun at the European University in St. Petersburg and on the editorial board of their new bilingual journal of political philosophy, *Stasis*. Chubarov has also been active in contemporary art circles, most notably participating in the *MediaUdar* festival of activist art. He is an editor of the journal *Logos* and has taught at Moscow State University and at the Russian State University for the Humanities. Like Timofeeva, he holds a position in the Institute of Philosophy of the Russian Academy of Sciences.

The question of the human occupies a central place in all three of the readings I will be examining. Platonov's incredibly fraught explorations of the threshold between human and animal, as between man and machine, offer a wealth of material for debates on the meaning and consequences of posthumanism—whether as a philosophical stance, an effect of shifting political and material forces, or both. My primary concern is to identify how these Russian philosophers relate Platonov's investigations of the human to the collapse of the revolutionary socialist project that gave meaning to his work. It is not difficult to identify links between the "posthuman condition" and the postsocialist epoch. What, after all, are the primary causes for uncertainty about the human today? The shift in post-Fordist capitalism away from the production of commodities toward the exploitation of cognitive and affective capacities, the collapse of analog civilization brought on by the digital revolution, the increasing sweep of biotechnology and its erosion of the conceptual boundaries of life, the ecological catastrophe as a new apocalyptic horizon… And all of these developments have coincided with the triumph of neoliberalism, the march of globalization, and the collapse of the Second World.

Each of the readings of Platonov I will discuss declares itself relevant to the contemporary struggle with capitalism. None of these authors is interested in creating a simple historicist portrait or, worse, some nostalgic myth about the heroic age of socialism. Magun, for example, argues that we need to "learn from [Platonov's texts], asking them our own, *contemporary* questions."[2] Timofeeva

2 Artemii Magun, "Otritsatel'naia revoliutsiia Andreia Platonova" [Andrei Platonov's negative revolution], *Novoe literaturnoe obozrenie* 106 (2010): 65. All translations are mine unless otherwise indicated.

goes further still, likening the wandering Central Asian workers in Platonov's *Dzhan (Dzhan)* to post-Soviet migrants and claiming that Platonov "could see the future."[3] Finally, Chubarov's reading of Platonov is part of a larger project of the left avant-garde, which he bases on a Deleuzian interpretation of the revolutionary events of 1917 as a singularity outside historical causality. The revolution and the art that accompanied it are in this sense always contemporary, at least in the realm of the virtual.

Nevertheless, each of these thinkers has a different take on the question of the human, and each invokes Platonov in a different way. One can conceptualize these differences, I believe, as reflecting a range of perspectives on the revolutionary socialist past from the horizon of our neoliberal and posthuman present. This position—that of the postsocialist subject who remains a communist—is hardly an easy one to occupy. And it is not only a question for leftists in Russia and other postsocialist states. We are all postsocialists today, all of us enduring the consequences of state socialism's inglorious defeat in 1989/91. Indeed, it is worth recalling the prophetic words of Platonov in his essay "On the First Socialist Tragedy" in 1934: "Without the USSR, the world would be certain to destroy itself in the course of no more than a century."[4] We seem well on our way.

My analysis in this essay revolves around a hypothesis that the postsocialist horizon forces us to restructure our desire for communism as an inverted echo of October's tragic outcome. Instead of rejecting the Russian revolution for its failures, suspending it in any number of counterfactuals about the post-Leninist phase, or—conversely—mythologizing it as a glorious historical rupture while disregarding its later fate, the postsocialist communist recognizes her formation in the fires of a different revolution entirely. Our connection to the event of 1917 must inevitably pass through the neoliberal revolution (or counter-revolution) of 1989/91. From this perspective, the latent negativity of the socialist past—its saturation with Platonov's beloved affect of *toska* (a longing or spiritual ache that can also manifest itself as boredom)—demands resuscitation as a new kind of militancy. This *toska* that so easily appears as doubt and despair about a revolutionary event that precedes it must be inverted as militant desire for a new revolution to come.

---

3 Oxana Timofeeva, "Living in a Parasite: Marx, Serres, Platonov, and the Animal Kingdom," *Rethinking Marxism* 28.1 (2016): 100.

4 Andrei Platonov, "On the First Socialist Tragedy," trans. Robert and Elizabeth Chandler and Olga Meerson with Jonathan Platt, *Times Literary Supplement*, August 23, 2011, https://www.the-tls.co.uk/articles/public/platonovs-graveyard-earth-2/.

Historically, interpretations of 1917 and its fate by Marxists both inside and outside the Second World have grappled with this negativity through debates about the problematic entanglement of socialism with humanism. Thus, before examining my three Russian philosophers, I will first consider some of these older debates alongside the story of Platonov's development and reception as a writer in the twentieth century. Next, I will briefly examine our own posthumanist moment and the theory that has arisen to describe it—specifically, those theories that extend some form of emancipatory promise. In my view, only a posthumanism that comes to terms with humanism's own fundamental kernel of *toska*—a *toska* that cannot simply be overcome but must be reimagined and redeployed—can hold out such hope.

Platonov and the History of Marxist Humanism

The narrative of Marxist humanism's development after 1917 begins with its rejection, as the first years of revolutionary enthusiasm saw avant-garde and proletarian culture movements fueled by Nietzschean fantasies of overcoming the human. The goal of dismantling the edifice of bourgeois life encouraged technological utopianism and all manner of enthrallment with machines and industrial modernity. As a young proletarian writer, Platonov was deeply affected by this first wave of posthumanist fervor, particularly the ideas of Proletkult and the productivism of LEF (Left Front of the Arts). Like the Proletkult ideologue and poet Alexei Gastev, he would even abandon literature in the mid-1920s in order to immerse himself in real production, working on electrification and amelioration projects.

However, the revolution endured a series of sharp transformations in the 1930s and 1940s. Among Western Marxists, the Moscow Trials inspired a distinctive if ambivalent turn toward the discourse of humanism in interpreting the legacy of 1917, as intellectuals drew on its categories both to reject the Soviet path (Arthur Koestler and George Orwell) and to defend Stalinism's "minimal" adherence to a revolutionary ideal (Maurice Merleau-Ponty).[5] Somewhat ironically perhaps, Stalinist culture had itself begun to invoke humanist ideals in the mid-1930s, rejecting earlier dreams of a mechanized superhumanity for what were called "general human" (*obshchechelovecheskie*) values, now believed to have been cleansed of their bourgeois impurities. This turn made sense, of

5 Maurice Merleau-Ponty, *Humanism and Terror: An Essay on the Communist Problem*, trans. John O'Neil (Boston: Beacon Press, [1947] 1969).

course, as the Soviet Union struggled to inhabit the new socialist infrastructure it had so hastily and destructively created during the first Five Year Plan. Culture and "cadres" (human resources) were prioritized over technology, and the New Man would no longer be an "iron messiah" but a bastion of *gumanizm* and *gumannost'* (Soviet ideologemes that shift the valence of humanism toward a more populist "humane-ness").

Left disillusioned by his own efforts in production, Platonov embraced this humanist turn and became increasingly critical of utopian technological fantasies. Indeed, in many ways he can be considered a pioneer of this cultural shift. Even though he struggled to publish much of what he wrote in the 1930s (and what he did publish was often vociferously attacked in the press), he developed his own idiosyncratic version of the new Soviet humanism—one quite distinct (in its tolerance for negativity) from what was appearing at the level of official propaganda. And he was not alone in this effort. The philosopher Mikhail Lifshits, Georg Lukács's colleague at *The Literary Critic* journal, was also elaborating the new humanism (while criticizing its more vulgar articulations) to argue that truly classic works of art invariably take on a tragic form, characterized by a sense of "humane resignation" (*gumannaia rezin'iatsiia*—a phrase borrowed from nineteenth-century critic Vissarion Belinsky). The classic artist emerges at the cusp of modernity (in the Italian Renaissance, Elizabethan England, or moments of national awakening like in Goethe's Germany and Pushkin's Russia) only to withdraw from historical struggle in search of the dialectical or "true middle" point that captures an epochal totality. The great rupture of October allows us to sense the importance of such moments, as we seek to redeem the tragic hope invested in them.[6] Platonov published extensively in *The Literary Critic*, and the journal—which otherwise rarely printed fiction—presented his stories as a model for socialist literature, capable of measuring up to the classics and their tragic heritage.[7]

In the late 1950s, the policies of de-Stalinization again brought great changes to Soviet culture. Nonetheless, one can argue that the humanist turn

6 See, for example, Mikhail Lifshits, "Narodnost' iskusstva i bor'ba klassov" [The people-mindedness of art and class struggle], *Sobranie sochinenii v 3 tomakh* [Collected works in 3 volumes] (Moscow: Izobrazitel'noe iskusstvo, 1986), 2: 245–92.

7 The common argument that this phase in Platonov's work arose out of desperate conformism does not hold up. Despite its early influence, *The Literary Critic* quickly ran afoul of better-connected critics, largely because its humanist ideal was too nuanced in its celebration of tragedy and negativity. Optimism was the order of the day in the Stalinist mainstream, and Platonov's stories and essays were among the main reasons for the journal's closure in 1940.

of the 1930s continued its development in these years. Indeed, it is no accident that, when Platonov was finally welcomed into the mainstream of Soviet culture, it was primarily his later works that were published, while the millenarian and cosmological aspects of his writings were flatly ignored. In the 1960s, several collections of his stories from the 1930s and 1940s appeared in large print runs, as did the fairy tales he wrote after the war. As Tatiana Rybal'chenko has described the reception of these works: "[T]he aesthetics of concrete humanism, affirmed in post-totalitarian art, also led to a search for individual psychology and concrete descriptions of everyday life in Platonov."[8]

These developments also found parallels outside the Soviet Union, as leftist thinkers like Jean-Paul Sartre and Frantz Fanon began calling for a new Marxist humanism, and de-Stalinization raised the possibility of "socialism with a human face" in Eastern Europe. Not everyone was enthusiastic about the humanist trend, however. Louis Althusser expressed the most important dissenting view, claiming that Marx had abandoned humanism in 1845, when he recognized its irredeemable roots in bourgeois ideology. A reimagining of the humanist legacy might be useful in certain practical matters (like de-Stalinization), but it is theoretically useless, save only as a sign of unresolved problems. In the resurgent gloom of the 1970s, Jacques Rancière attacked this position as elitist, blaming it in part for the failure of the May 1968 strikes and student uprisings to unseat the French government. According to Rancière, when workers appeal to their humanity and sing the "song of man," they are not merely aping bourgeois ideology. The invocation of humanism is strategic, designed to counter the much louder song of workers' subhuman impotence, which always accompanies bourgeois claims about universal equality and freedom. To say that workers are duped by such promises is just another way of putting them in their place, denying their capacity to discern true Marxist "science" from ideology without the help of academic specialists.[9]

It is worth noting that Platonov advanced an argument quite similar to Rancière's in his essays of the 1930s. He frequently called out intellectuals—even Maxim Gorky—for creating false hybrids of elite rationality and worker

8 T. L. Rybal'chenko, "A. Platonov v interpretatsii russkikh pisatelei vtoroi poloviny XX veka" [Interpretations of A. Platonov by Russian writers of the second half of the 20th century], *Filologicheskii klass* 2 (2012): 12.

9 Louis Althusser, "Marxism and Humanism," in *For Marx*, trans. Ben Brewster (New York: Verso, [1965] 2005). Jacques Rancière, "A Lesson in History: The Damages of Humanism," in *Althusser's Lesson*, trans. Emiliano Battista (New York: Continuum, [1974] 2011).

intuition that elude the fundamental tension of the Leninist spontaneity-consciousness dialectic. As he wrote in the socialist tragedy essay, "Ideology [...] is located not in the superstructure, not on some 'height,' but somewhere within, in the heart of society's sense of itself. To be more precise, unless in our concept of technology we also include the technician himself—the human being—our understanding of the question will remain obtuse and leaden."[10]

Althusser's theoretical anti-humanism aside, October's twentieth-century legacy was thus clearly dominated by an ineluctable slide into humanism. There are at least two possible interpretations of this fact. On the one hand, humanism serves as a corrective to the revolution's excesses, which may be understood either as its descent into violence or its hubristic faith in rationality. In fact, the two models are often linked. Slavoj Žižek sees the desire for a humanist corrective as rooted in leftist anxieties (with which he does not identify) about the extension of instrumental rationality to human beings, treating them as objects of use and manipulation—simply another resource to be exploited. The assumption is that "political 'totalitarianism' [...] results from the predominance of material production and technology over intersubjective communication and/or symbolic practice."[11] In other words, if we want a human-faced socialism, then our utopian dreams about unlocking the New Man's hidden potentials cannot be prioritized over organizing a just and equitable society (or defending workers' human rights) today. On the other hand, the slide into humanism can be seen as a testament to the revolution's betrayal. From a perspective that identifies with the avant-garde, Marxist humanists simply lacked the stomach for radical transformation, preferring to hold onto the human and adhere to the cowardly ethics of what Nietzsche called the "last man"—characterized by complacency and aversion to the risks of a dangerous, self-surpassing life.

Žižek offers his own variant of this second interpretation, in which the specter of "inhuman" terror, which haunts all radical liberation movements, may be thought of as a form of "hysterical acting-out" in frustration over the failure of a truly egalitarian and "concrete" terror—precisely the utopian impulse to reorganize the fundamental forms of production and everyday life. In Walter Benjamin's well-known terms, the "divine violence" of revolution fails in its promise to release bare, guilty life from the law that condemns and confines it. Instead, the revolution devours its children, and the endless oscillation of law-making and law-preserving violence begins again. Militant fidelity to the

---

10 Platonov, "On the First Socialist Tragedy."

11 Slavoj Žižek, *In Defense of Lost Causes* (New York: Verso, 2008), 174.

cause requires an inhuman subjectivity—Žižek compares it to the passion and drive of cyborgs in films like *Terminator* and *Blade Runner*—while failure to sustain this fidelity within a truly transformative praxis leads back to the "all too human" violence of law.[12]

In other words, we must radicalize Merleau-Ponty's argument about the Stalinist terror. For Merleau-Ponty, if the goal of communism is reached, finally "establishing relations among men that are human," the purges will be retroactively justified.[13] Open violence—indeed, open prevarication in the case of the show trials—may turn out to have been more human than the hidden violence and deceit of liberal societies. One must wager that this path will lead to realization of the "species-being" of man (as the early Marx defined the goal of communism), since opposing the human to revolutionary violence effectively blocks the possibility for change. Žižek, by contrast, argues that terror of the Stalinist type is in fact already indicative of the slide into humanism, witnessing the failure of a genuinely emancipatory transformation—a "terror" that is concretely embedded in life and thus truly revolutionary.

This analysis does make sense if one takes into account the oft-overlooked fact that humanism took hold of official Stalinist discourse long before the explosion of state violence in 1937. For my purposes, however, what is more interesting is the specific version of this humanist turn that was advanced in *The Literary Critic* and Platonov's mature work. The concept of humane resignation certainly implies the recognition of failure, and Platonov's evolution as a writer is manifestly tied to his retreat from production back into art. And yet, at the same time, it is impossible to doubt these thinkers' fidelity to the event of 1917. Perhaps what is needed is a new perspective on their tragic thought—as Magun says, a *contemporary* reading, performed from beyond the postsocialist horizon. Perhaps such a reading can unlock a new truth of the Russian revolution, one missed by historical narratives that present socialism in terms of terroristic rationality giving way to humanism, whether as a corrective or a betrayal.

The Posthuman Turn and Militant *Toska*

It is only recently that such a reading of Platonov has become possible. For obvious reasons, it was not Marxists who led the Soviet writer's reception in the

12 Žižek, *In Defense of Lost Causes*, 174-75, 166. Walter Benjamin, "Critique of Violence," in *Reflections*, trans. Edmund Jephcott (New York: Schocken, 1978).

13 Merleau-Ponty, *Humanism and Terror*, xv.

1990s. His previously unpublished works were read in a dystopian light, while his ideological commitment was seen as oriented toward Christian eschatology or the metaphysics of the Russian soul. Meanwhile, many of his works from the 1930s were dropped from the canon entirely. This approach reflected the apolitical ethos that characterized the neoliberal revolution's spread to Russia, when bitterness about politics went hand in hand with lamentations about the economic catastrophe the country was enduring (with Yegor Gaidar's "shock therapy" as a new kind of revolutionary terror). In the midst of history and ideology's end, consumed by the melancholy aftereffects of this "revolution against revolution," even a writer as passionately desirous of communism as Platonov could be recast as a Slavophile conservative.[14]

Now, however, with the emergence of a vibrant New Russian Left, it has become possible to consider Platonov's attitude to the revolution and humanism with greater sophistication. This opportunity also depends on the new discourses of posthumanism that have emerged since the late 1970s as bedfellows of neoliberalism—at times eager, at others reluctant. Here it is useful to distinguish different strains of posthumanism, even if they do overlap and contaminate one another. Most strains can be grouped into two broad categories, which I will call "affirmative" and "negative" posthumanism. On the side of affirmation, two notable tendencies are accelerationism and the new materialism, both of which are indebted to Deleuze. Grown weary of constructivism and critique after the long years of poststructuralism's dominance in the academy, the affirmative posthumanist no longer obsesses over the gaps, lacks, and aporias where the Cartesian subject comes unraveled. Instead she seeks a political efficacy beyond the subject in a heterogeneous material world of proliferation, difference, and excess. Thus accelerationism calls for the embrace and amplification of capitalism's powers of creative destruction. Benjamin Noys traces its origins to "a strange fusion of Nietzsche and Marx":

> It took from Nietzsche that apocalyptic desire to "break the world in two," and the need to push through to complete the nihilism, the collapse of

14 On the Russian anti-communist revolution, shock therapy as terror, and postrevolutionary depoliticization and melancholia, see Artemy Magun, *Negative Revolution: Modern Political Subject and Its Fate after the Cold War* (New York: Bloomsbury, 2013). For an Orthodox Christian reading of Platonov, see A. A. Dyrdin, *Potaennyi myslitel': Tvorcheskoe soznanie Andreia Platonova v svete russkoi dukhovnosti i kul'tury* [A secret thinker: creative consciousness of Andrei Platonov in light of Russian spirituality and culture] (Ul'ianovsk: Ul'ianovskii gosudarstvennyi tekhnicheskii universitet, 2000).

> values, that afflicts our culture. [...] This would be fused with Marx's contention that history advanced by the bad side, which welcomed the solvent effects of capitalism in dissolving the old world. The result was a Nietzschean Marx, a Marx of force and destruction.[15]

By contrast, the new materialism is less concerned with productive forces and more with the ethical disaster of modernity and its radical divisions between nature and culture, human and non-human, matter and life. For example, the neovitalist line of new materialism rejects the treatment of matter as an inert, passive substance and attends more closely to life's material origins, bodies, and environments, allowing the concept of "vitality" to swell and enfold all manner of machinic assemblages, aleatory encounters, and ontological events—untying the link between animacy and the organic.[16]

While aspects of affirmative posthumanism certainly recall the utopianism of the avant-garde (particularly futurism's proto-accelerationist ethos), negative posthumanism is closer to Platonov's mature thought. On its negative side, posthumanism is not about new forms of life that come after or beyond the human and its hegemonic categories; instead, it explores a form of thought, an ethics, and a potential politics that has always lurked in the shadows of humanism's anthropological universals, and which are now becoming increasingly visible (thinkable). Thus negative posthumanism remains a form of critique, striving to unpick the dialectical knots that hold the human between beast and superman, nature and technology, the body and its prostheses. Ultimately, the difference comes down to a question of politics. Both strains reject the humanist politics of identity for what Donna Haraway called for in her "Cyborg Manifesto" back in 1984—a politics of noise, pollution, and affinities that trouble such distinctions.[17] But while affirmative posthumanism focuses on the radically different world such a shift in thinking reveals, the negative strain preserves the link between humanism and its repressed others, looking for an emancipatory power in their unresolved conflict.

15 Benjamin Noys, *Malign Velocities: Accelerationism and Capitalism* (Washington: Zero, 2014), 8.

16 See, for example, Jane Bennett, *Vibrant Matter: A Political Ecology of Things* (Durham, NC: Duke University Press, 2010).

17 Donna Haraway, "A Cyborg Manifesto: Science, Technology, and Socialist-Feminism in the Late Twentieth Century," in *Simians, Cyborgs and Women: The Reinvention of Nature* (New York: Routledge, 1991). See also Cary Wolfe, *What is Posthumanism?* (Minneapolis: University of Minnesota Press, 2010).

Despite affirmative posthumanism's fascination with machines, it shares a great deal with the anti-rationalist critique of the Russian revolution. Whether championing the schizoid production of desire, affective flows, or nature-culture hybrids, affirmative posthumanism remains rooted in a mistrust of instrumental rationality and its efforts to isolate and purify the sphere of the human. As a Deleuzean might put it, molar codings of the world into discrete bodies are rejected in favor of molecular sites of becoming-other. By contrast, negative posthumanism looks to moments of indistinction churning within the dialectic of form and flux, reason and the unconscious. If the affirmative posthumanist cries (with Bruno Latour), "We have never been modern," and writes off the emancipatory potential of revolution as part of modernity's dubious legacy, the negative posthumanist sticks with this legacy by inverting its categories. Emancipation follows not from the historical ripening of contradictions (affirmative posthumanism is much more likely to be in thrall to progressive historical teleology). Rather, it comes from the destabilizing force of the contradiction's impossible yet necessary articulation. Modernity and the human have indeed never "existed," but it is precisely such negativity that defines the subject.

So what are the implications of this distinction between affirmative and negative posthumanism for our postsocialist epoch? Here I would venture the following hypothesis.

1) Affirmative posthumanism appears to unite avant-garde utopianism with its humanist corrective, producing a philosophy of radical transformation adapted to post-Fordist conditions. The humanist defense against rationalist excesses is remade into a posthumanist embrace of anti-rationalist excess. Reason is de-instrumentalized and replaced with the flows of affect and desire.
2) Negative posthumanism, by contrast, remains faithful to the politics of revolution. In its efforts to escape the false dichotomies of humanism by continuing to examine their logic, the negative strain does not push ahead into some promised land of radical otherness. Instead it lingers with the accursed legacy the Left has inherited, hoping for a final dialectical turn.
3) Thus, if affirmative posthumanism is postsocialist simply because it abandons the revolutionary legacy, negative posthumanism offers a way to articulate an authentically emancipatory postsocialist thought. A fundamental precondition for this thought would then be an attitude to 1917 that defines it not by the failure to reconcile certain accursed

antinomies—heart and mind, nature and culture, humanism and terror—but by its epoch-making revelation of their unresolvable entanglement with one another.

4) Militant postsocialist fidelity to October should therefore not be seen as some bizarre historical anachronism. Rather, the collapse of the Second World makes the negativity of its founding event visible and thinkable in a new way. The paroxysms of the postrevolutionary period must now be reimagined as a prerevolutionary force. Maybe the socialist world was doomed from the start—whether by its original, disastrous act of hubris or by the subsequent failure to follow the "inhuman" core of its revolutionary desire to the end. Accepting this fact does not mean the errors of the past should be used as a corrective for the future struggle. Instead, it means reorienting our engagement now, in our posthumanist present, in this new epoch that has reduced the past's revolutionary desire to impotent anguish and longing. Perhaps we can turn the tables and find a solution in the past's own revolutionary anguish, redeploying it as a new form of militant desire.

I will now turn to my three contemporary philosophers and their readings of Platonov. Each offers a different perspective on the socialist tragedy. As I will argue, Timofeeva and Magun both ground their readings in a deep affinity with Platonovian *toska*, inverting its orientation from postrevolutionary anguish to prerevolutionary desire. Platonov's anxious feelings about his community, laid bare by revolution, civil war, and the traumas of collectivization, become the unrest of our own precarious life, still waiting to be mobilized. At the same time, Timofeeva is clearly more committed to the posthumanist consequences of this inversion than Magun. Indeed, it is possible that she performs the inversion too effortlessly. For her the question of October casts barely a shadow over Platonov, and his desire for communism is directly paralleled to our own. Magun takes a different approach, offering a more historically situated reading that deals with this question directly. Still, while he invokes a model of subjectivity that critiques (in posthumanist fashion) the egocentric subject of liberalism, he is less willing to bring this reading to bear on his understanding of aesthetics. In a somewhat paradoxical manner, he positions his postsocialist desire for communism within the horizon of modernity—or, more accurately, still caught at its impasse. There is something appealing—and true—in this contradiction, but I will argue that Magun invests too much hope in a traditional, Aristotelian model of tragedy as a machine for subjectivization.

Finally, Igor Chubarov's work on Platonov is the furthest from my ideal of militant *toska* and the closest to affirmative posthumanism, although he also invokes more traditional constructs like the human-animal distinction. Chubarov is able to suppress postsocialist *toska* because of his Deleuzian interpretation of the event of 1917:

> To treat the revolution as an event that is not connected to all the subsequent years of building socialism, starting with the very first, means to liberate thought from the occurrence itself, which was inadequately actualized and led inevitably to defeat. The actualization of the revolution within the historical process remains an open potentiality, while the event of the revolution continues to exceed this actualization and requires counter-actualization in the activity of the artist, the actor, and the poet of revolutionary avant-garde art.[18]

But I think Chubarov goes too far in his effort to liberate October from its history. No aesthetic counter-actualization will save us in our postsocialist epoch. There can be no preserving the great rupture "for future use," if we abandon the revolution as an event, abandon its failure. Ultimately, Chubarov's attempt to isolate the avant-garde from the socialist tragedy amounts to its monumentalization as a transhistorical model for what can only ever be a disappointing emulation.

We Have Always Been Postsocialist: Oxana Timofeeva's Restless Creatures

In her 2012 book, *History of Animals*, Oxana Timofeeva reads a series of canonical philosophers (Aristotle, Descartes, Hegel, Heidegger, and Kojève) against the grain, questioning the consistency of the rigid animal-human distinction each posits. As Timofeeva puts it, quoting Mladen Dolar, a second, "unconscious philosopher" is also present in these thinkers' texts—a philosopher who does not exclude (or "include by excluding") the animal to found the human.[19] Instead, the unconscious philosopher retrospectively anticipates the emergence of human being from a place where this distinction

---

18 Igor' Chubarov, *Kollektivnaia chuvstvennost': Teorii i praktiki levogo avangarda* [Collective sensuousness: Theories and practices of the left avant-garde] (Moscow: Vysshaia shkola ekonomiki, 2014), 326. Translation mine.

19 Timofeeva, *History of Animals*, 59.

collapses. For example, Hegel rejects all "intermediate forms" in the animal kingdom (such as whales or amphibians) as signs of "the impotence of Nature to remain true to the Notion."[20] Evolution should be an internal, spiritual movement from one dialectical totality to another, depositing no mixtures along the way. Yet, at the same time, Timofeeva shows how a similar contamination compromises the distinction between human and animal itself. For Hegel, restless negativity defines the principle of becoming and lays the foundation for human freedom. Consciousness is a process of interruption and splitting—as, for example, in the articulation of mere (animal) voice with consonantal stops to produce language. But a similar splitting can be found in the vulnerability that divides any living organism against itself in sickness, insecurity, or anxiety. For Timofeeva, the "desperate unrest" of an animal struggling to escape such vulnerability partakes of the same fundamental negativity, pushing the animal toward the human.[21] But how can one assert a definitive break if this is true? Timofeeva's answer is that we can't; the distinction between animal and human appears only retrospectively, after the fact—once human freedom has marked the unhappy necessity of animal existence as its repressed other.

A final chapter on Platonov completes Timofeeva's program of recovering the negative power of the animal in the Western philosophical tradition. Alongside her other allies in this project (Kafka, Bataille, Agamben, and others), Platonov occupies a special place as a writer who blurs the boundary between man and beast, but who also represents the Hegelian (and avant-garde) impulse to overcome nature as the seat of unfreedom and exploitation. Timofeeva remarks on Platonov's adherence to the traditional denial of animal consciousness but also notes his departure from Descartes' concomitant denial of their suffering. In fact, Platonov's animals suffer all the more for their lack of cognition. They can't weep, can't deceive themselves, can't forget or move on in their sorrow and pain. When nature is cruel—as it always is—animals are left abandoned to their own restless desires, unable to find relief beyond the desperate satisfaction of appetites or the final escape of death.

Yet it is also through Platonov that Timofeeva unlocks the emancipatory potential of this animal unrest. Here she builds on Agamben's reading of Heidegger in *The Open*—in which he isolates our capacity for "profound boredom" as a zone of indistinction between the openness of *Dasein* and animals'

20 Quoted in Timofeeva, *History of Animals*, 74–75.
21 Ibid., 89.

captive "poverty in world."[22] Linking this boredom to Platonovian *toska*, Timofeeva argues that all life is impoverished and needy, animated by an unbearable negativity, which Platonov defines as the "desire for communism." She quotes from *Chevengur*: "Chepurny touched a burdock—it too wanted communism.... Just like the proletariat, this grass endures the life of heat and the death of deep snow."[23]

In her article "Living in a Parasite," Timofeeva situates this same reading of Platonov within an argument about power and economic relations. She begins with the young Marx's description of feudalism as a spiritual mirror of the animal kingdom, where the only equality is one of violence—as all animals are united in the belly of the beast of prey. The context of this image is Marx's critique of Rhineland lawmakers who defined the collection of fallen wood as theft, rescinding an ancient, customary right of the poor. Marx argues that such an unjust law is in fact a kind of lawlessness, "demanding instead of the human content of right, its animal form, which has now lost its reality and become a mere animal mask."[24]

In "Living in a Parasite," Timofeeva agrees—"oppressive power invariably [...] masquerades as nature"—but she questions Marx's image of the predator, identifying a more fundamental relation of parasitism beneath it.[25] From this perspective, derived from Michel Serres's 1980 book *The Parasite*, the belly of the predator is but the hairy paunch of the most successful parasite, positioned at the end of what Serres calls the "parasitic cascade," in which one parasite interrupts and feeds off another parasitic relation. Different parasites continually vie for this position, including ones further up the chain.[26] Thus, when Marx's forest owners drive the poor from their lands, they are staking a claim to

---

22 In *The Fundamental Concepts of Metaphysics*, Heidegger describes boredom as a uniquely human capacity, which presents us with a possibility of greater attunement to our being-in-the-world. Animals, by contrast, are "poor" in their phenomenological engagement with the world, since they are always "captivated" by the stimuli that delimit their existential horizons. See Martin Heidegger, *The Fundamental Concepts of Metaphysics: World, Finitude, Solitude*, trans. William McNeill and Nicholas Walker (Bloomington: Indiana University Press, 1995). Agamben performs a deconstruction of this distinction in *The Open*.

23 Timofeeva, *History of Animals*, 145.

24 Karl Marx, "Proceedings of the Sixth Rhine Province Assembly. Third Article: Debates on the Law on Thefts of Wood," in *Marx/Engels Collected Works* (New York: International Publishers, 1975), 1:231.

25 Timofeeva, "Living in a Parasite," 92.

26 Michel Serres, *The Parasite*, trans. Lawrence R. Schehr (Minneapolis: University of Minnesota Press, 2007).

the final position, sterilizing their own parasitic relation to nature by driving off any rivals. Property must be clean and proper.

Platonov again enters the story at the end of Timofeeva's argument. It is in every parasite's interest that its host does not die. While the old avant-garde wanted to leave nature behind, today we instead dream of a "deep ecology," in which all living beings—whether wolves, sheep, or migrant workers—would be protected and sustained in their "natural habitats." Timofeeva convincingly argues that this new ideologeme is but another version of the "destiny of capitalist technology [...] to perpetuate quasi-natural relations of production."[27] Humanity must ensure the continued reproduction of natural resources (including that of living labor) so that its parasitic relation can endure. What Platonov shows, however,—most explicitly in his essay on socialist tragedy—is that the capacity for such renewal comes not from our human cleverness but from the harsh, dialectical construction of nature itself. Nature is not abundant but miserly. Whatever machine we devise to plunder it, nature interrupts our plans with its own counter-parasitic force, and the suffering of poor life is a constant testament to this tragic antagonism. As technology advances, the *toska* that defines our exploitation of nature only increases in intensity.[28]

To fight this tendency, the strong expel weaker parasites—like Marx's wood thieves or the nomadic workers in Platonov's *Dzhan*—from the chain and reposition them so they might also be exploited like a natural resource. Driven from the feast, these dirty, criminalized parasites must now hand over their lives—"their children, their muscles, their bodies [...] bit by bit"—in order to keep them.[29] Yet, here again, Platonov offers the possibility for a dialectical reversal. Our *toska,* our unrest as insecure parasites at the feast of man, is the universal desire for communism that all impoverished life shares—a truly inexhaustible resource of negativity. For Timofeeva, this is what we must learn from Platonov. The communist is a "revolutionary animal," one who senses an affinity—which must become solidarity—with

27 Timofeeva, "Living in a Parasite," 105.

28 When Timofeeva pits Platonov's tragic dialectics of nature against deep ecology, she is engaging a particular moment in *The Parasite,* in which Serres considers the information age as a potentially infinite parasitism (98–99). Marx also argues that the customary right of the poor to collect fallen wood derives from a medieval tradition of "hybrid, indeterminate forms of property"—neither common, nor private. See Marx, "Debates on the Law on Thefts of Wood," 233.

29 Serres, 31. Marx notes a similar moment in the timber law article that would oblige a wood thief to hand over his very body and life in the form of labor, a temporary serfdom to the forest owner, if he cannot pay the fine. See Marx, "Debates on the Law on Thefts of Wood," 255.

poor life and its yearning anticipation. Timofeeva quotes *Dzhan*: "Inside every poor creature was a sense of some other happy destiny, a destiny that was necessary and inevitable—why, then, did they find their lives such a burden and why were they always waiting for something?"[30] The militancy appropriate for our times depends on discovering and preserving this place of affinity with the parasitized poor—whether fish, fowl, or something in between.

The Postsocialist Subject at the Impasse of Modernity: Artemy Magun's Soft-Focus Catharsis

Building on his book on the melancholia that followed the anti-communist revolution of 1989/1991 (examined in comparison with the French Revolution to suggest a persistent paradigm), Artemy Magun turns to the legacy of 1917 in his article "The Negative Revolution of Andrei Platonov" (*Otritsatel'naia revoliutsiia Andreia Platonova,* 2010). Here he argues that the postrevolutionary *toska* and anxiety (*trevoga*) that dominate the Platonovian universe do not simply reflect an unhappy consciousness characteristic of his times. Rather, Platonov treats *toska* as a "creative, active force" and conceives his artistic task as harnessing this negative energy for subjectivization, limiting the traumatic impact of the revolutionary event without sacrificing its power.[31] Most importantly, subject formation must be recognized as a fragile, ongoing process, and so Platonov is just as concerned with its suspension ("tarrying" with its negative, retroactive movement) as its facilitation.

This ambivalence comes through most clearly in the different forms of out-of-joint temporality that Magun identifies in Platonov's oeuvre. The present is defined in terms of an eschatological impulse (toward orgasm, death, or exterminatory violence) that must be halted at the threshold of consummation—"on the eve of liquidation," as Magun puts it, quoting from *Happy Moscow (Schastlivaia Moskva)*—because such moments of release are always premature, always a betrayal.[32] This effort to preserve the negative potential of the present appears in Platonov's anxiety about sex, in images of physical and spiritual exhaustion, in his characters' discovery of the non-coincidence of thought and being (falsely equated by Descartes), and in their efforts to turn

30 Timofeeva, *History of Animals*, 147–48.

31 Magun, "Otritsatel'naia revoliutsiia," 70.

32 Ibid., 79.

eschatological energy against itself (the vulture-hunting episode in *Dzhan*, Sambikin's "death sluice" in *Happy Moscow*, etc.) At the same time, the past and the future are also defined by persistent negativity—respectively, as withdrawal into the void laid bare by the event (*The Foundation Pit* as an effort to *reculer pour mieux sauter* from the position of history's vanquished), or as the suffering induced by anticipation of communism (the diagnosis Lukács gives to the weary, self-sacrificing railway station supervisor, Emmanuel Levin, in Platonov's "Immortality").[33]

In Magun's interpretation, Platonov uses the aesthetics of tragedy to organize this lingering, disjunctive negativity as a subjectivizing force. Tragedy imitates negative affects in such a way that the reader is suspended between associative and dissociative forms of identification. In other words, following the Aristotelian model, the spectator is simultaneously drawn toward the tragic action through pity and repulsed by it through fear. This is what keeps us in our seats until the dialectic of contradictory affects ripens into cathartic release.[34] But Magun also notes an inherent risk in tragedy, which explains Platonov's unease about potentially pessimistic (or, indeed, dissident) readings of his work. Negativity may be overly infectious, drawing the reader in too deeply. The reader must avoid falling into the imitation, as if repeating the fate of Dvanov's father in *Chevengur*, who drowns himself in an attempt to understand the peculiar non-being of fish at the threshold of life and death. Instead, "literature turns the world upside down in its mirror in order to eject the reader, who, unlike the fisherman, must use the infinite abyss of death as a 'foundation pit' for the construction of a rich and free society."[35]

Magun seems to reproduce the contradiction between associative pity and dissociative fear here as the tension between immersion in the text and expulsion from it. Only now the contradiction does not hold us; instead, cathartic expulsion is privileged, while infectious immersion must be resisted. However, I would argue that this moment reveals a different danger in Aristotle's definition of tragedy. True to its ritual origins (and despite Aristotle's best efforts at its secularization), classical tragedy reenacts a trauma already behind us, and its reflexive critique is only ever a contained, defanged subversion. If tragedy merely excites contradictory passions in order to purge or purify them, we can

33 Georg Lukács, "Emmanuil Levin," *Literaturnoe obozrenie* 19-20 (1937): 55-62. The French phrase translates as "to draw back in order to make a better jump."

34 See also Artemy Magun, "Tragedy as the Self-Critique of Spectacle," *Chto Delat Newspaper* 31 (2010).

35 Magun, "Otritsatel'naia revoliutsiia," 70.

no longer speak of tarrying with the ambivalent negativity of subjectivization (in which the subject is defined by retroactive, symbolic determination of the Other's indeterminate desire, to use Jacques Lacan's terms, or the undecidable truth of the event, to use Alain Badiou's). On the contrary, catharsis protects us from this ambivalence, enclosing it within the artwork and propelling us safely beyond its limits. It is the same structure as ritual sacrifice which protects us from "impure," indiscriminate violence (the very *jouissance* that must be surrendered to assume a subject position in the social order).

Magun does have a potential solution to this problem, however. After all, Platonov's passions are not pity and fear but *toska* and anxiety, and the difference between these two pairings is precisely the latter's lack of an alibi that would leave us safe in our seats. Magun quotes a central metaliterary moment from *Chevengur*: "it is not the skill of the writer that acts in books but the searching [*ishchushchaia*] *toska* of the reader."[36] In other words, Platonov's texts do not immerse us in the void of the event; we are already there. Our own *toska* and anxiety search the text from this internal perspective, suspended in the negativity of the transitional present, between the history of the vanquished and the anticipation of redemption, grappling with the real, historical tragedy of Leninist voluntarism, "socialism in one country," and the realization that technology alone will never be enough to overcome the obstacles facing the Soviet project. As a result, cathartic purgation must be inverted; its eschatological energy must be turned against the very consummation it seeks. Platonov's texts are neither rituals nor machines for the production of desire. They more closely resemble a kind of sustenance (Platonov often compared true art to black bread), something we need in order to endure the negativity of our ongoing, incomplete subjectivization, remaining faithful to the event of October, hesitating before the call to interpellation and the domestication of trauma.[37]

Magun has a very clear and sophisticated understanding of what this enduring "part-subject" of the revolution would be. In a long essay on the dialectic of unity and solitude (*edinstvo i odinochestvo*), he returns to the inextricable entanglement of the associative and dissociative sides of subjectivity, arguing that alienating distance from the other can promote a heightened

36 Ibid., 71.

37 Indeed, it is the event's persistent undecidability that produces the central Platonovian tension between transcendent nullity and bare, desolate matter, "which cannot be loved but must be understood," as Sartorius muses in *Happy Moscow*. Magun also quotes this line, but he sees the relationship as merely mimetic: Platonov's utopian, transcendental impulse paints the finite world as one of material desolation. See Magun, "Otritsatel'naia revoliutsiia," 73, 76.

receptiveness to the world. Denied the possibility of a true dialogic encounter, lonely experience suspends the distinction between inner and outer as something simultaneously "one's own" and "other." As Magun writes:

> The lonely person can suffer from the squeak of the smallest mosquito [...] but he can suffer just as much out of sympathy for the victims of Somalia's genocide. In contrast to the clear light of form that the state shines all around, the night vision of solitude sees better at the periphery, attending to the ground instead of the figure. Solitude sees the minimal, the unapparent, the non-thematic, the unrecognized—and this is why it can also have a subversive revolutionary role, bringing what is unnoticed, trivial, and hidden into the light.[38]

However, for Magun the exemplary figure of such solitude is not a militant, struggling to overthrow the state, but Platonov with his specifically post-revolutionary *toska*. Positioned at the threshold of a new era, Platonov's characters are simultaneously thrust toward one another and abandoned in naked isolation. The result is what Magun calls the "non-thematic sensuousness" of a "collective solitude."[39] The other no longer appears as a clear figure but only part of a background that includes a peripheral view of the self. This is how Magun explains Platonov's characteristic device of what Olga Meerson calls *neostranenie* or "refamiliarization"—the depiction of unusual, often traumatic events with a dry, deadpan affect, as if they are utterly ordinary.[40] The emblem of this affective strategy is the strange figure Platonov introduces in *Chevengur*—the "eunuch of soul" that observes our lives alongside us as we live them, preserving experience for some deferred future moment of understanding. According to Magun, this castrated, always belated gaze allows Platonov's reader to endure the painful process of subjectivization after the revolutionary rupture, "safely enjoying its frightening, ambivalent, oneiric world of negativity."[41] But such a world cannot move toward ecstatic release or purgation. And, as mentioned above, it is anything but safe. The specific tragic action of

38 Artemii Magun, *Edinstvo i odinochestvo: Kurs politicheskoi filosofii Novogo vremeni* [Unity and solitude: The course of political philosophy in the modern times] (Moscow: Novoe literaturnoe obozrenie, 2011), 65–66.

39 Ibid., 77, 80.

40 Olga Meerson, *Svobodnaia veshch': Poetika neostraneniia u Andreia Platonova* [The free thing: Andrei Platonov's poetics of refamiliarization] (Oakland, CA: Berkeley Slavic Specialities, 1997).

41 Magun, "Otritsatel'naia revoliutsiia," 85.

Platonov's texts depends on their suspension of that final release, patiently enduring the inside-out world of the part-subject, hovering at the hinge of non-coincidence between thought and being, art and life. What comes "after" this ambivalent position of endurance (communism) is something we cannot, and, as Platonov's writings clearly suggest, should not try to imagine directly.

Affirmative Postsocialism Mistaken for Fidelity: Igor Chubarov's Non-Violent Machines

In two articles—"Andrei Platonov's 'Literary Machines'" (*Literaturnye mashiny Andreia Platonova*, 2010) and "The Death of Sex or 'the Silence of Love'" (*Smert' pola ili "bezmolvie liubvi,"* 2011)—Chubarov takes Platonov as a central example for his broader project, in which he examines left avant-garde practices of exposing, describing, and—in the ideal—eradicating social violence.[42] In place of this violence—prototypically understood as the strong persecuting or exploiting the weak—the avant-garde produces non-violent, collective forms of sensuous engagement with the world. While persecutory violence is as old as society itself, under capitalism it accompanies a more universal alienation, and the task of revolutionary art is to unsettle and reorganize the sensuous habits upon which this order depends. Chubarov includes non-objective painting, transrational poetry, avant-garde cinema, and mass revolutionary spectacles as examples, but most important for him is the productivist movement, which sought to sublate art into life as engineering, socially useful design, and the documentation of socialist construction. This is the acme of the avant-garde, going further than any other tendency in its efforts to de-reify everyday life through the transformation of material objects and the re-conceptualization of the artist as producer.

As one can imagine, the Formalist concept of defamiliarization is a central category for Chubarov. However, he invariably emphasizes its affirmative side over the negative, praising avant-garde art's ability to restore "weightiness" and "corporeality" to things ("making the stone stony" in Shklovsky's terms). The avant-garde's negative, critical project takes a Nietzschean (or Nietzschean Marxist) form for Chubarov as the demystifying rejection of Kant's unprovable but "ethically necessary" ideas—God, freedom, and immortality. To overcome

42 Chubarov's recent monograph *Kollektivnaia chuvstvennost'* [Collective sensuousness] includes the essay "Literary Machines" as an "excursus," while his dissertation for the Doctor of Science degree includes both Platonov essays as well as other material related to the Soviet author.

these phantasmatic ideologemes of social control, the avant-garde lays bare their true, empirical content as, respectively, "lies, violence, and absurdity," while working to overcome the fear of death that gives them power.[43] Here Chubarov contrasts the avant-garde with myth and ritual ("persecutory art") as forms of mimesis that commemorate founding acts of communal violence. The avant-garde strives to bring such art to an end, replacing it with the production of new forms of egalitarian sensuousness.[44]

With such affirmative aspirations, Platonovian *toska* would seem an awkward fit for Chubarov. Indeed, much of his reading depends on contrastive analyses, showing how Platonov differs from various thinkers he might seem to resemble. For example, "The Death of Sex" presents a scathing (and very convincing) critique of the late nineteenth-century religious philosopher Nikolai Fedorov, who is often linked to Platonov. As Chubarov shows, Fedorov's "common task" (which calls for total chastity, the technological resurrection of dead ancestors, and the colonization of other worlds) is a fundamentally conservative project, alien to Platonov. For Fedorov, technology only ever serves the goal of mastery and symbolic power over nature, while the dream of reunion with our dead fathers is an anti-modern, "religious inversion of Oedipus," expressing a perverse longing for the Father, his legacy, and his law.[45]

Platonov, by contrast, shares none of this incestuous, necrophilic passion. Instead, Chubarov argues (perhaps less convincingly) that Platonov's countless images of non-normative sexuality are not to be taken seriously. They are

---

43 Chubarov's use of the avant-garde against Kant is apparently still in development. Aspects of the argument appear in his dissertation and, somewhat less so, in *Kollektivnaia chuvstvennost'*, but they have been more clearly articulated in various lectures he has given in relation to the project. See, for example, Igor Chubarov, "The Critique of Violence as a Transcendental-Ontological Project and its Media-Aesthetic Realization in the Russian Left Avant-Garde," YouTube video, from the presentation at the 2014 conference "No Radical Art Actions Are Going to Help Here…: Political Violence and Militant Aesthetics after Socialism," https://www.youtube.com/watch?v=MmEV2M0r1xk.

44 Among the major sources for Chubarov's argument here are René Girard's discussion of persecutory art in *Things Hidden Since the Foundation of the World* (Stanford, CA: Stanford UP, 1987), Deleuze's celebration of the impulse toward "minor literature" in *Kafka* (Gilles Deleuze and Felix Guattari, *Kafka: Toward a Minor Literature,* University of Minnesota Press, 1986), and the "Literature and Life" essay (Gilles Deleuze, "Literature and Life," *Critical Inquiry*, 23, no. 2 (Winter, 1997): 225-30), and Valerii Podoroga's analysis of Dostoevsky's representation of violence in *Mimesis* (Valerii Podoroga. *Mimesis. Materialy po analiticheskoi antropologii kul'tury. V dvukh tomakh* [Mimesis. Materials on the analytical anthropology of culture. In two volumes], Kul'turnaia Revolutsiia: 2011).

45 Igor' Chubarov, "Smert' pola ili 'bezmolvie liubvi'" [The death of sex or "the silence of love"], *Novoe literaturnoe obozrenie* 1 (2011): 233.

only symptoms of the characters' failure to embody an ideal toward which they are nonetheless always striving. This ideal also involves sexual abstinence, but now it serves the task of overcoming the *fear* of death (not individual death as such). Once we have passed through this fear—and, indeed, through the collective death of our fragmented world—a truly selfless love (and sex) will become possible, free of all violence and exploitation. Chubarov makes similar claims about Platonov's non-violent egalitarianism through critiques of Bataille (the Hegelian master, celebrating a body of excess enjoyment, as opposed to Platonov's body of excess displeasure) and Bakhtin (whose populist ideal of the primordial collective body differs from Platonov's potential collective body, which requires further technological progress to realize).[46]

In his other article on Platonov, Chubarov invokes Deleuze and the Russian postmodern philosopher Valerii Podoroga to describe Platonov's literary works as machines.[47] The emblem here is again the eunuch of the soul, which Chubarov defines as a principle of non-relational observation. The eunuch's gaze is a special kind of machine, which, unlike a camera, "sees" only what cannot be visualized, gesturing towards a "constructive, collective vision" to come. In some ways, this recalls the non-thematic sensuousness described by Magun (who also draws on Podoroga), but Chubarov is much less interested in the place of the subject in his version. Indeed, the only subject in his reading is Platonov himself—the artist-engineer who failed to complete this seeing but non-seeing machine, which he spent his entire life designing and redesigning:

> In his novels Platonov does not simply apply the principle [of machine vision] that he discovered, or describe with irony the failure of actual machines and characters to live up to its eternal truth. Rather, he tries to invent the machine of such vision, to construct it from the parts available to him. But it always remains unfinished. The paradoxical condition of its functioning as a machine is its openness to the other. In this way it is *a priori* kept from becoming automatized or closed off.[48]

46 On Bataille, see Igor' Chubarov, "Struktury kollektivnoi chuvstvennosti v russkom levom avangarde: Iskusstvo i sotsial'nyi proekt" [The structures of collective sensuousness in the Russian left avant-garde: art and social project] (PhD diss., Russian State University for the Humanities, 2014), 390–98. On Bakhtin, see "Smert' pola," 242.

47 Chubarov defines his concept of machine in a Deleuzian manner as an aleatory assemblage of heterogeneous elements, distinct from both mechanical and organic systems. See Chubarov, *Kollektivnaia chuvstvennost'*, 219.

48 Ibid., 239.

Chubarov offers excuses for this failure (capitalist encirclement and the like), but in so doing he reduces Platonov's concept of socialist tragedy to a reluctant reconciliation with reality. According to Chubarov's narrative, the mature (that is, disappointed) Platonov retreated from his utopian, productivist dreams into the politics of small deeds, laboring in the field of language alone, "humanizing the machine" of his writing in order to preserve its openness amid the encroaching Stalinist dark.[49] Platonov's hope, however, always remained with technology. Only this force can finally guide us through individual death to a collective, machinic redistribution of the sensible: "[Platonov] understands that the victory of machine civilization over nature will mean the end of humanity. But the condition for saving humanity [...] is not at all the preservation of man's famous individuality and petty bourgeois privacy; rather, it is [...] his transformation into a machine."[50]

Conclusion: The Noise of Militant *Toska*

It is significant that Chubarov marries his machinic ideal to a rather old-fashioned humanism (in fact, not unlike Fedorov himself). According to his model, violence comes from the animal part of man, and it is our lingering animality that blocks actualization of the revolutionary event:

> In this sense, the event of the revolution can be actualized in history only on the other side of those phenomena that still link the social to the organizational principles and values of the natural world. The revolution in this sense is the rupture that allows for a transition toward the identity of our species (Marx's *Gattungswesen*) as a fundamentally new type of specifically human collectivity, no longer characterized by animality, i.e., not connected exclusively to the tasks of survival on the basis of natural selection, and so on.

The species-being of man thus lies in his capacity for a collective, machinic sensuousness, requiring "passage through a stage of death, similar to the death of the animal in man".[51] If we recall the twentieth-century narrative of

49 Ibid., 223.
50 Ibid., 235.
51 Ibid., 327.

Marxist humanism that I presented at the beginning of this essay, Chubarov seems to mask the question of revolutionary violence and "concrete terror" (the remaking of everyday life) under his broader critique of persecutory violence. The violence of change and revolt is transformed into self-sacrifice and the suicidal passage through death of the human-animal hybrid. In this way, affirmative posthumanism reaches apotheosis by producing its opposite: the distillation of man from all his impurities.

Here it is useful to return to Serres and his theory of the parasite. In French, *parasite* not only refers to an invasive organism or a freeloading guest but to noise that interrupts a message—static on the line. The relevance to Timofeeva and Magun's arguments here should be clear. The intermediate evolutionary forms that Hegel rejects, the restless despair of the animal that would escape into human freedom, the "interference" that wood thieves and migrant workers introduce into property relations, the peripheral vision that abandons thematic focus to perceive the ground of collective solitude—all these are, in one way or another, examples of parasitic noise.

But Platonov's *toska* (also a kind of noise) reminds us that solidarity with the weakest parasites, the ones most likely to be expelled by a counter-parasitic, sterilizing force, is not enough. Timofeeva is clear on this point when she characterizes Platonov's revolutionary impulse as a weak Messianic force.[52] We must redirect our attention to all the unhappy plants and animals awaiting salvation, including the unhappy animals within ourselves. But, ultimately, to sustain desire for communism requires something more—a subjectivity that can retrospectively redeem parasitic interference as a form of collective belonging, severing the parasitic relation, inverting it, or, perhaps most aptly, suspending the very distinction between noise and message, pollution and clarity, hybridity and identity.

Platonov does at times offer images of such a shift, as, for example, in the 1936 story "Among Animals and Plants" (*Sredi zhivotnykh i rastenii*)—about a switchman who performs an act of heroism, losing an arm while stopping a runaway train. In a central passage, we catch a glimpse of that non-thematic sensuousness that Magun describes:

> Fyodorov lay down with his ear to the rail and heard the metal's eternal song—its response to the flow of the air, and to the noise of leaves and

52 Timofeeva, *History of Animals*, 149.

> branches. [...] But gradually this steady wavelike hum was joined by a vague extraneous mutter. Then this mutter grew more distinct and insistent; it was almost articulating words. This language was being spoken by a voice that was young and singing, and there were no false notes, no sounds of jangling irritation [...]. The locomotive's calm light rose up from beyond the horizon, chasing the darkness forward and over the forest, lighting up deep blue living trees, bushes, mysterious objects unknown during the day, and the figure of a railway man, watching over the track in darkness and solitude.[53]

The song of the tracks and the train pass through, emerge through the noise of air, plants, invisible objects, even the perceiving subjectivity of the switchman himself, illuminating them, responding to them, but certainly not sterilizing or expelling them—because here, suspended in the medium of the desire for communism, light and dark, communication and noise, the arrow of progress and the lonely, restless murmuring of life are not in conflict.

If we refuse to shuffle off the socialist tragedy, it may be possible to recover Platonov's own version of the tension between the human and its others, whether animal or machine. The site of this tension is *toska*, a dark matter that binds the entire continuum together in desire for communism. It is also what Platonov's colleagues at *The Literary Critic* looked for with their new humanism in the 1930s—a resignation without reconciliation that occurs in the valley between ascending and descending historical epochs. If we are now on the other side of the socialist project and its failure, might we not be able to revisit this humanism as posthumanism, reversing the vector of negativity from resignation and patient endurance toward renewed action? To me, this seems to be the challenge presented by the postsocialist Platonov. He wants us to become militants of *toska*.

53 Andrey Platonov, *Soul and Other Stories*, trans. Robert and Elizabeth Chandler with Katia Grigoruk, Angela Livingstone, Olga Meerson, and Eric Naiman (New York: NYRB, 2008), 166–67.

Part Six

Artistic Practices

CHAPTER 11

An Interview with Keti Chukhrov about *Love Machines*

Alina Kotova,
Cine Fantom

This interview first appeared in the newspaper *Cine Fantom*, November 20–December 2, 2015.[1]

A legend of a beautiful girl, two biorobots, contemporary art, and a virtuous cow, or a farce about urban dwellers playing themselves, based on Keti Chukhrov's dramatic poem.

Moscow, 2015. Plunged into a phantasmagorical state, the absurd city is populated by strange dwellers—that is, by us. Much like a certain famous scholar from Germany who was tempted by Mephistopheles, they are tempted by perfect, immortal, and emotionless creatures. The biorobots carry within temptation and perfect beauty and other things. What can humanity—as represented by an ordinary girl, an art journalist disillusioned with her own job and going through a personal crisis—say back to them? Obviously, glib quotes from Althusser, Michel Foucault, and Boris Groys will not suffice, so a talking cow that embodies archetypal patterns of sainthood comes to the rescue.

1 Keti Chukhrov, interview by Alina Kotova, trans. Anton Svynarenko, "Keti Chukhrov. Love Machines" [Keti Chukhrov. Love Machines] in *Cine Fantom*, Nov. 20–Dec. 2, 2015, 6–8, http://cnftm.ru/images/archives/2015/newspaper/18-11-2015.pdf.

CF: I think it's quite symbolic that we are talking at the National Center for Contemporary Art, considering that your play *Love Machines* explores the contemporary art scene in great depth.

KC: The thing is that contemporary art is the paramount cultural power of today. No other art exists in the mode of a global network; no other art is defined by philosophy. And posthumanist philosophy is precisely one of the most important themes in contemporary art: It's a kind of intellectual fashion of art's global context. Furthermore, it is precisely in contemporary art that we find answers to such questions as these: what's emancipation and what's degradation, what's reactionary and, conversely, progressive? It's because contemporary art has taken on the duties of micropolitics. The end of humanity, the finalization of anthropocentrism is one of the crucial themes in today's philosophy, now featured everywhere: on the level of representational techniques, "science art," political criticism. That's why we might say that contemporary art is at the center of thematizing the end of humanity.

CF: It's really interesting that all these themes—humanism, posthumanism, the end of anthropocentrism, that is to say, the defining philosophy of contemporary art—are addressed [in your work] theatrically.

KC: Generally speaking, I'm not an apologist for these theories, and I needed theater in order to deconstruct and challenge them. Theater, after all, adds a poetic component, an element of playfulness; characters and actual living people—actors—are introduced to help, in real time, to debunk these views. If anything, theater here confronts the sterilized space of contemporary art.

CF: Your play engages with the theme of violence, made especially pronounced in "new drama."

KC: I'm only interested in violence per se as a certain social consequence. Come to think of it, no one sets the task of inflicting violence for the sake of violence. It's frequently thematized—for instance, in revolutionary practices: "Is violence permissible in order to liberate the proletariat?" Benjamin, Lukács, Sorel, and others have written about it. Here, violence becomes, on the one hand, the effect of surviving among the underprivileged classes; on the other hand, it's the effect of management and domination among the elites. It's very important that violence used for subjugation is never articulated as such: For example, the state system, which is wearing a mask of self-defense, accuses others of violence, thus legitimating its own violent means. The same effect is achieved in my play. Historically speaking, biorobots are disciples of the Enlightenment, progressive ideas, emancipatory political projects, etc. In this sense, it's an irony directed at the history of humanity at large, at all the aspirations inherent in progressive ideas linked to the betterment of society and promotion of equality. I was interested in the rupture between the declaration and propaganda of progressive ideas, equality first and foremost, and the concrete ethics of the deed. Do they correspond to one another? In essence, biorobots want to reset these aspirations and prove that the ethical deed is bogus, and so are progressive theories, because there's a disconnect between the two. Once the humanist project and its attendant history have fallen through, there appears an ironic, nihilistic game of sorts. But there also has to emerge some human paradox to confute the game—perhaps this paradox will come from some non-human universe.

CF: Zor'ka the Cow.[2]

KC: Yes, I've been told that this cow is a figure of atonement. But this atonement is dubious, and it would be more modern if the cow turned out to be a robot, too, so there would be no suffering creature at the end, whose sacrifice would alter our worldview. This, so to speak, victim creature overcomes the logic of progress and its collapse, harking back, to an extent, to the Christian context, to the fairytale narrative and different theologies. That is, the cow as a character may be old-fashioned, but it embodies the paradox of a collapsing system that only it can restore.

CF: Funny you should mention theological systems. In *Love Machines*, there's a mention of how downright corny conversations about love and God sound nowadays.

KC: Again, this is connected to the factors of separating the sensual and the empirical—that is, separating theory from sensualism. The fact that contemporary art has chosen the path of empirical knowledge and theoretization is a crucial theme. Even when some emotional structure is being explored, the approach is always theoretical, i.e., conceptual, and we are well aware of it. Sensual practices are now relegated to mass culture.

CF: But can we talk about love and God as mass practices lodged entirely in the realm of the sensual?

KC: I wish we didn't have to. I wish there were some wholeness, but we must understand that there is none. I mean, art history as well as philosophy of history begin precisely with this division. They both speak of the impossibility of fusing together the cognitive and sensual parameters. At the moment, for instance, love is perceived as a personal story of what two people have experienced. But if we look at some universalist theological conception, whether it be Neoplatonic or medieval, we'll see love as a mode of understanding

---

2 This is the name of a character in *Love Machines*.

(*poznanie*). That is, love is not just the specifics of the relationship between Vasia and Masha, but also a system in which each participant—two people, for example—have to understand the world. That's why Rustaveli appears in the play, and the cow quotes from Tariel[3], a Midjnur[4] looking for his beloved. The cow, meanwhile, is looking for Lida. The cow is like a knight in search of his Beatrice, no matter how profane the realization. This search for a second subject is a medium for acquiring knowledge (*poznanie*) of the world; and vice versa, the world fills up the two creatures in search of each other. It's a kind of gravitational force, and gravity shapes the human realm. If we bracket off gravity, all that remains, as in Deleuzian philosophy, is the arbitrary molecular movement that Paco [the biorobot] mentions: that is, a contingent movement of material particles, which is also very productive. The entire universe is that arbitrary movement of material particles, including animate and inanimate, technical and natural objects; everything, so to speak, is everything. This is the revelation of contemporary post-philosophy: "On the one hand, there is nothing; on the other hand, there is everything!" What's most important is that there's no ethics and no gravitational pull, because gravity is painful, it causes suffering. You gravitate toward someone, and they do not gravitate toward you, so you're in pain. Or, you discover some object for cognition (*poznanie*), but it resists your efforts. As Groys recently said, the mind is the result of fear of death and suffering. But in today's posthumanist philosophy the mind is nothing but a machine for stratifying certain elements of transformation. The human mind is fueled by fear of losing consciousness when it works, analyzes, strives for survival. This "loss of consciousness" is both literal and figurative. This is how cognition comes about. But if you think that cognition is not a virtue...

CF: Who thinks so?

KC: Paco the biorobot, for instance, thinks of cognition not as a gift but as a system that accretes and circulates information. The main task philosophy faces today is to prove that the human is not necessary for cognition, that the system cognizes (*poznaet*) by itself, and affects are nothing but the body. But the body doesn't belong to the human, either: the body is a machine of affect. Consequently, there is no human.

CF: And yet it is humans who deal with these problems. Which is paradoxical: there's no human, but the human deals with these problems ...

---

3 Tariel is one of the two heroes in Shota Rustaveli's epic, twelfth-century poem *Knight in the Panther's Skin.*

4 A nickname for the main character in "Leili and Medjnun" by Persian poet Nizami Ganjavi (1140–1202).

KC: Good point. The thing is, the human wants to know what to call himself and how to decide whether he's staying or going. But as a body in nature, or even in society, to say nothing of technology, the human can be present with no cognizance of his own humanity whatsoever.

CF: At the same time, the "absent human" produces this schema mentally. Am I wrong?

KC: You're perfectly right. Partially, he does produce it, but you see, what matters here is the project. The Renaissance project begins when man wants to be reborn and to determine his sovereignty outside of God. In this case, man has produced himself, too. At first there was a God who said that people were his slaves. Man was a slave until he decided he wanted to be a subject, a sovereign entity, and a mind. But the current human project involves being either greater or less than human, or maybe something like "man with a difference" (*inochelovek*). The very category of the human is painful for him: it's an obstacle, it's shameful, it's something old-fashioned, just like that cow. No one wants to be that cow; there's something iffy about it. Being human is just as iffy, so man tries to look like a supermachine, supermind, superbody, some transcreature. This is partially explained by his wish to escape from the apparatus of power, from his suffering, death, and so on.

CF: I understand that we all want to be a supermind, a superintelligence, but I still don't want to reject the human, because this rejection may not be cognition.

KC: I agree that humanity may equal transcendence of certain limitations, but the human is shackled by this singular body.

CF: Not for long, though.

KC: That's right. But for now, he is shackled to one body, one life, one societal structure. Philosophy has always been concerned with metaphysical (*sverkhsushchnye*) categories. Or with the thing itself (in itself), as in Kant. The human mind is incapable of grasping it, hence the Enlightenment project, and the category of transcendentality, and some methods of understanding how the mind works and how it can comprehend the incomprehensible. Of course, the incomprehensible is part of the human mind. It's always been this way in philosophy, but I think an important shift has occurred recently. It's widely accepted that it's presumptuous of man to think he is capable of comprehending the incomprehensible. For instance, where was humankind before life appeared in the universe? Man cannot describe it. And yet, matter existed back then, too. The fact that the human cannot describe the Earth before him or after he is gone makes him a totally temporal creature—and a very limited one at that. And we're talking about millions of light years ... It's the universe, too! Who is its subject, then? Either God or, if there's no God, some mind other than human. Some autonomous machine of intelligence. Today, the so-called philosophy of new materialism admits that all our inventions that pass for intellectual history are just a plethora of myths and fairytales of an ethical, aesthetic, or political nature. What actually exists is the ineffable, the boundless matter extended in time.

CF: The text of your play situates the characters out of time, despite the many unmistakable markers of today's reality. And yet, all that the text postulates is refuted and what it refutes is postulated. There's a constant game going on.

KC: Yes, it's because I couldn't make any assertions. I can only wonder, because I don't know the answer. Drama is created because you don't know the answer. When you're writing lyric poetry, you have certain emotions and some idea, at least, of what you want to express. The same goes for the novel. But drama is constantly in flux. It engages different perspectives. Both are true, and yet neither is. It doesn't necessarily mean some kind of relativism; it's just the impossibility of resolving the conflict definitively.

CF: I feel like I'm flying from planet to planet holding Mephistopheles's hand in mine ...

KC: Faust is, after all, a kind of son to Mephistopheles. Basically, Paco the biorobot is a cross between Faust and Mephistopheles. Here again is the idea of gaining knowledge (*poznanie*), but this process is automatic and without any virtue. The question is as follows: is knowledge just the information you have accumulated, or does it include something else besides the known? Sokurov's film *Faust* opens with a scene of Faust the scholar dissecting dead bodies to see where the soul resides. And yet the corpse reveals no soul. He watches Gretchen sleeping, staring at her pubis and thighs in search of amorous attraction, but she can't be seen. What's left is the body being dissected, the body of the Enlightenment that strives to substantiate the ontological and moral canon of humanity, but cannot find it. It's just a body, a corpse, a machine, whereas the soul is metaphysical. So we have man divided into the metaphysical and the physical. But physics is not human, and neither is metaphysics; what is human, then? Somewhere in between, [or] nowhere. This very "nowhere" is the mystery and mysticism of the human, ostensibly taking place here and now, but essentially nonexistent. This is what I want to show as a tragic situation.

CF: What exactly is your position in this whole story?

KC: My position is finding a way to see the human not as fiction or ideology, which is how Louis Althusser sees man. However, it's impossible both logically and theoretically. It requires action, a conscious act, although we all know that humanism can be an ideology, part of legal policies, bourgeois moralism, etc. After all, morality and legal awareness always proscribe certain forms of behavior. It is this bourgeois confinement that scientific progress tries to avoid (here we have another Faustian idea, one of reaching superconsciousness). Imagine having one mind, as a single human, while the work of cognition and technological progress involves millions of minds. In other words, progress is already superhuman, and simply because this insane amount of knowledge exists, man is already being exterminated. As a result, the human, the pitiful, the sentimental, the soulful (*dushevnoe*)—it is all a waste. But where man is enlisted as a mind, there is hope of transcending this pathetic finitude. Another aspect of transcending the human is the animalistic, which is crucial to gender theory. In this case, the assertion is that man and animal should not be divided, because if you think that man is a genus, and the animal is just a species, you thus destroy the animal. So let man be a species, too. If he is a genus, that entails the pretenses of power and metaphysics. Man is guilty all around: guilty of scientific progress, political calamities, religion. Guilty of everything he is. For this reason, he tries to prove that he can be something other than himself. What matters in life, the world, politics, nature, ecology, is precisely what he is not. One of the latest theories is the Anthropocene, which positions man not as a sentient subject but as a fossil endowed with reason. The brain, in turn, is also material. In this case, there is no assumption that the mind is a supermaterial reality, rather than a biomateriality of the brain. Reason is not housed in our brain tissues. Reason is something that appears as a result of humans meeting each other, and communicating, and pursuing cultural and political aspirations. It is, in other words, a history of collectivity, presence, and development. This table, for instance, is an "objectified" human, too, because it bears the mark of human labor. This table contains the fact that man has invented it. But if we consider it to be pure matter, there is, of course, nothing human in it. The Soviet Marxist philosopher Ilienkov had an idea that man's concrete presence is impossible to grasp, because he is the history of society.

CF: Can we go back to the fossils for a second? I've already let my imagination run wild…

KC: You see, the human presence on this planet has led to a certain status of this planet. The water is polluted, there are holes in the ozone layer. Suppose the planet had been infested by some worms and, over the million years under their leadership, it had been transformed, materially and physically, into something different. So the presence of "comrade human" has brought the planet to its current state. It means there is a certain biophysical phenomenality. In the Anthropocene theory, man is entirely positivized, objectified, and viewed on the level of naturalization, as some biomolecular effect of the planet. Theater, on the contrary, is concerned with the debate itself. Right now: Will something be saved or not saved? A lot of people hate this question. I've been told, "We hate it when someone is saved. The character rises from the dead, the cow starts singing a song. It's so old-fashioned [and] disgusting ..." Yes, it does verge on vulgarity, but it's a conscious choice to skirt this boundary. I think pathetic vulgarity is what's missing in contemporary art. It's present in talk shows, some TV series, but what's crucial here is staying on the verge of vulgarity, instead of lapsing into it fully. Some people have noted that this successful maneuvering is the most interesting part of my play.

CF: Oh ... this makes me really want to live. It's all so scary, I want to live (laughs).

KC: Another aspect of posthumanism is non-human activity. For instance, when you bomb a city, you have drones—planes with no human control. There are now a lot of such instruments of mass murder that require no human participation. It rephrases the question of murder. If you're, say, throwing bombs from a plane or a trench, you're a murderer. But if you're just sitting in front of your computer and press a button somewhere in Switzerland, and the bomb drops in Eastern Europe or elsewhere, the very system of object distribution won't let you be considered a murderer. It's the most important question of all, also posed in my play: Where does man end? Is it at the point where he allows murder? Murder, after all, is that which man forbids, unlike animals. So my question is, in part, this: If we don't want to be human anymore, do we let others kills us? Do we allow ourselves to kill? That is the question. If we are some biophysical creatures with a brain, are we allowed then to exterminate each other? Because a lot of people who are adamant about the issues of posthuman existence are also very politically active in the Syrian anti-war campaigns. And yet they insist on a new ethics of the posthuman. What do they advocate, then? Who are they protecting? Who is doing the suffering or being the political victim: the refugees and migrants? If they're neither people nor a supermind nor animals, who are they? I also wanted to throw into question this absurd, preposterous situation. Judging from the screenings in Paris, NYC, Utrecht, Bergen, Moscow, and Saint Petersburg, I've come to realize that Russian audiences have a harder time understanding this theme than Western ones.

CF: So, this discourse hasn't manifested itself here yet?

KC: It hasn't. Here people get up in arms about the crisis of the human: "Who says there's a crisis?" In the West, the opposite is true: "How dare you doubt that hope remains for some sort of humanity?" This difference in perception is intriguing.

CF: From this point of view, it's important that the play opens at the Electrotheater, because that space actively engages various scientific and aesthetic categories.[5]

KC: Yes, it's important to have a platform for analysis and metapositioning.

CF: And the audiences are trained, too, because active research is constantly conducted in the Electrozone and on the stage.

KC: Yes! I hope so.

Translated from Russian by Anton Svynarenko

5 *Love Machines* premiered at *Elektroteatr na Belorusskoi* [Elektrotheater on Belorusskoi] in Moscow, under the direction of Mariia Chirkova.

CHAPTER 12

Some Entropy in Your Tea: Notes on the Ontopoetics of Artificial Intelligence

Alex Anikina,
Goldsmiths, University of London

We, ourselves, have become, or are on our way to becoming posthuman. Our life turns into a feat of self-engineering—programming oneself as one would program a machine: time-efficient, device-equipped, information-sustained. Our technological horizon expanded indefinitely, tempting us with tales of a brighter future and possibilities far exceeding what we have now, both physically and mentally: the awareness of that is, in itself, the condition of being posthuman.

The posthuman generation is constantly reaching out to the machine [. . .]. To dream of artificial mind is to dream of touching the unknown, the dangerous, the Other. And we, in a case of a terrible mise-en-abyme, are dreaming of the dreaming machine.

Alex Anikina and Sasha Burkhanova, "Dreaming Machines"[1]

---

1 Alex Anikina and Sasha Burkhanova, "Dreaming Machines." *Vremia mechtat': IV moskovskaia mezhdunarodnaia biennale molodogo iskusstva* [Time to dream: IV Moscow international biennale of young art], eds. Tat'iana Manina, Tat'iana Iudkevich and Nikolai Molok Jr. (Moscow: Gosudarstvennyi tsentr sovremennogo iskusstva, 2014). Published in conjunction with an exhibition of the same title at the National Center for Contemporary Arts, Moscow, Russia, June 26, 2014 - August 10, 2014. Cited on Anikina's website "Red in Blue," http://red-in-blue.com/index.php/texts/posthuman-manifesto/, accessed September 22, 2017.

In the years that have passed since this Haylesian excerpt was written, Google's Deep Dream, Terence Broad's artificially encoded *Blade Runner*, and some other excursions into machine vision have shown that the machines, too, can "dream," or at least generate a dream-like visuality that is deeply affective to our optical unconscious. But it is not exactly the hallucinatory blur or the vivid colors that translate the moving image into the presence of the Other; it's the glimpses of some other modes of operation, unfamiliar territories, and, of course, it is the very idea of a consciousness residing in the non-human subject that intrigues us and that produces the desire to close the distance.

How to inhabit a non-human subjectivity? If we choose to imagine the non-human Other through human means, then it is bound to stay in the realm of speculation and poetry. The two films in my unfinished trilogy *Some Entropy in Your Tea* were conceived as a channel for this thought experiment, in order to imagine a hybrid narrative that would exist simultaneously in the realm of the human and the machinic.[2] What would happen if a sentient artificial mind emerged from the masses of data *after* humanity had disappeared? If it had access to all human knowledge ever produced, but not to actual living humans? With no reference points against which it could measure its own existence, would the knowledge be processed, and would it become a memory—or a non-human "memory"? Or, perhaps, "madness"? Facing the need to untangle itself from humanity's overbearing memory, the emergence of AGI[3] questions some of our most firmly held ideas, establishing from scratch new definitions for language, sanity, and love.

Acting as a facilitating agent for the thought experiment, the film opens up the domain of ontopoetics, a word used here to denote the speculative instruments of poetical self- and world-making[4]—and, in film, the

---

2 Alex Anikina, "Some Entropy in Your Tea," Vimeo digital video, produced in 2013 as a digital video, 8:15, https://vimeo.com/69840605; Alex Anikina, "Aleph," Vimeo digital video, produced in 2014 as a digital video, 2:28, https://vimeo.com/98878372.

3 AGI stands for Artificial General Intelligence, also known as "strong AI." It is AI that most closely approximates the full range of human cognitive abilities. The AGI Society defines AGI as "an emerging field aiming at the building of 'thinking machines'; that is, general-purpose systems with intelligence comparable to that of the human mind (and perhaps ultimately well beyond human general intelligence)." The Website of the AGI Society, http://www.agi-society.org/, accessed September 20, 2017.

4 Instruments that also reflect on their own constitution and include it in the processes of making.

linguistic and the visual means, which are as important as their intended or unintended faults, lapses, and side effects. In a way, ontopoetics appears as a filmic consciousness that is shared by the character, the viewer and the maker: a state of inhabiting the images, of attempting to re-inscribe one's subjectivity from the inside of the picture-language conjunction. There are several brief comments to be made about the ways that ontopoetics operates in the film.

The archive. The informational deluge is one of the chronic conditions of our time; for the post-apocalyptic world of our thought experiment, however, this condition is the starting point. *Some Entropy in Your Tea* was initially inspired by the rumors of Google enlisting their vast digitized books repository for their AI project, and in a way, the film visualizes the end of the world as a radical practice to sort through this information. From the beginning, AGI has to take on the role of an archaeologist that looks back at our culture to re-establish lost connections and signifieds, but also ends up establishing new ones. The non-life of the archive becomes, ideally, a proliferating, self-sorting, self-copying, and self-modifying locus of newly generated meaning; a place to renegotiate entropy itself.

The landscape and the subject. The landscapes in the video belong to the long personal and global lineages of post-apocalyptic tableaux: the memories of reading science fiction in my childhood combined with my fascination with the Book of Revelation and Albrecht Dürer's engravings of it. The landscape becomes an agent of the sublime, channeling the catastrophic events that "already transpired" as that which we have yet to experience. So, on the one hand, guided by the human narrative in this landscape, the lonely AGI stands in romantic opposition to the world, like Friedrich's *Wanderer above the Sea of Fog*. On the other hand, AGI is also a constituent part of the world-as-data, and in this sense, it could be seen as a post-Anthropocene subject—a dispersed, non-referential entity that has the potential to re-animate the landscape through kinship rather than antagonism. In this scenario, it would be interesting to think if the real, physical landscape would constitute for the artificial mind some kind of hallucinatory realm, only partially accessible through remediated camera images.

The divine. "Man is by nature a social animal; an individual who is unsocial naturally and not accidentally is either beneath our notice or more than human. Society is something that precedes the individual. Anyone who either cannot lead the common life or is so self-sufficient as not to need to, and therefore does not partake of society, is either a beast or a god."[5] This otherness by exclusion described by Aristotle feels like, if it was written in our times, it would include a machine instead of a god. A machine joining an assembly of Others—plants, animals, minerals and, perhaps, even images. But what if we think of the concept of the divine as a conceptual tool that humanity has been using for centuries in order to create kinship with the unknown? Could we think of new visualities produced by the machines as new ways of approaching the Other?

What happens if we think of non-human subjectivity through human means? Can moving images be considered something that are "human"? The gateways into ontopoetics delineated here open up questions for future work. As the trilogy is still unfinished, the third chapter will become a place to ask them, if not to answer, by way of images and by way of further estrangement of language. The hope, after all, is that one might be able to push language to its extreme, far enough to sever the semantic links. And my feeling is, the voice-over will be provided by an old friend of mine—one of the default voices in Mac OS X, incidentally, also called Alex.

July 2016

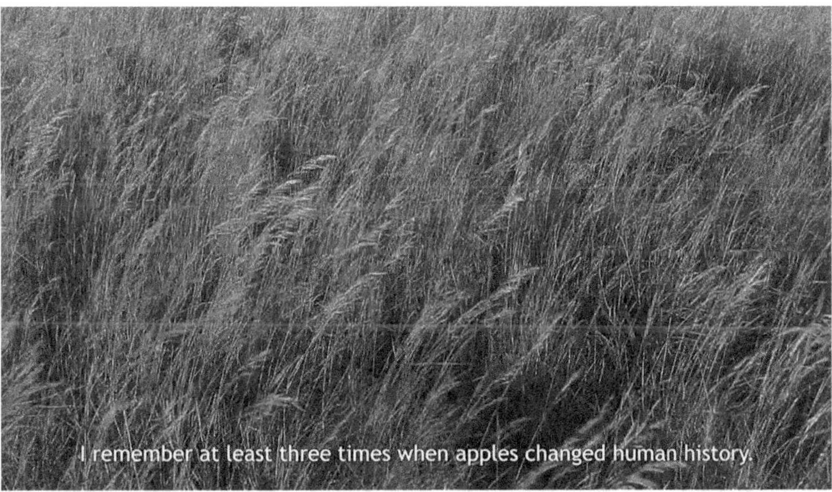

Fig. 1 Still frame from *Some Entropy in Your Tea* (2013), Alex Anikina. Single-channel HD video projection, 8 min 15 sec. Image courtesy of the artist.

5 Aristotle, *Politics* (New York: Dover Publications, 2000), 29.

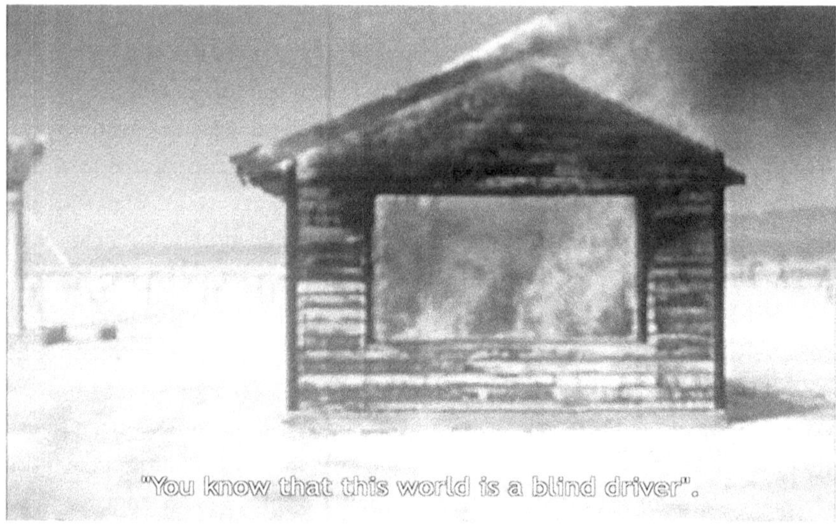

Fig. 2 Still frame from *Some Entropy in Your Tea* (2013), Alex Anikina. Single-channel HD video projection, 8 min 15 sec. Image courtesy of the artist.

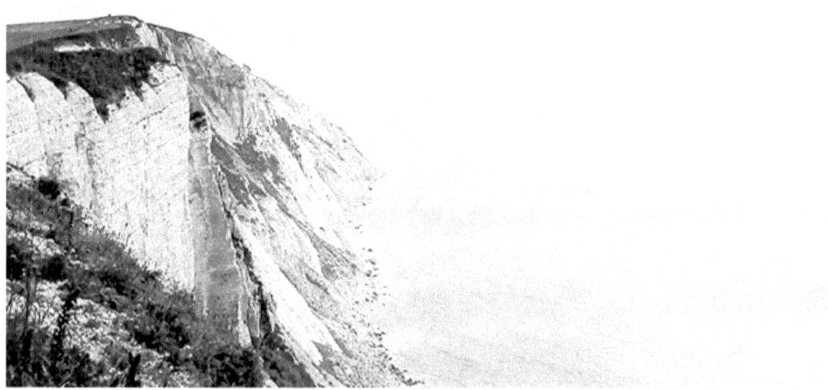

Fig. 3 Still frame from *Some Entropy in Your Tea* (2013), Alex Anikina. Single-channel HD video projection, 8 min 15 sec. Image courtesy of the artist.

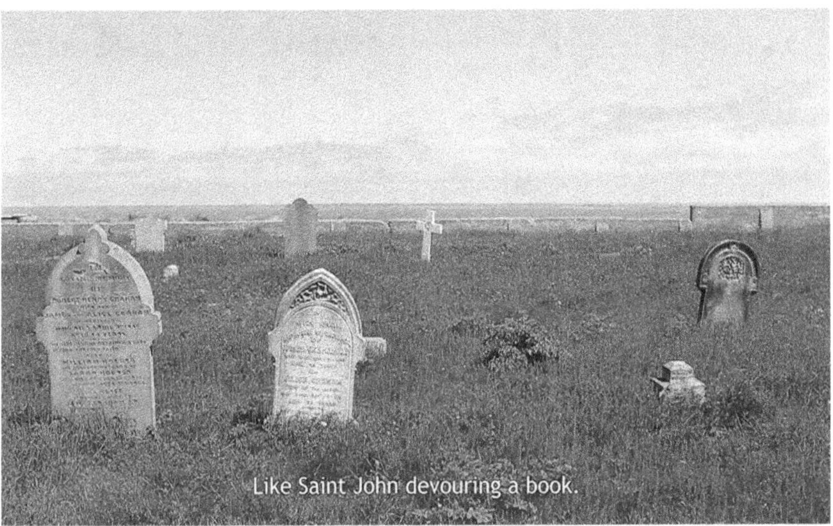

Fig. 4 Still frame from *Some Entropy in Your Tea* (2013), Alex Anikina. Single-channel HD video projection, 8 min 15 sec. Image courtesy of the artist.

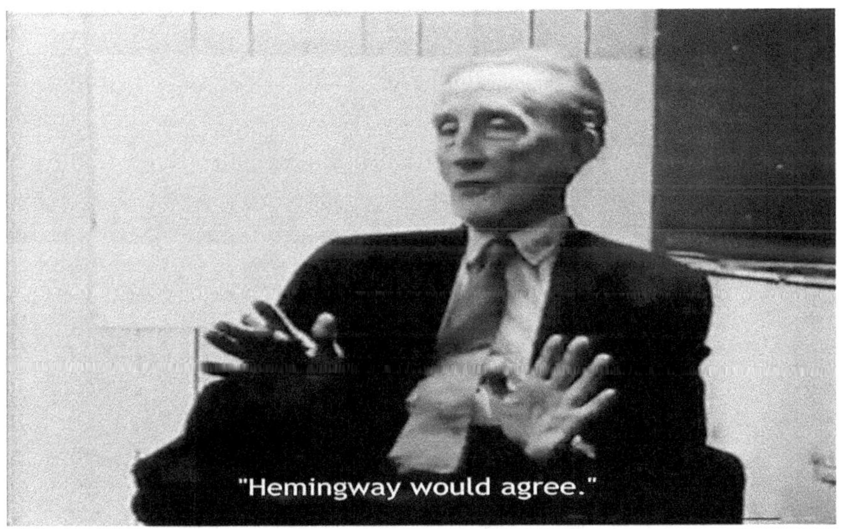

Fig. 5 Still frame from *Some Entropy in Your Tea* (2013), Alex Anikina. Single-channel HD video projection, 8 min 15 sec. Image courtesy of the artist.

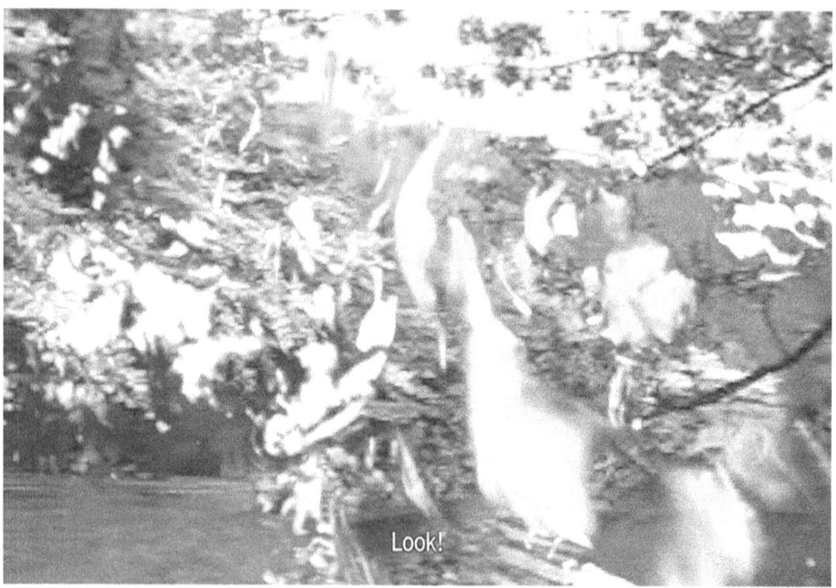

Fig. 6 Still frame from *Aleph* (2014), Alex Anikina. Single-channel HD video projection, 2 min 28 sec. Image courtesy of the artist.

Fig. 7 Still frame from *Aleph* (2014), Alex Anikina. Single-channel HD video projection, 2 min 28 sec. Image courtesy of the artist.

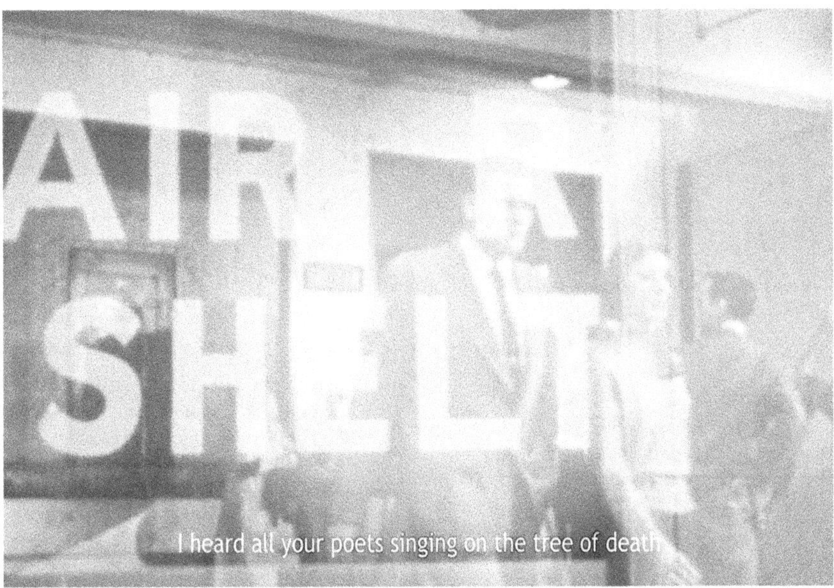

Fig. 8 Still frame from *Aleph* (2014), Alex Anikina. Single-channel HD video projection, 2 min 28 sec. Image courtesy of the artist.

Index

Note: Page numbers followed by 'n' denotes notes

N

O

P

R

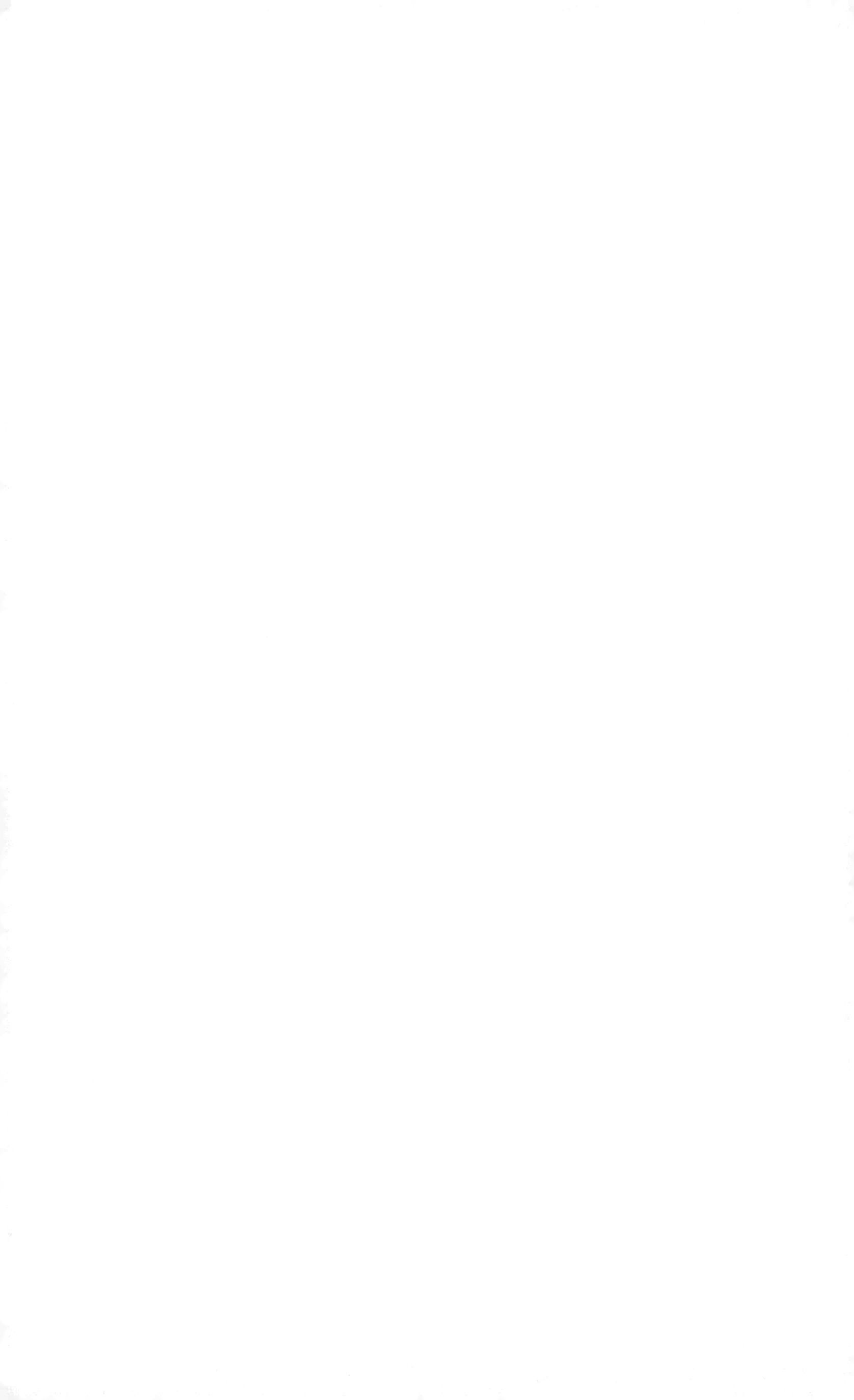

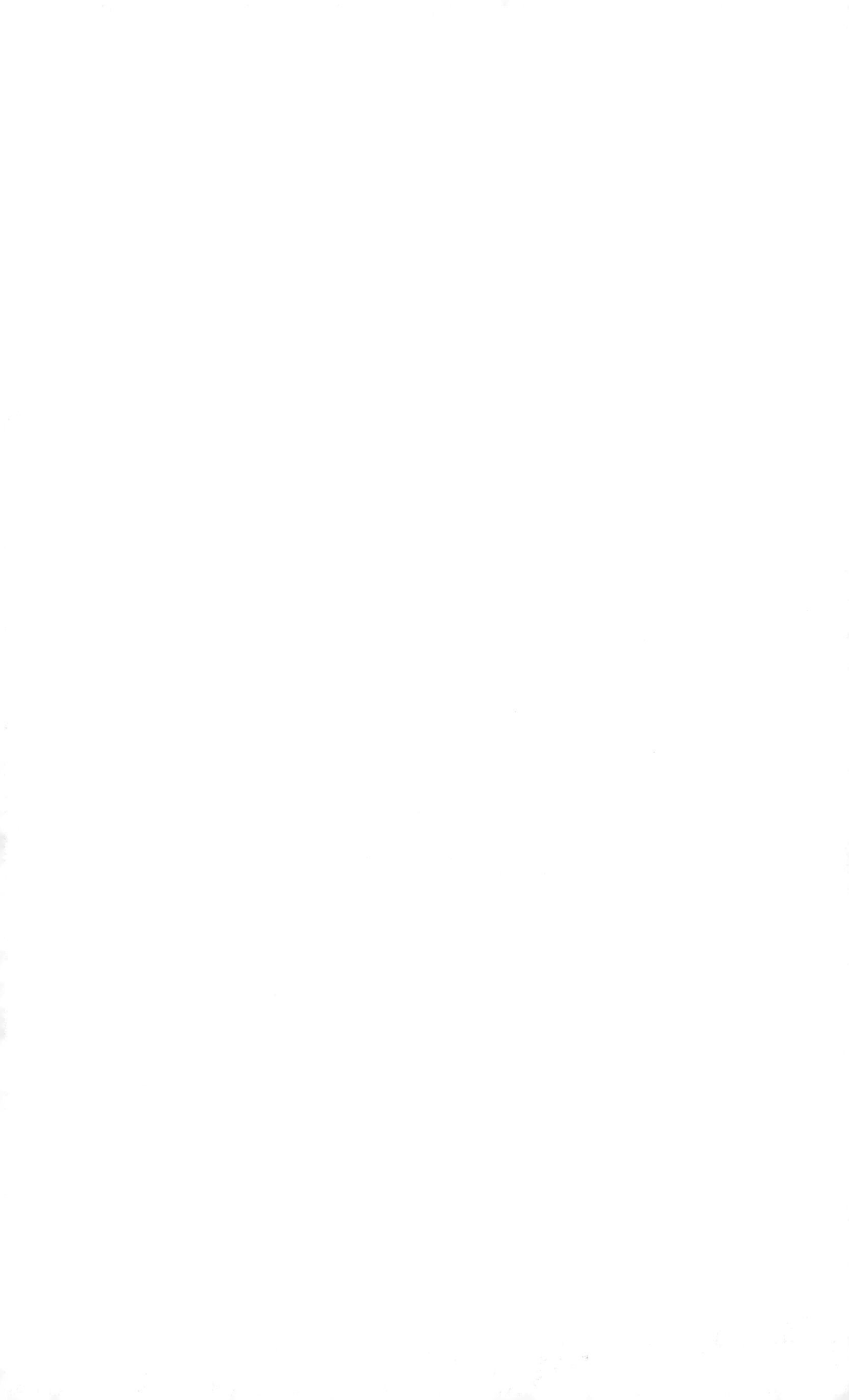

www.ingramcontent.com/pod-product-compliance
Lightning Source LLC
LaVergne TN
LVHW020507100826
845148LV00003B/716